MULTICULTURAL EDUCATION SERIES

James A. Banks, *Series Editor*

Multicultural Education, Transformative Knowledge,
and Action: Historical and Contemporary Perspectives
JAMES A. BANKS, Editor

MULTICULTURAL EDUCATION, TRANSFORMATIVE KNOWLEDGE, AND ACTION

Historical and Contemporary Perspectives

EDITED BY

James A. Banks

TEACHERS COLLEGE PRESS

Teachers College, Columbia University
New York and London

Published by Teachers College Press, 1234 Amsterdam Avenue, New York, NY 10027

Grateful acknowledgment is made to the following publishers for permission to reprint these publications:

Academic Press for Nathan Murillo (1977). The works of George I. Sánchez: An appreciation. In Joe L. Martinez, Jr. (Ed.). *Chicano psychology* (pp. 1–10). New York: Academic Press. Copyright © 1977 by Academic Press, Inc.

The American Educational Research Association for James A. Banks (1993). The canon debate, knowledge construction, and multicultural education. *Educational Researcher, 22*(5), 4–14; James A. Banks (1995). The historical reconstruction of knowledge about race: Implications for transformative teaching. *Educational Researcher, 24*(2), 15–25.

The Association for Supervision and Curriculum Development for James A. Banks (1994). Transforming the mainstream curriculum. *Educational Leadership, 51*(8), 4–8.

Carlson Publishing Company (Brooklyn, NY) for Allida M. Black (1993). A reluctant but persistent warrior: Eleanor Roosevelt and the early civil rights movement. In Vicki L. Crawford, Jacqueline Anne Rouse, & Barbara Woods (Eds.), *Women in the civil rights movement: Trailblazers & torchbearers, 1941–1965* (pp. 233–249). Bloomington: Indiana University Press.

Corwin Press for Cherry A. McGee Banks (1995). Intellectual leadership and the influence of early African American scholars on multicultural education. *Educational Policy, 9*(3), 260–280.

Howard University for James A. Banks (1992). African American scholarship and the evolution of multicultural education. *The Journal of Negro Education, 61*(3), 273–286; Michael R. Hillis (1995). Allison Davis and the study of race, social class and schooling. *The Journal of Negro Education, 64*(1), 33–41.

Penguin Books for excerpts from *This little light of mine: The life of Fannie Lou Hamer* by Kay Mills. Copyright © 1993 by Kay Mills. Used by permission of Dutton Dignet, a division of Penguin Books USA Inc.

Phi Delta Kappa for Gary Howard (1993). Whites in multicultural education: Rethinking our role. *Phi Delta Kappan, 75*(1), 36–41.

South End Press for an excerpt from G. Joseph & J. Lewis (Eds.). (1981). *Common differences: Conflict in Black and White feminist perspectives* (p. 19). Boston: South End Press.

The University of Tennessee Press for an excerpt from D. J. Garrow (Ed.). (1987). *The Montgomery bus boycott and the women who started it* (p. 45). Knoxville: University of Tennessee Press.

Library of Congress Cataloging-in-Publication Data

Multicultural education, transformative knowledge, and action : historical and contemporary perspectives / edited by James A. Banks. New York: Teachers College Press, 1996.

    p.   cm.

Includes bibliographical references (p.   ) and index.

ISBN 0-8077-3532-9 (cloth : alk. paper). — ISBN 0-8077-3531-0 (pbk. : alk. paper)

    1. Multicultural education—United States—History. 2. Educational change—United States—History. 3. Feminism and education—United States—History. 4. Minorities—Education—United States—History. I. Banks, James A.

LC1099.3.M855 1996

370.19ʹ6ʹ0973—dc20   96-1069

ISBN 0-8077-3531-0 (paper)
ISBN 0-8077-3532-9 (cloth)

Printed on acid-free paper

Manufactured in the United States of America

03 02 01 00 99 98 97 96   8 7 6 5 4 3 2 1

Contents

Preface

As the field of multicultural education moves down the road toward institutionalization and legitimacy, it is essential that its historical roots be documented, recognized, and linked to the current school reform movement. A major goal of the project from which this book developed, *Studies in the Historical Foundations of Multicultural Education,* is to document the ways in which the current multicultural education movement is both connected to and a continuation of earlier scholarly and activist movements designed to promote empowerment, knowledge transformation, liberation, and human freedom in U.S. society.

The chapters in this book document persistent themes in the struggle for human freedom in the United States since the late nineteenth century as exemplified in the scholarship and actions of people of color and their White supporters, many of whom were also in the margins of society. The historical research uncovered in this book reveals several important themes that connect multicultural education to the past and that can help to revitalize and energize it. One is that the margins of U.S. society, to which people of color have often been confined, have usually been the sites for preserving and defending the freedoms and rights stated in the founding documents of the United States when they were most severely challenged.

Groups such as African Americans, Jewish Americans, Latinos, and Japanese Americans were usually among the first to mobilize when antidemocratic actions and movements, such as institutionalized discrimination, immigration exclusion acts, and the internment of American citizens by the U.S. government, occurred. These historical developments have led historian Gary Okihiro (1994) to state that the groups in the margins of U.S. society have preserved and kept the nation's mainstream democratic values alive.

Cultural workers and scholars in the margins also have been persistent through time in developing and constructing transformative scholarship oppositional to racist and sexist mainstream scholarship institutionalized in the academic and popular worlds. An important aim of this book is to document the ways in which multicultural scholars and activists today—in their opposition to racist and sexist scholarship—are connected to historical progenitors such as W. E. B. DuBois, Carter G. Woodson, Franz Boas, Anna Julia Cooper, George Sánchez, and Carey McWilliams.

The conception of knowledge as intricately tied to action designed to further human freedom and justice is another significant idea that connects multicultural education today with its scholarly and activist progenitors. Early African American scholars such as W. E. B. DuBois and Carter G. Woodson believed that the construction of accurate knowledge would help to undercut stereotypes and misconceptions that supported institutionalized racism and discrimination. These scholars also believed that scholars had an obligation to participate in action that would help to make society more democratic and just.

This book is divided into five parts. The conceptual framework around which it is organized and the historical roots of multicultural education are described in Part I. This part also describes the ways in which transformative teaching is linked to the historical roots of multicultural education.

Case studies of individuals whose works exemplify the contributions of early transformative scholars to the historical foundations of multicultural education constitute Part II. The chapters in Part III describe the work of women scholars and activists who worked to transform society within a historical context. The ways in which women of color have faced triple oppressions—race, gender, and class—comprise an important theme that cuts across the chapters in Part III. Chapter 13, which describes the civil rights activities of Eleanor Roosevelt, is included to exemplify the ways in which Whites in mainstream society can become antiracist and transformative actors. These kinds of examples are essential as models for White scholars, teachers, students, and activists who want to become antiracists. Other examples not included in this book are John Brown, Helen Hunt Jackson, Lillian Smith, Carey McWilliams, and Morris Dees.

Part IV describes the rise and fall of the intergroup education movement and the emergence of research related to prejudice in the 1930s and 1940s. Intergroup education, a predecessor but not a direct root of the current multicultural education movement, emerged during the early decades of the twentieth century to deal with the "immigrant problem" caused by the massive numbers of immigrants from Southern, Central, and Eastern Europe who were entering the United States near the turn of the century. The intergroup education movement was revitalized during the period of rapid migration to the nation's cities and the related racial tension and violence during the 1940s. When the civil rights movement emerged in the 1960s, few traces of the intergroup education movement were evident. The rise and fall of the intergroup education movement offer important lessons to today's multiculturalists about school reform and the formulation of coalitions.

The final part of this book, Part V, bridges the past and the present. It describes school reforms that are needed to promote educational equity and guidelines for changing schools in ways that will make them more consistent with a culturally diverse and democratic society. Language revitalization, the role of Whites in multicultural education, and curricular reform are discussed in the chapters that constitute Part V. White readers should find the chapter on rethinking their role in multicultural education encouraging and empowering.

Our project on the history of transformative scholarship and multicultural education focuses on the construction of transformative knowledge within marginalized academic communities and on classroom teaching. For transformative teaching to occur, important connections must be made between knowledge construction and the communities in which students and teachers live. Also, both teachers and students mediate school knowledge in significant ways. Consequently, student–teacher interactions are important variables in transformative classrooms. Important links between communities and schools are described in Chapters 5 and 14. Chapter 5 describes how the African American community provided Woodson's organization and activities the financial support needed for survival. In the Springfield Plan—an intercultural education reform project initiated in 1939—community participation and involvement were essential components.

Our project to uncover the historical foundations of multicultural education is a pioneering effort. We hope it will encourage other scholars and graduate students to join and extend our work. We especially need more studies of early feminist scholars and activists, of non-African American scholars and activists of color, and of White scholars and activists such as Helen Hunt Jackson, Mary White Ovington, Carey McWilliams, Lillian Smith, and Morris Dees. African Americans are prominent in this initial effort not only because they were one of the first groups to force the nation to confront its contradiction of racism and the ideal of freedom, but also because Whites defined themselves in opposition to Blacks when they constructed their social identity and race in America, as Toni Morrison (1992) perceptively points out. African Americans have been at the center of the American identity and race struggle since the nation began.

The *Studies in the Historical Foundations of Multicultural Education* project, out of which this book emerged, is one of three interrelated projects of the Center for Multicultural Education at the University of Washington, Seattle. *Handbook of Research on Multicultural Education* (Banks & Banks, 1995) was the Center's first major project. Another Center project, funded by the Carnegie Corporation, is *The Synthesis and Dissemination of Knowledge About Multicultural Education.*

Studies in the Historical Foundations of Multicultural Education, which began in 1992, has as major goals the documentation of the history of multicultural education and transformative scholarship and the mentoring of graduate students. The work of graduate students is an integral part of the project. Most of the chapters in this book were first presented as papers in a faculty/student symposium series organized and sponsored by the Center for Multicultural Education at American Educational Research Association (AERA) annual meetings in three consecutive years: 1993, 1994, and 1995.

Studies in the Historical Foundations of Multicultural Education, which is continuing, is a collaborative project. I wish to thank the individuals who have helped to make it possible. Cherry A. McGee Banks, of the University of Washington, Bothell, has played a pivotal role in the project's conceptualization and implementation. She has been its strong intellectual supporter, has presented a paper each year in the AERA symposium series, and took the lead in writing the AERA proposal for the 1995 session.

I am grateful to the graduate students who have participated in the project since its inception, two of whom—Michael R. Hillis and Edward Taylor—are now university professors. I would like to acknowledge the papers written for the series and presented at the 1995 AERA symposium by Mary Henley and Heidi McKenna. Their papers are not included in this book because of its limited scope.

Several professors on campuses beyond the University of Washington participated in the AERA symposia that are the basis for this book. I would like to thank them publicly for their insightful and important contributions to the *Historical Series.* Professor Gloria Ladson-Billings (University of Wisconsin–Madison) and Professor Henry Yu (University of California, Los Angeles [UCLA]) wrote papers for the series. Professor Carlos J. Ovando (Indiana University) co-authored a paper with Karen Gourd—one of my graduate students—whom he also mentored. Professors Luanna Meyer (Syracuse University), Christine E. Sleeter (California State University–Monterey Bay), and Peter McLaren (UCLA) served as discussants in the 3 consecutive years in which we presented symposia at AERA.

I wish to thank the following individuals for their perceptive, helpful, and scholarly reviews of the chapters indicated: Professor Evelyn Hu-DeHart, University of Colorado, Boulder; and Professor Stanford M. Lyman, Florida Atlantic University—Chapter 9; Professor Ronald E. Butchart, University of Washington, Tacoma—Chapter 11; and Professor Robert E. Lowe, National–Louis University, Chapter 14.

I wish to extend warm thanks to Karen Gourd and Pamela Hart, research assistants at the Center for Multicultural Education, for undertaking many library, reference-checking, and computer tasks during the preparation of the manuscript for submission to the publisher. Karen Gourd worked on the manuscript intensively during its final stages. I am grateful to Brian Ellerbeck for his encouragement, perceptive reading of the manuscript, and helpful suggestions. I wish to thank Peter Sieger for his careful and prompt work on the production of the manuscript.

James A. Banks

REFERENCES

Banks, J. A., & Banks, C. A. M. (Eds.) (1995). *Handbook of research on multicultural education.* New York: Macmillan.

Morrison, T. (1992). *Playing in the dark: Whiteness and the literary imagination.* Cambridge, MA: Harvard University Press.

Okihiro, G. Y. (1994). *Margins and mainstreams: Asians in American history and culture.* Seattle: University of Washington Press.

PART I

Transformative Knowledge and Multicultural Education

The chapters that constitute Part I describe the major assumptions, concepts, and paradigms in this book. They focus on the nature and types of knowledge and describe the historical roots of the multicultural education movement. Chapter 1 describes the major types of knowledge conceptualized by J. A. Banks. This knowledge typology is the theoretical framework that guided the conceptualization of the project from which this book developed.

In Chapter 1, J. A. Banks describes five types of knowledge: *personal and cultural*; *popular*; *mainstream academic*; *transformative academic*; and *school*. J. A. Banks and the other authors throughout this book illustrate ways in which all knowledge is positional and reflects both the reality observed and the subjectivity of the knower. Multicultural education is a type of transformative knowledge. Transformative knowledge, which challenges institutionalized mainstream knowledge, makes explicit its value premises and its connection to action to improve society.

An important aim of Part I is to describe the connections between transformative scholarship done in earlier decades and transformative scholarship today. Chapters 2 and 3 describe the important roles that African American scholars have played in the construction of transformative knowledge since the late nineteenth and early twentieth centuries. The knowledge they constructed is an important root of multicultural education. Chapter 2 provides a general overview of the work of these scholars; Chapter 3 focuses on their roles as intellectual leaders and as challengers of the metanarrative constructed by mainstream scholars. A case study of the ways in which positionality influenced the construction of race from the turn of the century to the publication of *The Bell Curve* in 1994 is presented in Chapter 4. This chapter also describes the teaching implications of the construction and reconstruction of race.

CHAPTER 1

The Canon Debate, Knowledge Construction, and Multicultural Education

JAMES A. BANKS

A heated and divisive national debate is taking place about what knowledge related to ethnic and cultural diversity should be taught in the school and university curriculum (Asante, 1991; Asante & Ravitch, 1991; D'Souza, 1991; Glazer, 1991; Schlesinger, 1991; Sleeter, 1995; Woodward, 1991). This debate has heightened ethnic tension and confused many educators about the meaning of multicultural education. At least three different groups of scholars are participating in the canon debate: the Western traditionalists, the multiculturalists, and the Afrocentrists. Although there are a range of perspectives and views within each of these groups, each shares a number of important assumptions and beliefs about the nature of diversity in the United States and about the role of educational institutions in a pluralistic society.

The Western traditionalists have initiated a national effort to defend the dominance of Western civilization in the school and university curriculum (Gray, 1991; Howe, 1991; Woodward, 1991). These scholars believe that Western history, literature, and culture are endangered in the school and university curriculum because of the push by feminists, scholars of color, and other multiculturalists for curriculum reform and transformation. The Western traditionalists have formed an organization called the National Association of Scholars to defend the dominance of Western civilization in the curriculum.

The multiculturalists believe that the school, college, and university curriculum marginalizes the experiences of people of color and of women (Butler & Walter, 1991; Gates, 1992; Grant, 1992; Sleeter, personal communication, October 26, 1991). They contend that the curriculum should be reformed

Multicultural Education, Transformative Knowledge, and Action. Copyright © 1996 by Teachers College, Columbia University. All rights reserved. ISBN 0-8077-3531-0 (pbk.), ISBN 0-8077-3532-9 (cloth). Prior to photocopying items for classroom use, please contact the Copyright Clearance Center, Customer Service, 222 Rosewood Dr., Danvers, MA 01923, USA, tel. (508)750-8400.

so that it will more accurately reflect the histories and cultures of ethnic groups and women. Two organizations have been formed to promote issues related to ethnic and cultural diversity. Teachers for a Democratic Culture promotes ethnic studies and women studies at the university level. The National Association for Multicultural Education focuses on teacher education and multicultural education in the nation's schools.

The Afrocentrists maintain that African culture and history should be placed at the "center" of the curriculum in order to motivate African American students to learn and to help students to understand the important role that Africa has played in the development of Western civilization (Asante, 1991). Many mainstream multiculturalists are ambivalent about Afrocentrism, although few have publicly opposed it. This is in part because the Western traditionalists rarely distinguish the Afrocentrists from the multiculturalists and describe them as one group. Some multiculturalists also may perceive Afrocentric ideas as compatible with a broader concept of multicultural education.

The influence of the multiculturalists within schools and universities in the past 20 years has been substantial. Many school districts, state departments of education, and private agencies have developed and implemented multicultural staff development programs, conferences, policies, and curricula (Gollnick, 1995; New York City Board of Education, 1990; New York State Department of Education, 1989, 1991; Sokol, 1990). Multicultural requirements, programs, and policies also have been implemented at many of the nation's leading research universities, including the University of California, Berkeley, Stanford University, Pennsylvania State University, and the University of Wisconsin system. The success that the multiculturalists have had in implementing their ideas within schools and universities is probably a major reason that the Western traditionalists are trying to halt multicultural reforms in the nation's schools, colleges, and universities.

The debate between the Western traditionalists and the multiculturalists is consistent with the ideals of a democratic society. To date, however, it has resulted in little productive interaction between the two groups. Rather, each group has talked primarily to audiences it views as sympathetic to its ideologies and visions of the present and future (Franklin, 1991; Schlesinger, 1991). Because there has been little productive dialogue and exchange between the Western traditionalists and the multiculturalists, the debate has been polarized, and writers frequently have not conformed to the established rules of scholarship (D'Souza, 1991). A kind of forensic social science has developed (Rivlin, 1973), with each side stating briefs and then marshaling evidence to support its position. The debate also has taken place primarily in the popular press rather than in academic and scholarly journals.

VALUATION AND KNOWLEDGE CONSTRUCTION

I hope in this and other chapters to make a positive contribution to the canon debate by providing evidence for the claim that the positions of both the Western traditionalists and the multiculturalists reflect values, ideologies, political positions, and human interests. Each position also implies a kind of knowledge that should be taught in the school and university curriculum. In this chapter, I will describe a typology of the kinds of knowledge that exist in society and in educational institutions. This typology is designed to help practicing educators and researchers to identify types of knowledge that reflect particular values, assumptions, perspectives, and ideological positions.

Teachers should help students to understand all types of knowledge. Students should be involved in the debates about knowledge construction and conflicting interpretations, such as the extent to which Egypt and Phoenicia influenced Greek civilization (Bernal, 1987/1991). Students also should be taught how to create their own interpretations of the past and present, as well as how to identify their own positions, interests, ideologies, and assumptions. Teachers should help students to become critical thinkers who have the knowledge, attitudes, skills, and commitments needed to participate in democratic action to help the nation close the gap between its ideals and its realities. Multicultural education is an education for functioning effectively in a pluralistic democratic society. Helping students to develop the knowledge, skills, and attitudes needed to participate in reflective civic action is one of its major goals (Banks, 1991).

I argue that students should study five types of knowledge: personal/ cultural; popular; mainstream academic; transformative academic; and school. However, the philosophical position that underlies this book is within the transformative tradition in ethnic studies and multicultural education (Banks, 1991,1994; Banks & Banks, 1993). This tradition links knowledge, social commitment, and action (Meier & Rudwick, 1986). A transformative, action-oriented curriculum, in my view, can best be implemented when students examine different types of knowledge in a democratic classroom where they can freely examine their perspectives and moral commitments.

The Characteristics of Knowledge

Knowledge in this book means the way a person explains or interprets reality. *The American Heritage Dictionary* (1983) defines knowledge as "familiarity, awareness, or understandings gained through experience or study. The sum or range of what has been perceived, discovered or inferred" (p. 384). The conceptualization of knowledge used in this book is broad. We use knowl-

edge the way in which it usually is used in the sociology of knowledge literature, to include ideas, values, and interpretations (Farganis, 1986). As
postmodern theorists have pointed out, knowledge is socially constructed and
reflects human interests, values, and action (Code, 1991; Foucault, 1972;
Harding, 1991; Rorty, 1989). Although many complex factors influence the
knowledge that is created by an individual or group, including the actuality
of what occurred, the knowledge that people create is heavily influenced by
their interpretations of their experiences and their positions within particular social, economic, and political systems and structures of a society.

In the Western empirical tradition, the ideal within each academic discipline is the formation of knowledge without the influence of the researcher's
personal or cultural characteristics (Greer, 1969; Kaplan, 1964). However,
as critical and postmodern theorists have pointed out, personal, cultural, and
social factors influence the formulation of knowledge even when objective
knowledge is the ideal within a discipline (Cherryholmes, 1988; Foucault,
1972; Habermas, 1971; Rorty, 1989; Young, 1971). Often the researchers
themselves are unaware of how their personal experiences and positions
within society influence the knowledge they produce. Most mainstream historians were unaware of how their regional and cultural biases influenced their
interpretation of the Reconstruction period until W. E. B. DuBois published a
study that challenged the accepted and established interpretations of that
historical period (DuBois, 1935/1962).

Positionality and Knowledge Construction

Positionality is an important concept that emerged out of feminist scholarship. Tetreault (1993) writes:

> Positionality means that important aspects of our identity, for example, our gen-
> der, our race, our class, our age . . . are markers of relational positions rather than
> essential qualities. Their effects and implications change according to context.
> Recently, feminist thinkers have seen knowledge as valid when it comes from an
> acknowledgment of the knower's specific position in any context, one always
> defined by gender, race, class and other variables. (p. 139)

Positionality reveals the importance of identifying the positions and frames
of reference from which scholars and writers present their data, interpretations, analyses, and instruction (Anzaldúa, 1990; Ellsworth, 1989). The need
for researchers and scholars to identify their ideological positions and normative assumptions in their work—an inherent part of feminist and ethnic
studies scholarship—contrasts with the empirical paradigm that has dominated science and research in the United States (Code, 1991; Harding, 1991).

The assumption within the Western empirical paradigm is that the knowledge produced within it is neutral and objective and that its principles are universal. The effects of values, frames of references, and the normative positions of researchers and scholars are discussed infrequently within the traditional empirical paradigm that has dominated scholarship and teaching in U. S. colleges and universities since the turn of the century. However, scholars such as Myrdal (1944) and Clark (1965), prior to the feminist and ethnic studies movements, wrote about the need for scholars to recognize and state their normative positions and valuations and to become, in the apt words of Kenneth B. Clark, "involved observers." Myrdal (1944) stated that valuations are not just attached to research but permeate it. He wrote, "There is no device for excluding biases in social sciences than to face the valuations and to introduce them as explicitly stated, specific, and sufficiently concretized value premises" (p. 1043).

Postmodern and critical theorists, such as Habermas (1971) and Giroux (1983), and feminist postmodern theorists, such as Farganis (1986), Collins (1990), Code (1991), and Harding (1991), have developed important critiques of empirical knowledge. They argue that despite its claims, modern science is not value-free but contains important human interests and normative assumptions that should be identified, discussed, and examined. Code (1991), a feminist epistemologist, states that academic knowledge is both subjective and objective and that both aspects should be recognized and discussed. Code states that we need to ask these kinds of questions: "Out of whose subjectivity has this ideal [of objectivity] grown? Whose standpoint, whose values does it represent?" (p. 70). She writes:

> The point of the questions is to discover how subjective and objective conditions together produce knowledge, values, and epistemology. It is neither to reject objectivity nor to glorify subjectivity in its stead. Knowledge is neither value-free nor value-neutral; the processes that produce it are themselves value-laden; and these values are open to evaluation. (p. 70)

In her book, *What Can She Know? Feminist Theory and the Construction of Knowledge,* Code (1991) raises the question, "Is the sex of the knower epistemologically significant?" (p. 7). She answers this question in the affirmative because of the ways in which gender influences how knowledge is constructed, interpreted, and institutionalized within U.S. society. The ethnic and cultural experiences of the knower are also epistemologically significant because these factors influence knowledge construction, use, and interpretation in U.S. society.

Empirical scholarship has been limited by the assumptions and biases that are implicit within it (Code, 1991; Gordon, 1985; Harding, 1991). However, these biases and assumptions have been infrequently recognized by the scholars and researchers themselves and by the consumers of their works, such as other scholars, professors, teachers, and general readers. The lack of recognition and identification of these biases, assumptions, perspectives, and points of view frequently have victimized people of color such as African Americans, American Indians, Asian Americans, and Hispanics because of the stereotypes and misconceptions that have been perpetuated about them in the historical and social science literature (Gutiérrez, 1995; Ladner, 1973; Okihiro, 1994; Phillips, 1918; Rodríguez, 1995).

Gordon, Miller, and Rollock (1990) call the bias that results in the negative depiction of ethnic groups of color by mainstream social scientists "communicentric bias." They point out that mainstream social scientists often have viewed diversity as deviance and differences as deficits. An important outcome of the revisionist and transformative interpretations that have been produced by scholars working in feminist and ethnic studies is that many misconceptions and partial truths about women and ethnic groups have been viewed from different and more complete perspectives (Acuña, 1988; Blassingame, 1972; Harding, 1981; King & Mitchell, 1990; Merton, 1972).

More complete perspectives result in a closer approximation to the actuality of what occurred. In an important and influential essay, Merton (1972) notes that the perspectives of both "insiders" and "outsiders" are needed to enable social scientists to gain a complete view of social reality. Anna Julia Cooper, the African American educator, made a point similar to Merton's when she wrote about how the perspectives of women enlarged our vision (Cooper, 1892/1969, cited in Minnich, 1990):

> The world has had to limp along with the wobbling gait and the one-sided hesitancy of a man with one eye. Suddenly the bandage is removed from the other eye and the whole body is filled with light. It sees a circle where before it saw a segment. (p. viii)

A Knowledge Typology

A description of the major types of knowledge can help teachers and curriculum specialists to identify perspectives and content needed to make the curriculum multicultural. Each of the types of knowledge described below reflects particular purposes, perspectives, experiences, goals, and human interests. Teaching students various types of knowledge can help them to better understand the perspectives of different racial, ethnic, and cultural groups as well as to develop their own versions and interpretations of issues and events.

I identify and describe five types of knowledge (see Table 1.1): (1) personal/cultural knowledge; (2) popular knowledge; (3) mainstream academic

TABLE 1.1 Types of Knowledge

Knowledge Type	Definition	Examples
Personal/ Cultural	The concepts, explanations, and interpretations that students derive from personal experiences in their homes, families, and community cultures.	Understandings by many African Americans and Hispanic students that highly individualistic behavior will be negatively sanctioned by many adults and peers in their cultural communities.
Popular	The facts, concepts, explanations, and interpretations that are institutionalized within the mass media and other institutions that are part of the popular culture.	Movies such as *Birth of a Nation*, *How the West Was Won*, and *Dances with Wolves*.
Mainstream Academic	The concepts, paradigms, theories, and explanations that constitute traditional Westerncentric knowledge in history and the behavioral and social sciences.	Ulrich B. Phillips, *American Negro Slavery*; Frederick Jackson Turner's frontier theory; Arthur R. Jensen's theory about Black and White intelligence.
Transformative Academic	The facts, concepts, paradigms, themes, and explanations that challenge mainstream academic knowledge and expand and substantially revise established canons, paradigms, theories, explanations, and research methods. When transformative academic paradigms replace mainstream ones, a scientific revolution has occurred. What is more normal is that transformative academic paradigms coexist with established ones.	George Washington Williams, *History of the Negro Race in America*; W. E. B. DuBois, *Black Reconstruction*; Carter G. Woodson, *The Mis-education of the Negro*; Gerda Lerner, *The Majority Finds Its Past;* Rodolfo Acuña, *Occupied America: A History of Chicanos*; Herbert Gutman, *The Black Family in Slavery and Freedom 1750-1925.*
School	The facts, concepts, generalizations, and interpretations that are presented in textbooks, teachers' guides, other media forms, and lectures by teachers.	Lewis Paul Todd and Merle Curti, *Rise of the American Nation*; Richard C. Brown, Wilhelmena S. Robinson, & John Cunningham, *Let Freedom Ring: A United States History.*

knowledge; (4) transformative academic knowledge; and (5) school knowledge. This is an ideal-type typology in the Weberian sense. The five categories approximate, but do not describe, reality in its total complexity. The categories are useful conceptual tools for thinking about knowledge and planning multicultural teaching. For example, although the categories can be conceptually distinguished, in reality they overlap and are interrelated in a dynamic way.

Since the 1960s, some of the findings and insights from transformative academic knowledge have been incorporated into mainstream academic knowledge and scholarship. Traditionally, students were taught in schools and universities that the land that became North America was a thinly populated wilderness when the Europeans arrived in the sixteenth century and that African Americans had made few contributions to the development of American civilization (mainstream academic knowledge). Some of the findings from transformative academic knowledge that challenged these conceptions have influenced mainstream academic scholarship and have been incorporated into mainstream college and school textbooks (Hoxie, n. d.; Thornton, 1987). Consequently, the relationship between the five categories of knowledge is dynamic and interactive rather than static (see Figure 1.1).

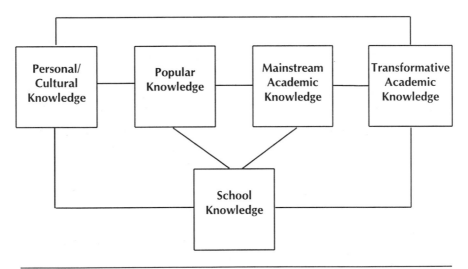

FIGURE 1.1 The Interrelationship of the Types of Knowledge
Although the five types of knowledge discussed in this chapter are conceptually distinct, they are highly interrelated in a complex and dynamic way.

THE TYPES OF KNOWLEDGE

Personal and Cultural Knowledge

The concepts, explanations, and interpretations that students derive from personal experiences in their homes, families, and community cultures constitute personal and cultural knowledge. The assumptions, perspectives, and insights that students derive from experiences in their homes and community cultures are used as screens to view and interpret the knowledge and experiences that they encounter in the school and in other institutions within the larger society.

Research and theory by Fordham and Ogbu (1986) indicate that low-income African American students often experience academic difficulties in the school because of the ways that cultural knowledge within their community conflicts with school knowledge, norms, and expectations. Fordham and Ogbu also state that the culture of many low-income African American students is oppositional to the school culture. These students believe that if they master the knowledge taught in the schools they will violate fictive kinship norms and run the risk of "acting White." Fordham (1988, 1991) has suggested that African American students who become high academic achievers resolve the conflict caused by the interaction of their personal cultural knowledge with the knowledge and norms within the schools by becoming "raceless" or by "ad hocing a culture."

Delpit (1988, 1995) states that African American students are often unfamiliar with school cultural knowledge regarding power relationships. They consequently experience academic and behavioral problems because of their failure to conform to established norms, rules, and expectations. She recommends that teachers help African American students learn the rules of power in the school culture by explicitly teaching them to the students. The cultural knowledge that many African American, Latino, and American Indian students bring to school conflicts with school norms and values, with school knowledge, and with the ways that teachers interpret and mediate school knowledge. Student cultural knowledge and school knowledge often conflict on variables related to the ways that the individual should relate to and interact with the group (Hale-Benson, 1982, 1994; Ramírez & Castañeda, 1974; Shade, 1989), normative communication styles and interactions (Heath, 1983; Labov, 1975; Philips, 1983; Smitherman, 1977), and perspectives on the nature of U.S. history.

Personal and cultural knowledge is problematic when it conflicts with scientific ways of validating knowledge, is oppositional to the culture of the school, or challenges the main tenets and assumptions of mainstream academic knowledge. Much of the knowledge about out-groups that students learn from their home and community cultures consists of misconceptions, stereotypes, and partial truths (Milner, 1983). Most students in the United States are socialized within communities that are segregated along racial, ethnic, and social-class lines (Feagin & Sikes, 1994; Hacker, 1992). Consequently, most American youths have few opportunities to learn firsthand about the cultures of people from different racial, ethnic, cultural, religious, and social-class groups.

The challenge that teachers face is how to make effective instructional use of the personal and cultural knowledge of students while at the same time helping them to reach beyond their own cultural boundaries (Au, 1993; Boykin, 1983). Although the school should recognize, validate, and make effective use of student personal and cultural knowledge in instruction, an important goal of education is to free students from their cultural and ethnic boundaries and enable them to cross cultural borders freely (Banks, 1991/ 1992, 1994).

In the past, the school has paid scant attention to the personal and cultural knowledge of students and has concentrated on teaching them school knowledge (Sleeter & Grant, 1991a). This practice has had different results for most White middle-class students, for most low-income students, and for most African American and Latino students. Because school knowledge is more consistent with the cultural experiences of most White middle-class students than those of most other groups, these students generally have found the school a more comfortable place than have low-income students and most students of color–the majority of whom are also low-income. A number of writers have described the ways in which many African American, American Indian, and Latino students find the school culture alienating and inconsistent with their cultural experiences, hopes, dreams, and struggles (Hale-Benson, 1982; Heath, 1983; Ramírez & Castañeda, 1974; Shade, 1989).

It is important for teachers to be aware of the personal and cultural knowledge of students when designing the curriculum for today's multicultural schools. Teachers can use student personal cultural knowledge as a vehicle to motivate students and as a foundation for teaching school knowledge (Ladson-Billings, 1994). When teaching a unit on the Westward Movement to Lakota Sioux students, for example, the teacher can ask the students to make a list of their views about the Westward Movement, to relate family stories about the coming of the Whites to Lakota Sioux homelands, and to interview parents and grandparents about their perceptions of what happened when the Whites first occupied Indian lands. When teachers begin a unit on the Westward Movement with student personal cultural knowledge, they can increase student motivation as well as deepen student understanding of the schoolbook version (Wiggington, 1991/1992).

Popular Knowledge

Popular knowledge consists of the facts, interpretations, and beliefs that are institutionalized within television, movies, videos, records, and other forms of the mass media. Many of the tenets of popular knowledge are conveyed in subtle rather than obvious ways (Cortés,1995; Dines & Humez, 1995; Giroux, 1994). Some examples of statements that constitute important themes in popular knowledge follow: (1) The United States is a powerful nation with unlimited opportunities for individuals who are willing to take advantage of them. (2) To succeed in the United States, an individual only has to work hard. You can realize your dreams in the United States if you are willing to work hard and pull yourself up by your bootstraps. (3) As a land of opportunity for all, the United States is a highly cohesive nation, whose ideals of equality and freedom are shared by all.

Most of the major tenets of American popular culture are widely shared and are deeply entrenched in U.S. society. However, they are rarely explicitly articulated. Rather, they are presented in the media and in other sources in the forms of stories, anecdotes, news stories, and interpretations of current events (Cortés, 1991, 1995; Greenfield & Cortés, 1991).

Commercial entertainment films both reflect and perpetuate popular knowledge (Bogle, 1989; Cortés, 1991, 1995; Greenfield & Cortés, 1991). While preparing to write this chapter, I viewed an important and influential film that was directed by John Ford and released by MGM in 1962, *How the West Was Won.* I selected this film for review because the settlement of the West is a major theme in American culture and society about which there are many popular images, beliefs, myths, and misconceptions (Chan, Daniels, García, & Wilson, 1994). In viewing the film, I was particularly interested in the images it depicted about the settlement of the West, about the people who were already in the West, and about those who went West looking for new opportunities.

Ford uses the Prescotts, a White family from Missouri bound for California, to tell his story. The film tells the story of three generations of this family, focusing on the family's struggle to settle in the West. Indians, African Americans, and Mexicans are largely invisible in the film. Indians appear in the story when they attack the Prescott family during their long and perilous journey. The Mexicans appearing in the film are bandits who rob a train and are killed. The several African Americans in the film are in the background silently rowing a boat. At various points in the film, Indians are referred to as *hostile Indians* and as *squaws.*

How the West Was Won is a masterpiece in American popular culture. It not only depicts some of the major themes in American culture about the winning of the West; it reinforces and perpetuates dominant societal attitudes about ethnic groups and gives credence to the notion that the West was won by liberty-loving, hard-working people who pursued freedom for all. The film narrator states near its end, "[The movement West] produced a people free to dream, free to act, and free to mold their own destiny."

Mainstream Academic Knowledge

Mainstream academic knowledge consists of the concepts, paradigms, theories, and explanations that constitute traditional and established knowledge in the behavioral and social sciences. An important tenet within the mainstream academic paradigm is that there is a set of objective truths that can be verified through rigorous and objective research procedures that are uninfluenced by human interests, values, and perspectives (Greer, 1969; Kaplan, 1964; Sleeter, 1991). This empirical knowledge, uninfluenced by human values and interests, constitutes a body of objective truths that should form the core of the school and university curriculum. Much of this objective knowledge originated in the West but is considered universal in nature and application.

Mainstream academic knowledge is the knowledge that multicultural critics such as Ravitch and Finn (1987), Hirsch (1987), and Bloom (1987) claim is threatened by the addition of content about women and ethnic groups of color to the school and university curriculum. This knowledge reflects the established, Western-oriented canon that historically has dominated university research and teaching in the United States. Mainstream academic knowledge consists of the theories and interpretations that are internalized and accepted by most university researchers, academic societies, and organizations such as the American Historical Association, the American Sociological Association, the American Psychological Association, and the National Academy of Sciences.

It is important to point out, however, that an increasing number of university scholars are critical theorists and postmodernists who question the empirical paradigm that dominates Western science (Cherryholmes, 1988; Giroux, 1983; Rosenau, 1992). Many of these individuals are members of national academic organizations, such as the American Historical Association and the American Sociological Association. In most of these professional organizations, the postmodern scholars—made up of significant numbers of scholars of color and feminists—have formed caucuses and interest groups within the mainstream organizations.

I am not claiming that there is a uniformity of belief among mainstream academic scholars, but rather that there are dominant canons, paradigms, and theories that are accepted by the community of mainstream academic scholars and researchers. Occasionally these established canons and paradigms are challenged within the mainstream academic community itself. However, they receive their most serious challenges from academics outside the mainstream, such as scholars within the transformative academic community whom I will describe later (Collins, 1990; hooks, 1994; Okihiro, 1994; Takaki, 1993).

Mainstream academic knowledge, like the other forms of knowledge discussed in this chapter, is not static, but dynamic, complex, and changing. Challenges to the dominant canons and paradigms within mainstream academic knowledge come from both within and without. These challenges lead to changes, reinterpretations, debates, and disagreements, and ultimately to paradigm shifts, new theories, and interpretations. Kuhn (1970) states that a scientific revolution takes place when a new paradigm emerges and replaces an existing one. What is more typical in education and the social sciences is that competing paradigms coexist, although particular ones might be more influential during certain times.

We can examine the treatment of slavery within the mainstream academic community over time, or the treatment of the American Indian, to identify ways that mainstream academic knowledge has changed in important ways since the late nineteenth and early twentieth centuries. Ulrich B. Phillips's highly influential book, *American Negro Slavery*, published in 1918, dominated the way Black slavery was interpreted until his views were challenged by researchers in the 1950s (Stampp, 1956). Phillips was a respected authority on the antebellum South and on slavery. His book, which became a historical classic, is essentially an apology for southern slaveholders (Smith & Inscoe, 1993). A new paradigm about slavery was developed in the 1970s that drew heavily on the slaves' view of their own experiences (Blassingame, 1972; Genovese, 1972; Gutman, 1976).

During the late nineteenth and early twentieth centuries, the American Indian was portrayed in mainstream academic knowledge as either a noble or a hostile savage (Hoxie, 1988). Other notions that became institutionalized within mainstream academic knowledge include the idea that Columbus discovered America and that America was a thinly populated frontier when the Europeans arrived in the late fifteenth century. Frederick Jackson Turner (1894/1989) argued that the frontier, which he regarded as a wilderness, was the main source of American democracy. Although Turner's thesis is now being highly criticized by revisionist historians, his essay established a conception of the West that has been highly influential in American mainstream scholarship, in the popular culture, and in schoolbooks. The conception of the West he depicted is still influential today in the school curriculum and in textbooks (Sleeter & Grant, 1991b).

These ideas also became institutionalized within mainstream academic knowledge: The slaves were happy and contented; most of the important ideas that became a part of American civilization came from Western Europe; and the history of the United States has been one of constantly expanding progress and increasing democracy. African slaves were needed to transform the United States from an empty wilderness into an industrial democratic civilization. The American Indians had to be Christianized and removed to reservations in order for this to occur.

Transformative Academic Knowledge

Transformative academic knowledge consists of concepts, paradigms, themes, and explanations that challenge mainstream academic knowledge and that expand the historical and literary canon. Transformative academic knowledge challenges some of the key assumptions that mainstream scholars make about the nature of knowledge. Transformative and mainstream academic knowledge is based on different epistemological assumptions about the nature of knowledge, about the influence of human interests and values on knowledge construction, and about the purpose of knowledge.

An important tenet of mainstream academic knowledge is that it is neutral, objective, and uninfluenced by human interests and values. Transformative academic knowledge reflects postmodern assumptions and goals about the nature and aims of knowledge (Foucault, 1972; Rorty, 1989; Rosenau, 1992). Transformative academic scholars assume that knowledge is not neutral but is influenced by human interests, that all knowledge reflects the power and social relationships within society, and that an important purpose of knowledge construction is to help people improve society (Code, 1991; Harding, 1991; hooks & West, 1991; King & Mitchell, 1990; Minnich, 1990). Write King and Mitchell: "Like other praxis-oriented Critical approaches, the Afrocentric method seeks to enable people to understand social reality in order to change it. But its additional imperative is to transform the society's basic ethos" (p. 95).

These statements reflect some of the main ideas and concepts in transformative academic knowledge: Columbus did not discover America. The Indians had been living in this land for about 40,000 years when the Europeans arrived. Concepts such as "the European Discovery of America" and "the Westward Movement" need to be reconceptualized and viewed from the perspectives of different cultural and ethnic groups. The Lakota Sioux's homeland was not the West to them; it was the center of the universe. It was not the West for the Alaskans; it was South. It was East for the Japanese and North for the people who lived in Mexico. The history of the United States has not been one of continuous progress toward democratic ideals (Appleby, 1992; Huggins, 1995). Rather, the nation's history has been characterized by a cyclic quest for democracy and by conflict, struggle, violence, and exclusion

(Acuña, 1988; Zinn, 1980). A major challenge that faces the nation is how to make its democratic ideals a reality for all.

Transformative academic knowledge has a long history in the United States. In 1882 and 1883, George Washington Williams (1849-1891) published, in two volumes, the first comprehensive history of African Americans in the United States, *A History of the Negro Race in America from 1619 to 1880* (Williams, 1882,1883/1968). Williams, like other African American scholars after him, decided to research and write about the Black experience because of the neglect of African Americans by mainstream historians and social scientists and because of the stereotypes and misconceptions about African Americans that appeared in mainstream scholarship.

W. E. B. DuBois (1868-1963) is probably the most prolific African American scholar in U.S. history. His published writings constitute 38 volumes (Aptheker, 1973). DuBois devoted his long career to the formulation of new data, concepts, and paradigms that could be used to reinterpret the Black experience and reveal the role that African Americans had played in the development of American society. His seminal works include *The Suppression of the African Slave Trade to the United States of America, 1638-1870,* the first volume of the Harvard Historical Studies (DuBois, 1896/1969). Perhaps his most discussed book is *Black Reconstruction in America: An Essay Toward a History of the Part Which Black Folk Played in the Attempt to Reconstruct Democracy in America, 1860-1880,* published in 1935. In this book, DuBois (1935/1962) challenged the accepted, institutionalized interpretations of Reconstruction and emphasized the accomplishments of the Reconstruction governments and legislatures, especially the establishment of free public schools.

Carter G. Woodson (1875-1950), the historian and educator who founded the Association for the Study of Negro Life and History and the *Journal of Negro History,* also challenged established paradigms about the treatment of African Americans in a series of important publications, including *The Mis-education of the Negro,* published in 1933. Chapter 5 describes Woodson's work and scholarship.

Transformative Scholarship Since the 1970s

Many scholars have produced significant research and theories since the early 1970s that have challenged and modified institutionalized stereotypes and misconceptions about ethnic groups of color, formulated new concepts and paradigms, and forced mainstream scholars to rethink established interpretations. Much of the transformative academic knowledge that has been produced since the 1970s is becoming institutionalized within mainstream scholarship and within the school, college, and university curricula. In time, much of this scholarship will become mainstream, thus reflecting the highly interrelated nature of the types of knowledge conceptualized and described in this chapter.

Only a few examples of this new, transformative scholarship will be mentioned here because of the limited scope of this chapter. Howard Zinn's *A People's History of the United States* (1980); *Red, White and Black: The Peoples of Early America* by Gary B. Nash (1982); *The Signifying Monkey: A Theory of African-American Literary Criticism* by Henry Louis Gates, Jr. (1988); *Occupied America: A History of Chicanos* by Rodolfo Acuña (1988); *A Different Mirror: A History of Multicultural America* by Ronald Takaki (1993); and *The Sacred Hoop: Recovering the Feminine in American Indian Traditions* by Paul Gunn Allen (1986) are examples of important scholarship that has provided significant new perspectives on the experiences of ethnic groups in the United States and has helped us to transform our conceptions about the experiences of American ethnic groups. Readers acquainted with this scholarship will note that transformative scholarship has been produced by both European Americans and scholars of color.

I will discuss two examples of how the new scholarship in ethnic studies has questioned traditional interpretations and stimulated a search for new explanations and paradigms since the 1950s. Since the pioneering work of E. Franklin Frazier (1939), social scientists had accepted the notion that the slave experience had destroyed the Black family and that the destruction of the African American family continued in the post-World War II period during Black migration to and settlement in northern cities. Moynihan, in his controversial book *The Negro Family in America: The Case for National Action* (1965), used the broken Black family explanation in his analysis. Gutman (1976), in an important historical study of the African American family from 1750 to 1925, concluded that "despite a high rate of earlier involuntary marital breakup, large numbers of slave couples lived in long marriages, and most slaves lived in double-headed households" (p. xxii).

An important group of African and African American scholars have challenged established interpretations about the origin of Greek civilization and the extent to which Greek civilization was influenced by African cultures. These scholars include Diop (1974), Williams (1987), and Van Sertima (1988, 1989). Cheikh Anta Diop is one of the most influential African scholars who has challenged established interpretations about the origin of Greek civilization. In *Black Nations and Culture,* published in 1955 (summarized by Van Sertima, 1989), he sets forth an important thesis that states that Africa is an important root of Western civilization. Diop argues that Egypt "was the node and center of a vast web linking the strands of cultures and languages; that the light that crystallized at the center of this early world had been energized by the cultural electricity streaming from the heartland of Africa" (p. 8).

Since the work by Diop, Williams, and Van Sertima, traditional interpretations about the formation of Greek civilization have been challenged by Bernal (1987/1991), a professor of government at Cornell University. The earlier challenges to established interpretations by Africans and African Americans received little attention, except within the African American community. However, Bernal's work received wide attention in the popular press and among classicists.

Bernal (1987/1991) argues that important aspects of Greek civilization originated in ancient Egypt and Phoenicia and that the ancient civilization of Egypt was essentially African. Bernal believes that the contributions of Egypt and Phoenicia to Greek civilization have been deliberately ignored by classical scholars because of their biased attitudes toward non-White peoples and Semites. Bernal has published two of four planned volumes of his study, *Black Athena.* In Volume 2 he uses evidence from linguistics, archeology, and ancient documents to substantiate his claim that "between 2100 and 1100 b.c., when Greek culture was born, the people of the Aegean borrowed, adapted or had thrust upon them deities and language, technologies and architectures, notions of justice and polis" from Egypt and Phoenicia (Begley, Chideya, & Wilson, 1991, p. 49). Because transformative academic knowledge, such as that constructed by Diop, Williams, Van Sertima, and Bernal, challenges the established paradigm as well as because of the tremendous gap between academic knowledge and school knowledge, it often has little influence on school knowledge.

School Knowledge

School knowledge consists of the facts, concepts, and generalizations presented in textbooks, teachers' guides, and the other forms of media designed for school use. School knowledge also consists of the teacher's mediation and interpretation of that knowledge. The textbook is the main source of school knowledge in the United States (Apple & Christian-Smith, 1991; Goodlad, 1984; Shaver, Davis, & Helburn, 1979). Studies of textbooks indicate that these are some of the major themes in school knowledge (Anyon, 1979, 1981; Loewen, 1995; Sleeter & Grant, 1991b): (1) America's founding fathers, such as Washington and Jefferson, were highly moral, liberty-loving men who championed equality and justice for all Americans; (2) the United States is a nation with justice, liberty, and freedom for all; (3) social-class divisions are not significant issues in the United States; (4) there are no significant gender, class, or racial divisions within U.S. society; and

(5) ethnic groups of color and Whites interact largely in harmony in the United States.

Studies of textbooks conducted by researchers such as Anyon (1979, 1981) and Sleeter and Grant (1991b) indicate that textbooks present a highly selective view of social reality, give students the idea that knowledge is static rather than dynamic, and encourage students to master isolated facts rather than to develop complex understandings of social reality. These studies also indicate that textbooks reinforce the dominant social, economic, and power arrangements within society. Students are encouraged to accept rather than to question these arrangements.

In their examination of the treatment of race, class, gender, and disability in textbooks, Sleeter and Grant (1991b) concluded that although textbooks had largely eliminated sexist language and had incorporated images of ethnic minorities into them, they failed to help students to develop an understanding of the complex cultures of ethnic groups, and an understanding of racism, sexism, and classism in American society. Moreover, textbooks described the United States as a nation that had largely overcome its problems. Sleeter and Grant write:

> The vision of social relations that the textbooks we analyzed for the most part project is one of harmony and equal opportunity—anyone can do or become whatever he or she wants; problems among people are mainly individual in nature and in the end are resolved. (p. 99)

A number of powerful factors influence the development and production of school textbooks (Altbach, Kelly, Petrie, & Weis, 1991; Fitzgerald, 1979). One of the most important is the publisher's perception of statements and images that might be controversial. When textbooks become controversial, school districts often refuse to adopt and to purchase them. When developing a textbook, the publisher and the authors also must consider the developmental and reading levels of students, state and district guidelines about what subject matter textbooks should include, and recent trends and developments in a content field that teachers and administrators will expect the textbook to reflect and incorporate. Because of the number of constraints and influences on the development of textbooks, school knowledge often does not include in-depth discussions and analyses of some of the major problems in American society, such as racism, sexism, social-class stratification, and poverty (Anyon, 1979, 1981; Sleeter & Grant, 1991b). Consequently, school knowledge is influenced most heavily by mainstream academic knowledge and popular knowledge. Transformative academic knowledge usually has little direct influence on school knowledge. It usually affects school knowledge in a significant way only after it has become a part of mainstream and popular knowledge. Teachers must make special efforts to introduce transformative knowledge and perspectives to elementary and secondary school students.

Teaching Implications

Multicultural education involves changes in the total school environment in order to create equal educational opportunities for all students (Banks, 1991; Banks & Banks, 1993, 1995; Sleeter & Grant, 1987). However, in this chapter I have focused on only one of the important dimensions of multicultural education—the kinds of *knowledge* that should be taught in the multicultural curriculum. The five types of knowledge described above have important implications for planning and teaching a multicultural curriculum. An important goal of multicultural teaching is to help students to understand how knowledge is constructed. Students should be given opportunities to investigate and determine how cultural assumptions, frames of references, perspectives, and the biases within a discipline influence the ways that knowledge is constructed. Students also should be given opportunities to create knowledge themselves and identify ways in which the knowledge they construct is influenced and limited by their personal assumptions, positions, and experiences.

I will use a unit on the Westward Movement to illustrate how teachers can use the knowledge categories described above to teach from a multicultural perspective. When beginning the unit, teachers can draw on the students' personal and cultural knowledge about the Westward Movement. They can ask the students to make a list of ideas that come to mind when they think of "the West." To enable the students to determine how the popular culture depicts the West, teachers can ask the students to view and analyze the film discussed above, *How the West Was Won.* They can also ask students to view videos of more recently made films about the West and to make a list of major themes and images. Teachers can summarize Turner's frontier theory to give students an idea of how an influential mainstream historian described and interpreted the West in the late nineteenth century and how this theory influenced generations of historians.

Teachers can present a transformative perspective on the West by showing the students the film *How the West Was Won and Honor Lost,* narrated by Marlon Brando. This film describes how the European Americans who went West, with the use of broken treaties and deceptions, invaded the land of the Indians and displaced them. Teachers also may ask students to view segments of the popular film *Dances with Wolves* and to discuss how the depiction of Indians in this film reflects both mainstream and transformative perspectives on Indians in U.S. history and culture. Teachers can present the textbook account of the Westward Movement in the final part of the unit.

The main goals of presenting different kinds of knowledge are to help students understand how knowledge is constructed and how it reflects the social context in which it is created, and to enable them to develop the understandings and skills needed to become knowledge builders themselves. An important goal of multicultural education is to transform the school curriculum so that students not only learn the knowledge that has been constructed by others, but also learn how to critically analyze the knowledge they master and how to construct their own interpretations of the past, present, and future.

Several important factors related to teaching the types of knowledge have not been discussed in this chapter but need to be examined. One is the personal/cultural knowledge of the classroom teacher. Teachers, like students, bring understandings, concepts, explanations, and interpretations to the classroom that result from their experiences in their homes, families, and community cultures. Most teachers in the United States are European American (87%) and female (72%) (Ordovensky, 1992). However, there is enormous diversity among European Americans that is mirrored in the backgrounds of the teacher population, including diversity related to religion, social class, region, and ethnic origin. The diversity within European Americans rarely is discussed in the social science literature or within classrooms (Alba, 1990) . However, the rich diversity among the cultures of teachers is an important factor that needs to be examined and discussed in the classroom. The 13% of U.S. teachers who are ethnic minorities also can enrich their classrooms by sharing their personal and cultural knowledge with their students and by helping them to understand how it mediates textbook knowledge. The multicultural classroom is a forum of multiple voices and perspectives. The voices of the teacher, of the textbook, of mainstream and transformative authors—and of the students—are important components of classroom discourse.

Teachers can share their cultural experiences and interpretations of events as a way to motivate students to share theirs. However, they should examine their racial and ethnic attitudes toward diverse groups before engaging in cultural sharing. A democratic classroom atmosphere also must be created. The students must view the classroom as a forum where multiple perspectives are valued. An open and democratic classroom will enable students to acquire the skills and abilities they need to examine conflicting knowledge claims and perspectives. Students must become critical consumers of knowledge as well as knowledge producers if they are to acquire the understandings and skills needed to function in the complex and diverse world of tomorrow. Only a critical and transformative multicultural education can prepare them for that world.

REFERENCES

Acuña, R. (1988). *Occupied America: A history of Chicanos* (3rd ed.). New York: Harper & Row.

Alba, R. D. (1990). *Ethnic identity: The transformation of White America.* New Haven: Yale University Press.

Allen, P. G. (1986). *The sacred hoop: Recovering the feminine in American Indian traditions.* Boston: Beacon Press.

Altbach, P. G., Kelly, G. P., Petrie, H. G., & Weis, L. (Eds.). (1991). *Textbooks in American society.* Albany: State University of New York Press.

The American heritage dictionary. (1983). New York: Dell.

Anyon, J. (1979). Ideology and United States history textbooks. *Harvard Educational Review, 49,* 361-386.

Anyon, J. (1981). Social class and school knowledge. *Curriculum Inquiry, 11,* 3-42.

Anzaldúa, G. (1990). Haciendo caras, una entrada: An introduction. In G. Anzaldúa (Ed.), *Making face, making soul: Haciendo caras* (pp. xv-xvii). San Francisco: Aunt Lute Foundation Books.

Apple, M. W., & Christian-Smith, L. K. (Eds.). (1991). *The politics of the textbook.* New York: Routledge.

Appleby, J. (1992). Recovering America's historic diversity: Beyond exceptionalism. *The Journal of American History, 79* (2), 419-431.

Aptheker, H. (Ed.). (1973). *The collected published works of W. E. B. DuBois* (38 vols.). Millwood, NY: Kraus-Thomson.

Asante, M. K. (1991). The Afrocentric idea in education. *The Journal of Negro Education, 60*(2), 170-180.

Asante, M. K., & Ravitch, D. (1991). Multiculturalism: An exchange. *The American Scholar, 60,* 267-275.

Au, K. H. (1993). *Literacy instruction in multicultural settings.* New York: Harcourt.

Banks, J. A. (1991). *Teaching strategies for ethnic studies* (5th ed.). Boston: Allyn & Bacon.

Banks, J. A. (1991/1992). Multicultural education: For freedom's sake. *Educational Leadership, 49* (4), 32-36.

Banks, J. A. (1994). *Multiethnic education: Theory and practice* (3rd ed.). Boston: Allyn & Bacon.

Banks, J. A., & Banks, C. A. M. (Eds.). (1993). *Multicultural education: Issues and perspectives* (2nd ed.). Boston: Allyn & Bacon.

Banks, J. A., & Banks, C. A. M. (Eds.). (1995). *Handbook of research on multicultural education.* New York: Macmillan.

Begley, S., Chideya, F., & Wilson, L. (1991, September 23). Out of Egypt, Greece: Seeking the roots of Western civilization on the banks of the Nile. *Newsweek, 118,* 48-49.

Bernal, M. (1987/1991). *Black Athena: The Afroasiatic roots of classical civilization* (Vols. 1-2). London: Free Association Books.

Blassingame, J. W. (1972). *The slave community: Plantation life in the antebellum South.* New York: Oxford University Press.

Bloom, A. (1987). *The closing of the American mind.* New York: Simon & Schuster.

Bogle, D. (1989). *Toms, coons, mulattos, mammies & bucks: An interpretative history of Blacks in American films* (new expanded ed.). New York: Continuum.

Boykin, A. W. (1983). The academic performance of Afro-American children. In J. Spence (Ed.), *Research directions of Black psychologists* (pp. 351–367). New York: Russell Sage Foundation.

Butler, J. E., & Walter, J. C. (1991). (Eds.). *Transforming the curriculum: Ethnic studies and women's studies.* Albany: State University of New York Press.

Chan, S., Daniels, D. H., García, M. T., & Wilson, T. P. (Eds.). (1994). *People of color in the West.* Lexington, MA: Heath.

Cherryholmes, C. H. (1988). *Power and criticism: Poststructural investigations in education.* New York: Teachers College Press.

Clark, K. B. (1965). *Dark ghetto: Dilemmas of social power.* New York: Harper & Row.

Code, L. (1991). *What can she know? Feminist theory and the construction of knowledge.* Ithaca, NY: Cornell University Press.

Collins, P. H. (1990). *Black feminist thought: Knowledge, consciousness, and the politics of empowerment.* New York: Routledge.

Cooper, A. J. (1969). *A voice from the South.* New York: Negro Universities Press. (Original work published 1892)

Cortés, C. E. (1991). Hollywood interracial love: Social taboo as screen titillation. In P. Loukides & L. K. Fuller (Eds.), *Beyond the stars II: Plot conventions in American popular film* (pp. 21–35). Bowling Green, OH: Bowling Green State University Press.

Cortés, C. E. (1995). Knowledge construction and popular culture: The media as multicultural educator. In J. A. Banks & C. A. M. Banks (Eds.), *Handbook of research on multicultural education* (pp. 169–183). New York: Macmillan.

Delpit, L. D. (1988). The silenced dialogue: Power and pedagogy in educating other people's children. *Harvard Educational Review, 58,* 280–298.

Delpit, L. (1995). *Other people's children: Cultural conflict in the classroom.* New York: New Press.

Dines, G., & Humez, M. (Eds.). (1995). *Gender, race, and class in media: A textreader.* Thousand Oakes, CA: Sage.

Diop, C. A. (1955). *Nations Nègres et culture.* Paris: Presence Africaine.

Diop, C. A. (1974). *The African origin of civilization: Myth or reality?* New York: Lawrence Hill.

D'Souza, D. (1991). *Illiberal education: The politics of race and sex on campus.* New York: Free Press.

DuBois, W. E. B. (1962). *Black Reconstruction in America: An essay toward a history of the part which Black folk played in the attempt to reconstruct democracy in America, 1860–1880.* New York: Atheneum. (Original work published 1935)

DuBois, W. E. B. (1969). *The suppression of the African slave trade to the United States of America, 1638–1870.* Baton Rouge: Louisiana State University Press. (Original work published 1896)

Ellsworth, E. (1989). Why doesn't this feel empowering? Working through the repressive myths of critical pedagogy. *Harvard Educational Review, 59,* 297-324.

Farganis, S. (1986). *The social construction of the feminine character.* Totowa, NJ: Russell & Russell.

Feagin, J. R., & Sikes, M. P. (1994). *Living with racism: The Black middle-class experience.* Boston: Beacon Press.

Fitzgerald, F. (1979). *America revised: History schoolbooks in the twentieth century.* New York: Vintage Books.

Fordham, S. (1988). Racelessness as a factor in Black students' school success: Pragmatic strategy or Pyrrhic victory? *Harvard Educational Review, 58,* 54-84.

Fordham, S. (1991). Racelessness in private schools: Should we deconstruct the racial and cultural identity of African-American adolescents? *Teachers College Record, 92,* 470-484.

Fordham, S., & Ogbu, J. (1986). Black students' school success: Coping with the burden of "acting White." *The Urban Review, 18,* 176-206.

Foucault, M. (1972). *The archaeology of knowledge and the discourse on language.* New York: Pantheon.

Franklin, J. H. (1991, September 26). Illiberal education: An exchange. *New York Review of Books, 38,* 74-76.

Frazier, E. F. (1939). *The Negro family in the United States.* Chicago: University of Chicago Press.

Gates, H. L., Jr. (1988). *The signifying monkey: A theory of African-American literary criticism.* New York: Oxford University Press.

Gates, H. L., Jr. (1992). *Loose canons: Notes on the culture wars.* New York: Oxford University Press.

Genovese, E. D. (1972). *Roll Jordan roll: The world the slaves made.* New York: Pantheon.

Giroux, H. A. (1983). *Theory and resistance in education: A pedagogy for the opposition.* South Hadley, MA: Bergin & Garvey.

Giroux, H. A. (1994). *Disturbing pleasures: Learning popular culture.* New York: Routledge.

Glazer, N. (1991, September 2). In defense of multiculturalism. *The New Republic,* pp. 18-21.

Gollnick, D. M. (1995). National and state initiatives for multicultural education. In J. A. Banks & C. A. M. Banks (Eds.), *Handbook of research on multicultural education* (pp. 44-64). New York: Macmillan.

Goodlad, J. I. (1984). *A place called school: Prospects for the future.* New York: McGraw-Hill.

Gordon, E. W. (1985). Social science knowledge production and minority experiences. *The Journal of Negro Education, 54,* 117-132.

Gordon, E. W., Miller, F., & Rollock, D. (1990). Coping with communicentric bias in knowledge production in the social sciences. *Educational Researcher, 14*(3), 14-19.

Grant, C. A. (Ed.). (1992). *Research and multicultural education: From the margins to the mainstream.* Washington, DC: Falmer Press.

Gray, P. (1991, July 8). Whose America? *Time*, *138*, 12-17.

Greenfield, G. M., & Cortés, C. E. (1991). Harmony and conflict of intercultural images: The treatment of Mexico in U.S. feature films and K-12 textbooks. *Mexican Studies/Estudios Mexicanos, 7,* 283-301.

Greer, S. (1969). *The logic of social inquiry.* Chicago: Aldine.

Gutiérrez, R. A. (1995). Historical and social science research on Mexican Americans. In J. A. Banks & C. A. M. Banks (Eds.), *Handbook of research on multicultural education* (pp. 203-222). New York: Macmillan.

Gutman, H. G. (1976). *The Black family in slavery and freedom 1750-1925.* New York: Vintage Books.

Habermas, J. (1971). *Knowledge and human interests.* Boston: Beacon Press.

Hacker, A. (1992). *Two nations: Black and White, separate, hostile, unequal.* New York: Ballantine Books.

Hale-Benson, J. E. (1982). *Black children: Their roots, culture, and learning styles* (rev. ed.). Baltimore: Johns Hopkins University Press.

Hale, J. E. (1994). *Unbank the fire: Visions for the education of African American children.* Baltimore: Johns Hopkins University Press.

Harding, S. (1991). *Whose science? Whose knowledge? Thinking from women's lives.* Ithaca, NY: Cornell University Press.

Harding, V. (1981). *There is a river: The Black struggle for freedom in America.* New York: Vintage Books.

Heath, S. B. (1983). *Ways with words: Language, life and work in communities and classrooms.* New York: Cambridge University Press.

Hirsch, E. D., Jr. (1987). *Cultural literacy: What every American needs to know.* Boston: Houghton Mifflin.

hooks, b. (1994). *Teaching to transgress: Education as the practice of freedom.* New York: Routledge.

hooks, b., & West, C. (1991). *Breaking bread: Insurgent Black intellectual life.* Boston: South End Press.

Howe, I. (1991, February 18). The value of the canon. *The New Republic,* pp. 40-47.

Hoxie, F. E. (Ed.). (1988). *Indians in American history.* Arlington Heights, IL: Harlan Davidson.

Hoxie, F. E. (n. d.). *The Indians versus the textbooks: Is there any way out?* Chicago: The Newberry Library, Center for the History of the American Indian.

Huggins, N. I. (1995). *Revelations: American history, American myths.* New York: Oxford University Press.

Kaplan, A. (1964). *The conduct of inquiry: Methodology for behavioral science.* San Francisco: Chandler.

King, J. E., & Mitchell, C. A. (1990). *Black mothers to sons: Juxtaposing African American literature with social practice.* New York: Lang.

Kuhn, T. S. (1970). *The structure of scientific revolutions* (2nd ed.). Chicago: University of Chicago Press.

Labov, W. (1975). *The study of nonstandard English.* Washington, DC: Center for Applied Linguistics.

Ladner, J. A. (Ed.). (1973). *The death of White sociology.* New York: Vintage.

Ladson-Billings, G. (1994). *The dreamkeepers: Successful teachers of African American children*. San Francisco: Jossey-Bass.

Loewen, J. W. (1995). *Lies my teacher told me: Everything your American history textbook got wrong*. New York: New Press.

Meier, A., & Rudwick, E. (1986). *Black history and the historical profession, 1915-1980*. Urbana: University of Illinois Press.

Merton, R. K. (1972). Insiders and outsiders: A chapter in the sociology of knowledge. *The American Journal of Sociology, 78*(1), 9-47.

Milner, D. (1983). *Children and race*. Beverly Hills, CA: Sage.

Minnich, E. K. (1990). *Transforming knowledge*. Philadelphia: Temple University Press.

Moynihan, D. P. (1965). *The Negro family in America: The case for national action*. Washington, DC: U.S. Department of Labor.

Myrdal, G. (with Sterner, R., & Rose, A.). (1944). *An American dilemma: The Negro problem and modern democracy*. New York: Harper.

Nash, G. B. (1982). *Red, White and Black: The peoples of early America*. Englewood Cliffs, NJ: Prentice-Hall.

New York City Board of Education. (1990). *Grade 7, United States and New York State history: A multicultural perspective*. New York: Author.

New York State Department of Education. (1989, July). *A curriculum of inclusion* (Report of the Commissioner's Task Force on Minorities: Equity and excellence). Albany: State Department of Education.

New York State Department of Education. (1991, June). *One nation, many peoples: A declaration of cultural interdependence*. Albany: State Department of Education.

Okihiro, G. Y. (1994). *Margins and mainstreams: Asians in American history and culture*. Seattle: University of Washington Press.

Ordovensky, P. (1992, July 7). Teachers: 87% White, 72% women. *USA Today*, p. 1A.

Philips, S. U. (1983). *The invisible culture: Communication in classroom and community on the Warm Springs Indian Reservation*. New York: Longman.

Phillips, U. B. (1918). *American Negro slavery*. New York: Appleton.

Ramírez, M., III, & Castañeda, A. (1974). *Cultural democracy, bicognitive development, and education*. New York: Academic Press.

Ravitch, D., & Finn, C. E., Jr. (1987). *What do our 17-year-olds know? A report on the first national assessment of history and literature*. New York: Harper & Row.

Rivlin, A. M. (1973). Forensic social science. *Harvard Educational Review, 43*, 61-75.

Rodríguez, C. E. (1995). Puerto Ricans in historical and social science research. In J. A. Banks & C. A. M. Banks (Eds.), *Handbook of research on multicultural education* (pp. 223-244). New York: Macmillan.

Rorty, R. (1989). *Contingency, irony, and solidarity*. New York: Cambridge University Press.

Rosenau, P. M. (1992). *Post-modernism and the social sciences: Insights, inroads, and intrusions*. Princeton, NJ: Princeton University Press.

Schlesinger, A. M., Jr. (1991). *The disuniting of America: Reflections on a multicultural society*. Knoxville, TN: Whittle Direct Books.

Shade, B. J. R. (Ed.). (1989). *Culture, style and the educative process*. Springfield, IL: Charles C. Thomas.

Shaver, J. P., Davis, O. L., Jr., & Helburn, S. W. (1979). The status of social studies education: Impressions from three NSF studies. *Social Education, 43*, 150-153.

Sleeter, C. E. (Ed.). (1991). *Empowerment through multicultural education*. Albany: State University of New York Press.

Sleeter, C. E. (1995). An analysis of the critiques of multicultural education. In J. A. Banks & C. A. M. Banks (Eds.), *Handbook of research on multicultural education* (pp. 81-94). New York: Macmillan.

Sleeter, C. E., & Grant, C. A. (1987). An analysis of multicultural education in the United States. *Harvard Educational Review, 57*(4), 421-444.

Sleeter, C. E., & Grant, C. A. (1991a). Mapping terrains of power: Student cultural knowledge versus classroom knowledge. In C. E. Sleeter (Ed.), *Empowerment through multicultural education* (pp. 49-67). Albany: State University of New York Press.

Sleeter, C. E., & Grant. C. A. (1991b). Race, class, gender and disability in current textbooks. In M. W. Apple & L. K. Christian-Smith (Eds.), *The politics of the textbook* (pp. 78-110). New York: Routledge.

Smith, J. D., & Inscoe, J. C. (Eds.). (1993). *Ulrich Bonnell Phillips: A southern historian and his critics*. Athens: University of Georgia Press.

Smitherman, G. (1977). *Talkin and testifyin: The language of Black America*. Boston: Houghton Mifflin.

Sokol, E. (Ed.). (1990). *A world of difference: St. Louis metropolitan region preschool through grade 6, teacher/student resource guide*. St. Louis: Anti-Defamation League of B'nai B'rith.

Stampp, K. M. (1956). *The peculiar institution: Slavery in the ante-bellum South*. New York: Vintage Books.

Takaki, R. (1993). *A different mirror: A history of multicultural America*. Boston: Little, Brown.

Tetreault, M. K. T. (1993). Classrooms for diversity: Rethinking curriculum and pedagogy. In J. A. Banks & C. A. M. Banks (Eds.), *Multicultural education: Issues and perspectives* (2nd ed., pp. 129-148). Boston: Allyn & Bacon.

Thornton, R. (1987). *American Indian holocaust and survival: A population history since 1492*. Norman: University of Oklahoma Press.

Turner, F. J. (1989). The significance of the frontier in American history. In C. A. Milner II (Ed.), *Major problems in the history of the American West* (pp. 2-21). Lexington, MA: Heath. (Original work published 1894)

Van Sertima, I. V. (Ed.). (1988). *Great Black leaders: Ancient and modern*. New Brunswick, NJ: Rutgers University, Africana Studies Department.

Van Sertima, I. V. (Ed.). (1989). *Great African thinkers: Vol. 1. Cheikh Anta Diop*. New Brunswick, NJ: Transaction Books.

Wiggington, E. (1991/1992). Culture begins at home. *Educational Leadership, 49*, 60-64.

Williams, C. (1987). *The destiny of Black civilization: Great issues of a race from 4500 B.C. to 2000 A.D.* Chicago: Third World Press.

Williams, G. W. (1968). *History of the Negro race in America from 1619 to 1880: Negroes as slaves, as soldiers, and as citizens* (2 vols.). New York: Arno Press. (Original works published 1882 & 1883)

Woodson, C. G. (1933). *The mis-education of the Negro.* Washington, DC: Associated Publishers.

Woodward, C. V. (1991, July 18). Freedom and the universities. *The New York Review of Books, 38,* 32–37.

Young, M. F. D. (1971). An approach to curriculum as socially organized knowledge. In M. F. D. Young (Ed.), *Knowledge and control* (pp. 19–46). London: Collier-Macmillan.

Zinn, H. (1980). *A people's history of the United States.* New York: Harper & Row.

CHAPTER 2

The African American Roots of Multicultural Education

JAMES A. BANKS

Consensus among scholars within multicultural education about its aims and boundaries is emerging. Most multicultural education specialists believe that a major aim of the field is to restructure schools, colleges, and universities so that students from diverse racial, ethnic, and social-class groups will experience an equal opportunity to learn (Banks, 1994; Banks & Banks, 1993, 1995; Gay, 1992; Grant, 1977). As schools, colleges, and universities are currently structured, some groups of students, such as middle-class White males, have a better chance for academic success than have others, such as African American males, especially those who live in low-income, inner-city communities (Gibbs, 1988; Lee & Slaughter-Defoe, 1995).

Although there is a high level of consensus among multicultural education theorists and specialists about the broad aims of the field, there is less agreement among them about its exact boundaries, dimensions, and specifics. Some theorists focus their work primarily on ethnic groups of color (i.e., African Americans and Latinos) (Baker, 1994; Bennett, 1990). Other theorists conceptualize multicultural education more broadly and include race, class, gender, and exceptionality—and the interaction of these variables—as important components of the field (Banks & Banks, 1993, 1995; García, 1991; Gollnick & Chinn, 1990). Banks (1994) makes an important distinction between *multiethnic education,* which focuses on ethnic and racial groups, and *multicultural education*, which deals with race, class, gender, and exceptionality and their interaction. However, this distinction rarely is made by other theorists and investigators.

CONCEPTUALIZING THE HISTORY
OF MULTICULTURAL EDUCATION

The way in which the history of a field is conceptualized is directly related to how its aims and boundaries are constructed. A history of multicultural education that conceptualizes it as a broad field that includes race, class, gender, and the interaction of the three results in a historical treatment with a scope broader than that of a history that conceptualizes multicultural education as a field focusing on people of color.

In this chapter, multicultural education is conceptualized as a broad interdisciplinary field that focuses on a range of racial, ethnic, and cultural groups as well as both genders. Due to space constraints, only some of the important aspects of the field's history will be discussed. This chapter thus focuses on the development of African American scholarship as one of the most important historical roots of the current multicultural education movement. The intergroup education movement of the 1940s and 1950s is another significant historical precedent of multicultural education that will be discussed and compared with the African American roots of multicultural education. However, as will be illustrated, intergroup education is a historical antecedent of multicultural education, not a root of the current movement. Chapter 14 provides a comprehensive discussion of the intergroup education movement.

The Early African American Studies Movement

The current multicultural education and Afrocentric movements are linked directly to the early study of African Americans undertaken by scholars such as George Washington Williams (1882, 1883/1989), W. E. B. DuBois (1899/1973, 1896/1973), Carter G. Woodson (1919/1968, 1921), Horace Mann Bond (1939), and Charles H. Wesley (1935/1969). The period from the publication of Williams's *History of the Negro Race in America* (1989/1882–1883) to the beginning of the 1970s can be conceptualized as one continuous period of African American scholarship because of the characteristics shared by these scholars, the problems they faced, the links in their research, the ways in which their scholarship was viewed by the mainstream popular and scholarly communities, and their struggles for acceptance and legitimacy (Meier & Rudwick, 1986). This period of almost 90 years also can be subdivided into more distinct periods, as was done by Franklin (1989), who divided it into four generations of scholars.

Most of the scholars working in Black studies prior to the 1950s were African Americans (Meier & Rudwick, 1986). Their research and publications were largely ignored by the White scholarly community and the wider society. Most of their research was published for African American audiences and institutions such as Black schools, colleges, churches, and fraternities. Much of it was published by African American presses and institutions such as the Associated Publishers, a division of the Association for the Study of Negro (now Afro-American) Life and History (ASNLH/ASALH), founded by Woodson and his colleagues.

Prior to the civil rights movement of the 1960s, most African American scholars were able to find jobs only in predominantly Black schools and colleges, where teaching loads were heavy and there was little support for scholarly research and writing (Meier & Rudwick, 1986; Platt, 1991). African American scholars such as Woodson, Wesley, Bond, and E. Franklin Frazier taught in predominantly Black institutions for the duration of their careers. Only a few African American scholars during this period (notably, Allison Davis at the University of Chicago, St. Claire Drake at Roosevelt University in Chicago, and John Hope Franklin at Brooklyn College) were able to obtain positions at predominantly White institutions prior to the 1960s. Franklin taught at predominantly Black colleges before he became chairman of the history department at Brooklyn College in 1956. He moved to the University of Chicago in 1964 and became chairman of its history department in 1967.

Most of the distinguished African American scholars from the turn of the century through the 1940s obtained their undergraduate degrees at historically Black colleges in the South and pursued their graduate education at prestigious White research universities such as Harvard and Columbia in the East and Chicago and the University of Wisconsin in the Midwest. DuBois received his doctorate from Harvard in 1895—the first Black to do so—and taught at Atlanta University. Woodson earned his doctorate from Harvard in 1912 and taught at Howard University and West Virginia State College, both historically Black colleges. Both Frazier and Charles S. Johnson, who became noted sociologists, studied under the influential sociologist Robert E. Park at the University of Chicago, received their doctorates there, and taught at historically Black colleges (Lyman, 1972).

The Focus of Early African American Scholarship

In the late nineteenth century, George Washington Williams published what is considered the first scholarly history of African Americans (Franklin, 1985). The two-volume study, *History of the Negro Race in America from 1619 to 1880* (1882, 1883/1989), was reprinted during the current ethnic studies period that emerged in the 1960s. The reissuing of Williams's two volumes in 1989 is evidence of the direct link between ethnic studies today and African American scholarship of the past. Other important books by these early scholars also have been reprinted for use by today's scholars, including such titles as:

> W. E. B. DuBois, *The Suppression of the African Slave Trade to the United States of America, 1638-1870* (1973); and *The Philadelphia Negro* (1973)
> Carter G. Woodson, *The History of the Negro Church* (1921)
> Charles H. Wesley, *Richard Allen: Apostle of Freedom* (1969/1935).

Although they brought new perspectives and insights to their fields of specialization and studied topics that had been neglected by White scholars, early African American scholars strove for objectivity in their work, wanted to be considered scientific researchers, and tried to avoid any hint that their works were value-laden, positional, or propagandist. Woodson considered himself a scientific historian and eschewed direct involvement in political or civil rights activities. He feared that such actions would endanger his attempts to establish his reputation as an objective historian (Meier & Rudwick, 1986). However, his highly polemical *The Mis-education of the Negro* (1933), his promotion of Negro History Week (now Black History Month), and his efforts to obtain funds from White foundations to keep the ASNLH alive were deeply partisan activities.

DuBois early became directly involved in social protest and civic action and took strong positions on justice and equality in many of his scholarly works. Nonetheless, he also strove to pursue a scientific study of African Americans, as evidenced by his fine scholarship in *The Suppression of the African Slave Trade* and *The Philadelphia Negro* and his aborted attempts to publish a multivolume *Encyclopedia of the Negro*. Like most scholars of color today who care deeply about the plight of their people, both Woodson and DuBois held scientific objectivity as an ideal, yet both became directly involved in action and social change.

The quest for scientific objectivity by early African American scholars should be understood within the context of the times in which they lived and worked. The Western empirical paradigm, borrowed from the European academic tradition and especially that of German universities, was the established paradigm within American universities and scholarship at the turn of the century and during the early years of the twentieth century. Scientific detachment and empiricism were the ideals toward which all scholars allegedly strove. Science was used to justify and rationalize the prevailing beliefs, norms, and practices of the day, including the pervasive stereotypes about African Americans (see Chapter 4 for a comprehensive discussion of these issues).

Gould (1981) has documented how scientific racism was created to justify the prevailing negative beliefs about Southern and Eastern European immigrants to the United States as well as discrimination against African Americans. Nativism, a movement whose major aim was to exclude Southern, Eastern, and Central European immigrants from the United States, was legitimized by scientific racism. This movement triumphed when the Immigration Act of 1924, which placed tight restrictions on the flow of immigrants from these regions, was enacted by Congress.

African American scholars of the period embraced the Western empirical paradigm because it was the most respected paradigm in use at the time. They also believed that the best way to counter the stereotypes and myths about African Americans was to use the prevailing and accepted paradigms and research assumptions to establish scientific facts about people of African descent. They contended that if science could be used to justify racism and stereotypes about African Americans, then that same science also could be used to construct knowledge that would contribute to empowerment and equity for African Americans. The use of the Western empirical paradigm thus became the most powerful weapon available to African American scholars for undercutting the pejorative depictions of African Americans that were pervasive in both the popular culture and the scholarly community (Franklin, 1989; Platt, 1991).

African American scholars also believed that the utilization of the scientific paradigm was the best and perhaps only way for them to attain legitimacy for their research. They were keenly aware that their work was dismissed by many White scholars as propaganda. DuBois was called a "racial chauvinist" and Woodson a "propagandist" by two influential Whites (Logan & Winston, 1982; Meier & Rudwick, 1986). DuBois and Woodson received little recognition from the White academic community during their lifetimes.

The Dilemma of African American Scholars

The conflicts and dilemmas that haunted early African American scholars such as DuBois and Woodson still face African American scholars today, if not in the same form and intensity. Franklin (1989) has written eloquently about the dilemma of the African American scholar, noting that while African American scholars are expected to pursue scientific truths in an objective and dispassionate fashion, many are committed to the uplift of their people. As a result, they often are marginalized by the mainstream scholarly community and their research may be held suspect, especially if it presents findings that challenge existing paradigms or describe African Americans in a more positive fashion than does that of most White scholars.

Further, regardless of their academic interests or specializations, African American scholars often are expected to be specialists in African American studies. In his own case, Franklin, who has tried in vain throughout his career to establish his primary identification as a southern historian, usually is regarded as a specialist in African American history. His book, *A Southern Odyssey: Travelers in the Antebellum North* (1976), which does not focus on African Americans, rarely is mentioned when his major works are listed. In this regard, Franklin's dilemma can be likened to that of the African American biologist Ernest E. Just. Manning (1983), in his richly textured biography of Just, describes the racism that Just experienced trying to teach and do research, and shows how it prevented Just from actualizing his full potential as a first-rate scientist.

The early period of African American studies is both similar to and different from that of the current period; yet, African American scholars of both periods share a quest to create scholarship about African Americans that depicts their experiences in a realistic, objective, and scientific fashion. Some of the new scholarship, especially Afrocentric scholarship (Asante, 1987, 1990), is much more explicit about its value claims and aims than was the early scholarship. Afrocentric scholarship today is also more explicit in its rejection of aspects of the Western empirical paradigm and its quest to create a new paradigm based on assumptions and perspectives that recognize the ways in which knowledge reflects positionality, interests, and values. However, like the current scholarship, the early scholarship on African Americans was not singular in focus. Many of the early scholars strove for objectivity; others pursued links with Egypt to highlight Black achievement and bolster Black pride (Drake, 1987).

One tradition within African American scholarship is directly linked to the current Afrocentric interest in Egypt and the importance of Egypt to the construction of interpretations about the role of Africa in the establishment of Western civilization. Drake (1987) has called these scholars, who included DuBois and other members of the American Negro Academy (founded in 1897), "vindicationists." A major goal of the vindicationists was to defend African Americans against intellectual attacks. He notes that "most educated black men and women had spoken and written during the two previous centuries against apologists for slavery who attempted to justify 'the peculiar institution' with the argument that Negroes were an inferior animal-like breed of [humankind] unfit to be treated like other people" (p. xvii).

Early Teaching of African American Studies

Most of the early African American scholars were teachers who became involved in social action. While they strove to achieve scientific objectivity in their published works, they did not view scholarship merely as an activity to build theories and explanations. Almost all of them were involved in some kinds of actions related to the uplift of the masses of African Americans. They generally believed that scholarship should be used to improve the conditions of their people and contribute to the formation of enlightened public and educational policies. For example, George Washington Williams became a legislator in Ohio; DuBois played important roles in the Niagara Movement and in the establishment of the National Association for the Advancement of Colored People (NAACP) (he also edited the NAACP's widely circulated *Crisis* magazine and wrote on a wide variety of topics related to social and political issues); and, according to Platt (1991), Frazier was a civil rights activist who had strong views on equity issues that he often expressed, to his professional detriment.

Carter G. Woodson and Early Black Ethnic Studies

Woodson probably had more influence on the teaching of African American history in the nation's schools and colleges from the turn of the century until his death in 1950 than any other scholar (Chapter 5 presents a comprehensive discussion of Woodson's career and contributions). With others, he established the ASNLH in 1912. He founded *The Journal of Negro History* in 1916 and served as its editor until his death. It stands as one of Woodson's most important contributions to the study and teaching of Black studies and to the multicultural education movement. In 1921 Woodson established Associated Publishers, a division of the ASNLH, to publish scholarly books and textbooks on African Americans. In addition to publishing Woodson's major books, Associated Publishers published important books by scholars such as Bond (1939) and Wesley (1935/1969).

Woodson, a former high school teacher, played a major role in popularizing African American history and in promoting its study in the nation's Black schools, colleges, churches, and fraternities. He initiated Negro History Week in 1926 to highlight the role that African Americans played in the development of the nation and to commemorate their contributions. In time, and with the vigorous promotion efforts by the ASNLH and its branches throughout the nation, Negro History Week, later expanded to Black History Month, became nationally recognized and celebrated. Woodson never intended for Negro History Week to be the only time of the year in which Black history was taught. Rather, he viewed it as a time to highlight the ongoing study of Black history that was to take place throughout the year.

In 1937 Woodson established *The Negro History Bulletin* to provide information on Black history to elementary and secondary school teachers. He also wrote elementary and secondary school textbooks that were widely used in Black schools, including *African Myths* (1928a), *Negro Makers of*

History (1928b), and *The Story of the Negro Retold* (1935). His widely used and popular text, *The Negro in Our History,* first published in 1922, has survived 11 editions.

The Intergroup Education Movement

The intergroup education movement during the 1940s and 1950s responded to the race riots and violent racial conflicts that occurred in the nation's cities in the early 1940s. Schools and colleges that trained teachers were pressured to create instructional units, projects, and activities to respond to the nation's racial crisis (Cook, 1951; Taba, Brady, & Robinson, 1952). A number of professional and civil rights organizations such as the American Council on Education, the National Council for the Social Studies, the Progressive Education Association, the National Conference of Christians and Jews, and the Anti-Defamation League of B'nai B'rith sponsored intergroup education projects, programs, and publications.

The intergroup education movement and the African American ethnic studies movement are related in several important ways (e.g., intergroup educators used ethnic content to help reduce student prejudice); however, there is little evidence that the movements were significantly linked. Rather, it appears that the African American ethnic studies movement of the 1940s and 1950s and the intergroup education movement were largely separate entities, despite the goals they shared. Neither Woodson nor any of his African American historian colleagues have chapters in any of the intergroup education publications examined by the author in a comprehensive review of intergroup education publications (Banks, 1995). Apparently, these two movements pursued their goals quite independently.

Several characteristics of the ethnic studies and intergroup education movements may explain, in part, why they remained quite separate. First, the two movements had some similar but also some very different goals. The primary goal of scholars such as Woodson, DuBois, and Franklin was to construct accurate knowledge about African Americans so as to invalidate misconceptions and stereotypes, and create more accurate versions of American history and life. The major aim of the intergroup education movement was to reduce prejudice, to develop interracial understandings, and to foster a shared national American culture (Taba & Wilson, 1946). Intergroup educators, most of whom were liberal White academics who worked in mainstream American institutions, placed more emphasis on a shared American identity than did African American scholars, who were more concerned about creating accurate images of African Americans, empowering African Americans, and building African American institutions.

The intergroup education movement and the ethnic studies movement had different origins, ideologies, and grew out of two distinct traditions. The ethnic studies movement, as formulated by scholars such as Williams, DuBois, Woodson, and Wesley, was born out of self-determination, ethnic pride, and survival. It was born within the African American community, supported primarily by African Americans, and fashioned by them. Consequently, it remained a lifelong career and commitment for most of its adherents. By contrast, the intergroup education movement was born in response to a national crisis, led by White professionals who were not linked to minority communities, and largely faded when the heat from the racial crisis faded and special funding for intergroup research and projects dried up.

The Ethnic Studies and Intergroup Education Movements Compared

The African American ethnic studies movement that was born during the late nineteenth and early twentieth centuries has experienced significant continuity from the turn of the century until today. Ethnic studies scholars frequently turned to the work of scholars such as Franklin and Woodson when the ethnic studies movement of the 1960s and 1970s emerged. The work of the early African American scholars provided an important intellectual foundation for the architects of today's multicultural education movement.

While the links among early ethnic studies and the new ethnic studies are direct, the current multicultural education movement and the intergroup education movement of the 1940s and 1950s are largely discrete in origin. This is partly because most of the vital signs of the intergroup education movement had vanished by the time the current multicultural education movement emerged. Significantly, eminent leaders of the intergroup education movement such as Hilda Taba and Lloyd A. Cook had, for the most part, left their work in intergroup education to pursue other academic and professional interests by the late 1950s. Taba became a well-known specialist in curriculum theory and elementary social studies (Taba, 1962, 1967). However, she incorporated some of the important ideas from her intergroup education work into her highly influential social studies curriculum and wrote, with Deborah Elkins (a professor at the City University of New York), the book *Teaching Strategies for the Culturally Disadvantaged,* which was published in 1966.

An important lesson that can be gleaned from the different fates of the African American ethnic studies movement and the intergroup education movement is that for educational reform movements related to diversity to be sustained over the long haul, they require the active involvement of scholars personally connected to and influenced by the fate of the movement, as well as sustained support by ethnic and minority communities. The ethnic studies movement headed by Woodson and his colleagues was supported by the African American community and was not totally dependent on the whims of established mainstream institutions for survival. Intergroup education had little grass-roots support from minority communities and was completely dependent on mainstream institutions for survival. The interest that the mainstream society—and its institutions and scholars—have in ethnic and minority issues is likely to ebb and flow with the times.

THE EVOLUTION OF THE MULTICULTURAL EDUCATION MOVEMENT

The major thesis of this chapter is that the early African American scholarship and the ethnic studies movement are an important historical foundation of the multicultural education movement. This section will describe how the major architects of the multicultural education movement were cogently influenced by early African American scholarship and the ethnic studies movement.

Gwendolyn C. Baker (1973), James A. Banks (1991), Geneva Gay (1992), and Carl A. Grant (1977) have each played significant roles in the formulation and development of multicultural education in the United States. Each of these scholars was heavily influenced by the early work of African American scholars and the African American ethnic studies movement. Each of them did early work in African American studies. Both Banks (1969) and Grant (1972) did their doctoral theses on Black studies topics. Banks attended and made presentations in the late 1960s and early 1970s at annual meetings of the ASNLH. At these meetings, he heard presentations by historians such as Franklin, Wesley, and Benjamin Quarles. Banks's early work was heavily influenced by African American historians, especially Franklin (1947) and Quarles (1964). His first published book is an African American history text for the middle school grades (Banks, 1970).

Baker (1973, 1977) developed one of the first multicultural teacher education programs in the United States while teaching at the University of Michigan, Ann Arbor. She has contributed to the development of theory and practice in multicultural education since its inception (Cross, Baker, & Stiles, 1977). Her work also was heavily influenced by early African American historical research and scholarship. Banks and Baker, who have worked jointly on a number of multicultural education projects for a period spanning 2 decades, met at an annual meeting of the ASNLH. Gay's work also has been heavily influenced and informed by African American scholarship in both history and anthropology. In the early 1970s she served as director of the ethnic studies program at the University of Texas, Austin. One of her books, co-edited with Willie L. Baber (an anthropology professor), focuses on African American culture and identity (Gay & Baber, 1987).

Unlike the intergroup education movement, scholars of color have played a major role in formulating the theory, research, and practice of the current multicultural education movement. Much of the early work of the African American architects of the multicultural education movement focused on teaching Black studies in the schools. Multiculturalists from other ethnic groups wrote articles about teaching ethnic studies related to their specific ethnic groups (e.g., teaching Mexican American studies [Cortés, 1973], and teaching Native American studies [Forbes, 1973]). The leaders of today's multicultural education movement are quite ethnically diverse. They include the African Americans mentioned earlier (Banks, Baker, Gay, and Grant) as well as H. Prentice Baptiste, whose early work focused on multicultural teacher education; European Americans such as Christine I. Bennett, Donna Gollnick, and Christine E. Sleeter; Latinos such as Carlos E. Cortés, Ricardo L. García, Hilda Hernandez, and Sonia Nieto; and Asian Americans such as Philip C. Chinn, Valerie O. Pang, and Derald W. Sue.

Ethnic studies dominated the first phase of the multicultural education movement in the United States (Banks, 1973). However, educators involved in the ethnic studies movement began to realize that ethnic content was a necessary but not a sufficient condition for restructuring schools so that students from diverse racial and ethnic groups would experience equality (Banks, 1981; Ramírez & Castañeda, 1974). The ethnic studies movement thus evolved into what Banks (1994) has called "multiethnic education," a movement designed to reform the total school environment, not just the curriculum. According to Banks, when multiethnic education is implemented, all components of the school structure are reformed, including the curriculum, teaching methods and materials, school policy, counseling, teacher attitudes and expectations, and the learning styles and languages accepted in the school.

As the multiethnic movement gained momentum and schools began to respond to some of the educational needs of African American students and other students of color, other groups who considered themselves on the margins of society began to demand that the school curriculum—and later other aspects of the school—be changed to reflect their perspectives, struggles, dreams, and realities. Women and people with disabilities became some of the most successful advocates for educational change and inclusion (Banks & Banks, 1993). Multicultural education evolved as a vehicle for school districts, colleges, and universities to respond collectively to the diverse and often conflicting demands of these various groups. However, the fact that multicultural education emerged out of conflict and expediency has haunted the movement since its birth. The challenge multicultural education faces as we enter a new century is one of determining how to transform its political liabilities into academic and scholarly strengths. Recognizing and strengthening the field's ties with African American scholarship and scholarship on other U. S. ethnic groups can facilitate this process (Banks & Banks, 1995).

Multicultural Education: Its Critics and Future

Multicultural education faces a rough road in the foreseeable future. Critics on both the right and the left are highly suspicious of it (Sleeter, 1995). The right claims that multicultural education promotes divisiveness and ethnic polarization rather than national unity (D'Souza, 1991; Schlesinger, 1991). The radical critics believe that multicultural education reinforces the status quo because it fails to challenge the current social structure that oppresses the poor, people of color, women, and people with different sexual orientations (Mattai, 1992; McCarthy, 1988). Suspicion and mistrust of multicultural education are two of the few sentiments shared by critics on both sides. However, as Sleeter (1989, 1995) notes, both groups support their arguments against multicultural education by largely dismissing the writings and research of its major theorists, by using examples of teaching and activities that violate the theoretical principles of multicultural education, and by ignoring many of the realities of today's classrooms.

Conservative critics such as Schlesinger (1991) and D'Souza (1991) pretend that the United States historically has been sociologically united and contend that multicultural education will divide it. That the nation was already sharply divided along class, race, and gender lines before the advent of multicultural education is conveniently ignored. A major aim of multicultural education is to cement and unify a deeply divided nation rather than to divide a united one. Those on the right assume that unity can be imposed on diverse groups and ignore the fact that national unity within a democratic society emerges only from a process of participation and negotiation.

Multiculturalists are too friendly with status-quo administrators and teachers for its critics on the left (e.g., Mattai [1992] and McCarthy [1988]), who fear that multicultural educators will be co-opted by participating in action and projects that give only the illusion of change. One need only reflect on the charades and illusions of change that have taken place under such school reform labels as gifted education, magnet schools, and whole language to understand that this is a real risk that multiculturalists, like any other group of school reformers, must take. The risk of being appropriated by the establishment is an essential part of any reform movement that challenges institutionalized paradigms and practices in the real world. However, multiculturalists have called for paradigm shifts and other school reforms that seriously challenge the status quo within the schools (Sleeter, 1989, 1995).

Despite the highly publicized criticisms it has received, grass-roots support for multiculturalism among teachers, students, school administrators, parents, and ethnic communities is growing by leaps and bounds. Multicultural education is a populist movement whose greatest support and possibilities come from teachers, students, and parents who are struggling to overcome inequality and address the culturally and ethnically diverse world of the present and future. The success that multicultural education is experiencing results in part from the demographic changes that are occurring in the nation and from the realization by teachers, parents, and the public that if students are to function effectively in the next century, they must have "multicultural literacy" (Banks, 1991)—that is, the knowledge, attitudes, and skills needed to function in a diverse world. Such broad-based support for multicultural education will propel it into the twenty-first century with not only enormous challenges but also the potential to help the United States to actualize its democratic legacy and ideals.

REFERENCES

Asante, M. K. (1987). *The Afrocentric idea.* Philadelphia: Temple University Press.

Asante, M. K. (1990). *Kemet, Afrocentricity and knowledge.* Trenton, NJ: Africa World Press.

Baker, G. C. (1973). Multicultural training for student teachers. *Journal of Teacher Education, 24* (4), 306–307.

Baker, G. C. (1977). Multicultural education: Two inservice approaches. *Journal of Teacher Education, 28,* 31–33.

Baker, G. C. (1994). *Planning and organizing for multicultural instruction* (2nd ed.). Reading, MA: Addison-Wesley.

Banks, J. A. (1969). A content analysis of the Black American in textbooks. *Social Education, 33,* 954–957, 963.

Banks, J. A. (1970). *March toward freedom: A history of Black Americans.* Belmont, CA: Fearon.

Banks, J. A. (Ed.). (1973). *Teaching ethnic studies: Concepts and strategies* (43rd Yearbook). Washington, DC: National Council for the Social Studies.

Banks, J. A. (Ed.). (1981). *Education in the 80s: Multiethnic education.* Washington, DC: National Education Association.

Banks, J. A. (1991). *Teaching strategies for ethnic studies* (5th ed.). Boston: Allyn & Bacon.

Banks, J. A. (1994). *Multiethnic education: Theory and practice* (3rd ed.). Boston: Allyn & Bacon.

Banks, J. A. (1995). Multicultural education: Historical development, dimensions, and practice. In J. A. Banks & C. A. M. Banks (Eds.), *Handbook of research on multicultural education* (pp. 3–24). New York: Macmillan.

Banks, J. A., & Banks, C. A. M. (Eds.). (1993). *Multicultural education: Issues and perspectives* (2nd ed.). Boston: Allyn & Bacon.

Banks, J. A., & Banks, C. A. M. (Eds.). (1995). *Handbook of research on multicultural education.* New York: Macmillan.

Bennett, C. I. (1990). *Comprehensive multicultural education: Theory and practice* (2nd ed.). Boston: Allyn & Bacon.

Bond, H. M. (1939). *Negro education in Alabama: A study in cotton and steel.* Washington, DC: Associated Publishers.

Cook, L. A. (1951). *Intergroup relations in teacher education* (College Study in Intergroup Education, Vol. 11). Washington, DC: American Council on Education.

Cortés, C. E. (1973). Teaching the Chicano experience. In J. A. Banks (Ed.), *Teaching ethnic studies: Concepts and strategies* (43rd Yearbook; pp. 181–199). Washington, DC: National Council for the Social Studies.

Cross, D. E., Baker, G. C., & Stiles, L. J. (Eds.). (1977). *Teaching in a multicultural society: Perspectives and professional strategies.* New York: Free Press.

Drake, St. C. (1987). *Black folk here and there: An essay in history and anthropology* (Vol. 1). Los Angeles: University of California, Center for Afro-American Studies.

D'Souza, D. (1991). Illiberal education. *Atlantic Monthly, 267,* 51–79.

DuBois, W. E. B. (1973). *The Philadelphia Negro: A social study.* Millwood, NY: Kraus-Thomson. (Original work published 1899)

DuBois, W. E. B. (1973). *The suppression of the African slave trade to the United States of America, 1638–1870.* Millwood, NY: Kraus-Thomson. (Original work published 1896)

Forbes, J. D. (1973). Teaching Native American values and cultures. In J. A. Banks (Ed.), *Teaching ethnic studies: Concepts and strategies* (43rd Yearbook; pp. 201–225). Washington, DC: National Council for the Social Studies.

Franklin, J. H. (1947). *From slavery to freedom: A history of Negro Americans.* New York: Knopf.

Franklin, J. H. (1976). *A southern odyssey: Travelers in the antebellum North.* Baton Rouge: Louisiana State University Press.

Franklin, J. H. (1985). *George Washington Williams: A biography.* Chicago: University of Chicago Press.

Franklin, J. H. (1989). *Race and history: Selected essays, 1938–1988.* Baton Rouge: Louisiana State University Press.

García, R. L. (1991). *Teaching in a pluralistic society: Concepts, models, strategies* (2nd ed.). New York: HarperCollins.

Gay, G. (1992). The state of multicultural education in the United States. In K. Adam-Moodley, (Ed.), *Beyond multicultural education: International perspectives* (pp. 41–65). Calgary, Alberta: Detselig Enterprises.

Gay, G., & Baber, W. L. (Eds.). (1987). *Expressively Black: The cultural basis of ethnic identity.* New York: Praeger.

Gibbs, J. T. (Ed.). (1988). *Young, Black and male in America: An endangered species.* Dover, MA: Auburn House.

Gollnick, D. M., & Chinn, P. C. (1990). *Multicultural education in a pluralistic society* (3rd ed.). Columbus, OH: Merrill.

Gould, S. J. (1981). *The mismeasure of man.* New York: W. W. Norton.

Grant, C. A. (1972). *An empirical study of the effects of relevant curriculum materials upon the self-concept, achievement and attendance of Black inner-city students.* Unpublished doctoral thesis, University of Wisconsin–Madison.

Grant, C. A. (Ed.). (1977). *Multicultural education: Commitments, issues, and applications.* Washington, DC: Association for Supervision and Curriculum Development.

Lee, C. D., & Slaughter-Defoe, D. T. (1995). Historical and sociocultural influences on African American education. In J. A. Banks & C. A. M. Banks (Eds.), *Handbook of research on multicultural education* (pp. 348–371). New York: Macmillan.

Logan, R. W., & Winston, M. R. (Eds.). (1982). *Dictionary of American Negro biography.* New York: W. W. Norton.

Lyman, S. M. (1972). *The Black American in sociological thought: A failure of perspective.* New York: Capricorn Books.

Manning, K. R. (1983). *Black Apollo of science: The life of Ernest Everett Just.* New York: Oxford University Press.

Mattai, P. R. (1992). Rethinking the nature of multicultural education: Has it lost its focus or is it being misused? *The Journal of Negro Education, 61,* 65–77.

McCarthy, C. (1988). Rethinking liberal and radical perspectives on racial inequality in schooling: Making the case for nonsynchrony. *Harvard Educational Review, 58,* 265–279.

Meier, A., & Rudwick, E. (1986). *Black history and the historical profession, 1915–1980.* Urbana: University of Illinois Press.

Platt, A. M. (1991). *E. Franklin Frazier reconsidered.* New Brunswick, NJ: Rutgers University Press.

Quarles, B. (1964). *The Negro in the making of America.* New York: Macmillan.

Ramírez, M., III, & Castañeda, A. (1974). *Cultural democracy, bicognitive development, and education.* New York: Academic Press.

Schlesinger, A. M., Jr. (1991). *The disuniting of America: Reflections on a multicultural society.* Knoxville, TN: Whittle Direct Books.

Sleeter, C. E. (1989). Multicultural education as a form of resistance to oppression. *Journal of Education, 171,* 51–71.

Sleeter, C. E. (1995). An analysis of the critiques of multicultural education. In J. A. Banks & C. A. M. Banks (Eds.), *Handbook of research on multicultural education* (pp. 81–94). New York: Macmillan.

Taba, H. (1962). *Curriculum development: Theory and practice.* New York: Harcourt.

Taba, H. (1967). *A teachers' handbook for elementary social studies.* Palo Alto: Addison-Wesley.

Taba, H., Brady, E. H., & Robinson, J. T. (1952). *Intergroup education in public schools.* Washington, DC: American Council on Education.

Taba, H., & Elkins, D. (1966). *Teaching strategies for the culturally disadvantaged.* Chicago: Rand McNally.

Taba, H., & Wilson, H. E. (1946). Intergroup education through the school curriculum. *Annals of the American Academy of Political and Social Science, 244*, 19–25.

Wesley, C. H. (1969). *Richard Allen: Apostle of freedom.* Washington, DC: The Associated Publishers. (Original work published 1935)

Williams, G. W. (1989). *History of the Negro race in America from 1619 to 1880: Negroes as slaves, as soldiers, and as citizens* (2 vols.). Salem, NH: Ayer. (Original works published 1882 and 1883)

Woodson, C. G. (1968). *The education of the Negro prior to 1861.* Washington, DC: The Associated Publishers. (Original work published 1915)

Woodson, C. G. (1921). *The history of the Negro church.* Washington, DC: The Associated Publishers.

Woodson, C. G. (1922). *The Negro in our history.* Washington, DC: The Associated Publishers.

Woodson, C. G. (1928a). *African myths.* Washington, DC: The Associated Publishers.

Woodson, C. G. (1928b). *Negro makers of history.* Washington, DC: The Associated Publishers.

Woodson, C. G. (1933). *The mis-education of the Negro.* Washington, DC: The Associated Publishers.

Woodson, C. G. (1935). *The story of the Negro retold.* Washington, DC: The Associated Publishers.

CHAPTER 3

Intellectual Leadership and African American Challenges to Meta-Narratives

CHERRY A. MCGEE BANKS

Scholars in multicultural education and early African American scholars share a tradition of intellectual leadership. As transformative leaders and leaders of reform, intellectual leaders frequently emerge in times of moral and social conflict. Their scholarship is used to explain, justify, and sanction social, political, and economic change. A central characteristic of intellectual leadership is thought grounded in moral power (Burns, 1978).

Key aspects of multicultural and early African American scholarship are selectively examined in this chapter to broaden, deepen, and refine our understanding of the link between the transformative nature of multicultural education and early African American scholarship. The exploration of the roots of multicultural education provides a basis for understanding issues in multicultural education within a historical context.

The term *early African American scholarship* is used in this chapter to refer to the work of George Washington Williams (Franklin, 1985), W. E. B. DuBois (1896/1973), Anna Julia Cooper (1892/1988), Carter G. Woodson (Woodson & Wesley, 1922/1962), and other African American scholars who wrote during the late 1800s and early 1900s. The work of W. E. B. DuBois (1896/1973, 1899/1973) serves as a primary reference. Multicultural education is defined as "a field of study and an emerging discipline whose major aim is to create equal educational opportunities for students from diverse racial, ethnic, social-class, and cultural groups" (Banks & Banks, 1995, p. xi).

This chapter is, by necessity, conceptually condensed. The author acknowledges, but does not examine, important areas such as the multiple roots of multicultural education (Banks, 1992a), the diverse and sometimes conflicting perspectives within early African American scholarship (Meier & Rudwick, 1986), and the extent to which both fields have been shaped by forces within the larger society. This chapter is exploratory and its central argument, that ideas and perspectives in early African American scholarship anticipated similar developments in multicultural education, is interpretative.

INTELLECTUAL LEADERSHIP

Intellectual leadership is a key concept that is woven throughout this chapter. It is used as an organizing concept because it captures the transformational quality of the work of early transformative scholars and multicultural education scholars. As intellectual leaders, their work is rooted in the needs, aspirations, and values of people on the margins of society.

Intellectual leadership requires not only that scholars focus their attention on analytical ideas and data; they also must recognize the social, political, and economic contexts of ideas and the normative aspects of data (Burns, 1978). They must try to unite analytical data with normative ideas. Burns (1978) argues that a true intellectual cannot be morally detached because such detachment stifles intellectual creativity. He states, "Moral detachment is itself at best a modal value and one hostile to the concerns of the free mind" (p. 141).

As scholars who are involved in the creation of knowledge, intellectual leaders help direct paradigmatic transitions wherein old paradigms are transformed in ways that result in new ones. The new paradigms can become mainstream paradigms of the future. The new paradigms also can provide an intellectual foundation for social change. The initial phases of social reform frequently are justified with scholarship and research. Kuhn (1970) states, "Led by a new paradigm, scientists adopt new instruments and look in new places . . . see new and different things when looking with familiar instruments in places they have looked before" (p. 111). By looking in new places and seeing new and different things, intellectual leaders can create knowledge that serves as a critical component of social change and action.

Intellectual leadership was important for early African American scholars and continues to be important for multiculturalists today. The transformational nature of their scholarship required early African American scholars in years past and multiculturalists today to grapple with complexities and gaps in research on groups on the margins of society; recognize the explicit and implicit biases that support the epistemologies in their academic disciplines; and build bridges between the objective and the subjective. The transformative knowledge created by early African American scholars and by multiculturalists stems from questions rooted in values, morals, and objectives. The primary characteristics of that knowledge is that it challenges the meta-narrative, encourages perspective-taking, and serves as a departure point and context for the exploration of enduring questions that must be confronted and resolved as we work to build a just society. Addressing these enormous epistemological and analytical problems frequently locates early African American and multicultural scholars in the borderlands. For intellectual leaders, the borderlands is that space between what is known and what is yet to be created.

All of the aspects of intellectual leadership discussed in this section are explored more fully in subsequent sections of this chapter that address the meta-narrative, perspective-taking, the borderland quality of the work of early African American and multicultural scholars, and the transforming power of intellectual leadership.

THE LEGACY OF EARLY AFRICAN AMERICAN SCHOLARSHIP TO MULTICULTURAL EDUCATION

Multicultural education has had a long and rich history. Its roots include contributions from diverse scholars and disciplines. A group of these diverse scholars and disciplines is described in Part II of this book. One of the most important roots of multicultural education lies in the rich intellectual soil of early African American scholarship described in Chapter 2. Multicultural education is the latest stage in the evolution of African American scholarship.

Key characteristics of early African American scholarship are reflected in the multicultural education literature (Banks & Banks, 1995). These characteristics include its interdisciplinary focus, its exploration of areas that lack legitimacy within mainstream scholarship, its challenge to dominant group hegemony, and its association with groups that have little cultural capital within the wider society. Taken together, these characteristics are the legacy of early African American scholarship to multicultural education.

Early African American scholars confronted questions of knowledge construction, borders and boundaries, and perspective-taking without naming them as such or openly challenging traditional scholarship. Their goal was to carve out and legitimize a knowledge base about African Americans (Franklin, 1989). The knowledge they created not only illuminated the Black experience; it had the potential to liberate the entire society. Scholars and activists such as DuBois (1899/1973) and Cooper (1892/1988) recognized that enduring human problems like racism affected not only African Americans; they were like ropes that tied all of humanity together in a common destiny and limited the potential of both the oppressor and the oppressed. In 1892, Anna J. Cooper, a scholar and social activist, wrote, "The cause of freedom is not the cause of a race or a sect, a party or a class . . . it is the cause of human kind, the very birthright of humanity" (pp. 120–121). In discussing the elimination of racism, DuBois (1899/1973) echoed Cooper's voice:

> It is a battle for humanity and human culture. If in the heyday of the greatest of the world's civilizations, it is possible for one people ruthlessly to steal another, drag them helpless across the water, enslave them, debauch them and then slowly murder them by economic and social exclusion until they disappear from the face of the earth—if the consummation of such a crime be possible in the twentieth century, then our civilization is vain and the republic is a mockery and a farce. (p. 388)

The need to address problems, such as racism and the challenges of creating a just society, has been carried forth from early African American scholarship to multicultural education. Multicultural educators are bringing the ideas and enduring questions of early African American scholars to the foreground and refining and broadening their vision for a more inclusive and just society.

Challenging Meta-Narratives

Challenging meta-narratives was at the heart of the intellectual leadership provided by early African American scholars. It is a legacy of early African American scholars to multiculturalists. Meta-narratives are stories that speak to the universality of the human experience and suggest that all people are tied together by overarching stories of humanized science and progress (Jackson, 1988). The Westward Movement, as typically portrayed in American history textbooks, is an example of a meta-narrative. Such meta-narratives are problematic because they do not tell the full story (Appleby, 1992; Huggins, 1995). The Westward Movement tells the story of European Americans moving West, but it does not tell the story of American Indians who lived in the West. By telling part of the story and leaving other parts of the story out, meta-narratives suggest not only that some parts of the story don't count, but that some parts don't even exist. The exclusive nature of meta-narratives, their canonized place in formal school curricula, and the extent to which they are woven into the societal curriculum result in meta-narratives producing a feeling of well-being and comfort within mainstream society and their validity rarely being questioned.

Early African American scholars challenged the idea that stories about a single group could be generalized to all humans (Woodson, 1915/1991). African American scholars, such as Carter G. Woodson and Charles Wesley (Woodson & Wesley, 1922/1962), recognized that the meta-narrative resulted in large gaps in the intellectual history of African Americans. They turned their attention to constructing stories that provided more opportunity for developing a deeper meaning for and understanding of the African American experience (Logan & Winston, 1982).

The Suppression of the African Slave Trade to the United States of America, 1638–1870 by W. E. B. DuBois (1896/1973) was the first scientific study in African American history. It challenged the meta-narrative by courageously highlighting the relationship between the slave trade and the economics and politics of slavery. It also raised questions about the moral leadership of our nation's early leaders and the role of the government in helping to maintain the oppression of African Americans. DuBois (1896/1973) states:

> No American can study the connection of slavery with United States history, and not devoutly pray that his country may never have a similar social problem to solve, until it shows more capacity for such work than it has shown in the past. It is neither profitable nor in accordance with scientific truth to consider that whatever the constitutional fathers did was right, or that slavery was a plague sent from God and fated to be eliminated in due time. (pp. 197–198)

DuBois's hope that *The Suppression of the African Slave Trade* would contribute to our understanding of slavery and the African Americans is borne out in Logan and Winston's (1982) description of this tome as "still an indispensable source for the study of this era of [humans'] inhumanity to [humans]" (p. 195).

The Philadelphia Negro (DuBois, 1899/1973) usually is considered the first scientific study in African American sociology. It is filled with copious details on life among Blacks in the late 1800s in a northern urban community. *The Philadelphia Negro* challenges the meta-narrative by rejecting Social Darwinism, which suggests, for example, that poor people are poor because of their inherent deficiencies. While acknowledging shortcomings among Philadelphia Blacks, DuBois presents data that suggest that numerous social, economic, and political factors were implicated in those shortcomings. DuBois (1899/1973) writes:

> In the realm of social phenomena, the law of survival [of the fittest] is greatly modified by human choice, whim and prejudice. And consequently no one knows when one sees a social outcast how far this failure to survive is due to deficiencies of the individual, and how far to the accidents or injustice of his environment. This is especially the case with the Negro. (p. 98)

Gunnar Myrdal (with Sterner & Rose, 1944) cited *The Philadelphia Negro* in *An American Dilemma* as a model study of an African American community. One of the reasons for Myrdal's admiration of *The Philadelphia Negro* was DuBois's painstaking adherence to the highest requirements of empirical research. Empirical research is a tool used by mainstream scholars to develop meta-narratives. DuBois used the tools of mainstream scholars to provide new insights on African Americans. *The Philadelphia Negro* provides a database for a broader understanding of African Americans. It locates the problems of African Americans within a social, economic, and political context. *The Philadelphia Negro* and *The Suppression of the African Slave Trade* are examples of research developed by early African American scholars that challenges meta-narratives and provides a database and a departure point for multiculturalists.

The tradition of challenging meta-narratives continues in multicultural education (Okihiro, 1994). The battle over the canon today is essentially a struggle over who will construct the meta-narrative (Gates, 1992). Multicultural educators such as Nieto (1992), Gay (1994), and Banks (1992b) reject the idea that single perspectives can define reality. They recognize that the meta-narrative is only one of many stories about the American experience and argue that multiple stories must be explored, ideas integrated, and people of all groups encouraged to work together to find common ground and to shape a shared national identity.

Perspective-Taking: A Tool Used by Multiculturalists to Challenge the Meta-Narrative

Nieto (1992), Gay (1994), and Banks (1992b) and other multiculturalists use perspective-taking to challenge the meta-narrative. They argue that for the American experience to be fully understood, it must be viewed from multiple perspectives. The idea of multiple perspectives challenges the very heart of the meta-narrative because it acknowledges the relationship of the knower to the known. It suggests that our values, experiences, and world views influence our understanding of the events we describe and the stories we write (Graff, 1992). Writes Palmer (1993), "The knower brings personal elements to every act of knowing—if only his or her commitment to be concerned about *this* phenomenon rather than *that*" (p. 58).

The aim of perspective-taking in multicultural education is not simply the accumulation of multiple perspectives. It should be used to help students understand the partial nature of knowledge and to recognize that the meanings drawn from texts are not universal. Perspective-taking problematizes the idea that knowledge is objective and can help students understand that knowledge is socially constructed (Banks, 1993b). Most important, perspective-taking provides a basis for each of us to learn from the other and reconstruct the known through a dialogue in which everyone participates as a respected knower (Palmer, 1993).

Because multiculturalists view perspective-taking as an essential part of creating an authentic unity, their work has been characterized as disuniting

America by assimilationists who are defenders of the established Western canon (D'Souza, 1991; Schlesinger, 1991). Multiculturalists have argued as fervently as any group for national unity (Banks, 1992b). However, multiculturalists differ in significant ways from assimilationists. Assimilationists assume that the nation is already united, whereas multiculturalists assume that the nation is polarized and deeply divided along racial, ethnic, gender, and class lines. Unlike assimilationists, multiculturalists do not believe that unity can be imposed through the use of meta-narratives. Nor do they believe that unity can be imposed by constructing a false dichotomy between assimilation and pluralism or by leaping over centuries of legal, social, and scholarly pronouncements of difference to declare that we are all part of the same human family (Ravitch, 1992; Schlesinger, 1991). Multiculturalists acknowledge the lack of unity in our society, confront the many barriers to it, and are working with others to construct a national unity that is inclusive and authentic (Banks, 1993a).

Insider and Outsider Perspectives. Merton's (1972) concepts of insider and outsider are useful to multiculturalists because they distinguish competing claims to valid knowledge about group life. Insiders believe that they have a valid view of their group because they are members of the group and therefore bring an understanding of the group's values, perspectives, and culture to their analysis. Outsiders, however, believe that their location outside the group results in a more valid and objective view of the group. Merton concludes that the perspectives of both outsiders and insiders provide important insights into social reality. Our understanding of a group remains incomplete when the perspective of either the insider or the outsider is overlooked (Merton, 1972).

Images of African Americans that have become institutionalized within the mainstream academic and scholarly communities historically have been constructed by people outside those communities (Kardiner & Ovesey, 1951; Phillips, 1918). The meanings embedded in these images often were constructed from the perspective of outsiders who did not have an understanding of the true essence and complexity of African American communities. This was especially pernicious because for many years outsider perspectives were the only ones that had legitimacy within the mainstream academic community (Park & Burgess, 1924/1937). During the 1960s, 1970s, and 1980s, insider perspectives began to gain recognition and legitimacy in U.S. history and social science, and new meanings about the African American experience were constructed (Billingsley, 1966; Blassingame, 1979; Franklin, 1989; Ladner, 1973).

Commenting on recent trends in African American history, John Hope Franklin (1989) noted that for many years it was considered a "fact" that Black people had been reluctant to become involved in radical activities. While this "fact" may have provided some insights into the African American experience, it was incomplete and flawed. African American scholars challenged the idea that Blacks were reluctant to become involved in radical activities. They argued that Black leaders were men and women of substance who encouraged the hopes and dreams among Black people to be free (Berry & Blassingame, 1982; Harding, 1981). Writes Franklin (1989): "Black people know quite well that it was a radical act for Frederick Douglass or Henry Highland Garnett to take the stands they did during the ante-bellum years" (p. 152). The polarity of the view that Blacks were radical when contrasted with the view that Blacks were reluctant to become involved in radical activities is understandable when it is recognized that one view is informed primarily by outsider perspectives and the other by perspectives from within.

While insider perspectives usually are identified as such, outsider perspectives often are concealed by the cloak of universality. African American historians, for example, usually are referred to as *Black* historians, whereas European American historians are simply *historians*. This duality situates African American scholarship in a more subjective and suspect position than European American male scholarship. It also makes it more difficult for outsiders to understand that the knowledge they construct is informed by an outside perspective. As a result, it is not uncommon for scholars who are outside a group to believe that they know more about the group than members of the group know about themselves. Such was the case in 1937 when Gunner Myrdal was invited by the Carnegie Corporation to direct a comprehensive study of Blacks in the United States (Southern, 1987). Myrdal, a Swedish economist, arrived in the United States in 1938 to begin work on what was called "the Negro problem" (Myrdal, with Sterner & Rose, 1944). African American scholars such as St. Clair Drake, Kenneth Clark, Ralph Bunche, and Allison Davis—who had worked for many years on issues related to race in the United States—were relegated to the role of support staff and researchers on the Myrdal study (Southern, 1987). It is ironic that the principal researchers, in a study that revealed a contradiction in real and idealized American values in race relations, were individuals who benefited from the privilege of being White in a society that discriminated against people of color.

A Multiculturalist's Position on Outsider/Insider Perspectives. While many scholars may agree that insider and outsider perspectives exist, it is not a simple task to determine who is an insider and who is an outsider. For example, can insider and outsider perspectives be identified by group membership? When Thomas Sowell (1981) and Shelby Steele (1990), two African American conservatives who are highly coveted by the mainstream popular media, comment on the African American experience, are they providing insider or outsider perspectives? Is it possible for members of a group to voice both insider and outsider perspectives? Since individuals belong to many groups, how can we determine which group has primacy in the formulation of an individual's perspective? Is it ever possible for one group identity to consistently have primacy in the formulation of an individual's perspective? When exploring issues of gender, does a woman's gender, social class, or race locate her voice as an insider or outsider?

Multicultural educators, such as Banks (1993b), Tetreault (1993), and Sleeter (1991), challenge students to grapple with these kinds of questions and to acknowledge their partial understanding of the complex issues involved. As students explore the questions above, they will find that there are no easy answers because the questions are inextricably intertwined with issues of identity, knowledge construction, and power. The answers change over time and context, and reflect the interests of the people who provide the answers. The questions provide a means for teachers and students to examine the ways in which intragroup diversity, positionality, and particularistic interests shape the construction of knowledge. By raising these kinds of questions, teachers are able to highlight the subjective component of knowledge and clarify its role in knowledge construction.

Some readers might conclude that the time spent considering these questions will not prove to be very fruitful. They may even argue that given postmodern perspectives on knowledge construction, the idea of insiders and outsiders is an anachronism. On the contrary, insider and outsider perspectives are important and helpful concepts. They call attention to the positionality of knowledge. Knowledge is not neutral. It is a political project that serves interests (Harding, 1986). Social change requires that we name those interests even when our efforts to do so are imperfect.

While group membership can inform our understanding of insider and outsider perspectives, it is not sufficient to determine them. Insider and outsider perspectives can best be situated by exploring and reflecting on a complex web of issues. Those issues include identifying who benefits from the perspective; the extent to which the person explicating the perspective locates herself in the group she is describing and is willing to embrace her descriptors of the group for herself and her children; and the extent to which the person is viewed as a member of the group by others both within and outside the group.

THE BORDERLAND STANCE OF MULTICULTURAL EDUCATION: A LEGACY OF EARLY AFRICAN AMERICAN SCHOLARSHIP

By embracing the idea of multiple perspectives, multicultural education embodies the idea of being a part of something while simultaneously being separate from it. It acknowledges the relationship of the part to the whole while maintaining the integrity of both the part and the whole. It eschews dualistic thinking. These are characteristics of the borderlands (Anzaldúa, 1987).

The borderland stance of multicultural education is informed by the bifurcated identity of African Americans that DuBois termed double consciousness. DuBois (1903/1969) wrote, "One ever feels his two-ness, an American, a Negro; two souls, two thoughts, two unreconciled strivings; two warring ideals in one dark body" (p. 45). The ambivalence embodied in double consciousness was a hallmark of DuBois's writing and research (Meier, 1966).

Paul Lawrence Dunbar (1973) also wrote about African Americans who simultaneously acknowledge contradictory realities. Dunbar referred to the idea of double consciousness in his poem "We Wear the Mask." In that poem, Dunbar states that African Americans were not allowed to present their true selves to Whites, but instead had to present themselves as Whites imagined them to be. Dunbar, like DuBois, understood the importance of situated identity, the roles that persons jointly construct to participate in a social act. Survival and upward mobility required African Americans to interact with Whites in ways that resulted in a bifurcated identity. "We Wear the Mask" is testimony to why African Americans were required to develop the skill to cross borders.

As a researcher, the concept of double consciousness provided a basis for DuBois to move beyond scientific ideals of objectivity and to subtly infuse humanistic perspectives into scientific inquiry. The subjects in his research were not a detached and distant "other." Throughout *The Philadelphia Negro* DuBois used "we" and "us." The use of those terms suggests that he identified with the people he was studying.

The borderland stance of multicultural education situates multiculturalists in a position that requires them to move beyond a focus on one group and to acknowledge the interconnectedness of ethnic, racial, gender, social-class, and other groups (Grant & Sleeter, 1985, 1986, 1988a, 1988b). It challenges multiculturalists to identify with multiple groups and to engage in social action to improve the circumstances of all people.

The interdisciplinary nature of multicultural education is another characteristic that reflects a borderland stance. As an interdisciplinary field, multicultural literature is spread across a wide range of disciplines including education, history, political science, economics, cultural anthropology, sociology, and psychology (Banks & Banks, 1995). Multicultural education, however, is not simply a conglomerate of different disciplines. Multiculturalists do not simply gather theories, concepts, and perspectives from mainstream disciplines and add a multicultural twist to them. While multicultural education reflects significant developments, concepts, and theories from various disciplines, its perspective is not that of mainstream disciplines. Many of the theories of mainstream disciplines have been used to legitimize oppressive practices, such as studies of race and IQ (Herrnstein & Murray, 1994; Jensen, 1969; Mensh & Mensh, 1991). Multiculturalists challenge, reinterpret, and reveal the extent to which mainstream disciplines have been influenced by social beliefs, ideology, myths, and stereotypes (Banks, 1993b, 1994; Sleeter, 1991).

The multicultural approach to an interdisciplinary perspective is grounded in the work of early African American scholars such as W. E. B. DuBois (1968), Carter G. Woodson (1915/1991), and Anna Julia Cooper (1892/1988). DuBois was trained as a historian but also worked as a sociologist. His interest in interdisciplinary approaches is reflected in his Atlanta Conferences, at which he brought people together from areas such as education, business, and medicine (Lewis, 1993). His goal was to integrate information from a broad range of fields, such as psychology, anthropology, and economics, into scientific and systematic studies of African Americans. His first 10-year cycle of conference studies produced publications such as *Mortality Among Negroes in Cities*, *The Negro in Business*, *The Negro Artisan*, *The Negro Church*, and *The Negro Common School* (DuBois, 1968). DuBois (1968) worked from 1896 to 1914 to "sharpen the tools of investigation and perfect our methods of work, so that we would have an increasing body of scientifically ascertained fact, instead of the vague mass of the so-called Negro problems" (p. 217).

The Challenge to Dominant Group Hegemony

The work of early African American scholars helped fill the intellectual void about African Americans and quietly challenged dominant group hegemony and the institutionalized stereotypes of Blacks (Woodson & Wesley, 1922/1962). The dearth of information about African Americans and their contributions to U.S. society reinforced the marginal status of African Americans and suggested that they had not played significant roles in U.S. history and culture. The paucity of research also cast doubt on the ability of African Americans to be scholars. As late as the turn of the century, few American leaders were willing to acknowledge that African Americans had the potential to become scholars (Franklin, 1989). In 1895, Theodore Roosevelt stated, "A perfectly stupid race can never rise to a very high plane; the Negro, for instance, has been kept down as much by lack of intellectual development as anything else" (cited in Franklin, 1989, p. 298). Roosevelt's statement reflected the widely held assumption that African Americans had not made significant contributions to U.S. society in the past and because of their lack of intellectual ability they should not be expected to do so in the future. This image not only limited the ability of African Americans to be viewed as scholars; it influenced their ability to secure funding for research. Within this context, the work of African American scholars often was viewed as less meritorious than "traditional" scholarship, even though most early African American scholars maintained high standards of scholarship (Franklin, 1989).

In 1906, DuBois made two major appeals to acquire funds to support the work of the Atlanta Conferences. The appeals were not successful. However, the Conferences eventually received funding through a grant that was secured by a White researcher. Commenting on this indirect method of funding Negro studies, DuBois (1968) concluded, "If there is a job to be done and a Negro fit to do it, do not give the job or responsibility to the Negro; give it to some white man and let the Negro work under him" (p. 225). DuBois (1968) stated that he could not imagine why an established center like Atlanta University would be ignored and funding preference given to someone who lacked expertise in and respect for Negro studies.

Multiculturalists Continue the Struggle for Legitimacy

Like early African American scholars, multicultural educators are struggling for legitimacy. However, unlike early African American scholars, who largely worked in obscurity, there is a spotlight on multicultural educators. This spotlight has made it particularly difficult to develop and maintain a clear view of the theory and practice in the field. Frequently the terminology, research, and writings of experts in the field are ignored. Writers, practitioners, and critics often create their own particularistic definitions and views of multicultural education (D'Souza, 1991; Schlesinger, 1991). Currently, there is a large and growing number of synonyms for multicultural education. These include *diversity, cultural pluralism, intercultural education*, and *global education*. The multiple synonyms for multicultural education and the definitions associated with them have led to misrepresentation of the field in the popular media, where its critics have focused their attack on multicultural education (D'Souza, 1991; Krauthammer, 1990; Schlesinger, 1991; Sleeter, 1995).

Practitioners and writers who do not have a clear understanding of the nature of multicultural education, its background, and its emerging scholarship tend to essentialize multicultural education as the study of ethnic heroes and holidays and the participation of students in superficial activities such as ethnic singing, eating, and dancing (Banks, 1992b; Grant & Gomez, 1995; Sleeter, 1995; Sleeter & Grant, 1987). The superficial image and multiple definitions of multicultural education do not acknowledge the essence of multicultural education, which includes social action and transformation (Grant, 1992; Nieto, 1992; Sleeter, 1991). Both transformation and social action have been key components of multicultural education theory since the 1970s (Banks, 1994; Cross, Baker, & Stiles, 1977).

The Future of Multicultural Education. The study and practice of multicultural education in the future will continue to face challenges from both within and without. The contemporary attacks on multicultural education may represent an important turning point for the field (D'Souza, 1991; Schlesinger, 1991). They indicate that the ideas presented by multiculturalists have gained enough legitimacy that their opponents believe that they must be discredited. The attacks also have held a mirror up to multiculturalists and revealed the extent to which the term *multicultural education* is used without regard to the work of major theorists in the field. This has forced multicultural theorists to recognize the need for standards and unity (Banks & Banks, 1995; Grant, 1992).

Multicultural education is entering a period of critical self-examination similar to that of other fields in their early development. During the 1970s, according to Leary (1990), social psychology went through a crisis of confidence. Serious questions were raised about "the relevance of its research for understanding and solving real world problems, the appropriateness of the prevailing philosophy of science, the usefulness of pervasive research paradigms and the general viability of the discipline as a behavioral science" (Leary, 1990, p. vii). About 20 years later, social psychology had taken its place as a legitimate area of study, and the crisis in the field had largely faded. Multicultural education is undergoing a period of introspection and reflection similar to social psychology's earlier crisis of theory, utility, intellectual isolation, and practice.

In the future multicultural education will need to more fully develop an academic presence as a legitimate area of study. It currently lacks full legitimacy and usually is seen as a stepchild in education. Standards for the field need to be developed. As DuBois (1968) did with the Atlanta Conference studies, scholars in multicultural education will have to engage in research that will refine our "tools of investigation and perfect our methods of work" (p. 217) so that we can more clearly identify and respond to the factors that prevent students from diverse racial, ethnic, social-class, and gender groups from succeeding in school. Studies that investigate the effect of multicultural education at the university level on attitudes and behaviors—and on the ability to work effectively with diverse populations—are essential. University programs designed to provide practitioners with multicultural skills and knowledge need to be reviewed and revised. They should reflect a common understanding of what it means to be a specialist in multicultural education.

Intellectual Leadership and Transforming Power

The commitment to social action through the transforming power of intellectual leadership is one of the most important legacies of early American scholars to scholars of multicultural education. The test of intellectual leadership is one of transforming power (Burns, 1978). Intellectual leaders must do more than create ideas. They must act. Action for intellectual leaders lies in the way they conceptualize purpose. To be effective social actors, intellectual leaders must conceive purpose in a way that analytically and creatively links ends and means and clarifies the implications of specific values for political action (Burns, 1978). Early African American scholars were intellectual leaders who were engaged in transforming the power of ideas into social action. Scholars such as Woodson and DuBois challenged the idea of inquiry for the sake of inquiry. Knowing was not enough for them. Their goal was to link knowledge to societal change.

Carter G. Woodson was involved in social action throughout his life. As a teacher and an advocate of African American history, he worked to secure a place for African Americans in U.S. history. In 1926, he inaugurated Negro History Week, which was designed to popularize the study of African American history. Woodson strategically placed the celebration of Negro History Week in February so that it would occur between the birthdays of Frederick Douglass and Abraham Lincoln (Goggin, 1993; Logan & Winston, 1982).

To ensure that materials were available on African American history, Woodson founded a publishing house, The Associated Publishers. It published texts that were used by African American children to learn about African American history and scholarly texts that were used in historically Black colleges (Wesley, 1935/1969; Woodson & Wesley, 1922/1962; Urban, 1992). Woodson also founded a scholarly journal, *The Journal of Negro History*. He edited the journal from its inception until he died on April 3, 1950 (Goggin, 1993; Logan & Winston, 1982).

DuBois's (1899/1973) research on Philadelphia Blacks is another example of the work of an early African American scholar whose transformative knowledge provided a basis for social action. DuBois used established methods of sociological inquiry to invalidate the idea that African Americans were inferior to Whites, to challenge the legitimacy of blaming low-income Blacks for their social, economic, and political problems, and to illustrate how these problems were symptoms of societal inequality (DuBois, 1968). This knowledge provided the scholarly support for African Americans to advocate for societal changes.

In the 1980s, James A. Banks (1984) conducted a series of studies on African Americans living in predominately White suburban communities. Like DuBois, who visited the homes of his subjects in *The Philadelphia Negro* to interview them, Banks gained access to his subjects and was able to complete his research because he was a member of the African American community. His findings challenged the established belief that African American children hated themselves and, along with the work of scholars such as William E. Cross, Jr. (1991), Margaret Beale Spencer (1990), and Janet Helms (1990), pointed out that understanding the meanings embedded in the responses of

African American children to self-concept and identity inventories was much more complex than previous research had indicated. The work of Cross, Banks, Spencer, and Helm is an example of transformative research that leads to paradigm shifts, action, and reform.

Ties That Bind

Multicultural education and early African American scholarship are both characterized by intellectual leadership and the development of transformative knowledge. Transformative knowledge links knowing, action, and societal reform. Like early African American scholars, multiculturalists acknowledge the objective–subjective nature of the research process and the implicit meanings embedded in concepts and definitions used to explore research questions, and pay attention to symbolic meanings and normative processes of subjects in the wider society.

The similarity between early African American and multicultural scholarship results from the influence of early African American scholars on multiculturalists and the liberatory goals of scholars in both groups. The Association for the Study of Negro Life and History provided opportunities for early multiculturalists to learn about the transformative scholarship of DuBois, Woodson, Cooper, and other early African American scholars. That scholarship provided a vision of U.S. society that was inclusive. It challenged the metanarrative, encouraged perspective-taking, and acknowledged life in the borderlands. The transformative scholarship of early African American scholars serves as a departure point and context for multiculturalists to explore, confront, and attempt to resolve enduring human problems and provides an intellectual foundation on which cultural workers can build a just and humane society.

REFERENCES

Anzaldúa, G. E. (1987). *Borderlands/la frontera: The new mestiza.* San Francisco: Spinsters/Aunt Lute Book Co.

Appleby, J. (1992). Recovering America's historic diversity: Beyond exceptionalism. *The Journal of American History, 79* (2), 419–431.

Banks, J. A. (1984). Black youths in predominately White suburbs: An exploratory study of their attitudes and self concepts. *The Journal of Negro Education, 53* (1), 3–17.

Banks, J. A. (1992a). African American scholarship and the evolution of multicultural education. *The Journal of Negro Education, 61* (3), 273–286.

Banks, J. A. (1992b). Multicultural education: For freedom's sake. *Educational Leadership, 49* (4), 32–36.

Banks, J. A. (1993a). The canon debate, knowledge construction, and multicultural education. *Educational Researcher, 22* (5), 4-14.

Banks, J. A. (1993b). Multicultural education: Characteristics and goals. In J. A. Banks & C. A. M. Banks (Eds.), *Multicultural education: Issues and perspectives* (2nd ed., pp. 3-28). Boston: Allyn & Bacon.

Banks, J. A. (1994). *Multiethnic education: Theory and practice* (3rd ed.). Boston: Allyn & Bacon.

Banks, J. A., & Banks, C. A. M. (Eds.). (1995). *Handbook of research on multicultural education.* New York: Macmillan.

Berry, M. F., & Blassingame, J. W. (1982). *Long memory: The Black experience in America.* New York: Oxford Press.

Billingsley, A. (1966). *Black families in White America.* Englewood Cliffs, NJ: Prentice-Hall.

Blassingame, J. W. (1979). *The slave community: Plantation life in the antebellum South.* New York: Oxford University Press.

Burns, J. M. (1978). *Leadership.* New York: Harper.

Cooper, A. J. (1988). *A voice from the South by a Black woman of the South.* New York: Oxford University Press. (Original work published 1892)

Cross, D. E., Baker, G. C., & Stiles, L. J. (Eds.). (1977). *Teaching in a multicultural society: Perspectives and professional strategies.* New York: Free Press.

Cross, W. E., Jr. (1991). *Shades of Black: Diversity in African-American identity.* Philadelphia: Temple University Press.

D'Souza, D. (1991). *Illiberal education: The politics of race and sex on campus.* New York: Free Press.

DuBois, W. E. B. (1968). *The autobiography of W. E. B. DuBois: A soliloquy on viewing my life from the last decade of its first century.* New York: International Publishers.

DuBois, W. E. B. (1969). *The souls of Black folk.* New York: Signet. (Original work published 1903)

DuBois, W. E. B. (1973). *The suppression of the African slave trade to the United States of America, 1638-1870.* Millwood, NY: Kraus-Thomson. (Original work published 1896)

DuBois, W. E. B. (1973). *The Philadelphia Negro: A social study.* Millwood, NY: Kraus-Thomson. (Original work published 1899)

Dunbar, P. L. (1973). We wear the mask. In A. Adoff (Ed.), *The poetry of Black America: Anthology of the 20th century* (p. 8). New York: Harper & Row.

Franklin, J. H. (1985). *George Washington Williams.* Chicago: University of Chicago Press.

Franklin, J. H. (1989). *Race and history: Selected essays, 1938-1988.* Baton Rouge: Louisiana State University Press.

Gates, H. L., Jr. (1992). *Loose canons: Notes on the culture wars.* New York: Oxford University Press.

Gay, G. (1994). *At the essence of learning: Multicultural education.* West Lafayette, IN: Kappa Delta Pi.

Goggin, J. (1993). *Carter G. Woodson: A life in Black history.* Baton Rouge: Louisiana State University.

Graff, G. (1992). *Beyond the cultural wars: How teaching the conflicts can revitalize American education.* New York: W. W. Norton.

Grant, C. A. (Ed.). (1992). *Research and multicultural education: From the margins to the mainstream.* Washington, DC: Falmer Press.

Grant, C. A., & Gomez, M. L. (1995). *Campus and classroom: Making schools multicultural.* Columbus, OH: Merrill.

Grant, C. A., & Sleeter, C. E. (1985). Race, class, and gender in an urban school: A case study. *Urban Education, 20,* 37-60.

Grant, C. A. , & Sleeter, C. E. (1986). Race, class, and gender in educational research: An argument for integrative analysis. *Review of Educational Research, 56,* 195-211.

Grant, C. A., & Sleeter, C. E. (1988a). Race, class, gender and abandoned dreams. *Teachers College Record, 90,* 19-40.

Grant, C. A., & Sleeter, C. E. (1988b). *Making choices for multicultural education: Five approaches to race, class, and gender.* Columbus, OH: Merrill.

Harding, S. (1986). *The science question in feminism.* Ithaca, NY: Cornell University Press.

Harding, V. (1981). *There is a river: The Black struggle for freedom in America.* New York: Vintage Books.

Helms, J. E. (Ed.). (1990). *Black and White racial identity: Theory, research, and practice.* New York: Greenwood Press.

Herrnstein, R. J., & Murray, C. (1994). *The bell curve: Intelligence and class structure in American life.* New York: Free Press.

Huggins, N. I. (1995). *Revelations: American history, American myths.* New York: Oxford University Press.

Jackson, J. M. (1988). *Social psychology, past and present: An integrative orientation.* Hillsdale, NJ: Lawrence Erlbaum.

Jensen, A. R. (1969). How much can we boost IQ and scholastic achievement? *Harvard Educational Review, 39,* 1-123.

Kardiner, A., & Ovesey, L. (1951). *The mark of oppression: A psychological study of the American Negro.* New York: W. W. Norton.

Krauthammer, C. (1990, February 5). Education: Doing bad and feeling good. *Time, 135* (6), 78.

Kuhn, T. S. (1970). *The structure of scientific revolutions* (2nd ed.). Chicago: University of Chicago Press.

Ladner, J. A. (Ed). (1973). *The death of White sociology.* New York: Vintage Books.

Leary, D. E. (Ed.). (1990). *Metaphors in the history of psychology.* New York: Cambridge University Press.

Lewis, D. L. (1993). *W. E. B. DuBois: Biography of a race.* New York: Henry Holt.

Logan, R. W., & Winston, M. R. (Eds.). (1982). *Dictionary of American Negro biography.* New York: W. W. Norton.

Meier, A. (1966). *Negro thought in America, 1880-1915.* Ann Arbor: University of Michigan Press.

Meier, A., & Rudwick, E. (1986). *Black history and the historical profession, 1915-1980.* Urbana: University of Illinois Press.

Mensh, E., & Mensh, H. (1991). *The IQ mythology: Class, race, gender and inequality.* Carbondale: Southern Illinois University Press.

Merton, R. K. (1972). Insiders and outsiders: A chapter in the sociology of knowledge. *The American Journal of Sociology, 78* (1), 9-47.

Myrdal, G. (with Sterner, R., & Rose, A.). (1944). *An American dilemma: The Negro problem and modern democracy.* New York: Harper.

Nieto, S. (1992). *Affirming diversity: The sociopolitical context of multicultural education.* New York: Longman.

Okihiro, G. Y. (1994). *Margins and mainstreams: Asians in American history and culture.* Seattle: University of Washington Press.

Palmer, P. J. (1993). *To know as we are known.* San Francisco: Harper.

Park, R. E., & Burgess, E. W. (1937). *Introduction to the science of sociology.* Chicago: The University of Chicago Press. (Original work published 1924)

Phillips, U. B. (1918). *American Negro slavery.* New York: Appleton.

Ravitch, D. (1992). A culture in common. *Educational Leadership, 49* (4), 8-11.

Schlesinger, A. M., Jr. (1991). *The disuniting of America: Reflections on a multicultural society.* Knoxville, TN: Whittle Direct Books.

Sleeter, C. E. (Ed.). (1991). *Empowerment through multicultural education.* Albany: State University of New York Press.

Sleeter, C. E. (1995). An analysis of the critiques of multicultural education. In J. A. Banks & C. A. M. Banks (Eds.), *Handbook of research on multicultural education* (pp. 81-94). New York: Macmillan.

Sleeter, C. E., & Grant C. A. (1987). An analysis of multicultural education in the United States. *Harvard Educational Review, 57* (4), 421-444.

Southern, D. W. (1987). *Gunnar Myrdal and Black-White relations: The use and abuse of an American dilemma 1944-1969.* Baton Rouge: Louisiana State University Press.

Sowell, T. (1981). *Ethnic America: A history.* New York: Basic Books.

Spencer, M. B. (1990). Identity process among racially and ethnic minority children in America. *Child Development, 6* (2), 290-309.

Steele, S. (1990). *The content of our character.* New York: St. Martin's Press.

Tetreault, M. K. T. (1993). Classrooms for diversity: Rethinking curriculum and pedagogy. In J. A. Banks & C. A. M. Banks (Eds.), *Multicultural education: Issues and perspectives* (2nd ed., pp. 129-148). Boston: Allyn & Bacon.

Urban, W. J. (1992). *Black scholar: Horace Mann Bond 1904-1972.* Athens: University of Georgia Press.

Wesley, C. H. (1969). *Richard Allen: Apostle of freedom.* Washington, DC: The Associated Publishers. (Original work published 1935)

Woodson, C. G. (1991). *The education of the Negro prior to 1861.* Salem, NH: Ayer. (Original work published 1915)

Woodson, C. G., & Wesley, C. H. (1962). *The Negro in our history.* Washington, DC: The Associated Publishers. (Original work published 1922)

CHAPTER 4

The Historical Reconstruction of Knowledge About Race: Implications for Transformative Teaching

JAMES A. BANKS

Since the 1960s and 1970s, efforts to revise the curriculum in the nation's schools, colleges, and universities to reflect the ethnic, cultural, and gender realities in the United States have stimulated a heated debate about the nature of knowledge. One of the important issues in the canon debate is whether personal/cultural knowledge should be considered legitimate knowledge (Banks, 1993). Another issue is the extent to which the actuality of what occurs and how people interpret their experiences and observations can be distinguished.

A clear and sharp distinction cannot be made between the actuality of what occurs and how an individual interprets the actuality. Knowledge is both subjective and objective (Code, 1991; Ladner, 1973). The knowledge created by the knower reflects both her subjectivity and the objective phenomena perceived. Code states that the "objective/subjective dichotomy is but one of several dichotomies that have structured mainstream Anglo-American epistemology" (p. 28). The attempt to sharply distinguish these two elements of knowing, and to label objective knowledge legitimate and subjective knowledge mere interpretation, is inconsistent with how human beings know. Knowledge "is, necessarily and inescapably, the product of an intermingling of subjective and objective elements" (Code, 1991, p. 30). An actuality that takes place is subject to multiple interpretations and can be analyzed from diverse perspectives.

African American feminist scholars such as Joyce A. Ladner (1973), Elsa Barkley Brown (1991), Paula Giddings (1984), and Marimba Ani (1994) have

Multicultural Education, Transformative Knowledge, and Action. Copyright © 1996 by Teachers College, Columbia University. All rights reserved. ISBN 0-8077-3531-0 (pbk.), ISBN 0-8077-3532-9 (cloth). Prior to photocopying items for classroom use, please contact the Copyright Clearance Center, Customer Service, 222 Rosewood Dr., Danvers, MA 01923, USA, tel. (508) 750-8400.

written informative and seminal analyses of the ways in which objective and subjective factors influence knowledge construction. These researchers describe the ways in which their socialization within African American communities enabled them to reject conceptions of African Americans as the "Other," and to construct more comprehensive, compassionate, and accurate descriptions of their communities because they were able to combine personal insights with scientific observations. Their research is made more difficult but also more deeply textured and enriched by the objective-subjective tension that arises when "insiders" study other "insiders" (Merton, 1972).

Recognizing that knowledge contains both subjective and objective elements does not mean we must abandon the quest for the construction of knowledge that is as objective as possible. One's location in the social structure is based partially on relations of race, social class, and gender; these are location frames that we see and view as significant. If we fail to recognize the ways in which social location produces subjectivity and influences the construction of knowledge, we are unlikely to interrogate established knowledge that contributes to the oppression of marginalized and victimized groups.

Hegemonic knowledge that promotes the interests of powerful, elite groups often obscures its value premises by masquerading as totally objective. This chapter describes how this process took place from the late nineteenth century to the 1940s, by examining how race was constructed and reconstructed during this period. To create and teach liberatory, transformative knowledge, we must not only be aware of the knowledge produced, but must understand that the knowledge producer is located within a particular social, economic, and political context of society. Feminist scholars call this phenomenon *positionality* (Tetreault, 1993). This chapter focuses on positionality as a factor in the construction of knowledge about race.

I examine the ways in which knowledge about race was constructed, deconstructed, and reconstructed from the turn of the century until the rise of Nazism during the 1930s and 1940s. First, I discuss the relationship between the social context and the racial theories and paradigms developed by intellectual leaders. Next, I describe how rigid and pernicious racial categories, stereotypes, and racist ideas were constructed in the late nineteenth century to justify colonization and slavery. I then describe how Franz Boas at Columbia University, Robert E. Park at the University of Chicago, and African American scholars and social scientists (e.g., W. E. B. DuBois at Atlanta University and Kelly Miller at Howard University) tried to reconstruct race during the late nineteenth and the early decades of the twentieth century.

The efforts made by selected scholars and activists to undercut Nazism during the 1930s and 1940s are then described. Next, I consider the extent to which the efforts to reconstruct race were successful, and the differences between the reconstructions made by Boas and Park and by African American scholars. In the final part of the chapter, I discuss the teaching implications of my historical analysis of the construction of race.

THE SOCIAL CONTEXT, KNOWLEDGE CONSTRUCTION, AND INTELLECTUAL LEADERS

The social, cultural, and political context in which the people who invented conceptions of race was situated had a cogent influence on the knowledge they constructed. Gould (1981) points out that both facts and theories are influenced by the cultural context of the knower: "Facts are not pure and unsullied bits of information; culture . . . influences what we see and how we see it. . . . The most creative theories are often imaginative visions imposed upon facts; the source of imagination is strongly cultural" (p. 22). Myrdal (as quoted in Gould) also described the cultural influences on knowledge construction: "Cultural influences have set up the assumptions about the mind, the body, and the universe with which we begin; pose the questions we ask; influence the facts we seek; determine the interpretation we give these facts; and direct our reaction to these interpretations and conclusions" (p. 23).

The views of race that individuals and academic organizations articulated and described were not independently invented by them, but were deeply embedded into the fabric of the social, economic, political, and structural institutions of the society in which these individuals were socialized. The social, economic, and cultural factors that influence the construction of ideas about race are much more cogent than the writings of individual intellectuals or the actions of specific intellectual groups and societies. The relationship between the social context of society (which includes the popular culture), the views of intellectuals, and the ideas about race that become institutionalized within a society, is complex. The views of popular writers, scholars, and social scientists both reflect and help to shape those within their communities and subsocieties. Consequently, the views, theories, and thoughts of intellectuals reveal the ways in which knowledge is constructed within society.

Individual intellectuals are influenced strongly by the cultures into which they are socialized. Although individual intellectuals are cogently influenced by the racial ideas within their societies, in complex societies such as the United States contradictory and competing conceptions of race, as well as other concepts, are institutionalized within different subsocieties. Throughout its history, the United States has been a multicultural society and consequently has been characterized by subsocieties, microcultures, and institutions that socialized individuals who had competing conceptions of race.

Consequently, race in the United States has been contested and reinvented to serve divergent interests and groups. Write Omi and Winant (1986):

> The meaning of race is defined and contested throughout society, in both collective action and personal practice. In the process, racial categories themselves are formed, transformed, destroyed, and re-formed. We use the term *racial formation* to refer to the process by which social, economic, and political forces determine the content and importance of racial categories, and by which they are in turned shaped by racial meaning. (p. 61)

When academics and public opinion leaders construct knowledge about race, they are influenced by the ideas, assumptions, and norms of the cultures and subsocieties in which they are socialized. Consequently, the ideas about race constructed by W. E. B. DuBois, an African American scholar who functioned within Black institutions, differed significantly from those constructed by Thomas Dixon, Jr., the lay historian who wrote the books (*The Clansman* and *The Leopard's Spots*) on which the popular film *The Birth of a Nation* was based (Franklin, 1989). Dixon's early socialization in North Carolina in the years immediately after the Civil War was an important factor that shaped his racist ideas epitomized in *The Birth of a Nation*. The early socialization of historian Ulrich B. Phillips in Georgia during the late 1800s strongly influenced his important study of slavery, which is very sympathetic to southern slaveowners (Smith & Inscoe, 1993).

The Emergence of Racism in the Nineteenth Century

While groups within all past societies have exhibited various forms of ethnocentrism, racism has not been a universal characteristic of human societies. Historians and social scientists often state that racism was a unique by-product of Western expansion into the Americas, Australia, Africa, and Asia in the nineteenth century (Franklin, 1968). However, van den Berghe (1967) refutes this claim. He maintains that racism has been independently invented in various parts of the world. Nevertheless, he contends that Western racism has been the most important and cogent version invented. He writes, "Through the colonial expansion of Europe racism spread widely over the world. Apart from its geographical spread, no other brand of racism has developed such a flourishing mythology and ideology" (p. 13).

As the Christian European nations conquered and colonized native peoples in Africa, Asia, Australia, and the Americas—and especially as slavery developed in the Americas—the Europeans needed an ideology that was consistent with both their Christian beliefs and the colonization of the native peoples of these lands. Racism developed as an ideology to meet both needs. To advance civilization, the native "savages" needed to be conquered to save their souls from hell and to bring Christianity to their lands. The Western Europeans, and especially the Anglo-Saxons in the United States, began to believe that it was their "manifest destiny" to colonize and Christianize the native peoples of the Americas and other lands (Horsman, 1981). To provide a justification for the colonization and conquering of native peoples, racism was developed into an elaborate ideology. Slavery was institutionalized in the Americas before racism was developed into an elaborate ideology indistinguishable from ethnocentrism in the nineteenth century (van den Berghe, 1967). The Western version of racism emerged as an ideology to justify the conquering and colonization of native peoples in the Americas, Africa, Australia, and Asia after these practices were institutionalized.

Prior to the development of colonization and before the mid-nineteenth century, a theory of the unity of humans had been developed in Europe and was highly influential (Horsman, 1981). This Enlightenment view held that "mankind was of one species, and that mankind in general was capable of indefinite improvement" (p. 98). However, by the 1840s race theorists in the United States and Europe had constructed and were defending theories of race that indicated there were innate differences among the races of humankind. Writes Horsman, "Scientists, by mid-century, had provided an abundance of 'proofs' by which English and American Anglo-Saxons could explain their power, progress, governmental stability, and freedom" (p. 43). Dr. Charles Caldwell constructed one of the first theories that challenged the unity of humans theory. In his book, *Thoughts on the Original Unity of the Human Race,* Caldwell (1830) argued that the Caucasian race was unquestionably innately superior to all others and that nature had endowed other races with less mental strength (Horsman, 1981). Caldwell's view, as well as those of other nativists and racists, became widespread and institutionalized during the nineteenth century (Gould, 1981; Horsman, 1981).

The science of phrenology, which involved studying the shape of the human skull in order to make inferences about mental and behavioral characteristics (Chernow & Vallasi, 1993), became a major weapon in the scientific quest to prove that some races were inferior to others. The phrenologists gained substantial influence during the 1820s and 1830s in part because of their use of scientific methods and assumptions to establish the superiority of some races. Horsman (1981) notes that the phrenologists "found in skulls and heads what they wanted to find: a physical confirmation of supposedly observed cultural traits" (p. 145).

The Construction of Knowledge about Race in the 1800s

As constructed in the mid- to late 1800s, race was conceptualized in a way that designated specific groups with clearly defined, biologically inherited physical and behavioral characteristics (Gould, 1981; Higham, 1972; Horsman,

1981). Some groups were defined as inherently superior to others. An important assumption that undergirded conceptions of race in the nineteenth century was that the environment or experiences of individuals or groups could do little to change their inherited racial characteristics. Consequently, the best way to ensure the survival and growth of Western civilization was to prevent racial mixture and to make sure that the superior races of humankind remained as pure as possible and were given the opportunities and resources needed to actualize their superior potential.

In considering race in the nineteenth century, it is important to realize that although groups of color, such as Africans and Native Americans, were considered to be at the bottom of the racial hierarchy, Whites were not considered one race. Scientific racists, nativists, and propagandists of the late nineteenth and early twentieth centuries considered some White races superior to others. The conception of Whites as one racial group is a rather recent phenomenon (Alba, 1990).

Late-nineteenth- and early-twentieth-century nativists made important and invidious distinctions between various White "races." These distinctions grew sharper as thousands of Southern and Eastern European immigrants entered the United States near the turn of the century. About 15 million immigrants arrived in the United States between 1890 and 1914, most of whom were from Southern and Eastern Europe (U. S. Bureau of the Census, 1993). Nativists and scientific racists were deeply concerned about the negative influences these predominantly non-Anglo-Saxon, Catholic immigrants would have on the development of civilization and democracy in the United States (Higham, 1972). They also were concerned about the negative effects these immigrants would have, through interracial marriage, on the development of the Anglo-Saxon race.

As the number of immigrants from Southern and Eastern Europe grew, and nativism in the United States increased, they became known as the "new" immigrants. They were distinguished from the "old" immigrants, who were largely from Northern and Western European nations. A myth developed and grew that the old and new immigrants were distinct in many important ways. The Dillingham Commission, in its 41-volume report, reinforced the popular belief that the old and the new immigrants were significantly different. Influential books by William Z. Ripley (1899) and Madison Grant (1916) not only warned about the ominous results from "racial" mixture, but also codified the distinctions among the various European races, which Ripley labeled the *Teutonic,* the *Alpine,* and the *Mediterranean.*

Madison Grant's *The Passing of the Great Race* (1916) was greatly influenced by the work of Ripley (1899). Grant had an intense hatred of Jews and the other new immigrants, and feared miscegenation. He warned in his book that the great Nordic race of America, "the white man par excellence" (p. 150), was in great danger of disappearing because of racial mixture with inferior

Whites, such as the Alpines, who are peasants, and the Mediterraneans, who possess fewer ideal characteristics than the Teutonic race. Grant described the great Nordic race as follows: "It is everywhere characterized by certain unique specializations, namely, blondness, wavy hair, blue eyes, fair skin, high, narrow and straight nose, which are associated with great stature, and a long skull, as well as with abundant head and body hair" (p. 150).

Efforts Within Minority Communities to Reconstruct Knowledge About Race: The Work of Franz Boas

Because they were socialized in ethnic communities on the margins of society and were not part of the mainstream, ethnic minorities such as Jewish Americans and African Americans often constructed ideas about race that conflicted with those institutionalized within mainstream society. Minority intellectuals, because they were outsiders with racial views that challenged those held by most insiders, "infused greater egalitarianism into scientific discourse" (Barkan, 1992, p. i). Their ideas grew out of their unique socialization, experiences with racism and anti-Semitism, and their ability to see the underdeveloped and unrecognized talents and gifts within their communities.

Jewish American and African American social scientists and activists constructed images and representations of themselves that were liberatory and oppositional to those created by powerful and hegemonic groups. Franz Boas, a German Jewish immigrant scholar who was a victim of anti-Semitism in his native Germany and in the United States, played a leading role in constructing a new racial paradigm that seriously challenged the institutionalized one (Herskovits, 1953; Hyatt, 1990). Boas bore dueling scars that resulted from fights triggered by anti-Semitic insults throughout his long life (Stocking, 1964).

When Franz Boas arrived in the United States in 1884, the conception of race that had been constructed in both his native Germany and the United States codified sharp distinctions among the races and held that some races were innately superior to others. From about 1894 until his death on December 21, 1942, Boas—and some of the influential anthropologists that he trained at Columbia University—tried to reinvent race and to deconstruct the notion that some races were superior to others.

Boas, who was a product of his times and cultures, did not believe in racial equality. He was not able to totally transcend some of the tenacious and pernicious assumptions and beliefs about race that were institutionalized and pervasive within Western society. However, to a significant extent he transcended the predominant racial biases and assumptions of his times and challenged the dominant racial paradigms that were institutionalized within both the scholarly and popular communities.

Boas challenged the dominant paradigm about race, which stated that some races were inferior to others and that the environment could have little influence on heredity. Craniometry, the science of measuring skulls, was the major method used to establish the relationship between race and intelligence. Boas did not try to deconstruct craniometry as a methodology or as a scientific practice. Rather, he tried to reconstruct race by using craniometry to marshal new findings and to interpret his findings differently. In 1907, he studied 18,000 immigrants and concluded that "the head forms of children born in the United States differed significantly from those of their parents" (Stocking, 1964, p. 84). Boas's findings about head forms challenged the established beliefs of the day, which held that head forms were not susceptible to environmental influences. Although Boas challenged the dominant paradigms about inferior and superior races, he accepted some of the important assumptions and findings of craniometry (Boas, 1928/1962).

While accepting many of the prevailing research methodologies, assumptions, and findings of his time, Boas (1928/1962) challenged the existing paradigms about race by reinterpreting these findings as well as by deriving new findings. Among Boas's most significant contributions to the reconstruction of race were his reinterpretations of the meanings of the craniological findings about race. Boas strongly contested the notion that there were pure racial types, that the form and size of the body were entirely shaped by heredity, and that superior intelligence is always related to brain size. He also introduced into his writings the important principle that the differences within a population are likely to exceed those between different population groups.

In an article published in *The Crisis*, the official journal of the National Association for the Advancement of Colored People edited by W. E. B. DuBois, Boas (1910) described the complex and highly developed cultures and civilizations of Africa in order to refute claims of Negro inferiority; argued that the mulatto population among Negroes was quite extensive; and refuted claims that mulattos were inferior to either pure race. Accepting the conventions of his day, Boas referred to the problems facing African Americans as "the Negro problem."

Challenges to Racial Theories from the Mainstream

As Boas and his Columbia University students and colleagues in anthropology were working to reinvent notions about race, Robert E. Park and his colleagues and students at the University of Chicago sociology department were conducting empirical studies about racial groups and revising ideas about race (Bulmer, 1984). The racial theories developed at Chicago by Park and his associates and students were more liberal than those within the mainstream and popular culture but did not challenge mainstream theories as much as the paradigms developed by Boas and African American scholars. These differences may result, in part, from the fact that the Chicago theories were grounded in mainstream Midwest society, whereas those developed by Boas and African American scholars emerged from the margins or "outside" of mainstream society. After 1918, Park became the dominant figure in sociology at Chicago. Before he came to Chicago Park had worked as a city journalist and had served as secretary for Booker T. Washington. He brought his keen interest in cities, urban problems, and African Americans to Chicago.

Park set forth his views on race in the influential *Introduction to the Science of Sociology* (with Burgess, 1921/1937), a required textbook used at Chicago from 1921 until at least the early 1950s. In the text treatment, which is reprinted from an article that Park published in 1918, he states that different racial groups have distinctive characteristics that are inherited biologically. He believed that racial characteristics were a product of both biological inheritance and environment. However, he maintained that inherent biological characteristics were an important cause of racial differences. Park (1921/1937) wrote:

> The temperament of the Negro, as I conceive it, consists in a few elementary but distinctive characteristics, determined by physical organizations and transmitted biologically. These characteristics manifest themselves in a genial, sunny, and social disposition, in an interest and attachment to external, physical things rather than to subjective states and objects of introspection, in a disposition for expression rather than enterprise and action. (p. 139)

Park (1921/1937) also stated that the Negro was "neither an intellectual nor an idealist, like the Jew; nor a brooding introspective, like the East Indian; nor a pioneer and frontiersman, like the Anglo-Saxon. He is primarily an artist, loving life for its own sake. His *metier* is expression rather than action. *He is, so to speak, the lady among the races*" (emphasis added; p. 139).

African Americans and the Construction of Knowledge About Race

Most scholars and activists of color argued that human racial groups were innately equal and that environmental conditions were the cause of any significant differences that were observed in their behavioral, psychological, and cultural characteristics (DuBois, 1899/1973; Miller, 1908; Woodson, 1933). Scholars and activists of color endorsed Enlightenment views, which held that all human beings had equal innate potential.

Black nationalist leaders such as Marcus Garvey went further than proclaiming the equality of the races and argued that African Americans should "glorify in their distinctive color, their proud past, and their bright future"

(Cronin, 1982, p. 255). Garvey blended racial pride and Black nationalism to create a cogent ideology and social movement that strongly appealed to the African American masses. Thousands of them joined his movement (Cronin, 1955/1969). He was one of the significant progenitors of today's Afrocentric movement.

African American scholars constructed ideas about race and images of their own groups not only to counteract those invented by others, but also because they believed that accurate information about race and ethnic groups would be antidotes to racist ideologies and misconceptions (Franklin, 1989). They did not challenge "race" as a construction, only particular conceptions of race (C. E. Cortés, personal communication, March 12, 1994). African American "race men" such as Kelly Miller, W. E. B. DuBois, Carter G. Woodson (Goggin, 1983), and Charles H. Wesley believed that accurate information about race and people of color would help to undercut pernicious misconceptions about race and thus help to reduce racism and discrimination (Meier & Rudwick, 1986). It was because of their faith in the power of objective knowledge (which was shared by anthropologists such as Franz Boas and Ruth Benedict) that they devoted so much of their time and energy to constructing new paradigms and data about race and culture.

One important institution within the Black community that codified and reflected its dominant racial attitudes, concepts, and paradigms was the American Negro Academy, founded in 1896 "to aid, by publications, *the vindication of the race from vicious assaults*, in all lines of learning and truth" (emphasis added; Moss, 1981, p. 24). The Academy was founded at a time when nativism, racism, and anti-Black feelings were rampant and extreme throughout the nation. More than 2,500 people were lynched in the United States between 1884 and 1900, most of whom were African Americans (Franklin, 1967). The *Plessy v. Ferguson* decision was handed down by the Supreme Court in 1896. It legalized apartheid throughout the South. Historian Rayford Logan called this period in African American history the "nadir," the lowest point (Janken, 1993).

African American Race Reconstructionists

African American scholars and leaders continued to "vindicate the race from vicious assaults" (Moss, 1981, p. 24), to reconstruct conceptions of race, and to construct oppositional representations throughout the late nineteenth century and the early and middle decades of the twentieth century. They rejected the concept of race that had been constructed by writers such as Grant and Ripley and reinvented conceptions of race in a way that emphasized the extent to which racial characteristics were malleable and subject to environmental influences. They also interrogated and demystified the ideas about the superiority of the Aryan race that were widespread during the late nineteenth and early twentieth centuries (Gould, 1981; Horsman, 1981). Another strategy of the African American vindicationists was to document the high level of civilizations in ancient Africa, including Egypt, and to describe the extent to which African civilizations had influenced those of Europe (DuBois, 1930/1977).

The members of the American Negro Academy "considered themselves to be the inheritors of the 'vindicationist' tradition, within which most educated black men and women had spoken and written during the previous two centuries against apologists for slavery who attempted to justify the 'peculiar institution' with the argument that Negroes were an inferior animal-like breed of mankind unfit to be treated as equals by other people" (Drake, 1987, p. xvii). Educated African Americans in the late nineteenth century, like many during the 1960s and 1970s (Ladner, 1973), considered the vindication of the race against "vicious assaults" an obligation that resulted from their fortunate status. Obtaining an education was not just an individual attainment but involved help from family and community. Education was a group achievement that incurred a group obligation. Consequently, an educated person had an obligation not just to herself or himself but to the community and the race. The purpose of knowledge was not just to build theory; knowledge should be used to improve the race and to make society more just.

The lives of many African American scholar-activists in the late nineteenth and early twentieth centuries exemplified a commitment to create knowledge to vindicate the race, to create more positive and realistic representations of the race, and to use knowledge to improve society. They failed, however, to challenge the idea of race itself.

Kelly Miller. One of the most prolific African American authors during the early twentieth century was Kelly Miller (Logan & Winston, 1982). Miller, who was born in 1863, was a mathematician who became interested in sociology because of its potential for contributing to the understanding of the race problem in the United States. Two collections of Miller's essays on the race question are *Race Adjustment: Essays on the Negro in America* (1908) and *Out of the House of Bondage* (1914). A major intent of Miller's essays was to refute the claim by William Z. Ripley (1899) and the writers he influenced that some races were innately inferior to others. Miller argued that the more advanced situation of the White race was due to environment and that when other races, such as Negroes, were given opportunities similar to those of Whites, they would experience an equal level of development. Miller (1914) stated that the positions of races historically have varied with conditions. Miller (1908) also urged social action that would substantially improve the condition of the Negro. He believed that racial self-respect impelled the Negro into some form of protest.

W. E. B. DuBois. In a prodigious scholarly-activist career that lasted from the late nineteenth century until the March on Washington in 1963, W. E. B. DuBois authored hundreds of publications that contributed greatly to a reconstruction of ideas about race and to the creation of oppositional and more realistic representations of African Americans. His empirical studies and other scholarly publications were transformative. They challenged dominant, institutionalized, and hegemonic perspectives and concepts about African Americans, other groups of color, and women.

DuBois rejected the notion that the Aryan race was superior to others and that there were higher and lower races. He believed that because the darker races of humankind were the majority in the world, the world's future was tied to their destiny. DuBois seriously challenged the institutionalized conceptions of race that canonized negative characteristics of African Americans by producing seminal empirical studies that provided new evidence to which he gave novel interpretations.

Near the turn of the century, the problems within African American urban communities—such as crime and poverty—often were used as evidence to support the assertion that African Americans were an inferior race. DuBois, as well as historians and social scientists such as Kelly Miller, Carter G. Woodson, Horace Mann Bond (Urban, 1992), and E. Franklin Frazier (Platt, 1991), produced empirical studies that documented the extent to which social conditions, such as racism and discrimination, contributed to the wretched conditions of most African Americans who lived in the nation's cities. The section on "Color Prejudice" in DuBois's seminal study, *The Philadelphia Negro* (1899/1973), vividly describes the depth and extent of the racism and discrimination that African Americans experienced in Philadelphia in 1896 and 1897. By quoting some of the hundreds of Black Philadelphians he interviewed, DuBois documented, with anguished voices, discrimination in housing, jobs, and public accommodations. African American social scientists such as DuBois, Bond, and Frazier tried to reconstruct race by using empirical evidence to undercut some of its basic assumptions and tenets. *The Philadelphia Negro* exemplifies this transformative research genre at its best.

The World War II Period, the Rise of Nazism, and the Reconstruction of Race

Ideas about inferior and superior races were still institutionalized and widespread throughout the Western world when Hitler began his triumphant and destructive march through Europe. However, social scientists, alarmed by the pernicious influence of Nazism, acted to construct and popularize ideas about race that were consistent with a democratic society. The racial paradigms within mainstream social science were becoming increasingly liberal and democratic.

As the Nazis spread their pernicious ideas throughout Germany and the rest of the Western world during the 1930s and 1940s, Franz Boas—as well as other influential social scientists—felt compelled to try to halt the influence of Nazism (Caffrey, 1989). His actions to fight anti-Semitism included becoming a founding member of the Lessing League (a New York organization that fought anti-Semitism) and working to facilitate the issuing of popular and widely read publications that would undercut and expose the pseudo-scientific theory on which Nazism was based.

During his 5 decades at Columbia University Boas was able to help establish anthropology as a respected academic discipline, to make the department at Columbia the ranking one in the United States, and to train the nation's most distinguished anthropologists. Ruth Benedict, of *Patterns of Culture* fame (1934/1959) and one of Boas's star students, was persuaded by her publisher and Boas to write a popular book and to participate in other ways to undercut Nazism and racism by popularizing and widely disseminating accurate information about race. In 1940 she published the first edition of *Race: Science and Politics* (1943), a book designed for the educated public that attempted to undercut pervasive myths about race by explaining how scientific findings refuted them. Benedict also joined the Commission on Intercultural Education, a commission of the Progressive Education Association, in 1936.

One of the most influential studies of this period was *An American Dilemma: The Negro Problem and Modern Democracy*, written by the Swedish economist Gunnar Myrdal (1944), with the assistance of Richard Sterner and Arnold Rose, two American social scientists. This important study, which drew heavily on the work of many African American social scientists such as Ralph Bunche and E. Franklin Frazier (and involved the participation of some of them), conceptualized the race problem in the United States as a moral dilemma. This dilemma resulted from the fact that most White Americans had internalized American democratic ideals (i.e., the American creed), and yet violated these ideals in their daily life by practicing racism and discrimination. Myrdal was optimistic because he believed that in their attempt to resolve their dilemma, White Americans would try to actualize human and civil rights. Myrdal (1944) makes a strong argument, and presents supporting evidence to support it, for the equal potential of the races and the power of environmental influences.

Knowledge About Race Is Reconstructed in Mainstream Social Science Discourse

By the late nineteenth century, rigid and racist ideas about the inherited characteristics of different racial groups were codified in established social science in the United States. Not only were groups of color such as American

Indians and African Americans regarded as inherently inferior, but the various White ethnic groups were perceived as different races, some inferior to others. Although many American leaders had inculcated Enlightenment ideas about the equality of humans during the Revolutionary period, these ideas faded as slavery became institutionalized and an ideology was needed to justify the enslavement of Africans in the United States.

Near the turn of the century, most academics legitimized and justified the dominant ideas and conceptions of race that were institutionalized in the colleges and universities and in the public imagination. Influential academics who legitimated racist ideas included the historian Ulrich B. Phillips (1918/1966) and sociologists George Fitzhugh (1854/1965) and Howard W. Odum (1910). Most academics reinforced dominant ideas about race during this period because they were socialized within institutions that benefited from the institutionalized conceptions. At the turn of the century, African Americans were only a few decades out of slavery. Consequently, they did, in fact, have low levels of education, high levels of poverty, and other characteristics that indicated low social, economic, and political status. The ways in which scholars interpreted these objective facts were influenced by their own positions within the social, economic, and political order. The ideas about race constructed by scholars were influenced by both the objective conditions they observed and their own personal and cultural perspectives and experiences.

The mainstream academics who challenged the institutionalized ideas about race in the late nineteenth and early twentieth centuries were lonely voices in the crowd. Franz Boas's experiences with anti-Semitism, his work with Eskimos, and his functioning in the liberal Jewish intellectual community in New York City may partially explain why he stood out from the crowd and seriously challenged the institutionalized conceptions of race when he arrived in the United States in 1884.

It is significant that Boas's ideas about race were in many ways more enlightened and consistent with today's theories than were those of Robert E. Park. Park's experiences among African Americans probably enabled him to have more enlightened views about race than many of his White colleagues. However, his upper-middle-class White background and socialization in the Midwest may explain in part why he was less able than Boas to transcend the predominant racial ideas and assumptions of his time.

DIFFERENCES BETWEEN WHITE AND AFRICAN AMERICAN RACE CONSTRUCTORS

The ideas of early African American scholars and social scientists differed significantly from those of Boas and Park, their contemporaries. These scholars completely rejected the notion of inherent racial differences and argued that the races were inherently equal and that environmental factors prevented people of color from being equal to Whites. The ideas and concepts about race that were constructed by African American scholars such as DuBois, Miller, and Woodson are highly consistent with today's social science race theories. African American social scientists were able to transcend the dominant ideologies and concepts about race institutionalized during their time.

Code's (1991) ideas about the interaction of the objective and the subjective in the formation of knowledge help to explain why African American social scientists, unlike Boas and Park, were able to completely transcend the dominant ideas about race during their time. The personal, family, and community experiences of these individuals within the Black world enabled them to see the possibilities for African Americans. They also believed that they were equal in ability to Whites and could, by extension, envision the intellectual and social potential of other African Americans. Because African American scholars were victimized by institutionalized racism and discrimination, they constructed ideas about race that would help to liberate themselves, as well as their communities, from institutionalized discrimination and oppression.

THE GENETIC EXPLANATION OF RACIAL DIFFERENCES LOSES GROUND

The work by scholars such as Boas, DuBois, Woodson, and Miller had some significant effects on changing the ways in which the academic world defined and conceptualized race. When Nazism reached its height in the 1930s and 1940s, important changes had taken place in the academic, if not in the public, conception of race. Mainstream scholars writing in the 1930s and 1940s, such as Ruth Benedict and Gunnar Myrdal, exemplified the emerging conception of race that was becoming institutionalized within academic discourse. Certainly much racist and anti-egalitarian academic work was written during this period, such as that on the nature of Black–White intelligence (Shuey, 1958). A number of psychologists during the 1930s and 1940s argued that intelligence tests indicated that Blacks were intellectually inferior to Whites.

Nevertheless, the dominant trend in the race literature among academics during the intergroup education period of the 1940s and 1950s and in subsequent years was toward the equality of the races. Although Darwinism and biological explanations of behavior became less legitimate and respected in academic discourse after the 1940s and 1950s, they remained a muted but tenacious paradigm within the academic community (Degler, 1991). The historic genetic paradigm was consequently an important foundation for genetic explanations that were exhumed in the 1960s and 1970s, and in 1994 (Herrnstein & Murray, 1994; Shockley, 1972; Shuey, 1958).

THE BELL CURVE LEGITIMIZES THE GENETIC EXPLANATION OF COGNITIVE ABILITY

The publication and public reception of *The Bell Curve* (Herrnstein & Murray, 1994) marks the renewed legitimacy and popularity of the genetic explanation of intelligence and of the argument that African Americans are genetically inferior to Whites. This book was on the *New York Times* best-seller list for a number of weeks and received major attention in the popular press. It was the subject of an entire issue of *The New Republic* (October 31, 1994) and of major stories in *The New York Times Book Review* (Browne, 1994), *The New York Times Magazine* (DeParle, 1994), *The New York Review of Books* (Lane, 1994), *The New Yorker* (Gould, 1994), and *The Nation* (Reed, 1994), as well as in many other mass circulation publications.

The Bell Curve is the most recent of a long list of publications that historically have defended and constructed the argument that some racial groups are genetically inferior to others. However, what distinguishes *The Bell Curve* from most earlier publications (e.g., Jensen, 1969) is the authors' argument that low-income people, including poor Whites, have less cognitive ability than the middle and upper classes. The Herrnstein and Murray hypothesis was first presented by Herrnstein in an article and a book published in 1971 (Herrnstein, 1971a, 1971b). Their theory is unique because it is one of the first theories about race since the turn of the century that makes a genetic distinction among groups of Whites. Ripley (1899) and Grant (1916) made distinctions among Whites based on ethnicity; the Herrnstein and Murray distinction is based on social class. In their theory, low-income Whites and African Americans share inferior genetic characteristics.

The major argument of *The Bell Curve* is consistent with the conservative political agenda for the 1990s. The book was published at a time when the nation was seriously rethinking its commitment to low-income groups and when the gap between the rich and the poor was growing sharply. A basic thesis of *The Bell Curve* is that people are poor because of their genetic characteristics, not because of the lack of social and economic opportunities in U. S. society. The top 20% of households in the United States received 11 times more income than the bottom 20% in 1992 ("Inequality," 1994). Poverty in the United States is also widespread and increasing. In 1991, approximately 24 million Whites, 10 million African Americans, and over 6 million Hispanics were living below the poverty level (U. S. Bureau of the Census, 1993, p. 475). Like the race theories that were constructed near the turn of the century, *The Bell Curve* reinforces some of the major societal sentiments of the times, such as calls for the closing of the nation's borders to foreigners and the radical reform of welfare and other programs targeted for low-income population groups. Writes Stephen Jay Gould (1994):

When a book garners as much attention as "The Bell Curve," we wish to know the causes. One might suspect the content itself—a startlingly new idea, or an old suspicion newly verified by persuasive data—but the reason might also be social acceptability, or even just plain hype. "The Bell Curve," with its claims and supposed documentation that race and class differences are largely caused by genetic factors and are therefore essentially immutable, contains no new arguments and presents no compelling data to support its anachronistic social Darwinism, so I can only conclude that its success in winning attention must reflect the depressing temper of our time—a historical moment of unprecedented ungenerosity, when a mood for slashing social programs can be powerfully abetted by an argument that beneficiaries cannot be helped, owing to inborn cognitive limits expressed as low I. Q. scores. (p. 139)

TRANSFORMATIVE TEACHING

Race is a human invention constructed by groups to differentiate themselves from other groups, to create ideas about the "Other," to formulate their identities, and to defend the disproportionate distribution of rewards and opportunities within society. These ideas about race, which are discussed in the previous sections of this chapter, can be used to integrate the school, college, and university curriculum with multicultural content and to teach students the ways in which knowledge is invented and reinvented through time. They also can be used to help transform the curriculum in U.S. history courses and units.

In the previous sections of this chapter, I focused on African Americans as a case study to illustrate how knowledge about race has been constructed and reconstructed through time. The concepts, ideologies, arguments, and methods used to construct racial concepts about African Americans were in most ways identical to those used to construct racial concepts and ideologies about American Indians, Mexican Americans, Asian Americans, and other groups of color. It is important for teachers to help students recognize the connections among the ways in which racial knowledge, concepts, and ideologies were constructed about the various groups of color. To emphasize the importance of these interconnections, the teaching examples below focus on American Indians.

Racializing the Other. Transformation is the process of changing the "nature, function, or condition" of a phenomenon (Morris, 1971, p. 1363). When teaching is transformed, the content of the curriculum, pedagogy, and the ways in which students learn are substantially modified. Research on classrooms and curriculum indicates that teaching at the upper and high school grades in most academic subjects is characterized largely by teacher talk, the mastery of low-level facts by students, and passive student learning (Goodlad, 1984; Shaver, Davis, & Helburn, 1979).

Transformative teaching and learning are characterized by a curriculum organized around powerful ideas, highly interactive teaching strategies, active student involvement, and activities that require students to participate in personal, social, and civic action to make their classrooms, schools, and communities more democratic and just. In their book *The Feminist Classroom,* Maher and Tetreault (1994) describe how college professors at six colleges and universities transformed their classrooms by integrating their curricula with multicultural content and engaging students in the process of knowledge construction.

One of the first steps in the construction of racial categories is the delineation of out-groups as the "Other." As Morrison (1992) and Todorov (1982) have pointed out, the Other often becomes essential for the in-group to create its own identity. Morrison describes how the presence of African Americans was necessary for Whiteness to be defined. She writes:

> It is no accident and no mistake that immigrant populations . . . understood their "Americanness" as an opposition to the resident black population. Race, in fact, now functions as a metaphor so necessary to the construction of Americanness that it rivals the old pseudo-scientific and class-informed racisms whose dynamics we are more used to deciphering. . . . Deep within the word "American" is its association with race. (p. 47)

Todorov writes, "It is in fact the conquest of America that heralds and establishes our present identity" (p. 5).

Constructing racial categories and stigmatizing out-groups not only have served as a source of self-identification for powerful and mainstream groups but also may have contributed to the development of some of their important ideas about freedom and democracy. In his study of the development of freedom in Western societies, Patterson (1991) concludes that slavery gave birth not only to group definition and group solidarity among the enslaving groups but also to freedom. In other words, freedom developed as an antidote to slavery.

Students can examine the ways in which ideas about the Other and racial categories were constructed when studying key events in the development of American history. A careful reading of Columbus's description of the Taino Indians when he arrived in the Caribbean will reveal how on his initial encounter with the Tainos Columbus began to conceptualize them as the Other, thus forming the basis for Indians to be perceived as a different and inferior race from Western Europeans. Columbus wrote about the Tainos in his diary (Jane, 1960):

It seemed to me that they were a people very deficient in everything. They all go naked as their mothers bore them, and the women also. . . . They should be good servants and of quick intelligence, since I see that they very soon say all that is said to them, and I believe that they would easily be made Christians, for it appeared to me that they had no creed. Our Lord willing, at the time of my departure I will bring back six of them to Your Highness, that they may learn to talk. (pp. 23–24)

When discussing the above and other excerpts from Columbus's diary, students can examine how Columbus perceived the Tainos, why, and how he used European ideas and concepts to determine whether they could become good servants; why they could not "talk"; and the meaning of his taking six of them back to Europe. Writes Todorov (1982):

Physically naked, the Indians are also, to Columbus's eyes, deprived of all cultural property: they are characterized, in a sense, by the absence of customs, rites, religion. (p. 35)
    In general, this [Columbus's] project of assimilation is identified with the desire to convert the Indians, to propagate the Gospel. We know that this intention is fundamental to Columbus's initial project. (p. 43)

Students also can examine the ways in which ideas and concepts about Indians have both changed and remained constant through time. The ideas that Columbus constructed about the Tainos can be compared and contrasted with those that Cortes and the Spanish conquistadors invented about the Aztecs. The Aztecs were defined by Cortes and his men as the Other in part because they engaged in human sacrifice in religious ceremonies, spoke a different language (Nahuatl), and had non-European gods. The conquistadors' project was to destroy the Aztec culture through either extermination or assimilation. The racial ideas the Spaniards invented about the Aztecs codified the major goals of their project in the Americas, which were to conquer the land and to Christianize the natives.

A study of the Westward movement in U. S. history will provide students with rich opportunities to continue their examination of the changing conceptions of racial ideas about Native Americans. In the seminal paper he presented at the meeting of the American Historical Association in 1893, Frederick Jackson Turner stated ideas about the Indians that deeply penetrated American popular and scholarly culture (Turner, 1989). He described the Western frontier as "the meeting between savagery and civilization" (p. 3). He characterized the Indians' homelands as the "western wilderness" (p. 5) and described how the European "settlers" brought civilization to the savage West: "The United States lies like a huge page in the history of society. Line by line as we read from west to east we find the record of social evolution.

It begins with the Indian and the hunter; it goes on to tell the disintegra-
tion of savagery by the entrance of the trader, the path-finder of civilization"
(pp. 6-7).

In Turner's racial schema, the Indians are the Other: savages who live in
an empty wilderness. The European settlers will bring civilization to the savage West and in the process create a unique form of American democracy.
Contemporary films such as *Little Big Man* and *Dances with Wolves* can be
used to extend students' study of continuity and change in the racial image
of American Indians. Most contemporary films about American Indians, which
reflect in many ways how the racial image of the Indian has become more
liberalized since the civil rights movement of the 1960s, maintain some of the
older conceptions of Indians as people who live in the wilderness. Most films
about Indians are set in a restricted time period in the past (Churchill, 1992).
Few deal with Indians in contemporary American society; most films depict
Native Americans as Plains Indians in the West for a period that does not
exceed 50 years.

The Changing Conceptions of Race. One of the most important teaching implications of this examination of the changing conceptions of race is
that students need to understand the extent to which knowledge about race
(as well as about other social phenomena), and even the very idea of race, is
a social construction that reflects both the objective reality as well as the subjectivity of the knower. Students should examine the ways in which the
construction of race reflects the social context, the historical times, and
the economic structure of society. Students also should understand that the
concept of race is still in the process of change and reconstruction. I have
illustrated how these understandings can be taught by having students
examine the changing racial image of the American Indian in U. S. society.

A study of race, as well as other social science concepts, can help students
to understand how the social context in which the knower is embedded
influences the knowledge that she or he produces. The European experience
and socialization of Columbus and Cortes strongly influenced how they
viewed and conceptualized the Indians as the Other without culture or
religion.

The Western empirical tradition has dichotomized the personal characteristics of the knower from the objective reality. An examination of the historical development of race can help students understand how the subjective characteristics of the knower, as well as the objective reality, influence
the knowledge the knower constructs, deconstructs, and reconstructs. Students can examine how this process has worked in the construction of knowledge about race, as well as examine how their own personal and family experiences influence their conceptions of ideas such as race, affirmative action,

and equal rights. They can carefully examine how they construct and reconstruct ideas, concepts, and interpretations.

Students who have a keen understanding of how knowledge is constructed, how it reflects both subjectivity and objectivity, and how it relates to power, will have important skills needed to participate in the construction of knowledge that will help the nation to actualize its democratic ideals (Banks & Banks, 1995). Students with these skills also will be able to interrogate the assumptions of knowers, and consequently will be less likely to be victimized by knowledge that protects hegemony and inequality. Students not only must be able to interrogate and reconstruct knowledge, they must be able to produce knowledge themselves if they are to be effective citizens in the multicultural world of the twenty-first century.

REFERENCES

Alba, R. D. (1990). *Ethnic identity: The transformation of White America.* New Haven: Yale University Press.

Ani, M. (1994). *Yurugu: An African-centered critique of European cultural thought and behavior.* Trenton, NJ: Africa World Press.

Banks, J. A. (1993). The canon debate, knowledge construction, and multicultural education. *Educational Researcher, 22* (5), 4–14.

Banks, J. A., & Banks, C. A. M. (Eds.). (1995). *Handbook of research on multicultural education.* New York: Macmillan.

Barkan, E. (1992). *The retreat of scientific racism: Changing concepts of race in Britain and the United States between the world wars.* New York: Cambridge University Press.

Benedict, R. (1943). *Race: Science and politics* (rev. ed.). New York: Viking.

Benedict, R. (1959). *Patterns of culture.* Boston: Houghton Mifflin. (Original work published 1934)

Boas, F. (1910). The real racial problem. *Crisis, 1* (2), 22–25.

Boas, F. (1962). *Anthropology and modern life.* New York: Dove. (Original work published 1928)

Brown, E. B. (1991). Mothers of mind. In P. Bell-Scott, B. Guy-Sheftall, J. J. Royster, J. Sims-Wood, M. DeCosta-Willis, & L. Fultz (Eds.), *Double stitch: Black women write about mothers & daughters* (pp. 74–93). Boston: Beacon Press.

Browne, M. W. (1994, October 16). What is intelligence, and who has it? *The New York Times Book Review,* pp. 3, 41, 45.

Bulmer, M. (1984). *The Chicago school of sociology: Institutionalization, diversity, and the rise of sociological research.* Chicago: University of Chicago Press.

Caffrey, M. M. (1989). *Ruth Benedict: Stranger in this land.* Austin: University of Texas Press.

Caldwell, C. (1830). *Thoughts on the original unity of the human race.* New York: E. Bliss.

Chernow, B. A., & Vallasi, G. A. (Eds.). (1993). *The Columbia encyclopedia* (5th ed.). New York: Columbia University Press.

Churchill, W. (1992). *Fantasies of the master race* (M. A. Jaimes, Ed.). Monroe, ME: Common Courage Press.

Code, L. (1991). *What can she know? Feminist theory and the construction of knowledge.* Ithaca, NY: Cornell University Press.

Cronin, D. E. (1969). *Black Moses: The story of Marcus Garvey.* Madison: University of Wisconsin Press. (Original work published 1969)

Cronin, D. E. (1982). Garvey, Marcus [Mosiah] (1887-1940). In R. W. Logan & M. R. Winston (Eds.), *Dictionary of American Negro biography* (pp. 254-256). New York: W. W. Norton.

Degler, C. N. (1991). *In search of human nature: The decline and revival of Darwinism in American social thought.* New York: Oxford University Press.

DeParle, J. (1994, October 9). Daring research or "social science pornography"? *The New York Times Magazine*, pp. 48-53, 62, 70-71, 74, 78, 80.

Drake, St. C. (1987). *Black folk here and there: An essay in history and anthropology* (Vol. 1). Los Angeles: Center for Afro-American Studies.

DuBois, W. E. B. (1973). *The Philadelphia Negro: A social study.* Millwood, NY: Kraus-Thomson. (Original work published 1899)

DuBois, W. E. B. (1977). *Africa—Its geography, people and products* and *Africa— Its place in modern history.* Millwood, NY: Kraus-Thomson. (Original work published 1930)

Fitzhugh, G. (1965). *Sociology for the South; or, the failure of free society.* New York: B. Franklin. (Original work published 1854)

Franklin, J. H. (1967). *From slavery to freedom* (3rd ed.). New York: Knopf.

Franklin, J. H. (Ed.). (1968). *Color and race.* Boston: Houghton Mifflin.

Franklin, J. H. (1989). *Race and history: Selected essays, 1938-1988.* Baton Rouge: Louisiana State University Press.

Giddings, P. (1984). *When and where I enter: The impact of Black women on race and sex in America.* New York: Bantam Books.

Goggin, J. (1983). Countering white racist scholarship: Carter G. Woodson and *The Journal of Negro History. The Journal of Negro History, 68* (4), 355-375.

Goodlad, J. I. (1984). *A place called school: Prospects for the future.* New York: McGraw-Hill.

Gould, S. J. (1981). *The mismeasure of man.* New York: W. W. Norton.

Gould, S. J. (1994, November 28). Curveball. *The New Yorker, 70* (38), 139-149.

Grant, M. (1916). *The passing of the great race.* New York: Scribner's.

Herrnstein, R. J. (1971a, September). I.Q. *Atlantic Monthly, 228*, 43-64.

Herrnstein, R. J. (1971b). *I.Q. in the meritocracy.* Boston: Little, Brown.

Herrnstein, R. J., & Murray, C. (1994). *The bell curve: Intelligence and class structure in American life.* New York: Free Press.

Herskovits, M. J. (1953). *Franz Boas: The science of man in the making.* New York: Scribner's.

Higham, J. (1972). *Strangers in the land: Patterns of American nativism 1860-1925.* New York: Atheneum.

Horsman, R. (1981). *Race and manifest destiny: The origins of American racial Anglo-Saxonism.* Cambridge, MA: Harvard University Press.

Hyatt, M. (1990). *Franz Boas: Social activist: The dynamics of ethnicity.* New York: Greenwood Press.

Inequality: For richer, for poorer. (1994, November 5). *The Economist, 333* (7888), 19–21.

Jane, C. (1960). *The journal of Christopher Columbus.* New York: Clarkson N. Potter.

Janken, K. R. (1993). *Rayford W. Logan and the dilemma of the African-American intellectual.* Amherst: University of Massachusetts Press.

Jensen, A. R. (1969). How much can we boost IQ and scholastic achievement? *Harvard Educational Review, 39* (1), 1–123.

Ladner, J. A. (Ed.). (1973). *The death of White sociology.* New York: Vintage Books.

Lane, C. (1994, December 1). The tainted sources of the *The Bell Curve. The New York Review of Books, 41* (20), 14–19.

Logan, R. W., & Winston, M. R. (Eds.). (1982). *Dictionary of American Negro biography.* New York: W. W. Norton.

Maher, F. A., & Tetreault, M. K. T. (1994). *The feminist classroom.* New York: Basic Books.

Meier, A., & Rudwick, E. (1986). *Black history and the historical profession, 1915–1980.* Urbana: University of Illinois Press.

Merton, R. K. (1972). Insiders and outsiders: A chapter in the sociology of knowledge. *The American Journal of Sociology, 78* (1), 9–47.

Miller, K. (1908). *Race adjustment: Essays on the Negro in America.* New York: Neale.

Miller, K. (1914). *Out of the house of bondage.* New York: Neale.

Morris, W. M. (Ed.). (1971). *The American heritage dictionary of the English language.* Boston: Houghton Mifflin.

Morrison, T. (1992). *Playing in the dark: Whiteness and the literary imagination.* Cambridge, MA: Harvard University Press.

Moss, A. A. Jr. (1981). *The American Negro Academy: Voice of the talented tenth.* Baton Rouge: Louisiana State University Press.

Myrdal, G. (with Sterner, R., & Rose, A.). (1944). *An American dilemma: The Negro problem and modern democracy.* New York: Harper & Row.

The New Republic. (1994, October 31), 5–37 [Entire issue].

Odum, H. W. (1910). *Social and mental traits of the Negro.* New York: Columbia University.

Omi, M., & Winant, H. (1986). *Racial formation in the United States: From the 1960s to the 1980s.* New York: Routledge.

Park, R. E., & Burgess, E. W. (1937). *Introduction to the science of sociology.* Chicago: University of Chicago Press. (Original work published 1921)

Patterson, O. (1991). *Freedom in the making of Western culture.* New York: Basic Books.

Phillips, U. B. (1966). *American Negro slavery.* Baton Rouge: Louisiana State University Press. (Original work published 1918)

Platt, A. M. (1991). *E. Franklin Frazier reconsidered*. New Brunswick, NJ: Rutgers University Press.

Plessy v. Ferguson, 163 U.S. 537 (1896).

Reed, A., Jr. (1994, November). Looking backward. *The Nation*, pp. 654–662.

Ripley, W. Z. (1899). *The races of Europe: A sociological study*. New York: D. Appleton.

Shaver, J. P., Davis, O. L., Jr., & Helburn, S. W. (1979). The status of social studies education: Implications from three NSF studies. *Social Education, 43* (2), 150–153.

Shockley, W. (1972). Dysgenics, geneticity, raceology: A challenge to the intellectual responsibility of educators. *Phi Delta Kappan, 53* (5), 297–307.

Shuey, A. (1958). *The testing of Negro intelligence*. Lynchburg, VA: Bell.

Smith, J. D., & Inscoe, J. C. (Eds.). (1993). *Ulrich Bonnell Phillips: A southern historian and his critics*. Athens: University of Georgia Press.

Stocking, G. W. (1964). Franz Boas. In E. T. James, P. M. Hosay, M. Caskey, & P. De Vencentes (Eds.), *Dictionary of American biography* (Supplement 3, 1941–1945; pp. 81–85). New York: Scribner's.

Tetreault, M. K. T. (1993). Classrooms for diversity: Rethinking curriculum and pedagogy. In J. A. Banks & C. A. M. Banks (Eds.), *Multicultural education: Issues and perspectives* (2nd ed., pp. 129–148). Boston: Allyn & Bacon.

Todorov, T. (1982). *The conquest of America: The question of the other*. New York: HarperCollins.

Turner, F. J. (1989). The significance of the frontier in American history. In C. A. Milner II (Ed.), *Major problems in the history of the American West* (pp. 2–21). Lexington, MA: Heath. (Original work published 1894)

Urban, W. J. (1992). *Black scholar: Horace Mann Bond 1904–1972*. Athens: University of Georgia Press.

U. S. Bureau of the Census. (1991). *Statistical abstract of the United States* (111th ed.). Washington, DC: U. S. Government Printing Office.

U. S. Bureau of the Census. (1993). *Statistical abstract of the United States* (113th ed.). Washington, DC: U. S. Government Printing Office.

van den Berghe, P. (1967). *Race and racism: A comparative perspective*. New York: Wiley.

Woodson, C. G. (1933). *The mis-education of the Negro*. Washington, DC: Associated Publishers.

The Historical Development
of Transformative Scholarship

"We stand on the shoulders of giants." This adage accurately describes the evolution of multicultural education and the extent to which it grew out of and extends the work of early scholars. The ethnic studies movement of the 1960s was the first phase in the evolution of multicultural education. The ethnic studies movement emerged directly from the work of scholars who did their work from the turn of the century through the 1940s and 1950s. Case studies of individuals and groups who did the pioneering work that constitutes the historical foundation of multicultural education are described in Part II.

The work and career of Carter G. Woodson is described in Chapter 5. Woodson, who is regarded as the "Father of African American history," was not only a scholar but worked tirelessly to promote the teaching of Black history in the nation's schools, colleges, and universities. His invention of "Negro History Week" was an important and effective vehicle for the popularization of African American history. Allison Davis, the University of Chicago anthropologist who interrogated and tried to reconstruct institutionalized theories about the intellectual abilities of Black children and who emphasized the importance of class on schooling, is discussed in Chapter 6.

Although African Americans were one of the first groups to challenge institutionalized conceptions of race, scholars from other ethnic groups also challenged these conceptions. It is important that their work be acknowledged and remembered. Beginning in the 1930s, George I. Sánchez challenged popular conceptions about the academic abilities of Mexican American students and contested segregated schools for Latino students. Chapter 7 details his work and career.

In Chapter 8, Carol Miller describes how two early Native American scholars, Mourning Dove and Ella Deloria, struggled to state their authentic voices through White scholars and interpreters who mediated their world views. In Chapter 4, readers of this book first met Robert E. Park, the renowned sociologist who taught at the University of Chicago from 1913 to 1932. In Chapter 8, Henry Yu describes how Park helped to construct the idea of the "Oriental problem" as well as provided opportunities for a small number of his Asian American subjects to participate in his studies as experts. Yu details the opportunities and dilemmas experienced by these Asian American graduate students and the problematic nature of the concept of the "Oriental problem."

CHAPTER 5

Carter G. Woodson and the Development of Transformative Scholarship

AGNES M. ROCHE

Carter G. Woodson (1875–1950) made important contributions to the fields of history and education. Often called the "father of Black history," Woodson probably influenced the teaching of African American history in schools and colleges more than any other single scholar. His historical scholarship based on African and African American perspectives challenged mainstream interpretations of history. His educational theories, articulated in *The Mis-Education of the Negro* (1933), challenged the paradigms on which Western education is based and offered an alternative approach to the education of African Americans.

Having received a Ph.D. in history from Harvard in 1912, Woodson founded, with others, the Association for the Study of Negro Life and History (now the Association for the Study of Afro-American Life and History) in 1915 and served as its director until his death in 1950. In founding the Association, Woodson hoped not only that his work would counter and correct the distorted and stereotypical views of mainstream historians, but that a more complete and accurate history would help African Americans think more positively about themselves, reduce prejudice in Whites, and broaden the perspectives of both groups.

This chapter examines the significance of Woodson's work as scholar, editor, publisher, and educator on the development of transformative knowledge about African Americans. Banks (1993) states that transformative knowledge challenges mainstream academic knowledge, which he defines as "the concepts, paradigms, theories, and explanations that constitute traditional Western-centric knowledge in history and the behavioral and social sciences" (p. 7). Transformative knowledge seeks to "expand and substantially revise established canons, paradigms, theories, explanations, and research methods" (p. 7). When disseminated, transformative knowledge provides possibilities for change. Dissemination is essential for transformative knowledge to lead to action. It is in the role of disseminator that Woodson left one of his most important legacies.

Woodson sought to disseminate historical knowledge on African Americans to two major audiences. He reached the scholarly community of historians through the Association's annual meetings that began in 1915, *The Journal of Negro History* founded in 1916, and monographs published by Associated Publishers, which he established, with others, in 1922. He influenced the general public, teachers, and students through Negro History Week established in 1926, the Association's annual meetings, teacher conferences, *The Negro History Bulletin* founded in 1937, and publication of textbooks and children's literature.

Woodson once commented to fellow historian, Luther Porter Jackson, "What is the use of knowing things if they cannot be published to the world?" (quoted in Goggin, 1983, p. 93). This idea was a driving force in his life. Mary McLeod Bethune (1935) expanded on the theme of "publishing to the world" to include the notion of translator and interpreter, two concepts closely related to the function of dissemination, in her address at the Association's twentieth anniversary meeting. She stated:

> Already we have an ample supply of investigators, but it appears to me that there is a shortage of readable and responsible interpreters, men and women who can effectively play the role of mediator between the trained investigator and the masses. (pp. 408–409)

Bethune served as the Association's president from 1936 to 1952 and undoubtedly had a hand in broadening the scope of its educational mission. She believed that the role of interpretation, not scholarly investigation, would become the major work of the Association in the future. She spoke of the social significance of the popularization of history for the community:

> The temptation of the scholar is to keep the new truth he finds stacked in the warehouse. It shocks his sense of scholarly dignity to see his discoveries hawked in the market place by the popularizer. But the social usefulness of scholarship and its findings depends upon its translation into the common tongue. . . . We must have the popularizer to stand between the masses whose knowledge of things is indefinite and the research worker whose knowledge is authoritative. (pp. 409–410)

Woodson founded *The Negro History Bulletin*, a magazine for students and the general reader, shortly after the twentieth anniversary meeting and during the early years of Bethune's presidency. Publication of the *Bulletin* appears to have been a response to her call. It also met the needs of his primary constituency, the African American community, which was the chief source of funding for the Association by the late 1930s (Goggin, 1983).

The challenge of disseminating historical knowledge to the general public, which Woodson addressed throughout his scholarly career, still confronts historians today. Results from a recent poll conducted by *The Journal of American History* indicated that "many historians were concerned that they were unable to communicate effectively with public audiences" (Winkler, 1995, p. A18). Thus, the significance of Carter G. Woodson for scholars and practitioners is that he not only produced historical scholarship for a scholarly audience, but also provided a model of how to translate, interpret, and create enterprises to make history more accessible to teachers, students, and the general public.

BIOGRAPHICAL SKETCH

Carter Godwin Woodson was born December 19, 1875, in New Canton, Virginia, to parents who were former slaves. Working in coal mines at an early age, he attended high school for less than 2 years, graduating at age 20. He studied at Berea College in Kentucky, received an L.B. degree, and subsequently volunteered to teach in the Philippines for 3 years (1903-1906). In 1908, he completed the requirements for both a bachelor's and master's degree at the University of Chicago. Woodson spent a year in residence at Harvard (1908-1909), completing his doctorate in 1912. He was the second African American to receive a Ph.D. in history from Harvard, W. E. B. DuBois being the first, in 1895. Woodson's 1912 dissertation, *The Disruption of Virginia*, treats West Virginia's secession from the original colony.

When Woodson graduated from Harvard, segregation and discrimination precluded him from obtaining employment in the best universities. The oppressive social and political atmosphere for African Americans in the nation's capital, where he lived and taught high school, caused him great concern. Woodrow Wilson's expansion of segregation in federal departments and the release of *Birth of a Nation* in 1915 motivated Woodson to do something to counteract the negative forces influencing the African American community (Franklin, 1989; Logan, 1973; Meier & Rudwick, 1986; Scally, 1977).

Two significant events shaped the direction Woodson's career would take. When the Washington, DC branch of the National Association for the Advancement of Colored People (NAACP), citing fear of a lawsuit, denied him permission to organize a boycott of White businesses that discriminated against African Americans, Woodson retorted:

> I am not afraid of being sued by white business men. In fact, I should welcome such a law suit. It would do the cause much good. Let us banish fear. We have been in this mental state for three centuries. I am a radical. I am ready to act, if I can find brave men to help me. (quoted in Scally, 1977, p. 653)

Another factor affecting Woodson's plans was the success of his first published scholarly work, *The Education of the Negro Prior to 1861* (1915), which gained him recognition as a historian among mainstream scholars (Scally, 1977). Moreover, investigation for this work "undoubtedly strengthened his belief in the reforming power of education" (Goggin, 1983, p. 6). Woodson began to envision a kind of organization that would use different strategies to combat segregation and discrimination than boycotts, demonstrations, and legal battles in the courts.

In the summer of 1915, while doing research at the University of Chicago, Woodson decided to form an association devoted to the "scientific" study of Negro life and history (Wesley, 1965). He met with cofounders William B. Hartgrove, J. E. Stamps, George Cleveland Hall, and Alexander L. Jackson on September 9, 1915 in Chicago (Goggin, 1983). The Association for the Study of Negro Life and History was incorporated in Washington, DC later that year.

While serving as director of the Association, Woodson taught briefly at Howard University (1919–1920), where he introduced major reforms in the history department (Winston, 1973), and at West Virginia Collegiate Institute (1920–1922). Grants from the Rockefeller and Carnegie Foundations in 1922 permitted him to leave college teaching to devote all his time to the work of the Association. In the early years, Woodson's work focused on obtaining and administering foundation grants, writing original research, serving as editor of the *Journal*, and training young scholars. His mentorship resulted in the "eventual placement of many excellent black historians on the history and social science faculties of the major black institutions" (Hine, 1986, p. 421), including Charles H. Wesley, A. A. Taylor, Luther P. Jackson, Lorenzo Greene, and Benjamin Quarles.

Woodson's conflicts with professionals in and outside the Association have been described in detail (Meier & Rudwick, 1986). In contrast to his "cantankerousness in the pursuit of truth" (Goggin, 1983, p. 311), he communicated effectively with ordinary people from all levels of the African American community—his major constituency—and impressed them as "a courtly, amiable, and witty gentleman" (Franklin, 1988, p. 166). He inspired hope and a sense of pride by presenting a positive portrayal of the Black experience. By stressing past achievements and triumphs over adversity, he tried to instill a sense of personal efficacy and community solidarity in order to foster social change.

In the early 1930s, Woodson refused to meet the demands of the philanthropic foundations to locate his enterprise at a Black college or university. He believed these institutions could not support the kind of research he had undertaken and that since Whites controlled many Black institutions administratively and financially, he could continue to produce scholarship from the Black perspective only if he maintained his autonomy (Meier & Rudwick, 1986). As a result, he lost foundation support, which greatly curtailed his research program. Thus, in the midst of the Depression, Woodson was forced to turn to the "impoverished Negro element of the United States" ("Annual Report," 1935, p. 366) for financial support. He insisted on maintaining his independent status, despite the threat it posed to the organization's survival: "No one has been able as yet to dictate to the Association for the Study of Negro Life and History what it should investigate, what it should publish, in what form it should appear or when it should be given to the public" ("Annual Report," 1942, p. 372).

Relieved from applying for grants from White philanthropists and subordinating himself to their research agendas, Woodson embraced the role of fund raiser, observing that "it is much better to obtain one dollar from each of 20,000 persons than $20,000 from one" (quoted in Goggin, 1983, p. 240). According to historian Lorenzo Greene (1965), "the secret of [Woodson's] success is that he has the courage to plan and confidence that, although the money is not presently available, his project will ultimately succeed" (p. 175).

With financial support now coming almost totally from the African American community, the work of the Association, as heralded by Mary McLeod Bethune at the twentieth anniversary celebration, focused more intensely on the teaching of African American history in the schools and dissemination of historical knowledge to the general public. When Woodson died in 1950, he had served continuously as editor of the *Journal* and *Bulletin* from their inception and as director of the Association for 35 years, often without a salary.

PRODUCTION AND DISSEMINATION OF TRANSFORMATIVE SCHOLARSHIP ON AFRICAN AMERICANS

The scholarly works of Woodson and his associates represent one of the earliest challenges to mainstream academic knowledge from the African American perspective. Annual meetings of the Association, articles, original documents, and book reviews published in *The Journal of Negro History*, as well as monographs, pamphlets, and books published by Associated Publishers, were the primary means Woodson used to counter White racist scholarship (Goggin, 1983, 1993).

The Journal of Negro History

Woodson and other Black scholars produced a number of works in the 1920s and 1930s that were published by Associated Publishers and in the *Journal*. A handful of White scholars also published their research in the *Journal* and through Associated Publishers. Historian Lorenzo Greene recalled that both Black and White scholars "turned to the *Journal of Negro History* if they desired to publish findings at variance with the currently accepted views of black people" (quoted in Goggin, 1983, p. 101). Woodson believed that an alternative press was needed because "if the Negro is to settle down to publishing merely what others permit him to bring out, the world will never know what the race has thought and felt and attempted and accomplished and the story of the Negro will perish with him" (quoted in Wesley, 1951, p. 20). He told readers that the purpose of the *Journal* was to exhibit the facts of Negro history, not to debate ways of solving the Negro problem (Meier & Rudwick, 1986). Because of the omissions and distortions in mainstream history texts, Woodson sought to produce evidence that would enable Blacks to "escape the awful fate of becoming a negligible factor in the thought of the world" (Woodson, 1925d, p. 600).

The *Journal* received approval from leading mainstream historians. Early recognition of the role Woodson would play in reshaping U.S. historiography came from his dissertation adviser at Harvard, Edward Channing. In a letter to Woodson, Channing (1920) wrote:

> Your "Journal of Negro History" is a most commendable undertaking. I have read every number as it has appeared and have derived great benefit from it in the preparation of my "History of the United States." We need sympathetic studies of the problem of the negro in times past and at the present day. To mention only one article: I think that the one on the "Negro in the Southern Army" was almost revolutionary in that it demanded a reconstruction of our whole idea of Southern society. It would be a great misfortune for the cause of historical truth for you to be obliged to suspend publication.

Although this letter may signify the well-wishes of a proud former teacher, the *Journal* undoubtedly succeeded, although perhaps modestly, in its initial attempts to compel historians like Channing to reconsider their writing of history from other perspectives.

Arthur Scheslinger, Sr., a member of the Association's Board of Directors in the 1930s and 1940s, recognized the *Journal*'s important contributions to scholarship. He noted that Woodson had "enlisted the interest and talents of historians of both races and maintained exacting standards of research and presentation which made the Journal rank with the best learned periodicals of the country" (quoted in Logan, 1973, p. 13).

Although few statistics are available, the circulation of the *Journal*, in contrast to the *Bulletin*, was small. The *Journal* had about 1,300 subscribers in the early 1940s, generally large libraries, universities, and scholars ("Annual Report," 1942). Publication continued regularly until 1980, and occasionally from 1981 through 1992.

Woodson's Scholarly Works

Woodson's first published scholarly treatise, *The Education of the Negro Prior to 1861* (1915/1991), provides a comprehensive coverage of the education of African Americans, both slave and free, prior to the Civil War. According to Franklin (1950), the book is "regarded by many as his most significant contribution in the area of original research" (p. 175). It contains a bibliography and appendix of documents, including letters, petitions, addresses, and minutes of meetings. Woodson identified significant traits of African American communities that emerged in the colonial and antebellum periods: a strong desire for education, the impulse to establish and support permanent educational institutions, and the increased ability of African Americans to assume roles as teachers and administrators of these institutions.

The most important scholarly works by Woodson and his associates were produced in the 1920s and early 1930s when the Association was supported by foundation grants. These works included: *A Century of Negro Migration* (1918), *The History of the Negro Church* (1921), and collections of source materials edited by Woodson: *Free Negro Heads of Families in the United States in 1830* (1925a), *Free Negro Owners of Slaves in the United States in 1830* (1925b), *Negro Orators and Their Orations* (1925c), and *The Mind of the Negro as Reflected by Letters Written During the Crisis, 1800–1860* (1926). Associated Publishers also published works by Woodson's research assistant, Alrutheus A. Taylor, *The Negro in South Carolina During the Reconstruction* (1924) and *The Negro in the Reconstruction of Virginia* (1926). In the mid-1920s, the Association sponsored studies of the social and economic conditions of African Americans, which led to *The Negro Wage Earner* (1930) with Woodson and Dr. Lorenzo Greene as co-authors, and Woodson's *The Negro Professional Man and the Community* (1934).

The Mis-Education of the Negro

Perhaps Woodson's most famous work is his most polemical one, a book of essays entitled *The Mis-Education of the Negro* (1933). Reprinted in 1969 and 1992, the work has been widely endorsed by African American scholars (Asante, 1991; Banks, 1993; Gordon, 1985; Hay, 1975). Woodson outlined an educational program to counter what he believed to be the widespread mis-education of African Americans. He cited as proof their acquiescence to segregation and political and economic exploitation. An educational system that taught Blacks to imitate and aspire to White culture at the same time that it taught the impropriety or the impossibility of becoming White guaranteed second-class citizenship. Woodson argued that mis-educated persons were not equipped to assume leadership roles in order to challenge segregation and exploitation. Moreover, their education only served to develop in them "attitudes of contempt toward their own people" (p. 1), whereas to be truly educated, a student must be prepared "to serve the lowly rather than to live as an aristocrat" (p. 149).

Woodson believed that knowledge about their past would help African American students aspire to positions of leadership and teach them about the value of community solidarity. As part of a long tradition, African Americans had built churches and schools, and joined with others sympathetic to the cause of racial justice, like the White abolitionists, to bring about societal reform. To become effective leaders, African Americans also needed to be able to think critically, because "the keynote in the education of the Negro has been to do what he is told to do," thereby making him "well prepared to function in the American social order as others would have him" (p. 134). Woodson would redefine higher education as "preparation to think" (p. 144) and base it on "a scientific study of the Negro from within to develop in him the power to do for himself what his oppressors will never do to elevate him to the level of others" (p. 144).

Woodson emphasized curriculum reform to counteract the mis-education caused by a curriculum and school atmosphere that perpetuated feelings of powerlessness and inferiority. Schools and colleges promoted a White supremacist ideology by teaching that the oppressor had accomplished everything worthwhile, while Blacks were "blank in achievement" (p. 6). Examination of catalogues of leading Black colleges revealed that courses were taught on ancient, medieval, and modern Europe, but not on Africa, whose civilizations contributed much to human progress. Moreover, a philosophy and ethics that had "justified slavery, peonage, segregation, and lynching" (p. xii) and that went unchallenged could result only in suppression of aspirations and mis-education of African Americans.

Woodson's educational philosophy, articulated in *The Mis-Education of the Negro*, influenced contemporary approaches to educational reform such as emancipatory citizenship education (Gordon, 1985), the Afrocentric approach (Asante, 1991), and multicultural education (Banks, 1993). After publishing *The Mis-Education of the Negro* in 1933, Woodson intensified his efforts to influence the teaching of African American history in schools and colleges.

DISSEMINATION OF TRANSFORMATIVE KNOWLEDGE TO SCHOOLS AND THE GENERAL PUBLIC

Woodson created a number of enterprises that influenced the teaching of African American history in the schools and disseminated historical knowledge about African and African American history to the general public.

Negro History Week

Woodson established Negro History Week "to dramatize the achievements of the race sufficiently to induce educational authorities to incorporate into the curricula courses on Negro life and history" ("Negro History Week Made Popular," 1941, p. 96). It was intended to be a culmination of study undertaken throughout the year. By 1935, historian Luther Porter Jackson determined that through Negro History Week "Negro History has found its way into the school curriculum . . . in twenty-one states or more [which] creates a demand for books, literature, and pictures on the Negro" (Jackson, 1935, p. 394). Two decades after its founding, Woodson concluded that Negro History Week had eclipsed other educational efforts of the Association ("Annual Report," 1943).

From its inception, Negro History Week was primarily a "Book Week." The annual event stimulated the writing and sale of books on every aspect of Negro life and history by White firms as well as Associated Publishers ("Annual Report," 1936). Woodson encouraged parents, as taxpayers, to become activists by calling on local school officials to demand that books and pictures bearing on Negro history be purchased for the schools. Some parents used the occasion to purchase books themselves, which they donated to city libraries to build up the Negro history section ("Annual Report," 1938). The Association also used Negro History Week as a time to promote the purchase of books, newspapers, and magazines for the home; the writing of family and local histories; and the collection, and transmission to the national office, of letters, diaries, and manuscripts ("Making Negro History Week Count," 1938). The collection of primary sources from the public that Woodson turned over to the Library of Congress comprised over 5,000 items (Romero, 1971).

In the 1940s, because so many schools had not yet taken the study of Negro history seriously, the Association continued to use Negro History Week as its primary means "to invite attention to this neglected task of our school systems" ("Annual Report," 1941, p. 417). Woodson reported in 1944 that "the large majority of the schools are still compelled to follow the regular courses in social studies which are projected altogether on the achievements of one race" ("Annual Report," 1944, p. 255). Incremental changes characterized

Woodson's curriculum reform efforts through Negro History Week, as indicated by this report:

> Schools may have to pass through several years of merely observing this celebration as a thing brought from afar, but gradually they become a part of the movement . . . ; and they make systematic effort[s] which count toward broadening their curricula sufficiently to include the study of all mankind. Textbooks have been accordingly revised, new works to meet the demand have been written, points-of-view have been changed, and a reign of tolerance has followed medieval racialism. ("Annual Report," 1940, p. 413)

The observance of Negro History Week spread to White schools in the 1940s because of substantial publicity the event received in mainstream educational journals ("Annual Report," 1941), its endorsement by state departments of education and superintendents of city schools, and allocation of funds for purchase of books bearing on the Negro ("Annual Report," 1947). Woodson felt that expansion of Negro History Week celebrations into White schools exposed students to "valuable knowledge which everyone in a democracy should possess" ("Annual Report," 1942, p. 375).

Negro History Week was not always celebrated as the founder intended. Woodson warned against too much race-consciousness or embitterment toward those "who have wronged the weak," because that "would place the Negro on the level with his oppressor" ("Annual Report," 1935, p. 370). He wanted the celebration to rise above "meaningless agitation and empty expressions of indignation" ("Annual Report," 1943, p. 377). He also cautioned against manipulation of the event by local leaders or propaganda organizations for political or publicity purposes ("Annual Report," 1935, 1945, 1946).

Objections to Negro History Week were raised by African Americans as well as other groups, citing the need to incorporate Black history into mainstream history and the discomfort the focus on them caused some African Americans (Cartwright, 1950). The Association, however, reaffirmed its mission with respect to Negro History Week in 1984:

> The Association for the Study of Afro-American Life and History, Inc., dreams of the day when the sharing and contributing of all Americans will be so appreciated, accepted and understood that there will no longer be a need for any ethnic group to call attention to its contributions. That day has not arrived, and until it does we shall continue to provide the information needed about the Afro-Americans in the United States and abroad. ("Key Questions and Answers," 1984, p. 13)

Woodson promoted the goal of inclusion of the contributions of all groups into the history of the nation and the world. According to historian Benjamin

Quarles, Woodson was "desperately anxious that the history of the Negro would be integrated into the history of the United States" (quoted in Romero, 1971, p. 261). It was the founder of Negro History Week, therefore, who above all looked forward to the day when it would no longer be needed.

Textbooks and Children's Literature

In 1922, Woodson published *The Negro in Our History*, a college textbook, which underwent several editions in his lifetime. By the third edition, Woodson reported that the book had been adopted for classroom instruction in about 100 schools and colleges (Woodson, 1925d). Alain Locke, the eminent Howard University philosopher, believed it belonged "to that select class of books that have brought about a revolution of mind" (Locke, 1927, pp. 100–101). The wide acceptance of *The Negro in Our History* prompted demands for texts more suitable to the lower grades. In response, Woodson wrote *Negro Makers of History* (1928b), a text for elementary schools based on *The Negro in Our History*, and *The Story of the Negro Retold* (1935), a condensed version of the college text for use in senior high schools.

Woodson, as author, editor, and publisher, made significant contributions to the emerging field of African American children's literature (Harris, 1990). He wrote *African Myths, Together with Proverbs* (1928a), a supplementary reader for the elementary grades, and *African Heroes and Heroines* (1939), a brief history of Africa and biographies of early African leaders. Prior to publishing *African Heroes and Heroines*, he selected teachers to test the materials in their classrooms with respect to suitability of arrangement, language, and illustrations ("Annual Report," 1931). Associated Publishers also published two well-received books by educator Jane Shackelford, *The Child's Story of the Negro* (1938), a book on Negro history for young children, and *My Happy Days* (1944), a photographic essay of a middle-class Black child and his family.

The Negro History Bulletin

In response to public demand for materials for the average reader and to provide a magazine for classroom use at low cost, Woodson began a monthly publication, *The Negro History Bulletin* (the *Bulletin*) in 1937 (Goggin, 1983). The magazine was "a new educational periodical designed to promote the study of the Negro among children by simplifying what is made too difficult for the young reader in books now available" ("Annual Report," 1938, p. 413). It was gratefully received by teachers and students, particularly in the South, where previously little material at low cost had been available for young readers. White educators, Woodson reported, also subscribed because they found the magazine "profitable in enriching the lives of the students who come under their direction and instruction" (p. 414).

Adopting a particular theme for the month, the *Bulletin* featured stories, historical narratives, biographical sketches, and photographs of both African Americans and Whites who made positive contributions to the race. Articles written by Woodson generally had no by-line. A "Children's Page" contained a column devoted to news from schools, questions for study, book reviews, and advertisements for books published by the Association. Woodson also used the Children's Page to write a mini-editorial to expound on his educational theories, describe an impressive celebration of Negro History Week or an encounter with a young student, or protest the circulation of *Little Black Sambo* in the public schools. He also wanted the *Bulletin* to be a vehicle for student expression, so he solicited and published plays and essays from students ("Annual Report," 1938).

The *Bulletin* featured stories about exemplary teachers and curriculum projects. Teachers wrote numerous articles pertaining to the teaching of Negro history in elementary and junior high schools (Lucas, 1939; Mixon, 1941; Turner, 1939; Tynes, 1939); high schools (Myers, 1939; Taylor, 1939); teachers colleges (Brooks, 1946; Browning, 1939); and colleges (Blythewood, 1939; Coleman, 1948; Heslip, 1943; Thompson, 1942). A number of articles of a more general nature dealt with the purpose and methods of teaching Negro history (Bailey, 1935; Brooks, 1939; Derricote, 1938; Harper, 1939; Reddick, 1937).

Although little data are available, Woodson reported that 4,000 subscribers were obtained during Negro History Week in 1938 ("Annual Report," 1938). Subscriptions, primarily from teachers and students, numbered between 4,000 and 5,000 in 1940 ("Annual Report," 1940). By 1942, the subscription level reached approximately 7,000. Favorable response to the *Bulletin* was second only to the popularity of Negro History Week. Woodson reported that:

> The management receives communications in which the subscribers refer to the *Bulletin* as "our magazine," "our periodical," and "our publication." These comments indicate that the people in need of this simplified history are thereby being reached. They not only read the magazine but send to the office suggestions and plans for such innovations as will assure a much more extensive service. ("What's Behind The Negro History Bulletin," 1943, p. 16)

In the early 1940s, the *Bulletin* held its subscription rate between 8,000 and 9,000, but postwar conditions saw a decline of about one-third of its subscribers ("Annual Report," 1945, 1946). The magazine sold for $1.00 but cost $2.00 to produce. In 1947, Woodson reported why he continued to publish the Association's "greatest liability" and its "greatest asset":

To raise the price would probably reduce the number of subscribers and thereby defeat the purpose of the publication. . . . The *Bulletin* is not only an aid to the study of the Negro but a channel for the publicity of the entire program for the study of the Negro. In this way the magazine has played a conspicuous part in the attainment of the objectives of the Association and thus justifies its existence. ("Annual Report," 1947, p. 415)

The *Bulletin* continued publication until 1992. Its longevity and success in providing supplementary material for classroom use and for a general readership is unmatched by other historical associations. For example, The Organization of American Historians, founded in 1907, did not begin its *Magazine of History* until April 1985. Similar to features in Woodson's *Bulletin*, the newer magazine includes sections devoted to various methods of teaching history, student discussions and articles, listing of resources, and reviews (*OAH Newsletter*, 1995). The American Historical Association, founded in 1895, thus far has not published a magazine for teachers and students.

Through textbooks, children's literature, and *The Negro History Bulletin*, Woodson laid the foundation for a transformative curriculum. To implement curriculum reform, he needed the collaboration and expertise of teachers at the elementary, secondary, and college levels.

THE ROLE OF TEACHERS IN THE DISSEMINATION OF KNOWLEDGE ON AFRICAN AMERICANS

With the publication of textbooks in the 1920s and the founding of Negro History Week in 1926, Woodson had begun the work of "translating" scholarly research into forms and language for schools and the general public, but this aspect of his mission became a greater priority in the late 1930s and 1940s. His influence on teachers, through the activities and publications of the Association, led to their assuming leadership roles in the promotion of the study of African American history at the school, district, and state levels.

The existence of segregated Black schools served as a facilitating factor of curriculum reform. Successful outcomes also depended on the presence of three other conditions: endorsement by White school officials of a particular district, county, or state, which was usually forthcoming ("Annual Report," 1935; Dreer, 1944); the ability to purchase or develop teaching materials, a more difficult condition to meet; and teachers' knowledge of and interest in engaging in the teaching of African American history, a condition that could not be presumed to be present even in all-Black schools ("Annual Report," 1935; Dreer, 1944; Williams, 1935).

The development of good translators and interpreters of the type Mary McLeod Bethune envisioned was critical to extending the curriculum reform movement begun by Woodson. As his influence spread, many teachers rose to fill the need. Woodson credited them for their contributions: "Important help has come from those teachers who have cheerfully given their time to [adapting materials] to the capacity of the children in the schools" ("What's Behind 'The Negro History Bulletin,'" 1943, p. 17).

Teachers who helped promote the educational work of the Association can be designated according to five main categories: distributors/subscribers/solicitors, curriculum innovators, field representatives, branch organizers, and educational researchers.

Distributors, Subscribers, and Solicitors

Many African Americans, especially teachers, devised ways to help Woodson in the dissemination of his publications. For example, an early supporter, Joseph A. Booker, President of Arkansas Baptist College, wrote to Woodson requesting that copies of *A Century of Negro Migration* (1918) be sent, at Booker's expense, to the governor of Arkansas and the secretary of the Little Rock Y.M.C.A. Booker wrote:

> As to commission for sales, I do not want to make a dollar on such a laudable enterprise; but I do desire some liberty in handing the book out to Southern white men whom I know will be greatly benefitted by it, and who will widely advertise the book. I have at least another list of perhaps one dozen leading men, editors, preachers, etc., among the white people in the various Southern states. (Booker, 1920)

In another letter, Booker (1924) reported that he had introduced Woodson's *The History of the Negro Church* (1921) into the theology curriculum of his college.

Teachers were the main subscribers to *The Negro History Bulletin*. Additionally, they solicited colleagues, neighbors, and churches for subscriptions; extended its circulation through delivery to newsstands; wrote articles, columns, poems, and stories; and volunteered as copy editors and proofreaders ("What's Behind 'The Negro History Bulletin,'" 1943).

Curriculum Innovators

Innovators included teachers who designed and implemented projects in Negro history at their schools. In some cases, teachers affected curriculum policy at the district or state level. Evidence of the activities of curriculum innovators appears in the *Bulletin*, which often featured exemplary teachers and programs, and recommendations for teaching Negro history effectively at various grade levels. Three models will be examined below.

Miss Lucille Duckett, a lifelong member of the Association and close associate of Woodson's, was a teacher at Monroe School, a laboratory school for Miner Teachers College in Washington, DC. Miss Duckett and her students undertook an interdisciplinary project in Negro history that Woodson observed and described in detail in the *Bulletin* ("A Method for Studying Negro Contributions," 1938). The students developed research questions on various topics and formed cooperative groups to carry out the project. Activities included interviewing older members of the community; writing original stories, poems, and songs; art projects; a classroom newspaper; making hand-bound books; and establishing pen pals with Negro students in other cities.

Rachel McNeill, an elementary school principal in Glassboro, New Jersey, published a unit of study in Negro history. She also helped form four centers in various parts of the state where teachers met to study Negro history and exchange teaching methods ("Rachel C. McNeill," 1943). Woodson felt her program "tops all the rest" because

> She is especially interested . . . in the background of the children whom she teaches. While the teacher must read many books and magazines she must read above all her own pupils. While the teacher may have much knowledge to impart to them the pupils know much with which the teacher should work. (p. 113)

Mrs. McNeill's approach resonated with ideas in Woodson's *The Mis-Education of the Negro* (1933). In that treatise, he proposed a research methodology to serve as a "preliminary step in establishing a curriculum for African Americans" (Gordon, 1985, p. 14). The methodology, based on observations he made of a fellow teacher in the Philippines, consists of using objects and experiences from the students' own environment and knowledge of local history and folklore to teach students about themselves and the world. This methodology challenged the mainstream model in which only the achievements and background of one race were emphasized ("Annual Report," 1944).

In April 1941, the Superintendent of the Chicago Public Schools, Dr. William H. Johnson, announced that the teaching of Negro history in the Chicago schools would be incorporated into the school curriculum (Morgan, 1943). At the heart of this historic development was a Chicago teacher and lifelong member of Woodson's Association, Madeline R. Morgan. Morgan had approached Johnson with the original curriculum proposal. He subsequently released her and a colleague from teaching to conduct research and write units in Negro history for various grade levels. Woodson and other scholars reviewed the project. Miss Morgan reported to the annual meeting that

These units of material are obligatory and have been sent to every public school in the city of Chicago. Nowhere in the United States has such a project been authorized for city-wide study. Such a study will not only serve as a source of inspiration to Negro youth, but as information to youth in general. (p. 66)

After the success of the Chicago experiment, other cities with large African American populations such as Boston, New York, Philadelphia, and Washington, DC followed suit by appointing committees to integrate the study of Negro history into their curricula ("Annual Report," 1943).

Field Representatives

The Association occasionally had funds to hire a field representative to extend its educational mission to more remote parts of the country. In the early 1940s, Hilda Grayson filled this role, calling on schools in various states and helping teachers prepare exhibits on some phase of Negro history for presentation at state teachers' conventions. In the 1941–1942 school year, for example, Miss Grayson organized exhibits at state teachers' meetings in South Carolina, Alabama, Mississippi, Delaware, Virginia, and West Virginia ("Hilda V. Grayson in the Field," 1942, p. 154).

Branch Organizers

Woodson opened new branches of the Association only if prospective leaders possessed a thorough understanding of the organization's aims and had the resources to carry them out; otherwise, he preferred to establish Negro History Clubs. A branch had to perform functions at the local level that were performed, largely by Woodson, at the national level, that is, conduct research, give lectures, and sponsor institutes. In 1937, Miss Jane Dabney Shackelford, a third-grade teacher, organized a new branch in Terre Haute, Indiana. She obtained the support of the local public school teachers and students at the State Teachers College to assist her in carrying out the functions of a local branch ("Annual Report," 1937). Well-qualified by education and experience, Miss Shackelford held a master's degree from Columbia University and through Associated Publishers made contributions to the field of African American children's literature (Shackelford, 1938, 1944).

Educational Researchers and Their Findings

Educational researchers conducted research at the school, district, state, or national level (Dabney, 1934; Dreer, 1944; Williams, 1935). Papers based on their findings were presented at the annual meetings and published in the

Journal or *Bulletin*. The researchers generally employed the survey method to determine to what extent Negro history was being taught in the schools.

Thomas Dabney (1934) conducted a survey for the Association to determine the number of courses in Negro history offered between 1925 and 1931 in high schools and colleges and to measure the results of the Association's work in encouraging the introduction of such courses. The Association determined it had most likely influenced curriculum changes in many schools, particularly through Negro History Week, since many courses were added to the curriculum of reporting schools after 1927. As yet, however, no Negro college, university, or teachers college required a Negro history course for graduation. Unfortunately, the Association did not have the resources or funding to conduct follow-up surveys in subsequent years.

Early research conducted by the Association's Committee on Findings found that a number of barriers to curriculum reform in all-Black schools were not insurmountable ("Proceedings," 1935). For instance, there seems to have been little or no opposition on the part of state and local school officials to the teaching of African American history as long as it was being taught to African American children in segregated schools. In the lower South, "in practically all cases in which superintendents and boards of education have been properly approached with the request to introduce such courses and projects in the schools they have been granted" (p. 2). The Committee concluded:

> The apparent laxity and inertia of principals and faculties in failing to request of school authorities permission to revise their curricula so as to include the study of Negro life and history must be viewed as an inexcusable dereliction of duty when they, the principals especially, should be the leaders in the construction of the much needed new program of education for teaching the Negro first about himself and then about other things in relation to himself. ("Proceedings," 1935, p. 12)

Absent restrictions imposed by White administrators, the greatest barrier to implementation of new courses seemed to be the "mis-education" of African American educators. The Association's mission consisted of finding ways to reach principals and faculties, to re-educate them, and to supply them with materials to expand and revise the curriculum.

The findings of the Committee on Findings and similar findings of a Texas high school study (Williams, 1935) were echoed in a survey of two Black high schools in St. Louis, Missouri by Herman Dreer (1944). Dreer mailed a questionnaire to teachers, visited libraries, and interviewed school personnel. One high school had excellent references in its library, including three of Woodson's books, but no formal course in Negro history. In the other high school, the library contained 100 titles on Negro life and history, but the books generally circulated only during Negro History Week.

Dreer discovered that both high schools had a stated but not an actualized policy that Negro history be integrated into the regular curriculum. Again, the barrier to implementation was not the local school district, which allowed teachers considerable flexibility in course planning, but individual teachers who had not assumed responsibility for teaching Negro history as part of their subject areas. Dreer concluded that only if teachers possessed the requisite knowledge and had the desire to teach it would Negro history be taught. Woodson would attribute the teachers' lack of knowledge and failure to understand the importance of teaching Negro history to the teachers' earlier "miseducation."

The surveys described above give only a suggestion of the extent of Woodson's influence on the teaching of African American history in the schools. A more accurate assessment of the link between the Association and its teacher members and the subsequent expansion and revision of the curriculum in African American schools awaits further research.

THE ANNUAL MEETINGS OF THE ASSOCIATION: DISSEMINATION OF KNOWLEDGE TO SCHOLARS AND THE GENERAL PUBLIC

Woodson insisted that the Association not charge an attendance fee to the annual meetings, which generally were held in cities with large African American populations, so that the poorest members of the Black community could participate (Goggin, 1983). Open to the general public, the meetings attracted an increasing number of White participants in the 1940s, including educational authorities and local and state politicians.

The annual meetings provided both Black and White scholars writing about African American history a professional outlet not afforded by other historical associations because of segregation and discrimination. The meetings also served to bridge the gap between scholars and nonscholars and were an important tool of adult education. They provided the African American community an opportunity to come together for intellectual stimulation, musical programs, art exhibits, poetry readings, theatrical performances, and visits to local historical sites and museums. Lay participants were exposed to ideas of leading scholars like Dr. Benjamin Quarles on "Douglass and the Meaning of Democracy" ("Proceedings," 1943), Dr. Charles H. Wesley on "The Negro's Struggle for Freedom in Its Birthplace" ("Proceedings," 1945), and Dr. James Leyburn (Yale University sociologist) on "The Disabilities from Which the Natives of South Africa Suffer" ("Proceedings," 1945). These papers gave meaning to Blacks' contemporary struggle for civil rights at home and abroad.

In sessions devoted exclusively to educational topics, teachers presented papers and exchanged ideas on philosophy, methods, progress, and problems in the teaching of African American history. A number of papers and forums debated the issue of whether Negro history should be taught in separate courses or integrated into the regular curriculum ("Proceedings," 1937, 1943, 1944, 1949, 1950). For those advocating separate courses, the argument against integration was that teachers were not trained adequately to be able to integrate the life and history of the Negro into regular courses ("Proceedings," 1937).

A greater consensus on the "why" than the "how" of teaching Negro history characterized the discussions at the annual meetings. The deliberations in the 1940s reflected a growing concern about the meaning of democracy in a country fighting to restore it abroad, while at home African Americans continually had to go before the courts in attempts to secure rights and privileges guaranteed by the U.S. Constitution. Because of the changing sociopolitical reality, the proposals for educational reform set forth by Woodson in *The Mis-Education of the Negro* (1933) took on greater urgency. Educators voiced their belief that the power to challenge discrimination and segregation would come through the development of greater self-understanding and community solidarity that the study of Negro history could provide. Moreover, there was general agreement that (1) Negro history should be taught to White as well as Black students, and (2) it should be taught to children at an early age so that they can develop "a more favorable attitude toward others than their parents who are so set in their ways that little change is possible" ("Proceedings," 1945, p. 6).

Through open admission and the design of the programs for the annual meetings, Woodson made the teaching and learning of history a community affair, devising yet another vehicle for the dissemination of historical knowledge on African Americans.

CONCLUSION

Without the Association for the Study of Negro Life and History founded by Carter Woodson, the development of African American history as an important field of inquiry undoubtedly would have been significantly delayed. Under Woodson's guidance, a number of African American scholars entered the field in the 1920s and 1930s and were able to publish their works through Associated Publishers and *The Journal of Negro History*. The Association collected many source documents that might otherwise have been lost. Equally important to Woodson, a generation of African Americans acquired knowledge about their past, presented in a positive light and through accessible means like the annual meetings, Negro History Week, and *The Negro History Bulletin*.

Through the Association, Woodson attempted to reach all levels of the African American community, scholars at home and abroad, and the general public, and he met with a considerable degree of success. While a major contributor to the development of transformative knowledge on African Americans, he likewise promoted the goal of an integrated history of all groups (Lindsay, 1950). Unquestionably, he desired that "in discussing a country's civilization, all peoples should be given credit for their contributions" ("The Annual Meeting," 1939, p. 35).

REFERENCES

The Annual Meeting of the Association for the Study of Negro Life and History. (1939). *The Negro History Bulletin, 3* (3), 35.

Annual report of the director. (1931). *The Journal of Negro History, 16* (4), 349–358.

Annual report of the director. (1935). *The Journal of Negro History, 20* (4), 363–372.

Annual report of the director. (1936). *The Journal of Negro History, 21* (3), 245–255.

Annual report of the director. (1937). *The Journal of Negro History, 22* (4), 405–416.

Annual report of the director. (1938). *The Journal of Negro History, 23* (4), 409–419.

Annual report of the director. (1940). *The Journal of Negro History, 25* (4), 407–415.

Annual report of the director. (1941). *The Journal of Negro History, 26* (4), 413–420.

Annual report of the director. (1942). *The Journal of Negro History, 27* (4), 371–379.

Annual report of the director. (1943). *The Journal of Negro History, 28* (4), 373–380.

Annual report of the director. (1944). *The Journal of Negro History, 29* (3), 251–259.

Annual report of the director. (1945). *The Journal of Negro History, 30* (3), 251–259.

Annual report of the director. (1946). *The Journal of Negro History, 31* (4), 385–391.

Annual report of the director. (1947). *The Journal of Negro History, 32* (4), 407–416.

Asante, M. K. (1991). The Afrocentric idea in education. *The Journal of Negro Education, 60* (2), 170–180.

Bailey, J. A. (1935). Perspective in the teaching of Negro history. *The Journal of Negro History, 20* (1), 19–26.

Banks, J. A. (1993). The canon debate, knowledge construction, and multicultural education. *Educational Researcher, 22* (5), 4–14.

Bethune, M. M. (1935). The Association for the Study of Negro Life and History: Its contributions. *The Journal of Negro History, 20* (4), 406–410.

Blythewood, M. L. (1939). In the college. *The Negro History Bulletin, 2* (5), 43.

Booker, J. (1920, July 24). Letter to Carter G. Woodson. Carter G. Woodson Papers, Reel No. 4. Washington, DC: Library of Congress.

Booker, J. (1924, January 16). Letter to Carter G. Woodson. Carter G. Woodson Papers, Reel No. 4. Washington, DC: Library of Congress.

Brooks, A. N. D. (1939). The problem for all groups. *The Negro History Bulletin, 2* (5), 38, 44.

Brooks, A. N. D. (1946). Teachers of Negroes. *The Negro History Bulletin, 10*(1), 14, 22.

Browning, J. B. (1939). In the teachers college. *The Negro History Bulletin, 2* (5), 42-43.

Cartwright, M. (1950). Negro History Week—1950. *The Negro History Bulletin, 13* (7), 153-154, 165-167.

Channing, E. (1920, March 30). Letter to Carter G. Woodson. Carter G. Woodson Papers, Reel No. 4., Washington, DC: Library of Congress.

Coleman, E. M. (1948). The teaching of Negro history in Negro colleges. *The Negro History Bulletin, 12* (3), 53-67.

Dabney, T. L. (1934). The study of the Negro. *The Journal of Negro History, 19* (2), 266-307.

Derricote, E. P. (1938). The Negro teacher at work. *The Negro History Bulletin, 2* (1), 5.

Dreer, H. (1944). The Negro in the course of study of the high school. *The Negro History Bulletin, 7* (7), 161-165.

Franklin, J. H. (1950). The place of Carter G. Woodson in American historiography. *The Negro History Bulletin, 13* (8), 174-176.

Franklin, J. H. (1988). Afro-American history: State of the art. [Review of *Black history and the historical profession, 1915-1980*]. *The Journal of American History, 75* (1), 162-173.

Franklin, J. H. (1989). *Race and history: Selected essays, 1938-1988*. Baton Rouge: Louisiana State University Press.

Goggin, J. (1983). *Carter G. Woodson and the movement to promote Black history*. Unpublished doctoral dissertation, The University of Rochester.

Goggin, J. A. (1993). *Carter G. Woodson: A life in Black history*. Baton Rouge: Louisiana State University Press.

Gordon, B. M. (1985). Toward emancipation in citizenship education: The case of African-American cultural knowledge. *Theory and Research in Social Education, 12* (1), 1-23.

Greene, L. J. (1965). Dr. Woodson prepares for Negro History Week, 1930. *The Negro History Bulletin, 28* (8), 174-175, 195.

Harper, C. L. (1939). Making Negro history a more important part of the curriculum. *The Negro History Bulletin, 2* (8), 71.

Harris, V. J. (1990). African American children's literature: The first one hundred years. *Journal of Negro Education, 59* (4), 540-555.

Hay, S. A. (1975). Carter G. Woodson's mis-education of the Negro: A revisit. *The Negro History Bulletin, 38* (6), 436-439.

Heslip, C. R. (1943). The study of the Negro in college and university curricula. *The Negro History Bulletin, 7* (3), 59-70.

Hilda V. Grayson in the field. (1942). *The Negro History Bulletin, 5* (7), 154, 167.

Hine, D. C. (1986). Carter G. Woodson, white philanthropy and Negro historiography. *The History Teacher, 19* (3), 406-425.

Jackson, L. P. (1935). The work of the Association and the people. *The Journal of Negro History, 20* (4), 385-396.

Key questions and answers. (1984). *The Negro History Bulletin, 47* (1), 13.

Lindsay, A. G. (1950). Dr. Woodson as a teacher. *The Negro History Bulletin, 13* (8), 183, 191.

Locke, A. (1927). [Review of *The Negro in our history*]. *The Journal of Negro History, 12* (1), 99–101.

Logan, R. W. (1973). Carter G. Woodson: Mirror and molder of his time, 1875–1950. *The Journal of Negro History, 58* (1), 1–17.

Lucas, J. O. (1939). In the elementary school. *The Negro History Bulletin, 2* (5), 40.

Making Negro History Week count. (1938). *The Negro History Bulletin, 1* (5), 12.

Meier, A., & Rudwick, E. (1986). *Black history and the historical profession, 1915–1980.* Urbana: University of Illinois Press.

A method for studying Negro contributions to progress. (1938). *The Negro History Bulletin, 2* (1), 3–4, 7.

Mixon, M. B. (1941). How the task was done. *The Negro History Bulletin, 4* (9), 200–201.

Morgan, M. R. (1943). Teaching Negro history in Chicago Public Schools. *The Negro History Bulletin, 7* (3), 57–58, 66.

Myers, E. D. (1939). In the high school. *The Negro History Bulletin, 2* (5), 41–42.

Negro History Week made popular. (1941). *The Negro History Bulletin, 4* (4), 96.

OAH Newsletter [Organization of American Historians]. (1995, February). Advertisement, *23* (1), A8.

Proceedings of the annual meeting. (1935). *The Journal of Negro History, 20* (1), 1–12.

Proceedings of the annual meeting. (1937). *The Journal of Negro History, 22* (1), 1–16.

Proceedings of the annual meeting. (1943). *The Journal of Negro History, 28* (1), 1–9.

Proceedings of the annual meeting. (1944). *The Journal of Negro History, 29* (1), 1–6.

Proceedings of the annual meeting. (1945). *The Journal of Negro History, 30* (1), 1–8.

Proceedings of the annual meeting. (1949). *The Journal of Negro History, 34* (1), 1–8.

Proceedings of the annual meeting. (1950). *The Journal of Negro History, 35* (1), 1–8.

Rachel C. McNeill, A resourceful teacher. (1943). *The Negro History Bulletin, 6* (5), 113, 118.

Reddick, L. D. (1937). A new interpretation for Negro history. *The Journal of Negro History, 22* (1), 17–28.

Romero, P. W. (1971). Carter G. Woodson: A biography. *Dissertation Abstracts International, 32* (05), 2580A. (University Microfilms No. AAC 7127548)

Scally, S. A. (1977). Woodson and the genesis of ASALH. *The Negro History Bulletin, 40* (1), 653–655.

Shackelford, J. D. (1938). *The child's story of the Negro.* Washington, DC: Associated Publishers.

Shackelford, J. D. (1944). *My happy days*. Washington, DC: Associated Publishers.

Taylor, A. A. (1924). *The Negro in South Carolina during the Reconstruction*. Washington, DC: Associated Publishers.

Taylor, A. A. (1926). *The Negro in the Reconstruction of Virginia*. Washington, DC: Associated Publishers.

Taylor, G. (1939). The teaching of Negro history in secondary schools. *The Negro History Bulletin*, *3* (3), 40-41.

Thompson, L. L. (1942). A college student looks at the problem of teaching Negro history to Negro college students. *The Negro History Bulletin*, *6* (3), 62-64.

Turner, L. K. (1939). The problem of teaching Negro history in the elementary school. *The Negro History Bulletin*, *3* (3), 35-36, 39-41.

Tynes, H. A. (1939). In the junior high school. *The Negro History Bulletin*, *2* (5), 41.

Wesley, C. H. (1951). Carter G. Woodson—as a scholar. *The Journal of Negro History*, *36* (1), 12-24.

Wesley, C. H. (1965). Our fiftieth year. *The Negro History Bulletin*, *28* (8), 172-173, 195.

What's behind "The Negro History Bulletin." (1943). *The Negro History Bulletin*, *7* (1), 16-20.

Williams, L. V. (1935). Teaching Negro life and history in Texas high schools. *The Journal of Negro History*, *20* (1), 13-18.

Winkler, K. J. (1995, January 20). Who owns history? *The Chronicle of Higher Education*, pp. A-10-11, A-18.

Winston, M. R. (1973). *Howard University Department of History: 1913-1973*. Washington, DC: Howard University.

Woodson, C. G. (1912). *The disruption of Virginia*. Unpublished doctoral dissertation, Harvard University.

Woodson, C. G. (1918). *A century of Negro migration*. Washington, DC: Associated Publishers.

Woodson, C. G. (1921). *The history of the Negro church*. Washington, DC: Associated Publishers.

Woodson, C. G. (1922). *The Negro in our history*. Washington, DC: Associated Publishers.

Woodson, C. G. (1925a). *Free Negro heads of families in the United States in 1830*. Washington, DC: Associated Publishers.

Woodson, C. G. (1925b). *Free Negro owners of slaves in the United States in 1830*. Washington, DC: Associated Publishers.

Woodson, C. G. (1925c). *Negro orators and their orations*. Washington, DC: Associated Publishers.

Woodson, C. G. (1925d). Ten years of collecting and publishing the records of the Negro. *The Journal of Negro History*, *10* (4), 598-606.

Woodson, C. G. (1926). *The mind of the Negro as reflected by letters written during the crisis, 1800-1860*. Washington, DC: Associated Publishers.

Woodson, C. G. (1928a). *African myths, together with proverbs*. Washington, DC: Associated Publishers.

Woodson, C. G. (1928b). *Negro makers of history*. Washington, DC: Associated Publishers.

Woodson, C. G. (1933). *The mis-education of the Negro*. Washington, DC: Associated Publishers.

Woodson, C. G. (1934). *The Negro professional man and the community*. Washington, DC: Associated Publishers.

Woodson, C. G. (1935). *The story of the Negro retold*. Washington, DC: Associated Publishers.

Woodson, C. G. (1939). *African heroes and heroines*. Washington, DC: Associated Publishers.

Woodson, C. G. (1991). *The education of the Negro prior to 1861*. Salem, NH: Ayer. (Original work published 1915)

Woodson, C. G., & Greene, L. (1930). *The Negro wage earner*. Washington, DC: Associated Publishers.

CHAPTER 6

Allison Davis and the Study of Race, Social Class, and Schooling

MICHAEL R. HILLIS

> Men after death . . . are understood worse than men of the moment, but heard better.
> Nietzche, quoted in W. H. Auden & L. Kronenberger, 1981, p. 235

Allison Davis and his important work should be remembered when the historical contributions that early African American scholars made to multicultural education are examined. Davis spent most of his professional life trying to understand the influences of race, class, and culture on learning (Davis, 1948). Despite his significant contributions to educational research, they are largely unrecognized in contemporary educational discourse. I will present a case for the need to re-examine his work, which contains important insights for multicultural education theory and practice (Banks & Banks, 1995).

Davis's research supports the tenet that educational institutions cannot work in isolation. Rather, education is strongly influenced by societal factors such as race, class, and the sociocultural context in which it occurs. Through his books—most notably *Children of Bondage: The Personality Development of Negro Youth in the Urban South* (1940 with John Dollard), *Deep South: A Social Anthropological Study of Caste and Class* (1941 with Burleigh B. Gardner and Mary R. Gardner) and *Social Class Influences upon Learning* (1948)—Davis showed that if students are to have successful educational experiences, it is essential to examine all facets of their lives.

This chapter examines the life and work of Allison Davis from three perspectives: first, biographical information to help place Davis within the context of his time and influences; second, an examination of his three major works, and a discussion of their relevance for contemporary researchers and educational practitioners; third, an examination of contemporary works in relation to his ideas, to elucidate his contribution to our present understanding of multicultural education.

A BIOGRAPHICAL PERSPECTIVE

Allison Davis was born in Washington, DC on October 10, 1902. He grew up at a time in U.S. history when the country was experiencing economic prosperity and tremendous change in the traditional structures of society. Having shown an abundance of academic promise while in high school, in 1920 Davis enrolled at Williams College in Massachusetts. He continued to excel academically at Williams, where he majored in English and graduated summa cum laude in 1924 with a bachelor of arts degree. Encouraged by his academic success as an undergraduate, Davis applied for and was accepted as a master's student at Harvard University in 1924, where he received a master's degree in English in 1925.

Between 1925 and 1932, Davis taught English literature at Hampton Institute (now Hampton University) in Virginia and was a research associate at the Institute for Human Relations at Yale. One of his students at Hampton was St. Clair Drake. Drake, who later became a noted sociologist, is a co-author of the classic study of Chicago, *Black Metropolis: A Study of Negro Life in a Northern City* (Drake & Cayton, 1945). In 1932, Davis returned to Harvard, where he received a master's degree in anthropology. After he completed his studies at Harvard, the Julius Rosenwald Fund awarded Davis a fellowship, which enabled him to study at the London School of Economics under the direction of Bronislaw Malinowski, author of *Magic, Science, and Religion* (1948), and Lancelot Hogben, author of *Political Arithmetic* (1938).

In 1933, as the United States was beginning to recover from the effects of the Depression, Davis and his wife, Elizabeth, returned from Europe and moved to Mississippi with Burleigh and Mary Gardner to conduct a social anthropological study. The Davises collected data on the African American participants in the study. Data on the White study participants were collected by the Gardners. The study focused on the class and caste system within the state and became the basis for the book *Deep South* (1941). After completing data collection, Davis began a 5-year teaching assignment at Dillard University, a historically Black university in New Orleans, Louisiana. In 1939, he received a second fellowship award, which enabled him to attend the University of Chicago. In 1940, Davis obtained a position at the University of Chicago. He completed his Ph.D. there in 1942.

Davis was the first African American professor to be hired at the University of Chicago, where he continued the studies he was pursuing on caste and class in American society. Davis made a transition in his research focus: He began to apply anthropological theories and research methodologies to the study of education. The reasons for this transition can only be hypothesized, but there are hints of this movement in some of his earliest writings. Davis (1939) saw the tremendous influence that education can have on an individual's life:

> We must make it possible for a much larger proportion of Negroes to obtain the kinds of occupations, income, education, and legal protection necessary for middle class training . . . and we must learn to do a new kind of remedial work with individuals, in which we direct them toward new class-goals and show them the techniques for reaching these goals. (pp. 273-274)

In 1948, Harvard University asked Davis to deliver the Inglis Lecture on Education. This lecture, which became the book *Social Class Influences upon Learning* (1948), synthesized the research he had been conducting in anthropology, sociology, and education. Davis also became one of the first African Americans to receive tenure at a predominantly White university when he was granted tenure at the University of Chicago in 1948.

In the 1950s, Davis started work on the nature of intelligence and how cultural factors often influence the measures used in assessment. He was one of the leading voices to call into question the assumptions that many educators held about IQ testing. This work resulted in two major books: *Intelligence and Cultural Differences* (Eells, Davis, Havighurst, Herrick, & Tyler, 1951) and the *Davis–Eells Test of General Intelligence* (Davis & Eells, 1953). This latter book presented a new test that was designed to measure intelligence in a culturally fair way. This test became known as the Davis–Eells Games Test. The authors state their rationale for this work:

> Pupils coming from the top and bottom social strata live in cultures which, though alike in certain fundamental American activities, are yet different in many other cultural habits and motives. At a great many points, therefore, their cultures differ with respect to the types of problems they teach each group to recognize and to solve. (Davis & Eells, 1953, p. 27)

In 1965, Davis, with Benjamin Bloom and Robert Hess, published *Compensatory Education for Cultural Deprivation*. The book was based on a conference held at the University of Chicago, June 8–12, 1964, "The Research Conference on Education and Cultural Deprivation." The purpose of the conference was to "review what [was] known about the problems of education and cultural deprivation, to make recommendations about what might be done to solve some of these problems, and to suggest the critical problems for further research" (Bloom, Davis, & Hess, 1965, n.p.). A number of distinguished social scientists participated in this important conference, including Anne Anastasi, Erik Erikson, Edmund W. Gordon, Lawrence Kohlberg, and Thomas Pettigrew. A year later, in recognition of his work and scholarship, Davis was appointed to the President's Civil Rights Commission.

In 1970, the University of Chicago appointed Davis the John Dewey Distinguished Service Professor of Education. Eight years later he retired from the University of Chicago at the age of 76. During his academic career Davis wrote many articles, chapters, and books. In recognition of his work, the American Academy of Arts and Sciences elected Davis as their first Fellow from the field of education. In 1983, Davis published his last book, *Leadership, Love, and Aggression: How the Twig is Bent*, an analysis of the personalities of Fredrick Douglass, W. E. B. DuBois, Richard Wright, and Martin Luther King, Jr. In October of that year, the African American faculty at the University of Chicago held a symposium in his honor, "Race, Class, Socialization, and Life Cycle." Shortly after this event Davis died at the age of 81.

PERSPECTIVES FROM DAVIS'S MAJOR WORKS

Children of Bondage: The Personality Development of Negro Youth in the Urban South

In *Children of Bondage* (Davis & Dollard, 1940), which resulted from the work initially begun by Davis in 1933, the authors attempt to assess how the personalities of African Americans in the urban South develop. The authors present seven case studies of adolescents. Each chapter follows a three-step progression: (1) the life history of the adolescent, (2) a psychoanalytic understanding of the personality presented, and (3) how the individual feels toward the White population. The case studies conclude with an analysis of how class and caste act as contributors to the socialization process.

When reading this book, it is important to place the authors' observations on personality development within the historical context of the 1930s. During this era, the two predominant strains of theoretical understanding were the schools of psychoanalysis and behaviorism. Davis and Dollard used psychoanalytic theory to guide their analysis of the personality of adolescents. It is unfortunate that time has not been kind to this theory, especially in the culture at large. Their work comes across as oversimplified 50 years later. However, it is important to see beyond this particular theoretical framework and examine how their observations can broaden our understandings of race and social class.

The ways in which Davis and Dollard describe the tremendous intra-ethnic diversity within the African American community are relevant for us today. As later scholars have pointed out (Allport, 1954; Banks, 1991), one of the major problems with stereotyping is that it fails to recognize the variation that exists within particular ethnic, cultural, and religious groups. *Children of Bondage* clearly indicates that the African American population in the South in the early 1930s was not a homogenous group. Rather, Davis and Dollard found that within what they conceptualized as the African American caste, they could divide class into three major groups (lower, middle, and upper). They subdivided these groups further (e.g., lower-lower class, middle-lower class, upper-lower class). Furthermore, from the study of these class positions, the authors observed that the issue of status limited interaction within the African American community.

Davis and Dollard also explicate the role that values, whether familial, cultural, or societal, play in the educational process. They write:

> The goals of white-collar or professional occupations and of middle-class status which are at the end of the school route, are not made to appear valuable, near, or certain for the lower-class child. He learns from his family and teachers that the chances for a person in his lower-class position to finish high school and college, and to become socially mobile through education, are so slight in view of the economic position and classways of his family, that they scarcely exist. (p. 286)

Consequently, most lower-class children perceive education as having little value in their lives. This study suggests that the job of educators is not only to develop educational programs for students who see value in education, but also to devise ways that will help all children recognize its value.

Deep South: A Social Anthropological Study of Caste and Class

Deep South (Davis, Gardner, & Gardner, 1941) presents the findings from the project the authors completed between 1933 and 1935. Because it contains much of the authors' original data, it is not as accessible to the lay reader as is *Children of Bondage*. Furthermore, although it was published after *Children of Bondage*, the material presented in *Deep South* provides the foundation for the theoretical propositions described in the earlier work.

The first section of the book examines the nature of class and caste, with a comparison between Black and White society. It presents information that reinforces the notion of intra-ethnic diversity suggested in *Children of Bondage*. The authors point out that although many of the Black families exceed the income levels for White families (an issue of class), because of their skin (an issue of caste) they remain in subordinate positions.

The second half of the book examines the nature of the economic system and its social consequences. For example, in the cotton economy of the South, "the occupational relationships between white and colored individuals are limited to the landlord–tenant relationships and the master–servant relationship" (p. 422). These relationships are complicated when we examine the Black–White relationships in urban areas. Rather than a situation in which the White landlord is always in a position of superiority, in the city Black–White relationships are more complex. Write Davis, Gardner, and Gardner (1941), "The economic relationship between the white and colored individual, that is, is not always that of white employers to a colored employee, so that occupational superordination does not always coincide with caste superordination, as it does on the plantation" (p. 422).

There are two major contributions from this work that remain valid for today's educators. The first is related to my earlier discussion of intra-ethnic diversity. This book clearly demonstrates that the points suggested in *Children of Bondage* about class and caste distinctions are based on solid evidence. It suggests, implicitly, why White people in the lowest economic class have the racial antagonism they often manifest. The authors make it clear that the only barrier separating many Whites and Blacks is their skin color; black and white skin color signals caste location. Consequently, those people in the superordinate position racially, but in a subordinate position economically, will be more inclined to exert a position of racial superiority.

Second, the authors point out that inequality can become entrenched in a society. Whereas we would hope that the one place where people are working for justice would be in the government sector, what we find instead is that "in actual operation of the governmental system certain groups are excluded entirely from participation, while others are limited drastically" (p. 483). This reminds the reader that racism not only exists in the lives of individuals, but also can become institutionalized. This institutionalized racism is part of the insidious nature of race relations that is often difficult to perceive and describe.

Social Class Influences upon Learning

In 1948, Davis delivered the Inglis Lecture at Harvard University, the purpose of which was to examine problems in the field of education and to suggest potential solutions. Davis considered the influence of social class on learning a major problem in education. His solution was a transformation of the schools as they were currently being operated.

Davis presented material that shows how social class can have a dramatic influence on the ways that children learn. As an example, Davis described how class status is a significant factor in the scores of individuals on a number of achievement tests. He wrote, "It is apparent that at least part of the difference must be due to the nature of the material in the tests themselves" (p. 45). This was quite understandable to Davis, who believed that human problem solving includes cultural learning. He argued that what we see in the differences manifested is a reflection of not simply innate differences but rather differences that arise out of a cultural group experience.

To support this idea, Davis turned to the work of Alfred Binet (1916), the developer of the first widely used intelligence test. Contrary to what many people may believe, Binet was acutely aware of the influence that culture plays in the assessment of intelligence. Davis points this out by quoting Binet at length from *The Development of Intelligence in Children* (1916). Davis states that "Binet and Simon proceed . . . to criticize certain of their own test-problems as depending, for their solution, largely upon home training in study habits and in specific information" (p. 73).

This limited nature of intelligence assessment also is manifested in class-room activities. Davis argued that because schools tended to emphasize a narrow range of behavior and activities, educators were failing to recognize that intelligence and school achievement are mediated by a broad range of variables: "From [their] middle-class culture, learned from [their] parents, teachers, and friends, both the teacher and professor of education have learned to regard certain mental interests and skills, certain moral values, as the 'best,' or 'most cultured,' or 'most intelligent'" (p. 89). The result is that those people who come from a culture or social class that is different from the mainstream will tend to be viewed as unsuccessful and lacking in academic potential. The result is that we end up asking students to change for the schools rather than changing the schools so that they satisfy the needs of the students.

This book remains important today. The ideas it contains foreshadow much of the work currently being done in education. As Davis suggested needed to happen, schools are beginning, albeit slowly, to broaden the focus of a school culture that "is a narrow selection of a few highly traditional activities and skills, arbitrarily taken from a middle-class culture as a broader whole" (p. 90).

This book enables readers to question how intelligence and cognitive ability are conceptualized. The publication, visibility, and influence of *The Bell Curve* (Herrnstein & Murray, 1994) and the responses to it (Jacoby & Glauberman, 1995; Perkins, 1995) have renewed the importance of Davis's theories, research, and arguments about the ways in which social class influences learning. Although many educators and researchers have broadened their definitions of intelligence (e.g., Gardner, 1983) since Davis first challenged the nature of intelligence tests, many school programs and practices, such as tracking and gifted programs, are based on traditional conceptions of intelligence (Oakes, 1985). The publication and visibility of *The Bell Curve* gave renewed legitimacy to traditional conceptions of intelligence that promote inequality. Davis's work is an antidote to these conceptions.

A PERSPECTIVE ON DAVIS AND HIS CONTRIBUTIONS TO MULTICULTURAL EDUCATION

Throughout the discussion above, I have tried to describe the areas of Davis's academic career that were the most influential. However, I also have tried to keep my analysis broad to paint a backdrop in which to frame his work in relationship to multicultural education. The remainder of the chapter will examine points of contact between Davis's work and the work currently being done in multicultural education (Banks & Banks, 1995).

Curriculum

Davis was concerned that classrooms represented only a narrow range of what children could or wanted to learn. He argued for a broadened curriculum most forcefully in *Social Class Influences upon Learning* (1948):

> In a dynamic society . . . the public school must aim to develop many different kinds of mental activities in pupils; to prepare children to deal with a much wider range of problems than those touched upon by the usual academic process; to encourage many kinds of mental talent and skills. (p. 39)

Multicultural education theorists strongly suggest that we need to change the nature of the school curriculum if we are to provide students with a solid education (Suzuki, 1979). A number of writers (Finn & Ravitch, 1987; Schlesinger, 1991) who believe that changing the curriculum to reflect diversity promotes particularism have seriously questioned this view. Other authors (Bloom, 1987; Hirsch, 1987) claim that we need to strengthen our commitment to the traditional curriculum, which has proven its worth through time.

Multicultural theorists believe that the current construction of our curriculum fails to reveal the entire picture of historical and social reality (Banks, 1993; Gay, 1990). They believe that curriculum reform should be undertaken not just to incorporate ethnic content, but also to help students understand the ways in which knowledge is constructed (Banks, 1995; McLaren, 1986; Weiler, 1988). Consequently, when Davis noted that there is a limited selection of views in the classroom, he was anticipating what many multicultural scholars are writing today (Banks, 1988; Gay, 1990; Sleeter & Grant, 1991).

The work of Davis, particularly *Social Class Influences upon Learning* (1948), points out that teachers during his time were teaching children from what we now call a Eurocentric perspective: "The present curricula are stereotyped and arbitrary selections from a narrow area of middle-class culture. Academic culture is one of the most conservative and ritualized aspects of human culture" (p. 97). The result of this education is that it reinforces behavior and patterns of thinking for middle-class students, while alienating those students who come from dissimilar situations.

An important goal of multicultural education is to broaden the curriculum and make it more representative. It is not about "particularism" or "political correctness." Rather, it is about recognizing that knowledge is a social construction (Banks, 1993; McLaren, 1986) and that we can more closely approximate the truth by presenting views in the curriculum that are representative and comprehensive.

Bias in Testing

A second point of intersection between Davis's work and multicultural education is in evaluation practices. As pointed out earlier in this chapter, Davis was one of the foremost scholars to examine the role that culture plays in our ability to make accurate assessments. Middle-class psychologists create most of the assessment devices used in schools, colleges, and universities (Samuda & Lewis, 1992). Consequently, it is little wonder that certain groups of students perform at higher levels than others. As Eells and colleagues (1951) noted, "The middle-class may be expected to prove superior on the present tests, because this group has had more training on the specific test problems or on closely related problems" (p. 28).

Whether tests can accurately measure the cognitive ability of students has been one of the most controversial areas within education. On one extreme of the debate, scholars suggest that there is nothing inherently wrong with the tests (Herrnstein, 1971; Herrnstein & Murray, 1994; Jensen, 1969). Rather, the tests simply show that there are systematic differences between the different ethnic groups in society. This position caused a great amount of debate when Jensen (1969) published his highly influential article in the *Harvard Educational Review*. Although few social scientists and practitioners today would take the extreme view of Jensen and Herrnstein, there are still many scholars who view current assessment practices as adequate. The publication of *The Bell Curve* in 1994 (Herrnstein & Murray) renewed the debate about the extent to which IQ is related to race.

On the other side of the debate, there are a number of scholars who believe that the way we evaluate students today is unfair (Mercer, 1989). Why? Because traditional tests have difficulty taking into account the effects of culture and experience (Gardner, 1995; Perkins, 1995; Samuda & Lewis, 1992). If we do not consider these effects, we may end up misdiagnosing students.

The misdiagnosis was demonstrated most forcibly in the 1986 *Larry P. v. Wilson Riles* court case, in which a student was placed in a school for the mentally retarded based on an achievement test score. The court's decision in this case forced the state of California to alter its method of assessment because the standardized tests were failing to assess students appropriately. This issue is exactly what Davis (1951) had maintained 20 years earlier:

> On the basis of these culturally biased IQs pupils are separated into so-called "fast" and "slow" groups in most systems. Moreover, school systems have attached so much importance to those culturally biased tests that they have often provided poorer buildings and equipment . . . because the pupils here are supposed to be "inferior" in mental abilities. (p. 255)

Trying to build culture into a measure of cognitive ability is a major problem. Because culture affects the way people process information and gives people different sets of experiences, it would appear that it would be nearly impossible to devise tests that do not reflect a particular culture. Davis and Eells (1953) address this point when they state that "the lifelong process by which culture helps to guide, develop, limit, and evaluate all mental problem-solving has not received sufficiently serious attention from either test-makers or educators" (p. 26). It was because of this situation that Davis and Eells constructed the Davis–Eells Games Test. This test, although not completely successful, was the first attempt to construct a measure that incorporated culture as a factor (Johnson, 1988). A later, and arguably more successful, attempt is the System of Multicultural Pluralistic Assessment (SOMPA) (Lewis & Mercer, 1978), an assessment device that attempts to gather data about an individual from a variety of sources. As Davis maintained many years earlier, we must try to expand our understanding of intelligence and understand that all students bring to the classroom a unique and positive way of performing.

Cultural Learning

Davis's (1948) research suggests that we need to pay more attention to how culture influences the learning process. As he noted:

> All human problem-solving, as anthropologists have indicated, includes cultural learning. Culture, we recall, may be defined as all behavior learned by the individual in conformity with a group. Culture "teaches" the individual not only to recognize certain phenomena, but also certain symbols of phenomena, and the logical relationships among them. Culture also sets the goals of human problems, and teaches the inferences (logic) which people in a particular culture regard as profitable. (pp. 59–60)

Multicultural education scholars have examined the influence of culture on learning with an emphasis on the classroom culture (Delpit, 1995; Irvine & York, 1995; Ladson-Billings, 1994; Shade, 1989).

In much of her work Gay (1981) describes the effects of culture on learning. She suggests that culture is important to understand not only in terms of background (i.e., how it affects the child away from school) but also in terms of how the culture of the educational climate affects learning. Gay defines climate as "the interpersonal interactions among students and teachers from different ethnic and cultural backgrounds" (p. 43). The consequences of this attention to climate is a realization that not all environments will be conducive to all students. The reason is related to the issue of "comfortability." If a student is in a situation where she feels uncomfortable, it follows that she will have a lessened ability to focus on learning tasks (Gilbert & Gay, 1985).

Davis (1945) viewed cultural differences as stemming not only from ethnicity (which is often how they are conceived), but also from social class variation. He wrote:

> A native-born white or colored child of inferior economic status undergoes acculturation when he begins to learn the culture of the school, for this culture is always different from that of the lower-class child's family. The culture of the school is everywhere middle-class. (p. 266)

If students find classrooms culturally alien, educators are faced with a more difficult task than if classrooms are culturally sensitive or culturally compatible (Delpit, 1995; Ladson-Billings, 1994). It is for this reason that educators must not only change the curriculum of a school, but also alter the culture and environment.

Baker (1981) states that the implementation of multicultural education requires not only curriculum reform but also reform of teaching, planning, and classroom organization. Merely incorporating new perspectives into the curriculum will not result in authentic educational reform related to diversity. Rather, curriculum reform without more fundamental restructuring of the school will result in classrooms that are not fundamentally changed. Most teachers will continue to teach in traditional ways (Cuban, 1973). To truly transform schools, we must change not only the curriculum but the total school culture.

Allison Davis and Education

The historical contributions of Allison Davis are important for understanding the historical development of multicultural education. Although preceding the current movement in multicultural education by more than 30 years, his pioneering works, *Deep South*, *Children of Bondage*, and *Social Class*

Influences upon Learning, provide a theoretical foundation upon which many of the goals and premises of multicultural education are built. Davis's work provides keen insights, data, and understandings that we should not ignore in today's educational debates. If, as Harrison (1988) suggests, Davis has been marginalized by the mainstream academic community, I believe we must work to bring his research and theories to the center. Davis's work can provide today's scholars and practitioners with helpful insights for research and practice. His voice ought to be heard; it has been silent for too long.

REFERENCES

Allport, G. W. (1954). *The nature of prejudice.* New York: Doubleday.

Auden, W. H., & Kronenberger, L. (1981). *The Viking book of aphorisms: A personal selection.* New York: Dorsett Press.

Baker, G. C. (1981). The teacher and multiethnic education. In J. A. Banks (Ed.), *Education in the 80s: Multiethnic education* (pp. 33–41). Washington, DC: National Education Association.

Banks, J. A. (1988). Approaches to multicultural curriculum reform. *Multicultural Leader, 1* (2), 1–3.

Banks, J. A. (1991). *Teaching strategies for ethnic studies* (5th ed.). Boston: Allyn & Bacon.

Banks, J. A. (1993). Multicultural education: Characteristics and goals. In J. A. Banks & C. A. M. Banks (Eds.), *Multicultural education: Issues and perspectives* (2nd ed., pp. 3–28). Boston: Allyn & Bacon.

Banks, J. A. (1995). The historical reconstruction of knowledge about race: Implications for transformative teaching. *Educational Researcher, 24* (2), 15–25.

Banks, J. A., & Banks, C. A. M. (Eds.). (1995). *Handbook of research on multicultural education.* New York: Macmillan.

Binet, A. (1916). *The development of intelligence in children.* Baltimore: Williams & Wiikins Company.

Bloom, A. (1987). *The closing of the American mind.* New York: Simon & Schuster.

Bloom, B. S., Davis, A., & Hess, R. (1965). *Compensatory education for cultural deprivation.* Chicago: Holt, Rinehart, and Winston.

Cuban, L. (1973). Ethnic content and "white" instruction. In J. A. Banks (Ed.), *Teaching ethnic studies: Concepts and strategies* (43rd Yearbook; pp. 103–114). Washington, DC: National Council for the Social Studies.

Davis, A. (1939). The socialization of the American Negro child and adolescent. *The Journal of Negro Education, 8,* 264–274.

Davis, A. (1945). Some basic concepts in the education of ethnic and lower-class groups. In H. Taba & W. Van Til (Eds.), *Democratic human relations* (16th Yearbook; pp. 263–279). Washington, DC: National Council for the Social Studies.

Davis, A. (1948). *Social class influences upon learning.* Cambridge, MA: Harvard University Press.

Davis, A. (1951). Socio-economic influences on learning. *Phi Delta Kappan, 32,* 253–256.

Davis, A. (1983). *Leadership, love, and aggression: How the twig is bent.* San Diego: Harcourt, Brace, Jovanovich.

Davis, A., & Dollard, J. (1940). *Children of bondage: The personality development of Negro youth in the urban South.* New York: Harper & Row.

Davis, A. & Eells, K. (1953). *Davis–Eells test of general intelligence.* Chicago: University of Chicago Press.

Davis, A., Gardner, B. B., & Gardner, M. R. (1941). *Deep South: A social anthropological study of caste and class.* Chicago: University of Chicago Press.

Delpit, L. (1995). *Other people's children: Cultural conflict in the classroom.* New York: New Press.

Drake, St. C., & Cayton, H. R. (1945). *Black metropolis: A study of Negro life in a northern city.* New York: Harcourt, Brace.

Eells, K., Davis, A., Havighurst, R. J., Herrick, V. E., & Tyler, R. (1951). *Intelligence and cultural differences.* Chicago: University of Chicago Press.

Finn, C. E., Jr., & Ravitch, D. (1987). What 17–year olds don't know is shocking, but boards can do more than fret. *American School Board Journal, 174* (10), 31–33.

Gardner, H. (1983). *Frames of mind: The theory of multiple intelligences.* New York: Basic Books.

Gardner, H. (1995). Scholarly brinkmanship. In R. Jacoby & N. Glauberman (Eds.), *The bell curve debate: History, documents, opinions* (pp. 61–72). New York: Times Books.

Gay, G. (1981). Interactions in culturally pluralistic classrooms. In J. A. Banks (Ed.), *Education in the 80s: Multiethnic education* (pp. 42–53). Washington, DC: National Education Association.

Gay, G. (1990). Achieving educational equality through curriculum desegregation. *Phi Delta Kappan, 72* (1), 56–62.

Gilbert, S. E., & Gay, G. (1985). Improving the success in school of poor Black children. *Phi Delta Kappan, 67* (2), 133–137.

Harrison, F. V. (1988). Introduction: An African diaspora perspective for urban anthropology. *Urban Anthropology, 17* (2–3), 111–141.

Herrnstein, R. (1971). IQ. *Atlantic Monthly, 228,* 43–64.

Herrnstein, R. J., & Murray, C. (1994). *The bell curve: Intelligence and class structure in American life.* New York: Free Press.

Hirsch, E. D., Jr. (1987). *Cultural literacy: What every American needs to know.* Boston: Houghton Mifflin.

Hogben, L. T. (1938). *Political arithmetic: A symposium of population studies.* New York: Macmillan.

Irvine, J. J., & York, D. E. (1995). Learning styles and culturally diverse students: A literature review. In J. A. Banks & C. A. M. Banks (Eds.), *Handbook of research on multicultural education* (pp. 484–497). New York: Macmillan.

Jacoby, R., & Glauberman, N. (Eds.). (1995). *The bell curve: History, documents, opinions.* New York: Times Books, Random House.

Jensen, A. R. (1969). How much can we boost IQ and scholastic achievement? *Harvard Educational Review, 39* (1), 1–123.

Johnson, S. T. (1988). Test fairness and bias: Measuring academic achievement among Black youth. *The Urban League Review, 11* (1–2), 76–92.

Ladson-Billings, G. (1994). *The dreamkeepers: Successful teachers of African American children*. San Francisco: Jossey-Bass.

Larry P. et al., Plaintiffs v. Wilson Riles, Superintendent of Public Instruction for the State of California et al., Defendants. (1986). No. C-71-2270 RFP. United States District Court for the Northern District of California.

Lewis, J. F., & Mercer, J. R. (1978). The system of multicultural pluralistic assessment (SOMPA). In W. A. Coulter & H. W. Morrow (Eds.), *Adaptive behavior: Concepts and measurement* (pp. 185–212). Orlando, FL: Grune & Stratton.

Malinowski, B. (1948). *Magic, science, and religion, and other essays*. Glencoe, IL: Free Press.

McLaren, P. (1986). *Schooling as a ritual performance*. Boston: Routledge & Kegan Paul.

Mercer, J. (1989). Alternative paradigms for assessment in a pluralistic society. In J. A. Banks & C. A. M. Banks (Eds.), *Multicultural education: Issues and perspectives* (1st ed., pp. 289–304). Boston: Allyn & Bacon.

Oakes, J. (1985). *Keeping track: How schools structure inequality*. New Haven: Yale University Press.

Perkins, D. (1995). *Outsmarting IQ: The emerging science of learnable intelligence*. New York: Free Press.

Samuda, R. J., & Lewis, J. (1992). Evaluation practices for the multicultural classroom. In C. Diaz (Ed.), *Multicultural education for the 21st century* (pp. 97–111). Washington, DC: National Education Association.

Schlesinger, A. M., Jr. (1991). *The disuniting of America: Reflections on a multicultural society*. Knoxville, TN: Whittle Direct Books.

Shade, B. J. (1989). Afro-American cognitive patterns: A review of the research. In B. J. R. Shade (Ed.), *Culture, style, and the educative process* (pp. 94–115). Springfield, IL: Charles C. Thomas.

Sleeter, C. E., & Grant, C. A. (1991). An analysis of multicultural education in the United States. In N. M. Hidalgo, C. L. McDowell, & E. V. Siddle (Eds.), *Facing racism in education* (pp. 138–161). Cambridge, MA: Harvard Educational Review.

Suzuki, B. H. (1979). Multicultural education: What's it all about? *Integrated Education, 17* (97), 42–50.

Weiler, K. (1988). *Women teaching for change: Gender, class, and power*. Boston: Bergin & Garvey.

CHAPTER 7

George I. Sánchez and Mexican American Educational Practices

NATHAN MURILLO

It is indeed fitting that the work of Professor Sánchez be remembered, for his career spans a time during which many events of importance to Chicanos occurred. Sánchez, virtually alone, stood at the beginning of the Chicano[1] *movimiento* (movement), and his writings focus on issues of continuing major concern to Chicano psychologists. We can gain strength and further direction for our efforts by looking to the leadership he provided.

George Isidore Sánchez was born in New Mexico in 1906 and died in 1972 during his sixty-sixth year. He began his professional career teaching in a one-room rural school in New Mexico. He later became a school principal and supervisor, college professor, director of research with the state department of education, and president of the New Mexico Educational Association. He obtained his master's degree from the University of Texas in 1931 and received his doctorate in education from the University of California, Berkeley, in 1934. From 1937 to 1938, Dr. Sánchez served as general technical adviser to the Ministry of Education and as director of the Venezuelan National Pedagogical Institute in Caracas. He returned to the University of New Mexico in 1938 to serve as associate professor of education and as research associate. In 1940, he became professor of Latin American education at the University of Texas at Austin and remained at the University of Texas, filling various posts there until his death. For example, from 1951 to 1959, he was chairman of the Department of History and Philosophy of Education, and from 1963 to 1972, he was director of the Educational Center for International Education.

During his distinguished career, Professor Sánchez served on numerous national and international commissions and boards and worked with many

---

1. Politically active Mexican American striving for justice and cultural equality.

Multicultural Education, Transformative Knowledge, and Action. Copyright © 1996 by Teachers College, Columbia University. All rights reserved. ISBN 0-8077-3531-0 (pbk.), ISBN 0-8077-3532-9 (cloth). Prior to photocopying items for classroom use, please contact the Copyright Clearance Center, Customer Service, 222 Rosewood Dr., Danvers, MA 01923, USA, tel. (508) 750-8400.

agencies. He was frequently called to Washington to serve as a consultant, especially in the area of Latin American affairs and education. In addition to these activities, he served as an editorial consultant for various journals, writing and contributing his own works as well. He continued to remain close to his people, and from 1941 to 1942 served as national president of the League of United Latin American Citizens.

PERSONAL AND PROFESSIONAL STRUGGLE

Although Sánchez devoted his life to helping the lowly and removing the burdens of ignorance, disease, and poverty from the long-suffering, within the Chicano movement he was personally hurt by criticism and rejection (T. Carter, personal communication, March 1976). Critics of Sánchez in the late 1970s claimed that he was not sufficiently militant in his efforts to achieve changes for Chicanos. Rather than militancy, he advocated persuasive methods and working within and through the system to foster evolutionary changes. He strongly believed in a concept of cultural dualism and accord whereby the Spanish-speaking could share in American society, contribute to it, and obtain its benefits. He always made it clear that the barriers that prevented this from occurring were caused by a failure on the part of the United States government to provide for the special needs of its Spanish-speaking citizens and by the racism of the dominant Anglo society. Perhaps Sánchez's own life serves as the best example of what he expected from the concept of cultural dualism. Nevertheless, his position against a move toward Chicano nationalism was not accepted by some.

Sánchez was a man willing to accept the consequences of expressing his own beliefs. Rejection by some of his own people must have wounded him deeply; yet, viewing his work from the perspective of time and historical setting, one can only admire his deeds while recognizing the personal penalties they incurred. Vaca noted, "Dr. Sánchez wrote some of his strongest criticisms of the American educational system vis-à-vis the Mexican American child in an atmosphere of patent societal and academic hostility" (Vaca, 1972). Despite his international reputation, there are indications that Sánchez suffered both professionally and monetarily for his outspoken views. In his monograph on the Navajo Indians, published in 1948, a point was made in the foreword that the statements made by Sánchez exaggerate the problems of Navajos and therefore do not reflect the opinion of the United States Indian Service. In the last years of his life, he continued to carry on his numerous activities although his health was poor and he experienced constant and severe physical pain. Thus, given the conditions under which he worked, his accomplishments appear significantly more remarkable.

According to Thomas Carter (personal communication, March 1976), a former student and later, for many years, a friend and colleague, Sánchez was modest in his manner of relating to others. He was always patient and understanding, living according to his humanistic beliefs. Thoroughly humanitarian in his outlook, he never ceased to work for the rights of others, no matter what their ethnic, racial, or national identities. Reviewing the writings of Sánchez, one is impressed with the range and depth of his knowledge. His persistence, determination, and courage were also conspicuous. In one instance, his research led him to discover the Mayan numerical concept of zero, a fact that had not been known previously to scholars in the field. He published his book on the subject himself because he was unable to find a publisher (Sánchez, 1961).

Educational Obstacles for Mexican Americans

Professor Sánchez became an educator because he saw clearly that education is the socializing agent of our society and mirrors its social values. He saw education as the primary vehicle for effecting changes in society and for progressing toward improved conditions for all its members. He devoted his career to making constructive changes in the educational system and to equalizing educational opportunities for every individual. He never ceased to place responsibility for the education of citizens, according to democratic principles, firmly on the government and its leaders, often criticizing government sharply for what he considered to be a default of leadership. His philosophy of education was pragmatic in that he believed education and educational systems should provide people with functional tools. In order to do this, education must remain flexible. He consistently viewed present reality in terms of its future potential and as the basis for effective planning. In this context, he felt that proper educational planning must consider all relevant social science theory and knowledge. Although his writings often presented historical material, he saw history mainly as the source of a necessary perspective to help guide constructive planning and change for the future.

Among the earliest of Dr. Sánchez's published works were articles on the intelligence testing of Spanish-speaking children, a subject that continues to be of major interest to Chicano psychologists. In an article published in 1932, Sánchez (1932a) attacked the notion that Spanish-speaking children are inherently inferior intellectually to English-speaking American children, as indicated by differences in IQ scores. Sánchez made it clear that no such conclusion could legitimately be drawn from the research literature, inasmuch as many studies showed environmental and linguistic factors to be significantly related to IQ scores. He emphasized the particular problems of bilingual children with language expression and language understanding and brought into serious question the interpretation of heredity as the primary basis for observed differences in IQ scores. Sánchez criticized those who accepted the IQ test results of Spanish-speaking children without paying attention to data obtained on other groups that showed clearly that factors beyond heredity could influence IQ scores.

In a second article published the same year, Sánchez presented data demonstrating an improvement in the IQ scores of Spanish-speaking children on repeated tests of intelligence (Sánchez, 1932b). Sánchez gave parallel forms of the Stanford achievement test and the Haggerty intelligence test to 45 Spanish-speaking children, grades 3 to 8, in New Mexico public schools. He administered these tests four times at approximately 5-month intervals from December 1928 to April 1930 and found that although there were marked correlations in all abilities tested, reading correlated most highly with all the other subtests. Reading had the highest correlation to intelligence. Sánchez concluded that environmental factors were significant and must be taken into account when test results of Spanish-speaking children were interpreted. Specifically, he saw English language ability as one of the most important variables resulting in different IQ scores among the Spanish-speaking children.

In 1934, Sánchez published an article strongly criticizing the misuse and misapplication of mental tests in measuring the intelligence of school children (Sánchez, 1934a). He directed his attack against those who blindly accepted the doctrine of individual differences and totally disregarded the importance of such fundamental facts as personal, social, cultural, and environmental differences and their effects on intellectual measurement. He reserved his greatest criticism for those who ignored bilingual and cultural factors in their interpretation of test results. He pointed out many times that the validity of any test was limited to the normative sample on which that test was based, and claimed that the facts of genetics and heredity were being "garbled" in order to champion the superiority of one "race" over another. He noted that IQ tests were continuing to be misapplied to bilingual children and that the results were being accepted uncritically.

Sánchez argued that the worth of any test instrument lay only in its proper interpretation and the assistance this provided in furthering the educational needs of the pupil. He wrote, "An IQ ratio, as such, *has no value*. It is only when that measure is used critically in promoting the best educational interests of the child that it has any worthwhile significance to the educator" (Sánchez, 1934a, pp. 766–767, emphasis original). He criticized the misuse of the Binet tests of vocabulary for bilingual students, indicating how the vocabulary was inappropriate for those students and therefore invalid as a measure of intelligence. He also objected to those who would simply translate a test from English into Spanish and expect it to assess the intelligence of bilingual children accurately. In his writings, he urged an examination of the responsibility of schools toward bilingual children in the achievement of desirable goals. He fostered the position that the school has the responsibility of creating experiences for bilingual children that make the knowledge sampled by an IQ test as common to them as to the Anglo children on whom the norms are based. He felt that only after equal opportunity had been given to bilingual children could failure to score high on an IQ test be considered a failure of the children.

Bilingual Education

In a second article published in 1934, Sánchez turned his attention to the importance of a basal vocabulary in English for bilingual children before they could actually participate meaningfully in their classrooms (Sánchez, 1934b). He also attempted to highlight the significance of language as a problem in the valid assessment of Spanish-speaking children. Using a standard 660 basal vocabulary list of English words, he compared the words to the vocabulary in the Stanford–Binet tests for 3- to 8-year-olds. In various subtests he found 82 words that did not appear on the criterion list. Since some of these specific words affected as many as six separate subtests, he reasoned that the influence of the "unknown" words was actually much more extensive than it appeared at first. He went on to examine in detail the effect of these words on test-taking and to examine other aspects of vocabulary such as homonyms and word usage. He gave examples of differences in word usage that might be particularly difficult and confusing to a child just acquiring a new vocabulary or new concepts in English. For example, "What do you call yourself?" becomes, "What is your name?" and, "How many years do you have?" becomes, "How old are you?" Assuming that the English vocabulary of the Spanish-speaking child upon entering school fell short of the prerequisite basal vocabulary, Sánchez concluded that the Spanish-speaking child had to be properly equipped with at least the rudiments of the English language before progress in school could be expected. He placed the responsibility for this directly on the schools.

Sánchez's concern for improving the educational opportunities of Spanish-speaking children led him to promote bilingual, bicultural educational programs. In the article just discussed, he raised a question about the extent to which the schools build or add on to the experiences and language that Spanish-speaking children bring with them. Sánchez believed curriculum should be determined by what is in the community and that education should begin with the language of the community and the experiences of the children. He noted that for Spanish-speaking children the schools proceeded in the opposite direction, creating innumerable difficulties and all but insurmountable obstacles. Sánchez viewed learning a language as natural. Acquiring a second language became a problem primarily when one language was seen as less valuable than another and this attitude was internalized by the child, causing confusion and conflict. Sánchez reminded us again in 1958 that all language development proceeds from experience. He emphasized that bilingualism should be viewed as a prize, not a problem (Hughes & Sánchez, 1958).

In several writings, Dr. Sánchez evaluated the educational status of the Spanish-speaking in the United States. In these publications, he presented abundant data consistently showing that the schools failed to educate these students. In assessing responsibility for the shocking conditions his investigations and data analysis invariably revealed, Sánchez was forced to conclude that government had failed in its duty to these citizens and to the democratic principle of equal educational opportunity for all. In fact, Sánchez's first major work, his dissertation (Sánchez, 1934/1974), was aimed at evaluating the status of education for children of Spanish descent and educational practices as they affected these children. His study showed that bilingual students warranted special attention because of their unique educational problems. He deplored the common practice of segregating Spanish-speaking children because it is contrary to the aims and ideals of educational theory. In his estimation, this practice limited the educational opportunity for Spanish-speaking students in the New Mexico school system. He attributed the deficiencies he found primarily to an administrative policy that discriminated against children of Mexican American heritage and to lack of financial support to the predominantly Spanish-speaking schools.

Governmental Neglect of the Spanish-Speaking Community

Governmental neglect of the health, educational, and economic needs of Spanish-speaking people was portrayed by Sánchez most movingly in what is perhaps his best-known book, *Forgotten People: A Study of New Mexicans,* first published in 1940. In this work he described the geographical and cultural isolation these people endured for close to 400 years. He traced the relationship between the United States government and the Spanish-speaking people of New Mexico from the time that land became a territory of the United States.

Sánchez described the Spanish-speaking New Mexican as severely handicapped, both socially and economically, because of a gap between the impacted New Mexicans and the Anglo culture that surrounded them. Comparing education in New Mexico with education in other states in terms of economic support and pupil achievement, Sánchez found it third from the bottom. He wrote that the problem of educating a bicultural people was never recognized by the United States government. As a consequence, children were systematically forced out of the schools. He provided figures on expenditures for education in various portions of the state, which showed that the areas where most of the Spanish-speaking people lived received far less money than others. He pointed out that even though the United States government provided help to the American Indian, the Indian still lags behind; and that the Spanish-speaking New Mexican, also in desperate need, had received no help whatsoever. He concluded that the inferior status of the New Mexican was caused by the failure of the government to recognize the special character of the people and their needs when it forced this group into American society.

Attempts at Educational Reform

Again, writing in 1941, he emphasized that educational backwardness is not a product of a society's physical or mental constitution but a direct result of the circumstances of a society's history and environment. He believed that the condition of educational backwardness in New Mexico was directly related to the policies of the United States government. He wrote, "It is astonishing to have to come to the conclusion that the administration of affairs in New Mexico during the nineteenth century by the United States was lacking in all salient benefits of good, sympathetic, democratic government" (Sánchez, 1941, p. 65). He noted that between 1846 and 1910, the statistics on education in New Mexico clearly showed the limited educational opportunities. For him, these statistics also symbolized eloquently the cultural deterioration that he saw as the inevitable result of that condition.

Sánchez was not content merely to criticize. At every opportunity, he provided programs, made recommendations, and discussed problems directed toward ameliorating conditions and improving the educational system to meet the needs of the people. For example, in 1939 he published a detailed discussion of the issues and problems, as he saw them, involved in planning the distribution of state school funds. His purpose was to ensure the equalization of educational opportunity for the educationally disadvantaged. At that time the state legislatures and the federal government were developing plans for the appropriation of school funds. Sánchez insisted that there had to be some relationship between educational theory and the financial formula adopted. In other words, he wanted to ensure that the way the funds were spent would actually improve the educational system in accordance with sound educational theory. He wrote that educational need should be measured by standards that take into consideration the absence of educational opportunity indicated by such conditions as illiteracy, unsatisfactory health status, nonattendance in school, and child labor. Recognizing the enormity of the problem and concerned that local and state governments might not be strong enough to accomplish equalization, Sánchez (1939) wrote:

Furthermore, the standard financial pattern and the measures of educational need utilized in an equalization plan must be such that, when applied to a given community, they will reveal the degree to which the educational situation in that community is in conformity with the total situation symbolized by the standard. In addition, the remedial nature of equalization forces us to recognize that its primary purpose is not served until the equalization funds are applied to overcome education handicap upon which need has been determined. To the extent that this application will not result without implementation within the plan itself, to that extent an equalization law must be made compulsory rather than permissive—to that extent is central control essential to the very function of the law whose ultimate purpose is the equalization of educational opportunity. (pp. 26–27)

Sánchez believed equal distribution of money raised in different communities to be politically justified when it is recognized that education is both a duty and a right of government.

In his proposals for educational reform in New Mexico, Sánchez (1940/1967) suggested broad remedial measures. He established as a first priority that citizens be provided with a satisfactory livelihood in the form of food and economic security. To this end, he proposed a plan whereby the government would develop an economic base, purchasing land and establishing a land-use management program. His second priority was establishing a cultural balance through education, which he emphasized would have to be more than "routine." The educational program he proposed had to be identified with the needs of the people and the setting from which it operated. For example, the programs for reading and writing could not be disassociated from poor health, civic ineffectiveness, and inefficient farming methods. The educational program he proposed was action oriented, designed to overcome existing deficiencies in the social and economic life of the people. In order to do this, the program would require adaptation to the customs and traditions, to the language and historical background, of the people. He called for a pooling of resources and cooperative efforts across all agencies and all levels of government. It was his contention that major problems could be solved if every element of government would put forth the necessary effort.

In stressing the responsibility of government to provide educational opportunity to the New Mexican, Sánchez wanted to ensure that this group of people would make their proper contribution to the larger society. Although his humanitarian nature caused him to be concerned primarily with alleviation of human misery, he also recognized the loss to the country of human resources in terms of cultural enrichment, loyalty of the citizens, and other potential losses that were a consequence of the government's failure to provide for the educational needs of a significant number of its citizens.

Segregation and Racism in Mexican American Schools

Sánchez did not overlook the issue of segregation in the schools, and he made strong, forceful arguments against such practices and the racism behind them. For example, Sánchez wrote in defense of the Mexican American Pachuco youths who were being condemned on all sides after the "zoot-suiter" riots in Los Angeles in 1943. He turned the tables on White society, which was complaining that it had been victimized by Pachucos: "The crimes of youth should be punished, yes, but what of the society which is an accessory before and after the fact?" (Sánchez, 1943, p. 13). Continuing, he wrote:

> The frequent prostitution of democratic ideals to the cause of expediency, politic vested interests, ignorance, class and "race" prejudice, and to indifference and inefficiency is a sad commentary on the intelligence and justice of a society that makes claim to those very progressive democratic ideals. The dual system of education presented in "Mexican" and "White" schools, the family system of contract labor, social and economic discrimination, educational negligence on the part of state and local authorities, "homogenous groupings" to mask professional inefficiency—all point to the need for greater insight into a problem which is inherent in a "melting pot" society. The progress of our country is dependent upon the most efficient utilization of the heterogeneous masses which constitute its population—the degree to which two million or more Spanish-speaking people, and their increment, are permitted to develop is the extent to which a nation should expect returns from that section of its public. (Sánchez, 1943, p. 13)

He castigated investigations on the causes of the Mexican American youth riots as going off "on a tangent witch hunting in anthropological antecedents for causes which lie under their noses" (Sánchez, 1943, p. 13). His fear that the real causes of the rioting would be missed was confirmed when the Los Angeles city council failed to confront the issue of negligence by public service agencies to the needs of the Mexican American community and, instead, spent time deliberating over a city ordinance that would outlaw zoot suits.

Sánchez pointed out many examples of racism against Mexican Americans in the Southwest. Regarding segregated schools, he perceived that although they ostensibly were established for pedagogical reasons, such schools did not conform to any sound philosophy of education. He observed that only pseudopedagogical reasons would call for shorter school terms, ramshackle school buildings, and poorly paid and untrained teachers for "Mexican" schools, and criticized the argument that segregated schools were justified because the Spanish-speaking children suffered under a language handicap. He stated explicitly that the "Mexican problem" was not a Mexican problem, but an American problem "made in the USA."

Writing in 1943, Sánchez foresaw that the racist social attitudes evident in this country would create crime, disease, ignorance, internal discord, and international animosity. He saw the Pachuco as a symbol of a cancerous growth within the majority group gnawing at the core of democracy and the American way of life.

Returning to the subject of segregation in a later paper published in 1951, Sánchez made a careful legal case review and analysis of segregated classes and schools. He showed conclusively that such practices were illegal. Further, he put forward practical suggestions for optimal classroom learning when both Spanish-speaking and English-speaking children are together. He concluded, "The 'pedagogical' reasons usually offered to justify segregation are not supported by competent authority; and those reasons must be regarded either as professional blunders, or worse still, as evidence that educational principle is being prostituted to racialism" (Sánchez, 1951/1974, p. 58). About a year before he died, Sánchez participated in a symposium on Mexican Americans and educational change. He summarized his views in this way:

> While I have championed the cause of educational change for American children of Mexican descent for more than 45 years, and while I have seen some changes and improvements in this long-standing dismal picture, I cannot, in conscience or as a professional educator, take any satisfaction in those developments. The picture is a shameful and an embarrassing one. (Sánchez, 1974, p. 14)

Sánchez's Legacy

Perhaps Chicano psychologists will be wise enough to learn from George I. Sánchez, the man and the teacher. It is not enough to recognize that this dedicated Chicano was perhaps more responsible than any other for laying the foundation of present-day Headstart and bilingual-bicultural educational programs. If we are to follow his direction, we must assume greater responsibility and continue to develop a more forceful leadership role within our profession and across the country by using our specialized knowledge and research skills with greater discernment and increasing effect. We must press government harder at all levels for positive programs devoted to research, education, and health improvement and take an active part in the development of such programs, insisting that they be guided by empirical information gathered on Chicanos rather than by myths, stereotypes, or warped ideology. Within the profession of psychology, our task is both immediate and great. The Chicano psychologist continues to be almost completely ignored by the American Psychological Association, not to mention state and local organizations. Despite all evidence, which consistently shows the desperate need for Chicano psychologists, neither the professional organizations nor recognized training centers have taken any significant step toward encouraging Chicanos into the profession. The equalization of educational opportunity for Chicano psychologists, beyond financial support, entails dual-cultural psychological training to make the program more meaningful and relevant to students who want to work for the improvement of their people.

Psychological training in graduate schools has been Anglo oriented and Anglo dominated. As Sánchez pointed out regarding the education of the Spanish-speaking child, all group and ethnic differences generally have been ignored, with no attention paid to resultant differences in psychological orientation, cognition, attitudes, or patterns of behavior. This has been especially detrimental in the area of mental health, where such factors are most important in that they frequently provide a basis for what is considered "normal" or "abnormal." At present, Chicano psychotherapists must become qualified according to Anglo criteria, in order to work with Anglo clients. Yet Anglo therapists frequently assume they are already adequately qualified to work with Chicanos, especially if they have some knowledge of Spanish, even though there may be vast cultural differences between them and their clients. As in the field of education, where bilingual, bicultural specialization is important, a recognized specialization probably should be developed for psychotherapists who choose to provide services to Latinos.

REFERENCES

Hughes, M. M., & Sánchez, G. I. (1958). *Learning a new language 1957-1958*. (General Service Bulletin 101). Washington, DC: Association for Childhood Education International.

Sánchez, G. I. (1932a). Group differences and Spanish-speaking children—A critical review. *Journal of Applied Psychology, 16*, 549-558.

Sánchez, G. I. (1932b). Scores of Spanish-speaking children on repeated tests. *Journal of Genetic Psychology, 40*, 223-231.

Sánchez, G. I. (1934a). Bilingualism and mental measures: A word of caution. *Journal of Applied Psychology, 18*, 765-772.

Sánchez, G. I. (1934b). The implications of a basal vocabulary to the measurement of the abilities of bilingual children. *Journal of Social Psychology, 5*, 395-402.

Sánchez, G. I. (1939). The equalization of educational opportunity—Some issues and problems. *The University of New Mexico Bulletin, 10*, 3-47.

Sánchez, G. I. (1941). New Mexicans and acculturation. *New Mexico Quarterly Review, 11*, 61-68.

Sánchez, G. I. (1943). Pachucos in the making. *Common Ground, 4*, 13-20.

Sánchez, G. I. (1948). *The people: A study of the Navajos*. Washington, DC: United States Indian Service.

Sánchez, G. I. (1961). *Arithmetic in Maya*. Published privately. Austin, TX.

Sánchez, G. I. (1967). *Forgotten people. A study of New Mexicans.* Albuquerque: Calvin Horn. (Original work published 1940)

Sánchez, G. I. (1974). Concerning segregation of Spanish-speaking children in the public schools. In A. Castañeda, M. Ramírez, III, C. E. Cortés, & M. Barrrera (Eds.), *Education and the Mexican American* (pp. 14–21). New York: Arno Press. (Original work published 1951)

Sánchez, G. I. (1974). The education of bilinguals in a state school system. In C. E. Cortés (Ed.), *Education and the Mexican American* (pp. 1–166). New York: Arno Press. (Original work published 1934)

Sánchez, G. I. (1974). Educational change in historical perspective. In A. Castañeda (Ed.), *Mexican Americans and educational change.* New York: Arno Press.

Vaca, N. C. (1972). *George I. Sánchez memorial lecture.* University of California, Berkeley.

CHAPTER 8

Mediation and Authority: The Native American Voices of Mourning Dove and Ella Deloria

CAROL MILLER

Early scholarship on American Indian cultural and intellectual traditions in most cases was initiated, conducted, or overseen first by non-Native explorers and missionaries and later by academics. In some cases these tasks were undertaken by patrons and reformers whose motivations frequently emerged from their self-identification as "friends of the Indian" (Berkhofer, 1978, p. 172). By the beginning of the twentieth century, many non-Native anthropologists and Indian-rights advocates believed that they had an obligation to gather, edit, and publish materials about indigenous peoples. Indians often were involved in a variety of ways, most frequently as informants or in other roles generally meeting a "white need, as Christians or chroniclers of their own cultures" (Murray, 1991, p. 57). Mary Louise Pratt (1992) uses the problematic term "autoethnography" to describe these "instances in which the colonized subjects undertake to represent themselves in ways that engage with the colonizer's own terms" (p. 9), noting also that elements of resistance and circumvention are contained within these representations. Historically, however, non-Native influences, occurring in varying degrees and forms, have mediated the published voices of American Indians speaking about their cultural traditions and circumstances. Only today are these problematic mediations of Native authority and point of view—and the sometimes contending issues of intellectual property and purpose that result—being fully examined (e.g., Brown, 1993; Murray, 1991).

A crucial part of that examination logically should concentrate on the countering presence of what Dakota anthropologist Bea Medicine (1980) has

Multicultural Education, Transformative Knowledge, and Action. Copyright © 1996 by Teachers College, Columbia University. All rights reserved. ISBN 0-8077-3531-0 (pbk.), ISBN 0-8077-3532-9 (cloth). Prior to photocopying items for classroom use, please contact the Copyright Clearance Center, Customer Service, 222 Rosewood Dr., Danvers, MA 01923, USA, tel. (508) 750-8400.

called "the emic [native] perspective" (p. 23). From unique positions as cultural insiders, Native people certainly found ways to act with differing degrees of autonomy in the production and dissemination of information about their own cultures. The writings of two American Indian women, Mourning Dove (Okanogan) and Ella Deloria (Dakota), both working primarily in the first half of the twentieth century, provide illuminating sites for an examination not only of the processes of non-Native mediation but of the ways in which the emic perspective asserts itself in counterbalancing outcomes. Attention to these complex interactions also provides an opportunity for transformative teaching and learning about broader issues of cultural transaction and competing constructions of knowledge.

INSIDER VOICES AND MEDIATED AUTHORITY: MOURNING DOVE AND ELLA DELORIA

Mourning Dove was the literary name taken by Okanogan writer Christal Quintasket, credited as the author of the first novel by an American Indian woman (*Cogewea the Half-Blood*, originally published in 1927). Although she also transcribed a number of traditional Okanogan tales in *Coyote Stories* (Mourning Dove, 1934/1990), more significant for this chapter are her novel *Cogewea* (1927/1981) and her collected personal and communal reminiscences, published as *Mourning Dove, A Salishan Autobiography* (1990) more than 50 years after her death in 1936.

Ella Deloria's substantial written work included extensive bilingual transcriptions of traditional stories and an influential Dakota grammar (Picotte, 1988). Of particular relevance to this analysis of mediation, authority, and transformative knowledge, however, are Deloria's popular-audience, anthropological exposition of Dakota culture, *Speaking of Indians* (1944), and her posthumously published fictional narrative of gender and kinship relations in the traditional camp circle, *Waterlily* (1988).

In a sense, Mourning Dove's *Cogewea* and her culture-based memoir—and Deloria's anthropological and narrative treatments of Dakota cultural practices—may be seen as companion pieces of cross-textual referencing that not only reveal direct and indirect processes of influential mediation but also show the ways in which these writers use particular instances of traditional knowledge as sources of circumvention and restoration.

Mourning Dove's *Cogewea the Half-Blood*

Mourning Dove (whose Indian name was Humishuma) was born into an Okanogan/Colville family in the Pacific Northwest in 1888. As a migrant worker, she experienced poverty and physical hardship, and completed only a few years of formal schooling. Despite harsh living conditions, she pursued a literary career throughout her adulthood (Mourning Dove, 1927/1981). The process of collaboration that brought her novel *Cogewea* to publication but also significantly mediated her narrative voice is accessibly documented in Dexter Fisher's introduction to the 1981 Bison edition. It is true that without the help of Lucullus McWhorter, founder of *American Archaeologist* and "journalist-Indian hobbyist, literary patron" (Miller, 1989, p. 160), *Cogewea* probably would never have been published. McWhorter exhorted Mourning Dove to record the storytelling traditions of her people and supported her in the publication of the novel, which was her real ambition. McWhorter's motivation, according to Fisher (1981), was his perception of the imminent corruption of American Indian cultures by "intermarriage and the influence of white civilization" (p. viii). McWhorter's vision of Native peoples as a vanishing race was shared by almost all of White America (Berkhofer, 1978). Consequently, his exhortation to Mourning Dove to record traditional tales rather than concentrate on *Cogewea,* the story she herself wanted to tell, was at once earnest and manipulative: "Helping hands are held out to her, and the trail will not be so rough as it appears," he wrote to Mourning Dove as an imagined third person whose cultural responsibility was to assume the mantle he was thrusting upon her (Fisher, 1981, p. viii). He also wrote that "her race blood will be of actual benefit to her in this work. It is a duty she owes her poor people, whose only history has been written by the destroyers of her race" (p. viii). She should, he told her, show the world "her nobility of purpose to perpetuate the story of her people in their primitive simplicity" (p. ix).

A deconstruction of McWhorter's urging speaks worlds about the initial characteristics of his mediation of Mourning Dove's voice and intentions. In fact, the trail he wished to set her upon was very rough indeed for a woman of limited education who had few material resources. That she tried to assume the role of (auto)ethnologist that McWhorter cast for her is evidenced not only from the stories she was able to gather but from her assumption of even the professionalized terminology of the task: "A whiteman has spoiled my field of work," by paying informants for stories, she complained at one point (Fisher, 1981, p. viii). However, a greater obstacle was another sort of field of work—where she toiled as a migrant worker, frequently trying to write in a tent at night after a long day's labor. Her perseverance is an indication that her own motivations may have been more complex than McWhorter's desire to perpetuate the record of a vanishing race.

Although Fisher (1981) states that a manuscript of *Cogewea* had already been drafted when Mourning Dove met McWhorter in 1914, the novel was not published until 13 years later. Many circumstances, including World War I and hesitations on the part of the publisher, intervened. By the time the novel was finally published in 1927, McWhorter's mediation had increased so significantly that Mourning Dove's own authorship was questioned. Long after the novel was published, she acknowledged with gratitude McWhorter's critical part in getting it into print. But Fisher (1981) notes significantly that "Mourning Dove was completely overwhelmed by the final product in which she suddenly realized the full extent of McWhorter's influence" (p. xv). In fact, the appropriative character of McWhorter's mediation is a poignant subtext in her letter to him immediately after she saw the book in print: "I have just got through going over the book *Cogewea*, and am surprised at the changes that you made. I think they are fine, and you made a tasty dressing like a cook would do with a fine meal . . . I felt like it was some one elses [*sic*] book and not mine at all. In fact the finishing touches are put there by you, and I have never seen it" (Fisher, 1981, p. xv).

Mourning Dove's self-effacement implicitly acknowledges the inequities of relationships of power that were at work in her interaction with McWhorter. Two decades later, Zora Neale Hurston would assume a similarly self-effacing posture in her correspondence with her controlling patron, Mrs. R. Osgood Mason (hooks, 1990, p. 138). As hooks points out, however, it is simplistic to conclude that Hurston's refusal to acknowledge Mason's paternalism was an endorsement of it. An enforced monologue, in such instances, appears to be more or less a collaborative dialogue (Brown, 1993). Mourning Dove's letter to McWhorter illustrates an inevitable ambivalence resulting from her part in an apparent collaboration that became in actuality a mediation, and to some degree an appropriation, of authorial property. This ambivalence is a significant indication of the influences of mediation in the writings produced by Mourning Dove and by Deloria. Although the nature of mediation is different in the work of each writer, its effects require careful analysis to bring into focus not only the complexity of the cultural negotiations actually going on, but the ways in which each writer circumvented impositions of even the sympathetic dominant voice.

Readers may see a particularly compacted example of both ambivalence and circumvention in the dedication that begins *Cogewea* (Mourning Dove, 1927/1981). On one level, Mourning Dove's evocation of the memory of her grandfather and "the crowded death huts and burial cairns of a nation" (Mourning Dove, 1927/1981, n.p.) seems directly in line with McWhorter's goal that her writing should perpetuate the story of her people as they vanish from the American scene. Additionally, her self-representation as "one who ever yearns for the uplifting of her most unhappy race," suggests some degree of engagement with McWhorter's, if not the colonizer's, terms (Mourning Dove, 1927/1981, n.p.). But on closer analysis, beneath the ambivalence of the surface, Mourning Dove reveals not romanticized nostalgia but quite resonant Native values. Her celebration of her grandfather's "good deeds," for example, derives from Okanogan terms of chiefly leadership, the commemoration of which, she asserts, will in the form of song "forever mingle with the mighty roar of the falls of the Swa-Neck-Qah" (Mourning Dove, 1927/1981, n.p.). She secures his veneration by tying it to tribal place—the salmon waters of the Okanogan homeland—and casts tribal presence in place forward into eternality rather than backward into an anachronous past. Further, she straight-forwardly acknowledges causation and responsibility in the destruction resulting from contact with White culture, and an accompanying inconclu-siveness about "uplift" evades any direct equation with assimilation.

McWhorter's mediation at other points throughout the text has received some measure of critical attention (Brown, 1993; Fisher, 1981; Miller, 1989). Didactic invective about injustices suffered by Indians; the insertion of McWhorter's own anthropological research about tribal histories, language, and cultural practice; allusive epigraphs that introduce chapters; and the pervasive presence of hybridized rhetoric employing in turn a sort of dime-novel argot and an inflated linguistic romanticism—all point to McWhorter's narrative presence and influence. Page by page, passage by passage, it is per-haps impossible to distinguish Mourning Dove's words from her mediator's. Throughout, readers may be tempted to speculate—whose authorial "voice," for example, employs the ironically rich nomenclature of "Caucasian" and "American" to distinguish White from Indian? Who is responsible for the scene in which Cogewea, angered by a book in which she finds "an unjust presen-tation of Indian sentiment and racial traits," concludes that the writer, instead of "extending a helping hand," had dealt the hero "a ruthless blow" (Mourn-ing Dove, 1927/1981, p. 88)?

At many points, however, Mourning Dove is able to establish a more clearly identifiable authority as cultural insider. Thematically, for example, *Cogewea* is as centered on conflicted identity, "the disjuncture between myth and reality [at which] American Indian novelists most often take aim, and out of which the material of their art most often arises" (Owens, 1992, p. 4), as any more contemporary narrative by Scott Momaday (1968), Leslie Silko (1977), or Louise Erdrich (1984). Specifically, Mourning Dove delineates the dilemma of mixed-bloods as "just go-between people shut within their own diminu-tive world" (1927/1981, p. 41). And although the novel makes use of non-Native formulas of melodramatic plotting and language—Mourning Dove had, after all, learned to read from the "penny dreadful" novels of a young White orphan taken in by her family (Mourning Dove, 1990, p. xvi)—these are posed against other structural components reflective of ancestral orality.

The text is infused with the traditional storytelling carried on by the Stemteema, the grandmother, who voices the instructive weight of Okanogan oral tradition as a counter to the general influences of contact and the spe-cific duplicity of Cogewea's White suitor, Densmore. Elements of Okanogan spirituality are important components of the narrative development—evidenced by the significance of the Sweat House, for example, and the buffalo skull that speaks to Cogewea as a spirit helper at the story's conclusion. As Fisher (1981) points out, "In Okanogan culture, the Sweat House was consulted in matters ranging from love and war to success in hunting and gambling" (p. xxii). Mourning Dove (1927/1981) consistently positions the sweat as an important cultural practice. Her acknowledgment of the general importance of spirit power in the conduct of individual life is, in fact, represented in both *Cogewea* and the autobiography at many points (Mourning Dove, 1927/1981, 1990).

Despite the pervasive presence of the conventions of high melodrama within many passages, the conclusion of *Cogewea* is closely constructed by Native American narrative patterns of less directly resolved conflict and resolution. Although Cogewea has been physically abused and left to die by Densmore, there is no actual showdown between the Cogewea/Jim contingent and the villain, no overt confrontation in which good triumphs over evil to its face. Mourning Dove's awareness that there could be no circumstances in which Indians could expect equitable treatment within the legal system of White society is reflected in her story's outcome, as well as in the earlier episode in which Jim is almost arrested or perhaps worse when he speaks up against the refusal of the judges to recognize Cogewea as the winner of the Ladies' Race. Readers must be satisfied instead with the purely poetic justice conveyed in one brief paragraph describing Densmore's chagrin at learning belatedly of Cogewea's inheritance (Mourning Dove, 1927/1981).

Additionally, the novel's ending is an illustration of William Bevis's (1987) identification of "homing in" as a fundamental strategy of American Indian narrative. The mixed-bloods Cogewea and Jim end up together, no longer self-perceived as "go-betweens in a diminutive—diminished—post-contact setting" (p. 41), but at home in the natural world viewed from the spiritual center represented by Buffalo Butte. "See how magnificent those grand old mountains are in the moonlight. Isn't this a splendid world?" Cogewea asks rhetorically. "Yes! it is jus' 'bout right—when not too cold nor too hot—nor nothin' wrong with the corral fencin'," Jim replies (p. 284). In both structure and theme, the story resolves itself in the restoration of lives in a harmonious adaptive balance, an American Indian epistemology as clear in Mourning Dove's conclusion as in Leslie Silko's *Ceremony* (1977), published 50 years later.

Ultimately, then, McWhorter's mediation of *Cogewea the Half-Blood* is contextualized and contained by attention to the insider voice, which places the story demonstrably within Mourning Dove's narrative agenda, simultaneously participating in and circumventing McWhorter's. When Mourning Dove's ambivalence in *Cogewea* is juxtaposed against her more recently published personal and cultural reminiscences, collected in *Mourning Dove, A*

Salishan Autobiography (1990), edited by Jay Miller, a reconstruction of more culturally particular knowledge—and resulting pedagogical transformations that can occur in the teaching and learning environment—is even more clearly evident.

MOURNING DOVE'S MEDIATED "AUTOBIOGRAPHY"

Much may be learned from the previously unpublished manuscripts edited by Miller. It is certainly true that, decades after Mourning Dove's death, readers are fortunate to have access to them. As Brown (1993) points out, however, in an important paper summarizing the extent of Miller's editorializing role, intrusive interventions appear to constitute a mediation ultimately as pervasive as McWhorter's, resulting in a similar if more subtle alteration of Mourning Dove's own purposes. Fundamentally, for example, her loosely organized accounts of traditional tipi life giving way to assimilative adaptations do not conform to the conventions of the generally non-Native genre of autobiography. Rather, they fall more naturally within storytelling traditions foregrounding communal well-being over personal identity.

Furthermore, in addition to justifiable, although extensive, correction of Mourning Dove's ungrammatical language, Miller assumes an interpretive stance toward her materials and the details of her life, which ultimately does not serve her well, casting for her a "frenetic, imbalanced persona" (Brown, 1993, p. 286) and ignoring a more generous reading of biographical data that would take into account the consequences of marital abuse and medical misdiagnosis. Miller's extensive commentary in endnotes—frequently judgmental rather than informative in tone and substance—contains elements of paternalism, condescension, and projection. When, for example, Mourning Dove (1990) observes that as a child she did not like dolls, preferring instead to play with the bows and arrows made by her father or to listen "to old men tell stories of warfare or horrible bloodshed" (p. 23), her apparent point is to illustrate something about her adventurous child's spirit. But Miller as editor and mediator deflects the meaning of the anecdote with a corrective footnote: "These references to warfare are a fiction, presumably inserted to accommodate a white audience" (p. 200). The cumulative effect of such commentary diminishes the authority of Mourning Dove's voice in recounting and interpreting her own experience, supplanting it with a judgmental, dominant perspective.

Her authority is plainly present, however, when the insider perspective is given exposure and credence. The ambivalence that accounts for the divided voice of *Cogewea* is contextualized and mitigated here by a more direct and consistent valuing of traditional identity and experience, as may

be seen from the opening passage of *Mourning Dove: A Salishan Autobiography*:

> There are two things I am most grateful for in my life. The first is that I was born
> a descendant of the genuine Americans, the Indians; the second, that my birth
> happened in the year 1888. In that year the Indians of my tribe, the Colvile (Swhy-
> ayl-puh), were well into the cycle of history involving their readjustment in liv-
> ing conditions. They were in a pathetic state of turmoil caused by trying to learn
> how to till the soil for a living, which was being done on a very small and crude
> scale. It was no easy matter for members of this aboriginal stock, accustomed to
> making a different livelihood (by the bow and arrow), to handle the plow and
> sow seed for food. Yet I was born long enough ago to have known people who
> lived in the ancient way before everything started to change. (1990, p. 3)

In the paragraph above, Mourning Dove lays out the major ideas and signals the purpose of her account, using what she clearly considered the fortunate circumstance of her Native identity and her own birth and upbringing at
this critical historical moment as a path of understanding to her people's
broader experience. What she feels important to tell about that experience
follows—in the first section, descriptions of her happy childhood in the growing (and extended) family headed by her authoritative mother, and of the
spiritual and domestic practices that structured passage from childhood to
adulthood. In a second section, she presents a more distanced selective portrait of a Native society in transition from the psychological well-being
derived from its traditional sources of livelihood—salmon fishing and
hunting—to the less congenial practice of farming, and an account of competition with White settlers for control of traditional homelands (Mourning
Dove, 1990).

What emerges overall is a validation and reassertion of fundamental
values of indigenous cultural life in the face of hardship and change:

> The big snow destroyed all the ponies, preventing us from searching for food,
> and the melting snow caused the rampage that wiped out everything else. We
> had to start over and became stronger than before as a result. . . . We learned the
> important thing about being Indian was willingness to share whatever we had
> and the determination to survive with renewed intent and wisdom after any
> calamity. (Mourning Dove, 1990, p. 165)

Recurring references here—and, as we shall see, in Deloria's work as well—
highlight these two characteristics of cultural being—sharing and the stamina
to survive—as distinctly Indian. Other passages articulate a clear predilection
for traditional rather than assimilated ways of living: "My people loved the
free life and were reluctant to stay in one place," she writes (p. 167). Later,

she points out her family's uneasy transition to the presumed improvements of ranch life: "Once the cabin was finished we used it only occasionally. Usually we lived in a tipi in the backyard, where Mother cooked over a camp fire on warm, sunny days. We enjoyed this lifestyle much more" (pp. 173–174).

In the chapter meaningfully titled "The Invasions of Miners and Settlers," Mourning Dove (1990) speaks unequivocally with the authority of the emic voice. Her account of the opening of the Colville Reservation in 1896, first to mining interests, then to allotment surveyors, and eventually to White homesteaders, has none of the ambivalence in *Cogewea* about conflicted identity or contending cultural interests. Describing onslaughts of White invasion, her imagery is that of infestation: "Whites were swarming over the reservation"; they "came in hordes, startling the peaceful isolation of my people" (p. 177). Recounting the participation of the chief Aropaghan, bribed into giving permission for the surveyors to begin their work, and of the half-breeds who acted as interpreters, she speaks clearly as an insider expressing disapproval and sorrow: "The half-breeds sold their birthright for a job, and people said the chief sold their reservation for a pair of underwear" (p. 183).

William Bevis (1987) argues that Native American identity "is not a matter of finding 'one's self,' but of finding a 'self' that is transpersonal and includes a society, a past, and a place" (p. 585). The converging individual and communal experiences and values Mourning Dove chooses to express here merge into just such a transpersonal identity. When the charged melodrama of the plot of *Cogewea* and its divided voices are cross-referenced with this perspective, that text is itself inversely mediated—additionally contextualized and reconstructed by Mourning Dove's evolving presentation of an ultimately consistent tribal sense of knowing and being.

ELLA DELORIA'S PROFESSIONAL AND CULTURAL IDENTITIES

Ella Deloria's *Speaking of Indians* (1944) and *Waterlily* (1988) proceed from differing sources and influences of mediation but offer a similar interaction illustrating how a reconstruction of knowledge may occur when the insider voice is accounted for. Deloria's circumstances were very different from Mourning Dove's. Born into a prominent Native family in South Dakota in 1889, Deloria earned a baccalaureate degree in 1915 at Teachers College, Columbia University, where she was recruited by Franz Boas as a "linguistic informant and ethnological entrepreneur" (Medicine, 1980, p. 23). Working with Boas intermittently until his death in 1942, she produced several books, including a bilingual collection of traditional stories and a *Dakota Grammar* (Boas & Deloria, 1941).

Boas had revolutionized the practice of anthropology by advancing concepts of cultural relativism over inherent racial superiority (Banks, 1995). Linguistic and ethnological field work among Deloria's Dakota people was one of many projects Boas sponsored to support his conception of anthropology as "a field that might stand in opposition, trying to correct the false proclamations of the superiority of one culture, one way of life, over another" (hooks, 1990, p. 136). Even so, however, Boas's study of other cultures did not entirely avoid the baggage of colonialism or "totally transcend some of the tenacious and pernicious assumptions and beliefs about race that were institutionalized and pervasive within Western society" (Banks, 1995, p. 18).

In her merging of professional and cultural identities, Deloria, who grew up Christian, developed the skills of the anthropologist, and was "educated in the 'modern' tradition, . . . was well-suited for the role of cultural mediator" (Medicine, 1980, p. 23). She undertakes this role in *Speaking of Indians* (1944), but her desire to explain and justify what she significantly calls "a scheme of life that worked" (p. 24) is itself mediated by three factors: the dominant culture influences of her academic training, the highly charged circumstances of the historical moment in which she wrote, and the overlay of Christianity.

As Clifford and Marcus (1986) write, "The predominant metaphors in anthropological research have been participant observation, data collection, and cultural description, all of which presuppose a standpoint outside—looking at, objectifying, or, somewhat closer, 'reading' a given reality" (p. 11). The text Deloria produces is clearly marked by a respect for and loyalty to Dakota traditions. These are viewed, however, from a perspective that blends Boasian professionalism—the assumed perspective of the objective observer—and Deloria's Christian upbringing. Even her title suggests that she is gazing from the outside in: She is primarily speaking *of*, not *to*, Indians. She writes a sentence that captures her own particular form of ambivalence: "We may know about a people, but we cannot truly know them until we can get within their minds, to some degree at least, and see life from their peculiar point of view" (Deloria, 1944, p. 18).

Intermittently but recurringly, Deloria asserts the superiority of Christian faith over Dakota spirituality, equates assimilation with progress, and defends White appropriation of the American continents. "A relatively small group of mankind," she writes, "could not rightly refuse to share their vast rich domain with others; they could not rightly prevent its exploitation for the good of the many. I do not think there is a Dakota who would doubt the rightness of that, if only he understood" (1944, p. 79). Even this problematic passage, however, contains a cultural logic when it is viewed from an emic perspective that acknowledges the profoundly civilizing power of the Dakota kinship system within traditional camp life. As Deloria (1944) describes it, the ultimate aim of this functional scheme of life was to obey kinship rules—to be a good relative—for in that attainment resided civilized human behavior and social harmony. Thus, as in Mourning Dove's indigenous cosmology, the principle of sharing as a function of kinship and communal well-being would have been entirely logical to Deloria's Dakota people. Kinship accounted for the meeting of minds that made potential relatives out of strangers; it guaranteed kindness and unselfishness; it created a balance of social coercion and tolerance. Systems of biological and social kinship included everyone in a great Ring of Relatives and ensured a sense of stability. "Be related, somehow," Deloria (1944) wrote, "to everyone you know; make him important to you; he also is a man" (p. 49).

Deloria (1944) includes in her description of this functional communal life a discussion of complementary gender roles, education, spirituality, and economics, justifying as natural her desire to show the best of the traditional past. When she speaks about post-contact experience, she describes the "new order" as a storm, a black curtain "screening out the declining sun" (p. 78), a "surprise attack" (p. 79) that caught people unprepared. She lists the slaughter of the buffalo, the battle with Custer, the killing of Sitting Bull, and Wounded Knee as the "decisive blows," the "death-dealing shafts hurled into Teton-Dakota life, the final reasons for change" (p. 79). This is not equivocal language.

Yet as both anthropologist and Dakota woman, Deloria (1944) appears to view her own simultaneous identities as necessarily equivocal. She counts herself among a people "used to accepting fate with fortitude and dignity" (p. 84), but this cultural characteristic is mediated by a highly charged historical moment—the height of World War II, with its dramatically accelerating social change and propulsion into an unpredictable future. Ultimately, she uses her opportunity to speak from both the outside and the inside to call for sympathetic understanding by non-Natives, but also to argue that Indian people must be stakeholders in the coming postwar era. Using the power of both voices, she suggests the cultural logic of a system of progress that builds upon traditional loyalties and autonomy motivated by the powerful appeal to tribehood.

At about the same time that Deloria was publishing the ethnological analysis *Speaking of Indians* (1944), which linked the traditional camp circle to contemporary Dakota experience, she also was working on an expanded narrative recreating camp-circle life. Although she apparently had completed a draft by 1944 and submitted the manuscript to several publishers in the years following the war (DeMallie, 1988, p. 241), it was rejected because of fears about the lack of a large enough readership to ensure profitability. *Waterlily* was finally published in 1988 and reprinted 2 years later in an edition that "reproduces the manuscript in its entirety" (Deloria, 1988, p. xi), with apparently minimal changes designed to reduce redundancies and outdated phrases "out of keeping with the tone of the story" (Deloria, 1988, p. xi). The text itself is followed by a brief biographical sketch by Agnes Picotte (1988) and an afterword by Raymond DeMallie (1988), who suggests that its most interesting feature is the "blurring" of categories of ethnographic description with fictional methodology (p. 241). In fact, DeMallie asserts that one way to understand *Waterlily* may be as an anthropological "experiment with the medium of fiction as an effective way of explicating ethnographic fact" (p. 243).

More significant from a Native point of view, however, is how distanced *Waterlily* (1988) is from the mediating influences that marked *Speaking of Indians* (1944), and how, as a result, the narrative functions within Dakota storytelling tradition. Locating her narrative in a primarily ahistorical moment, Deloria is emancipated from conversations of modernity, assimilation, or the other framing components of cultural transaction that marked the earlier book. Reworking and expanding information about kinship and traditional community interactions first presented in *Speaking of Indians* (1944), in *Waterlily* Deloria (1988) foregrounds story rather than ethnographic analysis.

Since literary closure is not a conventional feature of American Indian storytelling—since, in fact, "the end of a story may . . . be thought of as a pause" (Rice, 1992, p. 175)—there is an internal cultural coherence rather than redundancy in the telling and retelling undertaken by both Deloria and Mourning Dove. As Robert Warrior (1995) correctly asserts, Deloria is engaged "in the recovery of Native intellectual traditions. . . . In this function, her work is similar to that of Mourning Dove" (p. 24). A remarkable aspect of *Waterlily* (1988)—true as well for Mourning Dove's "autobiography"—is that this process of recovery is enabled by re-creation of domestic social relations rather than by more familiar domains emphasizing warrior leadership or subsistence processes.

Deloria's particular vantage in this text is as uncontended insider—a Dakota woman writing about the mostly undisrupted social experience of Dakota camp life only a generation or two earlier. The storytelling form and her assumption of the role of storyteller allow her to establish a virtually unmediated authority deriving from the manner in which her narrative illuminates four culturally particular Dakota virtues: generosity and sharing; bravery; fortitude; and wisdom. These are, in fact, ongoingly resonant properties of tribal life for many Native people. Deloria shows these properties to be integrated inextricably throughout all aspects of personal, societal, and ceremonial practice, revealing them by means of stories about the unfolding lives of Waterlily and her interwoven biological and social kinship families. They are universally inclusive, applying to and acknowledged by both men and women and by all age groups, and demonstrated by people's behavior and by the values and structures that undergird Dakota communality. She writes, "The measuring and valuing of self was only possible in camp-circle life. . . . Thus only did people learn to be responsible for and to each other and themselves" (p. 216).

Personal and collective generosity, bravery, fortitude, and wisdom are modeled instructively at every point of the narrative—in childbirth, the socialization and education of children, courtship and marriage, social and spiritual ceremonial practice, gender and generational relationships, in good times and disastrous ones. Deloria's emic voice is consistent and essentially unmediated, guiding contemporary reader/listeners toward cultural comprehension and acceptance while presenting an alternative to what historian Vine Deloria, Jr. (1985) has called the "chaotic and extreme individualism" (p. 20) offered by White society. In *Waterlily* (1988) Deloria is not only speaking of Indians, she is speaking to them—about the present and future as well as the past.

RECOVERING CULTURAL AUTHORITY: IMPLICATIONS FOR TRANSFORMATIVE TEACHING AND LEARNING

"The success or failure of American Indian communal societies has always been predicated not upon a set of uniform, unchanging beliefs, but rather upon a commitment to the groups and the groups' futures" (Warrior, 1995, p. xx). This commitment undergirds the writing of Mourning Dove and Ella Deloria. Their objective is not merely to gain the sympathy of White audiences; they transcend the desire to leave behind a record of a dying way of life. Both reveal a usable past, a "scheme of life that worked" (Deloria, 1944, p. 24), and by articulating the functional components of their traditional cultures, they illuminate the potential for a regenerative American Indian—and American—present and future. Ultimately, their work is contemporarily functional when it speaks clearly and authentically to multiple audiences, Native and non-Native. In the classroom setting, however, this can occur only when teachers and learners are willing to engage themselves in the ongoing processes and effort of reconstructing knowledge—specifically here, of identifying the presence, forms, and consequences of authorial/editorial mediation, of delving into the historical, cultural, political, and creative *contexts* that produced the *texts*, and subsequently being responsive to cultural authority.

Without such a reconstruction, one outcome is that the voices of Mourning Dove, Deloria, and the many other writers and scholars who have struggled to become producers of useful knowledge about their own and their cultures' experience are silenced or distorted. Beyond the unacceptable consequences of such a loss for American Indian people and other nondominant groups, an educational setting that does not take into account the relational dynamics of inquiry risks that its students may never develop the analytical skills necessary to understand that knowledge, like culture itself, is a "process that resists any final summation" (Clifford & Marcus, 1986, p. 16). In the transformative classroom, strategies of teaching and learning address the dynamic and transactional character of what and how we know, by (1) illuminating context and purpose; (2) examining relationships of power; (3) clarifying the complex interactions of sometimes contending authorities; and, in instances in which culturally grounded materials are involved, (4) giving credit to emic interpretations (Medicine, 1980).

Even within this more accurate frame of understanding, the work of Mourning Dove and Ella Deloria represents no final word in the proliferating "interplay of voices and positional utterances" (Clifford & Marcus, 1986, p. 12) of cultural discourse. The power of transformative knowledge, certainly not contained within the classroom, inevitably and naturally derives from the communities and contexts in which people live. Optimally, however, students may become empowered participants in this interplay, better prepared to recognize and respond to representations that reinscribe stereotypes and chronicle American Indian experience as merely "part of the recurrent effort of Whites to understand themselves" (Berkhofer, 1978, p. 111). In an educational environment of more informed and equitable transaction among contemporary America's many participant cultures, Mourning Dove and Ella Deloria have the best chance of finally speaking for themselves.

REFERENCES

Banks, J. A. (1995). The historical reconstruction of knowledge about race: Implications for transformative teaching. *Educational Researcher, 24* (2), 15-25.

Berkhofer, R. F., Jr. (1978). *The White man's Indian*. New York: Vintage Books.

Bevis, W. (1987). Native American novels: Homing in. In B. Swann & A. Krupat (Eds.), *Recovering the word* (pp. 580-620). Berkeley: University of California Press.

Boas, F., & Deloria, E. (1941). *Dakota grammar: Memoirs of the National Academy of Science* (Vol. 22). Washington, DC: U.S. Government Printing Office.

Brown, A. K. (1993). Looking through the glass darkly: The editorialized Mourning Dove. In A. Krupat (Ed.), *New voices in Native American literary criticism* (pp. 274-290). Washington, DC: Smithsonian Institution Press.

Clifford, J., & Marcus, G. E. (Eds.). (1986). *Writing culture: The poetics and politics of ethnography*. Berkeley: University of California Press.

Deloria, E. (1944). *Speaking of Indians*. New York: Friendship Press.

Deloria, E. (1988). *Waterlily*. Lincoln: University of Nebraska Press.

Deloria, V., Jr. (1985). Out of chaos. *Parabola, 10* (2), 14-22.

DeMallie, R. J. (1988). Afterword. In E. Deloria, *Waterlily* (pp. 233-244). Lincoln: University of Nebraska Press.

Erdrich, L. (1984). *Love medicine.* New York: Bantam Books.

Fisher, D. (1981). Introduction. In Mourning Dove's *Cogewea the half-blood* (pp. v–xxix). Lincoln: University of Nebraska Press.

hooks, b. (1990). Saving Black folk culture: Zora Neale Hurston as anthropologist and writer. In *Yearning: Race, gender, and cultural politics* (pp. 135–143). Boston: South End Press.

Medicine, B. (1980). Ella C. Deloria: The emic voice. *MELUS,* 7 (4) 23–30.

Miller, J. (1989). Mourning Dove: The author as cultural mediator. In J. A. Clifford (Ed.), *Being and becoming Indian: Biographical studies of North American frontiers* (pp. 160–182). Chicago: Dorsey Press.

Momaday, S. (1968). *House made of dawn.* New York: Harper & Row.

Mourning Dove. (1981). *Cogewea the half-blood.* Lincoln: University of Nebraska Press. (Original work published 1927)

Mourning Dove. (1990). *Coyote stories* (H. D. Guie, Ed.). Lincoln: University of Nebraska Press. (Original work published 1934)

Mourning Dove. (1990). *Mourning Dove: A Salishan autobiography* (J. Miller, Ed.). Lincoln: University of Nebraska Press.

Murray, D. (1991). *Forked tongues: Speech, writing and representation in North American Indian texts.* Bloomington: Indiana University Press.

Owens, L. (1992). *Other destinies: Understanding the American Indian novel.* Norman: University of Oklahoma Press.

Picotte, A. (1988). Biographical sketch of the Author. In E. Deloria, *Waterlily* (pp. 229–231). Lincoln: University of Nebraska Press.

Pratt, M. L. (1992). *Imperial eyes: Travel writing and transculturation.* New York: Routledge.

Rice, J. (1992). *Deer women and elk men.* Albuquerque: University of New Mexico Press.

Silko, L. M. (1977). *Ceremony.* New York: Penguin.

Warrior, R. A. (1995). *Tribal secrets: Recovering American Indian intellectual traditions.* Minneapolis: University of Minnesota Press.

CHAPTER 9

Constructing the "Oriental Problem" in American Thought, 1920–1960

HENRY YU

This chapter examines the history of the "Oriental problem" as an intellectual and institutional construction in America, beginning with the Survey of Race Relations in the Pacific in 1924 and ending with its demise during the 1960s (Bulmer, 1984; Matthews, 1977). As I have argued in *Thinking About Orientals* (Yu, 1995), the "Oriental problem" had a profound effect on definitions of race and culture in America. In this chapter, I will describe more specifically how a number of American social scientists came to be interested in Chinese and Japanese immigrants, how they tried to understand their place within American society, and how their theories about "Orientals" affected the self-identities of the Chinese and Japanese American intellectuals who helped research the "Oriental problem."

Terms, definitions, and theories that sociologists at the University of Chicago originally formulated to understand the experiences of people they had defined as "Orientals" in the United States often were used by Chinese and Japanese American scholars to understand themselves and their own roles in American society. In particular, Chinese and Japanese American scholars seized the role offered to them by the Chicago sociologists as valued interpreters occupying the margin between "Oriental" and White Americans. Intellectuals who were categorized as "Orientals" used sociology as a powerful tool for analyzing the difficulties that Asian immigrants had suffered in the United States, but they also used sociological theories as a language for expressing their own existential situations. Since relatively little research was conducted on Asian immigrants during most of the twentieth century (in comparison, for instance, to studies of African Americans or European immigrants), the

Chicago sociologists' definition of the "Oriental problem" dominated thinking about Asians in America.

The term "Oriental" had a long history before American social scientists appropriated it to describe the Chinese and Japanese on the West Coast. From medieval European descriptions of Islamic enemies through eighteenth- and nineteenth-century European categorizations of the "Near" and "Far East," the definitions of who and what was "Oriental" have said much about the European need to create a monolithic "Other" whose description defines and orders the self-conception and identity of Europe (Said, 1979). As Edward Said points out in *Orientalism*, the "Oriental" category speaks more about those who have defined the Orient than about those who purportedly are being defined.

Even before the Chicago sociologists came to study Asian immigrants on the Pacific coast in the 1920s, the term *Oriental* was used to refer to American immigrants from China and Japan. Racial nativists, who campaigned for an America centered around native-born White Protestants, and labor organizers (agitating against Chinese immigrants in the 1860s and 1870s and Japanese immigrants in the 1890s and 1900s) both had lumped the Chinese and Japanese together as "Orientals" (Chan, 1991; Saxton, 1971). Protestant missionaries, often allies to the Asian immigrants, also had mirrored the nativists' characterization of the Far East as an exotic locale completely foreign and opposite to all that was American.

Robert Park did not invent the term *Oriental* to describe Asians in America. He did, however, create a specific definition that constructed certain meanings for the existence of Asians in the United States. Because Chicago sociologists such as Park, Emory Bogardus, Roderick McKenzie, and William Carlson Smith defined the "Oriental problem" as the shared experiences of Chinese and Japanese in being excluded from the White experience of successful assimilation, they further reinforced a lumping together of Chinese and Japanese under the rubric of "Orientals." For most of the twentieth century, almost any analysis of Asian immigrants began with the question of Oriental assimilation. The intellectual construction of the "Oriental problem" categorized and defined Asian immigrants in America, and its legacy would continue through the rise of Asian American consciousness movements and to the present day.

THE SURVEY OF RACE RELATIONS AND THE "ORIENTAL PROBLEM," 1924–1926

In the summer of 1923, the Institute of Social and Religious Research, a philanthropic organization in New York City that had funded many reform-minded social research projects, began looking into the feasibility of conducting a research survey investigating the "race problems" on the West Coast of the United States. By the end of the year, the Institute had committed $25,000 for a Survey of Race Relations on the Pacific coast to be conducted in 1924–1925 and had appointed as research director, Robert Ezra Park, the most prominent figure in American sociology since he joined the faculty of the University of Chicago in 1913. As director of the survey, Park constructed the problem to be studied, directed the lines of inquiry, and recruited researchers from every prominent university on the Pacific coast. The survey, as originally envisioned by the Institute, was intended to be an all-encompassing project, setting out to examine every aspect of what the missionaries termed the "Oriental problem." As Eliot Mears (1925), executive secretary of the survey, wrote in a press release:

> Is there an Oriental Problem in America? If so, where is it? What are its manifestations? What do we know of our Chinese, East Indians, Filipinos, and Japanese? How do they contribute to our wealth and welfare? To what extent are our impressions in accordance with the facts? These are some of the questions which The Survey of Race of Relations is trying to answer. (p. 1)

At the beginning, the Institute, which originally had conceived the survey, and the sociologists who were brought in as researchers disagreed not only about what exactly was meant by the phrase "Oriental problem," but also about the ultimate purpose of the survey. A large number of former Protestant missionaries to Japan and China staffed the Institute of Social and Religious Research, and many were still actively involved in either domestic or YMCA International mission projects. The fund-raising staff of the survey, who often doubled as research field workers, were drawn heavily from existing YMCA networks on the West Coast, and they as well as almost all of the missionaries were highly sympathetic to the plight of Asian immigrants in America. Prominent clergymen associated with the Institute in New York, such as the Reverend Sidney Gulick of the Federation of the Churches of Christ in America, had long-standing connections to missions among Asians and had been the most vocal champions of Asian immigrants against the series of anti-Asian laws that culminated in the 1924 exclusionary acts passed by Congress.

For the missionaries, the "Oriental problem" was the prejudice and misunderstandings of Whites concerning "Orientals," and the purpose of the survey was to lessen this problem. The religious activists clearly believed that once the truth about the lives and contributions of Asian immigrants in the United States was known, understanding and a lessening of anti-Asian feeling could be promoted.

For Robert Park and his team of sociologists, the purpose of the survey ended strictly with the goal of finding out more about "Orientals," and indeed the knowledge gathered would be categorized according to their own research questions and methodologies. Theories about assimilation, race relations, and social organization, all phenomena strictly defined by them, ordered their analysis of the relations between "Orientals" and Whites. The divisive and polarized political debate on the West Coast concerning the presence of Asians was an interesting phenomenon in itself and worthy of study, but mitigating conflicts was not one of the goals of the sociologists. Park remarked that he had been brought in

> to answer questions . . . that were then the subject of discussion in the newspa-
> pers and in individual groups of people interested in social politics all over the
> state. However, I was convinced in my own mind, no matter how these ques-
> tions were answered, it would not alter very greatly the existing relations between
> the Oriental and the Occidental population. (quoted in Raushenbush, 1979,
> p. 107)

Park's pessimism about the ameliorative effects of the survey were connected with his pessimism about the effectiveness of planned moral reform.
The role of sociology was not the improvement of society; indeed, Park often
professed a deep-felt distaste for the motives of do-gooders:

> The first thing you have to do with a student who enters sociology is to show
> him that he can make a contribution if he doesn't try to improve anybody. . . .
> The trouble with our sociology in America is that it has had so much to do with
> churches and preachers. . . . The sociologist cannot condemn some people and
> praise others. (quoted in Raushenbush, 1979, p. 97)

Before 1924 the discussions about "Orientals" in the United States (po-
lemic, academic, or both) had been dominated by the political issue of anti-
Asian legislation—in other words, by the incendiary "yellow peril" tracts of
nativists and the moral discourse of the missionaries who opposed them. With
the passing of the 1924 immigration legislation excluding Asians, the issue of
whether to allow Asian immigration lost much of its significance, and along
with it faded the dominant terms for debate concerning "Orientals." The newly
emerging social science definitions of the "Oriental problem" were thus left
as the language for discussing Asians in America.

As the survey proceeded, Park and his researchers worked hard to define
the "Oriental problem" from the perspectives of their own research interests,
using theories and concepts that Park had developed earlier while researching European immigration to the East Coast, as well as newer theories that
the researchers developed directly from their work on the Chinese and Japanese. The theoretical questions and concepts developed during this time
would define the "Oriental problem" within American sociology for the next
30 years.

Robert Park's interest in race relations and immigration was long-standing. Before joining the University of Chicago, he had worked for years as Booker T. Washington's press secretary at Tuskegee Institute and had worked on an extensive study of American immigration. In Park's then recently completed book on American immigration, *Old World Traits Transplanted* (Park & Miller, 1921), he and his colleague William I. Thomas had used Thomas's conceptions of the disorganization and reorganization of immigrant communities to survey the progress, or lack of progress, toward Americanization of all the major groups who had recently migrated to the United States (Park & Miller, 1921). (Thomas did not appear as one of the authors of the study because of a scandal that led to his dismissal from the University of Chicago.) Interestingly, Park and Thomas had conducted most of the study in New York's Lower East Side, lending the work a marked leaning toward Eastern European immigration, and although a chapter on Japanese immigrants had been included in *Old World Traits Transplanted*, it was based almost wholly on data from previously published sources. The Pacific Coast Survey offered Park an opportunity to see race relations on the West Coast firsthand and to apply his knowledge of European immigration and Southern race relations to Asian immigration.

One of the most important of the theoretical frameworks that Park brought to the survey was the interaction cycle, also called the immigrant, the race relations, or the assimilation cycle, which Park and Thomas had developed and applied in the *Old World Traits Transplanted* project. Park asserted that any two well-ordered cultures or groups coming into contact, for instance, immigrant groups with "native stock" Americans, would undergo a similar series of social interactions and changes: competition, conflict, accommodation, and assimilation. This natural process began with competition, the bedrock of Chicago theories of social interaction and a holdover legacy from American sociology's social Darwinist roots. As groups competed economically for limited resources (jobs, land, or status), the competition between them, which heretofore might not have been conscious, transformed into a declared conflict between the self-conscious groups. Park emphasized that the groups were defined as and turned into communities by this conflict. The accommodation stage occurred whenever one of the groups won the conflict or, more commonly, some mitigation of the conflict was achieved; for instance, one of the groups withdrew into a ghetto or accepted a subordinate economic status and avoided competitive situations.

Assimilation, the natural end to the cycle, was inevitable as groups communicated and began to share memories, experiences, and histories; social intercourse was virtually unavoidable, and the mixing of disparate peoples was the rule rather than the exception. Successful nations invariably were the result of the inevitable assimilation of heretofore separate social groups.

As Park (1928/1950) would later write, translating his understanding of America into that of the world: "Every nation, upon examination, turns out to have been a more or less successful melting-pot" (p. 346).

The questions that Park had brought from *Old World Traits Transplanted* to the West Coast race relations survey involved the progress of "Orientals" in this assimilation cycle. If the assimilation cycle was inevitable as a natural process, then why was there such a widespread assumption that "Orientals" were unassimilable? Were they in fact assimilating? And if they were not, what was holding them back? Something had jammed the natural cycle, and it was up to the sociologists to find out what or who it was. In Park and Burgess's *Introduction to the Science of Sociology* (1921), the so-called green bible of the Chicago sociologists (named for the textbook's distinctively colored binding), Park had connected the situation of the Japanese not only with that of the Chinese in America, but also with race relations in the South (Park & Burgess, 1921):

> The chief obstacle to the assimilation of the Negro and the Oriental are not mental but physical traits. It is not because the Negro and the Japanese are so differently constituted that they do not assimilate. If they were given an opportunity, the Japanese are quite as capable as the Italians, the Armenians, or the Slavs of acquiring our culture and sharing our national ideals. The trouble is not with the Japanese mind but with the Japanese skin. The Jap is not the right color.
>
> The fact that the Japanese bears in his features a distinctive racial hallmark, that he wears, so to speak, a racial uniform, classifies him. He cannot become a mere individual, indistinguishable in the cosmopolitan mass of the population, as is true, for example, of the Irish, and, to a less extent, of some of the other immigrant races. The Japanese, like the Negro, is condemned to remain among us an abstraction, a symbol—and a symbol not merely of his own race but of the Orient and of that vague, ill-defined menace we sometimes refer to as the "yellow peril." This not only determines to a very large extent the attitude of the White world toward the yellow man but it determines the attitude of the yellow man toward the White. It puts between the races the invisible but very real gulf of self-consciousness. (p. 761)

It was awareness of physical difference that led to distinctions among races. Consciousness of some boundary called *race* led to prejudice, but since prejudice could be overcome only by the sharing of experiences and memories, producing the empathy and understanding that characterized assimilation as defined by Park, the isolation caused by prejudice cut off communication, producing yet more isolation and prejudice. Isolation was thus a dead-end result defying the interaction cycle.

The inability of "Orientals," no matter how much effort they expended, to achieve the last step of the assimilation cycle because of race-consciousness among Whites and the resulting feelings among "Orientals" of exclusion and inferiority became one of the main aspects of the "Oriental problem" as outlined by Park. This conscious linking of immigration questions involving assimilation with theories about race relations in general was to be Park's signature contribution to American theories of race and ethnicity, and it would form the basis of sociological research on "Orientals" for the next 3 decades.

The first step Park took in organizing the survey was to set up a team of social scientists to coordinate the research. All the prominent universities on the West Coast were represented on the research team and, remarkably, all but one of the local research directors were Chicago graduates. Emory Bogardus, professor and later long-standing chairman of the sociology department at the University of Southern California, had received his doctorate from Chicago in 1911. William Carlson Smith, also at USC, had just completed his doctorate at Chicago in 1920. Roderick McKenzie of the University of Washington was a recent student of Park's and had received his degree from Chicago in 1921. The researchers' close ties to Chicago were not altogether surprising, since the sociology department at Chicago had been the first in the country and remained one of the most renowned institutions for graduate studies. Park naturally recruited his own or his Chicago colleagues' former students, many of whom were now members of fledgling sociology departments around the country. The stature of the Chicago department in the first half of the twentieth century helps explain how the Chicago sociologists' definitions of the "Oriental problem" extended far beyond their own immediate circle.

One of the important legacies of the Survey of Race Relations and the Chicago sociologists' involvement in it was the emphasis on the Chinese and Japanese as the constituent representation of the "Oriental" type. The boundaries of the "Oriental problem" originally had been broadly conceived to include Chinese, Japanese, Filipino, East Indian, and even Mexican immigrants (obviously reflecting the central importance of labor conflicts within political debates about Oriental immigration). By the time the Chicago sociologists had defined their perspective on the "Oriental problem," attention had become focused mainly on the Chinese and Japanese. The reasons for this were almost entirely institutional—the missionaries who helped set up the survey had connections to the Chinese and Japanese Christian associations on the West Coast, and, just as important, there simply were more Chinese and Japanese immigrant institutions (newspapers, Chinese Benevolent Associations, Japanese Associations, Chinese and Japanese student groups) at the time. The informants available to the survey were invariably direct products of institutional ties, and thus the amount of information on Chinese and

Japanese immigrants dominated the survey's data. Park himself was particularly interested in the role of immigrant institutions in the process of assimilation, and thus furthered the importance of institutions in the research. It became common to consider the Chinese and Japanese as typical "Orientals," and this practice was perpetuated by the Chicago school's continuing definition of the two groups as being representative of the "Oriental problem" in America.

The intellectual construction of the "Oriental problem" involved not only the delineation of a set of questions, problems, and assumptions deemed to be interesting and worth researching, but also certain ideas about a proper method of investigation and a certain language for presenting both the questions and the findings. The most important step toward achieving a coherent research program was the rigid adherence to standardized terms and definitions. Emory Bogardus (1936), one of the principal research heads, later described the problems the sociologists had with maintaining definitions and with disciplining research workers into the Chicago school's understandings of social interaction:

> The Pacific Coast Race Relations Survey in 1924 had not proceeded far before it was evident that different research workers were using even common terms, such as race, community, competition, in different ways, and hence were misunderstanding each other. Moreover, the layman used the same terms in his own and still different ways. Thus, the determination of a careful, accurate, and basic usage of terms is a minimum essential. (p. 11)

For Park and his Chicago-trained colleagues, there may have been little difficulty keeping terms straight, but for many of those under their direction who were actually researching and collecting the materials for the survey, the widely disparate conceptions of commonly employed terms became a methodological nightmare. This confusion of tongues highlighted the need for researchers who were trained in the language of Chicago sociology and its research methodology. Unlike many previous research surveys, which had relied on social workers or church networks to supply volunteers, the sociologists turned to university students to answer their need for amenable, disciplined researchers.

During the survey, the University of Washington and the University of Southern California became the focal points for a distinctive kind of research that was becoming the hallmark of Chicago sociological studies: the collecting of life-histories. The subjects of these life-histories were "Orientals," or people who had had contact with "Orientals." It was "attitudes" that Park and his researchers were interested in, especially the underlying social forces that had led to the formation of these attitudes. Park came up with a series of questionnaires that were designed to elicit extensive answers revealing a person's attitudes about other races, assimilation, intermarriage, and other subjects in which the sociologists were interested. The gathering of the hundreds of life-histories for the survey involved several dozen university students, and it created a need for translators to bridge the linguistic gap between the researchers and the many non-English-speaking subjects.

The need for such help was revealed by such instances as the project of an undergraduate named Ruth M. Fowler, who in January 1925 tried to conduct for her Economics 203 course at Stanford University a study of Japanese immigrants' food consumption patterns in San Jose and Santa Clara counties. The intrepid surveyor designed an elaborate form that asked the subjects to detail what they had eaten at each meal for a month, as well as an inventory of weekly food purchases and their costs. The extraordinary thing is not that Fowler received a paltry number of her surveys back in the end, but that any were returned at all, considering the language barriers and the amount of work her survey entailed.

"Oriental" interpreters were at a premium. In June 1924, both William Smith and Robert Park had requested money to hire people to help translate from Japanese, Chinese, and Filipino newspapers, as well as to interview for life-histories. In the end, the survey relied heavily on students who were of Chinese or Japanese heritage for informants; one such person was Flora Belle Jan, an 18-year-old American-born Chinese student and aspiring writer who had been educated in American schools and occasionally wrote for newspapers in her hometown of Fresno, as well as for the *San Francisco Examiner.*

Flora Jan is an excellent illustration of the position in which Asian Americans involved in the Survey of Race Relations were placed. Not only did they help the survey researchers gather data, but they also were at all times subjects for the survey: Flora Jan became an exemplar, for many of the researchers, of an assimilated Chinese. Park wrote to William Thomas that Jan was "the most emancipated girl I have ever met. Clever, sophisticated, Americanized," and J. Merle Davis, the executive secretary of the survey, reported to Park that she was the "only Oriental in town . . . who has the charm, wit and nerve to enter good White society" (Raushenbush, 1979, p. 113). Winifred Raushenbush, Park's personal research assistant, became particularly enamored with Flora Belle Jan, singling her out in a report in 1925 as an example that "assimilation is going on," as well as mentioning Jan in her own book about Park written 50 years later.

In the decades following the end of the survey, the position of Chinese and Japanese American students as inside observers—the studier as well as the studied—became a recurring role as Chicago sociologists maintained an interest in the "Oriental problem" and a string of graduate students with Asian backgrounds entered the Chicago department.

KNOWLEDGE AND SELF-IDENTITY: THE MARGINAL MAN THEORY AND ASIAN AMERICAN INTELLECTUALS

Between 1924 and 1960, approximately 20 graduate students in the departments of sociology and anthropology at the University of Chicago worked on topics dealing with Asians in the United States and Hawaii. Most were themselves of Chinese or Japanese background, either having come from China for college or having been born in America of immigrant parents. They came from a variety of social, family, and economic backgrounds: Several were from landed gentry in China or Japan; one was the son of a laundryman in the United States; another was the daughter of a merchant importing Chinese goods to Montana. There were five women among the group, and one of them, Rose Hum Lee, went on to become the first woman in the country to head a sociology department (further information on Rose Hum Lee, perhaps the most fascinating and revealing of the sociologists, may be found in Yu, 1995). After completing their doctoral dissertations or master's theses, the students went on to a variety of careers, usually academia and social work; one became a movie actress. They came from and went to different places, but they all had one thing in common when they were at Chicago—they researched some aspect of "Orientals" in America.

The students may have come to the University of Chicago from other lives, and after they left they may have gone on to do other things, but for the time they were at the Chicago sociology department, the "Oriental problem," as it was defined by the sociologists, allowed the students to speak about certain things in a certain way to a certain audience. Chicago sociologists often used the image of a theatrical stage as a metaphor for social interaction, and it is interesting how the "Oriental" students who became researchers within American social science found within the role of social scientist a powerful way to understand their place in American society.

For those researchers of the "Oriental problem" who were not of Asian ancestry, their work on the "Oriental problem" was purely in the role of researcher. They may have had a deep interest in their research for personal reasons, or it may have come out of a constellation of arbitrary factors, but rhetorically their self-identities remained fairly uninvolved in their research. Indeed, the social scientists' ideal of neutral, detached analysis encouraged the furthest emotional distance between the object of study and the studier. For Asian American students, the ideal of detachment from the subject remained the same, but for many of them, the role of studier often was intimately connected with their sense of self-identity, since they were also being asked to play the role of the studied, to be an "Oriental." The position of the "Oriental" researcher as both studier and studied provides an example of how the social science project of studying the "Oriental problem" constructed dual roles for the Asian American researchers involved. In their roles as researchers, they could identify, and be identified, with their other role as "Orientals" in ways which non-Asian researchers never would.

As much as the Chinese and Japanese American students were in demand for the utility of the skills that sociologists associated with their "Oriental" identity (i.e., their knowledge of languages and also their ability to enter as insiders the Chinatowns and Japantowns that were perceived as social spaces with barriers erected against outsiders), their specific identification with the communities or social groups they studied was always downplayed within the rhetoric of their writings. Since it was important to avoid even the hint of bias on the part of the sociologist, within the texts that most successfully achieved the genre of the sociological monograph, the identity of the studier was erased. In contrast, the ideal of neutral analysis never forced non-Asians to extend their worries about bias all the way to issues over their own identity—that a sociologist studying the "Oriental problem" may have been sixth-generation Pennsylvania Dutch never entered into questions of the objectivity of his or her analysis. For Chinese and Japanese American sociologists, there was an uncomfortable tension because their identity as a member of the studied group was both a detriment and a bonus. This tension over the effects and value of "Oriental" identity extended far beyond issues of impartiality.

Some of the most interesting effects of the students' work on the "Oriental problem" were the ways in which the sociological theories they learned and then espoused came to engage their self-identities (the actors taking to heart their own speeches, so to speak). The best example, perhaps, was the role of the marginal man. The theoretical concept of the marginal man, borrowed from German social scientist Georg Simmel's conception of the stranger and retooled by Robert Park, held a special resonance for many University of Chicago scholars with immigrant backgrounds—Asian, Jewish, Eastern and Southern European—because it seemed to mirror the perception that many intellectuals held of being "caught between two worlds." The theory served as a language of discontent that named, and reified, internal conflicts between perceived American and traditional traits. But not only did concepts such as the marginal man serve the scholars as descriptive expressions of personal situations, they helped to embed social phenomena in a larger theoretical framework that suggested greater ramifications and possible solutions.

In his article "Human Migration and the Marginal Man," published soon after the end of the Survey of Race Relations, Park (1928/1950) gave his fullest description of the ramifications of what he termed *mobility*, a term that encompassed not only the physical movements of peoples, but also the attendant social effects. In a process analogous to Ferdinand Tonnies's *gemeinschaft/gesellschaft* distinction, increased mobility and contact broke down traditional, well-ordered societies, producing not only changes in customs and mores, but also an emancipation of the individual. A new type of social interaction produced a new type of person. Contrary to sociological theories that had decried this breakdown in social organization (for instance, Emile Durkheim's *anomie*), Park celebrated this new social type, the "marginal man," as being freer and more creative, released from the bonds of custom and tradition. Although a price was to be paid in confusion resulting from lack of direction and control, Park had no doubt that the attendant gains in freedom and empathy, a cosmopolitan ability to move among and understand different cultures without the blinders of ethnocentrism, were more than compensatory.

As Fred Matthews (1977) noted, within the framework of Park's theories, the marginal man had an important role to play in the racial and cultural relations of the future. Robert Park's admiration for Flora Belle Jan, the Chinese American journalism student he had met through the survey, makes sense within this framework. It was not her mere emancipation from traditional Chinese society, but the ability for self-conscious appreciation of both American and Chinese values afforded her by this emancipation, that made her, for Park, an exemplar of the marginal man. She could understand both worlds and, more important, she could help each understand the other.

Park and his colleagues had brought to the Survey of Race Relations not only theoretical constructs ready to be used to interpret the natural process (and progress, since the immigrant cycle of assimilation had a normative element) of race relations on the West Coast, but also a universal context for it. For Park, the marginal man in many ways marked modernity and the future. The racial conflicts in the Pacific states were the attendant effects of human mobility and migration; on a grander scale, however, the result was the creation of a higher order of consciousness. The confrontation and negotiation between incommensurable social and cultural demands resulted in the ability to empathize with different values and beliefs, a modern and often urban cosmopolitanism. The irony was not lost on Park that this higher order of sensibility was often to be found in individuals who had been marked as outcasts or outsiders, and not among the smug Anglo-Saxons who were so often depicted as the acme of civilization. That this cosmopolitan ability to empathize with and understand diverse beliefs also marked the sociological perspective was no mere coincidence to Park—sociology was quite obviously a modern science.

Many American-born students of Chinese or Japanese ancestry explicitly saw themselves as marginal men and seized upon the theory's powerful description of marginal men as cultural translators. Shotaru Frank Miyamoto, born in Seattle in 1912, was the son of Japanese immigrants. His father, who operated a furniture business, tried hard to move his family outside the bounds of the tight-knit community of approximately 6,000 Japanese Americans in Seattle, and although Frank Miyamoto knew many of the Japanese in town, he was raised outside the geographic and social territory of Japantown. In his master's thesis in sociology at the University of Washington, Miyamoto explored what was widely regarded as the extraordinary social solidarity of the Japanese community in Seattle, a phenomenon that sociologists had speculated might have retarded the assimilation of the Japanese in America and a phenomenon that Miyamoto and his family had tried in many ways to escape.

Since the days of the Survey of Race Relations, the University of Washington's sociology department possessed a strong Chicago presence, as well as a deep research interest in the Japanese community. Roderick McKenzie, the Chicago sociologist who was at Washington during the survey, had since left the university, but he had been replaced by Jesse Steiner, a former mission teacher in Japan who had written his doctorate at Chicago about the Japanese in the United States. Steiner quickly became Miyamoto's academic advisor and mentor. Steiner encouraged Miyamoto to pursue a doctorate at Chicago, and in 1939, soon after completing his master's at Washington, Miyamoto went to the University of Chicago.

Miyamoto (1939), while describing to Ernest Burgess his life history and the reasons for his interest in sociology (Burgess had all graduate students in the introductory graduate seminar produce "background papers" as one of their first exercises), explained how his becoming a sociologist had much to do with his cultural background:

> The strongest criticism of American society which I felt as a child was concerning the matter of race prejudice. Because of my father's early desire of finding a better home than those offered in the Japanese community, our family rode at the forefront of an ecological invasion, and we took the brunt of White-American disapproval. I felt deeply the injustice of the whole affair, and naturally began searching for means by which these injustices might be removed. Thus, the problems of Japanese-American relations came to take on personal meaning for me. (p. 3)

Becoming a sociologist allowed Miyamoto to understand the social forces that had affected his youth—race prejudice resulting from the "ecological invasion" (a technical term used by Chicago sociologists) of which his family was just a small part. The science of sociology gave Miyamoto a powerful language for naming the problems of the Japanese in America, so much so that his life before becoming a sociologist could be interpreted through the theories of sociology. In a statement that showed the deep effect of the concept of the marginal man on his self-identity and memory, Miyamoto (1939) remarked how it was the circumstance of the Japanese culture being superimposed upon the American culture, vividly contrasting the two, that further stimulated my interest in social problems. It led me, at certain points, to be critical of the one or the other of the cultures, for from my particular perspective, I felt a step removed from both and no strong subjective attachment to either. In this way I was developing the attitude of detachment fundamental to the sociologist—I was becoming, in a sense, a "marginal man." (p. 3)

In his grammar school days, Miyamoto had dreamed of becoming a novelist, but like many Japanese and Chinese American students of that time, the almost nonexistent career prospects due to racial discrimination led him to a "safer" career option in college, in his case, engineering. He disliked what he felt was the cold and inhuman nature of engineering, though, and with his first exposures to sociology courses, his interests began to turn. As the "science of human society," sociology appeared to be both analytical and humanist at the same time, and, better yet, there seemed to be a genuine interest in Asian immigrants within the discipline. Miyamoto's choice to become a sociology major seemed to him at the time to be on a whim, almost by chance, but with his "increased powers as a social analyst" (p. 1) gained through training, he began to see that there had been an array of factors in his background that had determined his later interest. It was no accident that his understanding of his path toward becoming a sociologist was configured in the language of sociology.

The power that the Asian American students found in sociology had much to do with their ability to analyze and explain the larger contexts for events in their personal lives. Miyamoto used the theories and concepts of sociology to understand portions of his youth, as well as his own consciousness of being an observer unattached to any particular community. The theoretical descriptions of the marginal man engaged strongly with Miyamoto's own understandings of himself and his role in the world.

Utilizing theories of the "Oriental problem" such as the assimilation cycle and the marginal man, Asian American intellectuals could transform their understandings of themselves, but they also could remake definitions of race and culture in the United States. The theories of the "Oriental problem" had been defined by the interests of American sociology (and thus aimed to answer academic questions), but they also argued for the inclusion of Asians in American society. The research of the "Oriental problem" had left no doubt that, if allowed, Asian immigrants and second-generation, American-born Asians could assimilate American culture as well as any other immigrant group.

The description of young Asian American intellectuals as marginal men between two cultures gave them a way of understanding their role in the modern world, but the idea that Chinese and Japanese American sociologists could explain Asian communities to interested scholars led to another important result: These Asian American sociologists occupied an authoritative position as the expert voices for "Orientals" in America. The "Oriental problem" as a research project created an interest in "Oriental" Americans as objects of study, and it also produced a demand for Chinese and Japanese American students to act as interpreters for "Orientals" in America. This expert position had both its benefits and its costs. The authority and expertise granted the Chinese and Japanese sociologists allowed them to explain the difficulties and discrimination suffered by Asian communities in America, but there was also the threat of the scholars becoming so identified with the knowledge they possessed that they became "professional Orientals," listened to only if they spoke about their own subjects of expertise. In other words, they were forced to prove themselves as serious scholars by becoming knowledgeable about more than just "Orientals." If they did not, there was always the danger of being typecast—the academic equivalent of bit actors consigned to playing only small "Oriental" roles in Hollywood movies.

USING SOCIOLOGY: PAUL SIU
AND THE CHINESE LAUNDRYMAN

In being asked to study the problems of "Orientals" in America, Chinese and Japanese American sociologists could use the opportunity to detail the psychological and social damage that resulted from denying Asians inclusion into American society. Perhaps the best example of this was Chinese American sociologist Paul Chan Pang Siu. In 1953, Siu presented to the sociology department at the University of Chicago a doctoral dissertation entitled "The Chinese Laundryman: A Study of Social Isolation" (Siu, 1987). Siu had researched the bulk of his study during the 1930s—by the time he defended his Ph.D. in 1953, he was 47 years old and had spent almost 30 years of his life among Chinese workers toiling in Chicago and Boston.

The lonely existence of Chinese immigrant bachelors in the United States was a phenomenon most Americans had witnessed in small laundry shops and chop suey restaurants scattered across the country, but it fell to Paul Siu to explore and explain the lives of these men. Using Chicago sociology theories to explain what he labeled the "sojourner" mentality of Chinese male immigrants, Siu wrote the richest and most detailed portrait of Chinese America that Chicago sociologists would ever produce.

Using an abundance of colorful excerpts from Chinese laundrymen's chatting and talking about their lives, Paul Siu (1987) described the immigrants' nonidentification with American life. The Chinese men had responded to the prejudice and discrimination they encountered in America with a sojourner attitude; according to Siu, the sojourner was "an individual who clings to the heritage of his own ethnic group and lives in isolation" (p. 4). Faced with racial discrimination, and unable to have social relationships with anyone except other Chinese, ethnocentrism became a defensive measure for the Chinese laundryman: "In leisure time and social events, the Chinese have a world of their own which is based upon the social solidarity of the families, the clans, and the kinship system" (p. 138).

Laundry work, as an economic and social mode of behavior, served as the point of entry for the Chicago sociologists' understanding of the "Oriental problem" in America. Paul Siu agreed with Robert Park's earlier analysis of the Chinese as stuck in the assimilation cycle, unable to escape the dead-end result of social isolation. Chinese male workers, unable to obtain most jobs in the American labor market because of discriminatory hiring, had been forced to make the accommodation of working jobs for which they did not compete with White workers, for instance, jobs in laundries and noodle restaurants. This accommodation to racial conflict lessened the hostility that Whites felt toward the Chinese, and Siu followed Park in explaining that it also cut the Chinese off from communication with other social groups in America. What began, therefore, as an accommodation in response to racial discrimination and violence, now served to maintain the isolation of the Chinese laundry worker. He was unable to progress to the final stages of the assimilation cycle.

The inability of the Chinese to assimilate in the continental United States was the source and origin of all their social problems. Chinese laundrymen were denied a viable social life in America, so they concentrated their lives around making enough money to become rich and return to China. According to Siu, the Chinese male immigrant's goal of a triumphant journey home defined the sojourner attitude; he was a migrant, unable and unwilling to consider settling down in the United States.

Paul Siu, for a number of reasons, had difficulties acquiring the validation of institutional academia. He had conducted all the research for his laundryman project as a graduate student during the 1930s, but had been unable to complete his dissertation because of a lack of funding. Finally, after more than 15 years working as a social worker in Chicago and Boston, with the final deadline approaching and his advisors retiring, Siu was able to return in 1953 to the University of Chicago and complete his doctoral defense.

Like most of the theses and dissertations produced by Chinese and Japanese American students at the University of Chicago, Siu's study received little scholarly attention beyond the small network of sociologists interested in "Orientals." Siu's dissertation languished in the obscurity of the University of Chicago's library stacks until 1980, when historian John Kuo Wei Tchen came across the work while conducting research on Chinese laundry workers in New York. In 1987, *The Chinese Laundryman* was finally published,

34 years after it had been completed and almost 50 years after it had been researched.

The revival of Siu's thesis, strangely, indicated the wane of the theories of the "Oriental problem." The new interest in Siu's work signaled the rise of a new intellectual construction of Asian immigrants, one that validated Siu in a very different manner than the "Oriental problem" and, ironically, one that arose from an opposition to the theories of the "Oriental problem."

The creation of interdisciplinary Asian American studies programs in the 1970s was a movement that in many ways tried to distance itself from the theories and texts of the early "Oriental problem" researchers. The Asian American activists saw the Chicago school's theories on race relations and immigration, born in the 1920s, as backward and outdated, and deliberately maligned many of the earlier researchers. Many of the Chinese and Japanese American researchers who had become sociologists came under attack as proassimilationist apologists.

Robert Park, whose ideas exemplified the Chicago school's definitions of race and culture, was labeled a conservative and a racist by many Asian American activists (Takagi, 1973). In the 1920s, Park had been progressive in his attempts to move scholarship away from biological definitions of race toward social and psychological explanations for behavior. Arguing against any notion that Negroes and "Orientals" were biologically inferior, he had ascribed differences between Whites and "colored" peoples to learned cultural traditions. His notions of culture, though, could be almost as essentializing as earlier racist notions. As James A. Banks (1995) has noted, Park's ideas about the Negro in 1921 contained a conflation between biologically and socially inherited characteristics; indeed, he could still refer to the Negro as "the lady among the races" (Park, 1921). After Park's work on immigrants with W. I. Thomas, his own work on "Orientals," and his student Charles Johnson's work on the Negro in Chicago, Park's views on culture became increasingly devoid of biological fixations. Beginning in the 1920s and continuing into the 1940s, the Chicago school would come to provide the theoretical foundation for the cultural assimilation of immigrants and racial minorities. By the 1960s, of course, as more structural analyses of American society began to question the validity of the assimilation cycle, cultural assimilation was no longer seen as the solution to America's race problem but as one of its primary sources (Gordon, 1961; Lyman, 1970).

Although the historians born of the Asian American activist movement rejected much of the "Oriental problem" paradigm, they also recognized the importance of the sociologists' work. When Paul Siu's (1987) study of Chinese laundrymen was rescued from the obscurity of the archive, it was hailed for the manner in which its insider perspective reflected the genuine experience of Chinese immigrant life. The sociological analysis became secondary to the rich portrayal of laundrymen, and because Chicago sociologists were some of the only scholars to have studied Asians in the United States, their work could not be dismissed. Often, though, their studies were mined for authentic voices of Asian immigrants, as sources for firsthand quotations of Asian immigrants. The genesis of the quotations, and their path through the interpretive frameworks of Chicago sociology, went unaddressed.

The intellectual construction of the "Oriental problem," first defined in the 1920s, may have disintegrated as a coherent and cohesive framework by the 1960s, but it still left important legacies. In particular, the sociologists, by defining the "Oriental problem" as the shared experiences of Chinese and Japanese in being excluded from the White experience of successful assimilation, had continued and further reinforced a lumping together of Chinese and Japanese under the rubric of "Orientals." Ironically, this externally imposed aggregation of Chinese and Japanese Americans laid one of the foundational elements for Asian American consciousness in the 1970s, as the "Oriental" suffering from similar types of oppression was transformed from the problem of sociology to an empowering awareness of shared social and political identity.

The boundaries of who was now Asian American curiously mirrored the boundaries of who had been "Oriental." The new pan-ethnicity of Asian groups and its relationship to earlier definitions of the "Oriental" was no accident, since the newer definition was a conscious attempt to replace the pejorative and stereotypical meanings of the Orient with the neutral geographic origin of Asia. The connection between mostly Chinese and Japanese Americans initially, and among Filipino, Korean, Vietnamese, Cambodian, Thai, and South Asians in America later on, was no more natural than the rubric of "Oriental." The recently constructed nature of the term *Asian American* is sometimes forgotten these days, and exploring the historical connection between the two terms reveals much about how a specific kind of discrimination against "Orientals" during most of American history has been a foundational element for a shared sense of Asian American consciousness. In other words, the "Oriental problem" as a social definition had a great effect on how Chinese and Japanese Americans were seen, on how they saw themselves, and on how those who no longer wanted to see themselves as "Oriental" would come to redefine themselves. Considering oneself as Asian American is a different intellectual, social, and political experience from thinking of oneself as an "Oriental," but the changed definition still existed, and exists, within a world in which Asians are considered different and somehow exotic. As I have examined elsewhere (Yu, 1995), Asians are still portrayed as a unique group— a model minority that is not a problem with American immigration, but an exemplar of how it should work.

It is truly ironic that portrayals of Asian immigrants as an assimilation problem are now ellided by a focus on their seemingly phenomenal ability to overcome every obstacle thrown in their way. Indeed, Asians in America are, rhetorically, a better and better model with each listing of an obstacle overcome: Chinese Exclusion in 1882, complete exclusion of Asians in 1924, internment of Japanese Americans in 1942. The perversity of the mythology of the model minority lies in the way it glorifies the suffering of Asians in America, erasing the bitter world described by Paul Siu (1987) and transforming the poignant story he told into a generic narrative of redemption through endurance. Recent examples of Asian American economic success are cited by politicians on the right (and by many Asians themselves) as the salutary effects of being forced to overcome discrimination, as if Asians have somehow become better because of what they have suffered. The apotheosis of Asians in America is perverse precisely in the way in which it mirrors the historical denigration of "Orientals" in America. One of the legacies of the "Oriental problem" has been to single out Asians as an exemplar, whether of what is wrong with America or, strangely, what is right about what is wrong with America.

Perhaps the most interesting legacy of the "Oriental problem" in American sociology was how it gave Chinese and Japanese American intellectuals entrance into an exclusive academic world. As in much of American society in that period, the opportunity to enter academia often came at a cost. To offer to explain "Orientals" to American social scientists was at the same time to accept validation as an expert authority on "Orientals," an intellectual role that could be as limiting as the designation of "Oriental" identity that accompanied it. Who was seen to speak for whom was a judgment almost always made by sociologists interested in "Orientals" for their own reasons, and whatever opportunities to speak were offered to "Oriental" intellectuals, were strictly circumscribed. That Chinese and Japanese American sociologists used those opportunities to understand themselves and the communities that they studied has to be considered a significant accomplishment.

REFERENCES

Banks, J. A. (1995). The historical reconstruction of knowledge about race: Implications for transformative teaching. *Educational Researcher, 24* (2), 15-25.

Bogardus, E. S. (1936). *Introduction to social research.* Los Angeles: Suttonhouse.

Bulmer, M. (1984). *The Chicago School of Sociology: Institutionalization, diversity, and the rise of sociological research.* Chicago: University of Chicago Press.

Chan, S. (1991). *Asian Americans: An interpretive history.* Boston: Twayne.

Gordon, M. (1961). Assimilation in America: Theory and reality. *Daedalus, 90,* 263-285.

Lyman, S. (1970). *The Asian in the West.* Reno and Las Vegas: University of Nevada, Desert Research Institute.

Matthews, F. H. (1977). *Quest for an American sociology: Robert E. Park and the Chicago School.* Montreal: McGill University Press.

Mears, E. G. (1925). The survey of race relations. Excerpt from *The Stanford Illustrated Review.* Papers of the Survey of Race Relations. Stanford University, Hoover Institution Archives.

Miyamoto, S. F. (1939). Background paper. In Ernest W. Burgess Papers. University of Chicago, Regenstein Special Collections, Box 170, Folder 1.

Park, R. E. (1950). Human migration and the marginal man. In E. C. Hughes, C. S. Johnson, J. Masuoka, R. Redfield, & L. Wirth (Eds.), *Race and culture: The collected papers of Robert E. Park* (Vol. 1, pp. 345-356). Glencoe: Free Press. (Original work published 1928)

Park, R. E., & Burgess, E. W. (1921). *Introduction to the science of sociology.* Chicago: University of Chicago.

Park, R. E., & Miller, H. A. (1921). *Old world traits transplanted.* New York: Harper & Brothers.

Raushenbush, W. (1979). *Robert E. Park: Biography of a sociologist.* Durham, NC: Duke University Press.

Said, E. (1979). *Orientalism.* New York: Random House.

Saxton, A. (1971). *The indispensable enemy: Labor and the anti-Chinese movement in California.* Berkeley: University of California Press.

Siu, P. C. P. (1987). *The Chinese laundryman: A study of social isolation* (J. K. W. Tchen, Ed.). New York: New York University Press.

Takagi, P. (1973). The myth of assimilation in American life. *Amerasia Journal, 2,* 149-159.

Yu, H. (1995). *Thinking about Orientals: Race, migration, and modernity in twentieth-century America.* Unpublished doctoral dissertation, Princeton University.

PART III

Women Transformative Scholars and Activists

In the past, women of color have been as invisible in African American, Hispanic American, American Indian, and Asian American history as they have been in White history. Women of color have been struggling to become visible and to experience equity in U. S. society since the nation began. This title of an early book in Black women's studies encapsulates the struggle of women of color against invisibility and for inclusion: *All the Women Are White, All the Blacks Are Men, but Some of Us Are Brave* (Hull, Scott, & Smith, 1982).

The chapters in this part describe the work of women scholars and activists who challenged institutionalized and pernicious conceptions of race and who took actions to change and reform society to make it more democratic, just, and humane. In Chapter 10, Gloria Ladson-Billings describes how African American women have struggled historically against the triple oppressions of race, gender, and class. She discusses womanist exemplars of history, activism, and scholarship.

After the Civil War, the newly freed Blacks in the South were eager to learn to read and write (Anderson, 1988; Bullock, 1967). Edward Taylor, in Chapter 11, describes how African American women teachers in the North, out of a sense of duty and calling, headed South to teach the newly freed Blacks during and after the Civil War. The work of Mary McLeod Bethune, another educator who worked tirelessly because of her commitment to help uplift her people, is described in Chapter 12. The final chapter in this part, Chapter 13, describes how Eleanor Roosevelt, an influential White leader and president's wife, took risks to take stands on civil rights issues that made a difference. Roosevelt is an excellent exemplar for White cultural workers who want to become antiracists.

REFERENCES

Anderson, J. D. (1988). *The education of Blacks in the south, 1860–1935.* Chapel Hill: University of North Carolina Press.

Bullock, H. A. (1967). *A history of Negro education in the South: From 1619 to the present.* Cambridge, MA: Harvard University Press.

Hull, G. T., Scott, P. B., & Smith, B. (Eds.). (1982). *All the women are White, all the Blacks are men, but some of us are brave: Black women's studies.* Old Westbury, NY: Feminist Press.

CHAPTER 10

Lifting As We Climb: The Womanist Tradition in Multicultural Education

GLORIA LADSON-BILLINGS

> We are frequently just a sister away from our healing. We need a woman, a sister who will see in our destitution a jagged image of what one day could be her own story. We need a sister whose genuine mercy—not pity which is episodic, random, and moody—is steadfast, consistent and free.
>
> R. Weems, 1988, p. 17

Careful attention to the construction of "new knowledge" in the social sciences reveals the emergence of scholarship that addresses issues and perspectives informed by race, class, and gender (Anzaldúa, 1987; Asante, 1987; Code, 1991; Gordon, 1990; Warrior, 1995). Scholars of color have been conceptualizing alternative ways of knowing since the turn of the century (DuBois, 1903; Woodson, 1933). The legitimacy of these perspectives is growing with the increasing challenges to literary and historical canons (Gates, 1992). Every permutation of knowledge and perspective has within it additional forms. Thus, the assertion of an African American or Black perspective evokes Native American (Allen, 1986), Mexican American (Gutiérrez, 1995), Chinese American (Chan, 1991), and other ethnic and cultural perspectives (Okihiro, 1994; Takaki, 1993). Together, these perspectives may be seen as constituting a multicultural perspective. These new forms cross categorical lines and create new scholarly categories. Not only does a perspective informed by race or ethnicity exist; a perspective informed by gender is increasingly important in the arts and sciences (Bleier, 1986; Davis, 1981; MacKinnon, 1987; Maher, 1987). As if operating in parallel worlds, Black studies scholarship and femi-

nist scholarship failed to address their possible linkages in any important way
until the 1980s (Bethel & Smith, 1979; Butler, 1991; Carby, 1987; Frankenberg,
1993; Lourde, 1984). No one, male or female, Black or White, has just one
identity. How we come to understand our multiple identities provides opportunities for understanding and investigating their intersections (McCarthy,
1988). Joseph (1981) appropriately addresses the issue:

> Three women are standing before a covered mirror. At a given signal the cover
> will be removed and the following question will be put to them:
>> Mirror, mirror, on the wall,
>> What is the greatest oppressor of us all?
> The mirror is unveiled and all three see their reflections bouncing back.
>   Woman number one sees her Blackness. "It is my Blackness that is most domi-
> nant. That is what makes for my oppression. And who oppresses Blacks? Whites.
> So it is White racism that is the greatest oppressor. Yes, racism oppresses!" So
> thinks woman number one. Woman number two says, "I see myself as female,
> and as such, dominated and controlled by men. Men and their sexism oppress
> women, so sexism is the greatest oppressor of us all."
>   Woman number three observes her reflection and sees her gender, race, and
> class. "My femaleness, my color, and my class are sources of exploitation. Who
> is exploiting me? The question deserves *serious consideration* [emphasis added].
> An immediate response will not do." (p. 19)

Thus, with *serious consideration* a perspective that considers both feminists and Blacks has emerged. Pulling on both traditions and at the same time
different from both, the "womanist" perspective has developed. Novelist Alice
Walker (1984) began using the term "womanist" to describe Black feminists
who were courageous women committed to whole people, both men and
women. This chapter discusses the historical and intellectual intersections
of the womanist tradition within both White feminism and multicultural
education.

Historical evidence suggests that African American women have grappled
with issues of race and gender since their arrival in the Americas (Giddings,
1984; Lerner, 1972). However, more recently, African American women have
worked toward defining the special characteristics of both racial and sexual
oppression and experiences. This work is best expressed in womanist scholarship (Collins, 1990; Joseph, 1981).

In the first section of this chapter I discuss the importance and power of
self-definition (and self-determination) in the development of womanist scholarship. I also discuss the tensions between feminist and womanist scholarship and those between Black studies and womanist studies. I conclude this
section by arguing for the legitimacy of a womanist scholarly tradition as a
unique, yet complementary, aspect of multicultural education.

In the second section of this chapter, I use three categories—*history*, *activism*, and *scholarship*—to introduce specific African American women as examples of the womanist tradition. Although I have selected particular Black women as examples in each category, this does not imply that they do not fit into others. However, because of space limitations, it is necessary to make selective (and personal) judgments about how examples might best be used.

History is important because without it we lose the ability to depict ourselves as actors in our own and others' lives. We lack perspective and point of view without our own history. The second category, activism, is used to detail the front-line role Black women have played in struggles against racism and sexism. Not merely "supporters," Black women have played an important role in defining and shaping the course of social justice in the United States (Hine, 1990; Lerner, 1972; Sterling, 1984). Finally, scholarship provides us with an opportunity to document the history and activism of Black women, while at the same time allowing us to create new paradigms and ways of knowing.

The chapter concludes with a discussion of the linkages that exist between the womanist and multicultural traditions. I suggest that although multicultural education is greater than the sum of its parts, the womanist tradition is a part that must be examined and included if multicultural education is to achieve its stated goals of equity and reform (Banks, 1995; Gollnick, 1995; Grant & Sleeter, 1986).

THE IMPORTANCE OF DEFINITION

If Black women don't say who they are, other people will and say it badly for them.

B. Christian, 1985, p. xii

In *The Disuniting of America*, Arthur Schlesinger (1991) states that the majority of African Americans repudiate the notion that there is a connection between themselves and the continent and cultures of Africa. Schlesinger's "evidence" for this claim are polls and surveys taken by the *Washington Post*-ABC and the Joint Center for Political and Economic Studies that indicate most African Americans prefer to be called "Black." In this decontextualized assertion, Schlesinger makes an unwarranted leap that ignores the ongoing "naming" dilemma that African Americans have faced since their arrival in the Americas. At one time, African Americans chose "Negro" over "Black." At another time "colored" was favored over "Negro" (Taulbert, 1989). This evolution/revolution of terms of identification was made necessary by the inhumane conditions that account for African Americans being in America in the first place. Thus, as African Americans struggle to define themselves, the need to grapple with seemingly unimportant issues like, "How shall we be called?" rests at the crux of their ability to be both self-defined and self-determined.

Women in this society have had similar "naming" struggles. The genteel term "lady" is now considered pejorative by many feminists. The preferred term for women who work inside the home is no longer "housewife" (as if a woman is married to her house) but rather "homemaker." Women who work outside and within the home have gained recognition, making the phrase "working mother" obsolete since all mothers work regardless of whether they are paid. And women have worked to uncover sexism in our language (e.g., "mankind" and the generic "he"). All of these changes represent symbolic and real shifts in thinking about the role of women in U.S. society. It is likely that women have the same visceral reaction to being called "girls" by men that African American men have to being called "boys" by Whites.

The special situation of African American women who carry the stigmata of race and gender (and often, class) makes the question of naming oneself more complex. African American women rarely experienced the condescending status of "femininity" conferred on White women. However, they did not enjoy the privileges of masculinity (McIntosh, 1988) and remained in an undefined position that alternately appeared to be bondage to some (Truth, 1992) and "freedom" to others. Indeed, aspects of African American folk wisdom suggest that "White men and Black women are the freest people in America." The reference to White men and their freedom appears obvious, but Black women were considered "free" because of historical stereotypes. Black women's early roles as keepers of both White and Black households made them appear "indispensable" but not a threat to White men.

In an attempt to produce both a clarifying and a liberating vision of African American women, scholars such as Collins (1989) have argued that "since Black women have access to both the Afrocentric and the feminist standpoints, an alternative epistemology used to rearticulate a Black women's standpoint reflects elements of both traditions" (p. 756). Thus, rather than an either/or dichotomous definition of African American women as either members of a racial group or members of a gender group, we must entertain a both/and orientation as members of both a racial and a gender group, or sometimes members of one in relation to the other, to understand African American women's perspectives and allegiances (King, 1987).

These dual allegiances do not make for easy interchange between Black women and (White) feminism or Black women and Black (male) studies. Knowing that the concerns of White women do not represent the universe of feminist concerns, and that the concerns of African American men do not represent the universe of Black concerns, means creating the intellectual, social, and emotional space for a Black women's epistemology. The development of a Black women's or womanist discourse represents the recognition of voices that are at the same time Black and female, voices that challenge at least two oppressions simultaneously.

Three ways that African American women have struggled against these oppressions have been as active participants in the construction of enduring histories, as leaders and catalysts for social justice, and as scholars committed to doing research and scholarship that will make a difference in the material and psychic lives of people now and for generations to come. I discuss womanist exemplars of history, activism, and scholarship in the next section.

WOMANIST EXEMPLARS OF HISTORY, ACTIVISM, AND SCHOLARSHIP

History: Sojourner Truth

I will use the life and work of Sojourner Truth as an example of the historical roots of the womanist tradition. Born Isabella Baumfree in about 1797 in Ulster County, New York, Sojourner Truth is in many ways the embodiment of the womanist movement (Hendricks, 1989; Painter, 1990; Yellin, 1989). Having endured beatings, rape, an arranged marriage, and the sale of one of her children, Sojourner Truth nevertheless maintained her sanity and dignity and became an outstanding champion for the rights of African Americans and women. She became a free woman in 1828 under a New York law that banned slavery.

Not content to stand quietly by and allow White abolitionists or White women to champion the cause of freedom that held special meaning for her as an African American woman, Truth spoke out on both causes despite the threat and actuality of violence. Clearly, many other Black women serve as historical examples of the dual perspectives of race and gender (for example, Harriet Tubman, Ellen Craft, Frances Ellen Harper). However, Sojourner Truth is the exemplification of these dual perspectives that lay the foundation for what has become known as the womanist perspective.

Sojourner Truth's uncompromising decision to fight both oppressions—racism and sexism simultaneously—made her the "most notable and highly regarded African American woman in the nineteenth century" (Washington, 1993, p. ix). Unwilling to be silenced or defined by either Black men or White women, Sojourner confronted men like Frederick Douglass and women like Harriet Beecher Stowe. When Douglass insisted that the Black man must rise up and throw off the shackles of slavery by his own might, Sojourner Truth, a pacifist, reminded him that Blacks were dependent on their faith as a key to liberation. "Is God Almighty dead?" Sojourner shouted back at Douglass's pronouncement (Washington, 1993, p. x). The power of her question forced Douglass to modify his assertion.

According to Washington (1993), "Douglass was both put off and enchanted by this uneducated woman who considered herself his equal in discourse and intelligence, if not in literacy and posturing" (p. x). This assessment by Douglass is interesting in light of the fact that Sojourner could neither read nor write, and he was considered one of the most eloquent speakers of his time. She declared, "I cannot read a book, but I can read the people" (cited in Washington, 1993, p. xvi).

Washington (1993) also states that Harriet Beecher Stowe "seemed genuinely impressed, and perhaps discomfited, by this sinewy African American woman in Quaker dress" (p. xi). Stowe's own words (as quoted in Sterling, 1984) paint a telling picture:

> I do not recollect ever to have been conversant with any one who had more of that silent and subtle power which we call personal presence than this woman. Her tall form is still vivid to my mind. . . . She seemed self possessed and at her ease; in fact there was almost an unconscious superiority, not unmixed with a solemn twinkle of humor, in the odd composed manner in which she looked down on me. (p. 150)

It is important to note that Sojourner Truth emerged during the nineteenth century's "cult of true womanhood." White womanhood was defined by four cardinal virtues—"piety, purity, submissiveness and domesticity" (Washington, 1993, p. xxx). Of course, African American women could not be thought of in terms of the first two—piety and purity—because they were "objectified as sexual beings and laborers" (Washington, 1993, p. xxx).

Undaunted by White constructions of Black women, Sojourner Truth is a shining example of the power and will of Black women to determine for themselves the course and meaning of their actions. As a warrior for the rights of both Blacks and women, Sojourner Truth reminds Black women of their dual responsibility to work through the challenges and gifts of Blackness and womanhood. In her most often quoted speech, "Ain't I a woman?" she challenges the narrow constructions of womanhood and of White men and women alike by enumerating the ways in which she is marginalized by men and White women (Washington, 1993):

> I have plowed and reaped and chopped and mowed, and ain't I a woman? I have heard much about the sexes being equal. I can carry as much as any man, and eat as much too, if I can get it, and bear the lash as well. And ain't I a woman? I have borne thirteen children and seen most sold off to slavery and when I cried out with my mother's grief, none but Jesus heard me. And ain't I a woman? (p. 118)

One young Black woman, Josephine J. Franklin (quoted in Washington, 1993) who wrote Sojourner in 1864, illustrates both the pride and solidarity we all must feel as we come to understand her history:

> This is the second epistle I have addressed to you. . . . You asked me if I was of your race. I am proud to say I am of the same race that you are, I am coloured thank God for that; I have not the curse of God upon me for enslaving human beings, did I say I was proud yes thrice proud of my race. . . . Although crushed and enslaved kept back and rejected, their talents will shine and in some way they will show their superiority. (p. xiv)

BLACK WOMEN ACTIVISTS

Educate a man and you educate an individual;
Educate a woman and you educate an entire family.
                                    Malcolm X, quoted in Cone, 1991, p. 279

A second category of Black women who help to illustrate the womanist tradition is one I term "activists." Only a few examples will be discussed. Sojourner Truth also could be included in this category. However, for the purpose of this discussion, Ida Wells, Septima Clark, and Fannie Lou Hamer will serve as examples.

Ida B. Wells

Ida B. Wells was born in 1862 in Holly Springs, Mississippi, during slavery's last years (DeCosta-Willis, 1995; Greaves & Archambault, 1989). After emancipation, she took advantage of available schooling and progressed to college-level studies. Unfortunately, yellow fever swept through the Mississippi Valley and took the lives of both her parents and one of her brothers. Rather than allow her siblings to be separated and parceled out to relatives, Wells—the eldest at 16—gave up her studies and went to work as the sole provider for four brothers and sisters.

Wells worked initially as a teacher but began a budding career as a journalist when she reported an incident in which a train conductor forcibly ejected her from the first-class car. Before long Wells's forceful writing was in demand by many African American newspapers. She wrote reviews of lectures and plays as well as forceful political essays (Duster, 1972; Sterling, 1988; Thompson, 1990).

Perhaps no incident crystallized for Wells what her true mission in life was more than the lynching of Black grocers Thomas Moss, Calvin McDowell, and

Henry Stewart in Memphis, Tennessee, in 1892. The only "crime" committed by these men was the opening of a grocery store in direct competition with a White grocer. So incensed was Wells by the murders that she urged the residents of Memphis to "save [their] money and leave a town which will neither protect [their] lives and property, nor give [them] a fair trial in the courts, but takes [them] out and murders [them] in cold blood" (as quoted in Giddings, 1984, p. 26). With her urging, hundreds of Blacks left Memphis. Their leaving caused several White-owned businesses to teeter on the edge of bankruptcy.

Before her firsthand experience with the lynching murders of Moss and his associates, Wells—like many prominent African Americans—was beginning to believe the "big lie" promoted by southern White men (and expressed by mainstream publications) that Black men were "reverting" to "African savagery" and raping White women. According to Giddings (1984):

> The charge was leveled so consistently against Black men, and came from such impeccable sources, that the whole nation seemed to take it for granted. Not only *Harper's* but other scholarly and reputable magazines and newspapers wrote about the "new crime." The liberal reformer, Jane Addams, though opposed to lynching, nevertheless believed that Black men had a proclivity for rape. Even some Blacks began to wonder. (pp. 27-28)

Aware of the barbaric way in which Moss, Thomas, and Stewart had been murdered, Wells decided to investigate every lynching she could (DeCosta-Willis, 1995; Greaves & Archambault, 1989). Ultimately, she researched the circumstances of 728 lynchings that had taken place over a decade. She learned that "only a third of the murdered Blacks were even *accused* of rape, much less guilty of it" (Giddings, 1984, p. 28, emphasis original). Instead, she discovered that most African Americans were killed for "crimes" like "race prejudice," "quarreling with Whites," and "making threats." Her investigations revealed that African American women and children also were lynched.

In addition to reporting the truth about lynching, Wells began to expose evidence of interracial sexual liaison initiated by White women. Her editorial detailing the pursuit of Black men by White women so inflamed Whites that Wells's newspaper office was burned to the ground while she was in Philadelphia. She also was permanently banished from the South.

Black women, whose finances underwrote the publication of Wells's "Southern Horror: Lynch Law in All Its Phases," sponsored a testimonial in 1892. Two hundred and fifty African American women honored Wells for revealing that "all Blacks, regardless of class or achievement, were vulnerable" to the arbitrary and capricious sanctions of Whites (Giddings, 1984, p. 31).

In addition to her work as a journalist, Wells was a prime mover in the establishment of the National Association for the Advancement of Colored

People (NAACP). However, the tradition of male dominance and Wells's fiercely independent personality kept her name from the initial list of the organization's founders. Her name was later restored to the list. However, Wells was involved in continuing feuds with the leadership for what she saw as its lack of conviction to the lives of African Americans. About Mary White Ovington, the chairwoman of the NAACP's executive committee, Wells stated:

> She has basked in the sunlight of the adoration of the few college-bred Negroes who have surrounded her but has made little effort to know the soul of the Black woman; and to that extent she has fallen far short of helping a race which has suffered as no White woman has ever been called upon to suffer or to understand. (Duster, 1972, p. 51)

Wells believed that some members of the NAACP's executive committee were more concerned with the growing Black middle and professional class than with the working- and lower-class masses. Wells's own work was aimed at highlighting the plight of all Black people in the United States and underscoring the vulnerability of Black men and women to the arbitrary application of laws and sanctions in their communities.

Septima Clark

In characterizing the civil rights movement of the 1950s and 1960s, theologian Cone (1991) states, "The most glaring and detrimental limitation of Martin [Luther King's] and Malcolm [X's] leadership was not seeing sexism as a major problem connected with and as evil as racism" (p. 273). However glorified and mythologized the presentation of the story of the civil rights movement, it is incomplete without a discussion of the role Black women played in the fight for social justice. One such freedom fighter was Septima Clark (Brown, 1986; Lanker, 1989).

Septima Poinsette Clark was born on May 3, 1898, in Charleston. She taught school on St. Johns Island, South Carolina (Lerner, 1972). The death of her husband in 1924—just 3 years after they were married—left her with a small child to support. Determined to continue as a teacher, Clark left her son to be raised by his grandmother while she taught in Columbia, South Carolina, and obtained a master's degree at Hampton Institute. Later she began teaching in the Charleston, South Carolina, public schools where she was active in civic work. Clark worked in what was then considered radical activities to improve interracial relations. As a result of her work in interracial relations, Clark lost her teaching job as well as her retirement pay in South Carolina and was unable to teach anywhere in the state. She became director of workshops and later director of education at Highlander Folk School in Monteagle, Tennessee (Brown, 1986).

Highlander Folk School is a "movement halfway house" (Morris, 1984), "an established group or organization that is only partially integrated into the larger society because its participants are actively involved in efforts to bring about a desired change in society" (p. 139). The philosophy of Highlander Folk School was that oppressed people know the answers to their own prob-lems and that the role of teachers is to help them start talking about their problems, "to raise and sharpen questions, and to trust people to come up with the answers" (Morris, 1984, p. 139). Thus, the staff of Highlander began its work by going into oppressed communities, identifying potential leaders, and recruiting them for participation in Highlander workshops. The early work of Highlander brought together coal miners, labor organizers, and leaders of educational organizations. Workshop participants formulated solutions to their problems. Additionally, Highlander required that some action be performed in the community to test the feasibility of the proposed solutions (Morris, 1984).

Clark worked with Esau Jenkins. A Black community leader with little formal education, he was committed to helping the Black citizens of St. Johns Island, South Carolina, learn to read and write so they could vote and partici-pate in politics. Working with Myles Horton, founder of the Highlander Folk School, Clark and Jenkins spent several months on St. Johns Island learning from and about the people there (Brown, 1986; Morris, 1984). Clark and Jenkins learned that although plenty of money from both the state and the federal government had been spent for existing literacy programs, most people were not becoming literate. The reason for these failures, they surmised, was that adult learners were treated like children (Morris, 1984). Participants in the state and federally supported programs were made to sit at children's desks and read child-like words, phrases, and sentences. Horton, Clark, and Jenkins knew that this was not the way to teach adults (Brown, 1986; Morris, 1984).

Jenkins became the main teacher for the St. Johns Island adult learners. Morris (1984) states that Clark was "the theoretician of the [Highlander Folk] Citizenship School" (p. 152). Morris describes the teaching strategy used by Clark, Jenkins, and Bernice Robinson, a Black beautician:

> The method employed in the school followed Highlander's axiom that the oppressed had to be educated through their own concrete experiences. Robinson began a class by asking the participants what they wished to learn. Many of the students wanted to learn to write their names in the Bible, others wanted to write to their sons in the military, and some wanted to make out money orders. . . . Many ingenious methods were used. People were taught to write words they had sung for years. Newspapers were brought in, and words taken from them were woven into new paragraphs. (Morris, 1984, p. 152)

Adams (1972) reported:

> At the end of three months and thirty-six classes in all, the first fourteen students took the voting test. Eight of them registered. And before the first citizenship school ended its size had more than doubled from fourteen to thirty-seven, just opposite of the "regular" reading school. (p. 512)

Within 3 years, citizenship schools were springing up everywhere. Writes Clark, "[People] were being taught in kitchens and outside under trees in the people's yards" (quoted in Morris, 1984, p. 154). The demand for citizenship schools soon far outdistanced the ability of Clark and Jenkins to prepare teachers to teach them. One of Clark's greatest gifts was to recognize the talent and ability of people to teach for liberation. When she began her work as organizer of citizenship schools, she said:

> We went into various communities and found people. I sat down and wrote out a flyer saying that the teachers we need in a citizenship school should be people who are respected by the members of the community, who can read well aloud, and who can write their names in cursive writing. . . . We were trying to make teachers out of people who could barely read and write. But they could teach. (quoted in Brown, 1986, p. 47)

To meet the growing need for citizenship school teachers, Clark and Jenkins moved the citizenship training center to Highlander and "established a procedure whereby future citizenship teachers came to the mountain and received their training in just five days" (Morris, 1984, p. 154). As a result of the untiring effort of Jenkins and Clark, citizenship schools began to appear throughout South Carolina and Georgia. However, in 1961 Clark's work with the Citizenship School would take on new meaning (Adams, 1972; Brown, 1986; Morris, 1984).

In 1961 Martin Luther King, Jr. and the Southern Christian Leadership Conference (SCLC) were looking for a vehicle through which to educate and mobilize the masses of Black people for the cause of civil rights (Brown, 1986; Morris, 1984). Encouraged by Myles Horton, SCLC took over the Citizenship School. Clark remained the primary director. SCLC used the Citizenship School "to prepare Blacks for the movement" (Morris, 1984, pp. 237–238). In addition to literacy instruction, the Citizenship School taught participants how to protest, question unequal power distribution, and become more politically active. The Citizenship School staff recruited teachers by traveling throughout the South. Citizenship recruits, according to Clark,

> had a special job of going into the community and getting the community ready to accept Dr. [Martin Luther] King with his way of speaking . . . [to prepare them]

to listen to a Black man and to know that the government of that state can be handled by Blacks as well as Whites. They didn't know it before. We used to think everything White was right. We found out differently, though. (quoted in Morris, 1984, p. 239)

Both Highlander and the Citizenship School "graduated" many distinguished participants of the struggle for African American liberation—Hosea Williams, Rosa Parks, John Lewis, James Bevel, Martin Luther King, Jr., C. T. Vivian, Fred Shuttlesworth, and Bernice Robinson.

In her reflections about the civil rights movement and its leadership, Septima Clark refrained from the romantic characterization that has come with time. She was honest about the marginalization of women:

In those days I didn't criticize Dr. [Martin Luther] King other than asking him not to lead all the marches. Like other Black ministers, Dr. King didn't think too much of the way women could contribute. I see this as one of the weaknesses of the civil rights movements, the way the men looked at women. . . . I think that the work the women did during the time of civil rights is what really carried the movement along. The women carried forth the ideas. I think the civil rights movement would never have taken off if some women hadn't started to speak up. (quoted in Brown, 1986, pp. 77–78)

Fannie Lou Hamer

One of the notable people to attend the SCLC Citizenship School was Fannie Lou Hamer. Mills's (1993) biography of Fannie Lou Hamer provides an extensive chronology of her life. Born Fannie Lou Townsend in 1917, she was the youngest of 20 children born to Jim and Ella Townsend. She was born to the hard life of sharecropping in the rural Mississippi Delta. She began working in the fields at the age of 6. Her opportunity to attend school was circumscribed by the harsh economic realities and the planting and harvesting seasons. In 1944 she married Perry Hamer and settled on the W. D. Marlow plantation just outside of Ruleville, Mississippi. Although she never had children of her own, she did, in the spirit of "other mothering" (Collins, 1990), raise two daughters, Dorothy Jean and Vergie. As a victim of the prevailing racial cruelty toward Black women, Fannie Lou was sterilized without her knowledge or permission in 1961.

In August 1962, Hamer began traveling the road that would make her a legend in civil and human rights. She attended a mass meeting of the Student Non-Violent Coordinating Committee (SNCC) in Ruleville, Mississippi. From there she unsuccessfully attempted to register to vote and was subsequently evicted from the Marlow plantation. Hamer credited SNCC with providing her the voice and courage to fight for social justice:

> If SNCC hadn't of come into Mississippi, there never would have been a Fannie
> Lou Hamer. . . . They treated me like a human being, whether the kids was White
> or Black. I was respected with the kids, and they never told nobody what to say,
> nobody. Everything you heard us screaming and saying . . . nobody tell us to say
> that. This is what's been there all the time, and we had a chance to get it off our
> chests, and nobody else had ever give us that chance. . . . They brought every
> hope into the state of Mississippi. (Mills, 1993, p. 41)

At the same time, SNCC knew Hamer was a special person. Writes Mills
(1993):

> Fannie Lou had a presence. She was smart. And as a poor Black southern share-
> cropper, she represented the soul of the people whom the movement wanted
> to represent. As disfranchised people were starting to assert themselves, she
> stepped forward, voicing her own concerns and those of her neighbors. She had
> a personal story, which would only grow more compelling the more she endured.
> And she had a voice with which to tell it. Virtually everyone whose path crossed
> hers remembered first and foremost her singing and her speaking. (p. 41)

Hamer attended one of SCLC's Citizenship Schools in Dorchester, Georgia. She was later selected for further training as a prospective Citizenship
School teacher. As a part of this training she had the opportunity to interact
with other grass-roots activists and scholars such as Vincent Harding and John
Henrik Clarke (Mills, 1993).

Although she worked tirelessly for the cause of civil and human rights from
that first mass meeting sponsored by SNCC in 1962, it would be 2 years later
at the Democratic National Convention that the nation would get its first
glimpse of Hamer's power and eloquence. Hamer challenged the Mississippi
Democratic Party in her role as a spokesperson for the Mississippi Freedom
Democratic Party (MFDP). She met with the Mississippi Democratic Party's
credentials committee and began her testimony with the words, "Mr. Chairman, and the credentials committee, my name is Mrs. Fannie Lou Hamer, and
I live at 626 East Lafayette Street, Ruleville, Mississippi, Sunflower County,
the home of Senator James O. Eastland and Senator Stennis" (Mills, 1993,
p. 119). Hamer told the story of how she had tried to register to vote, had
been evicted from her home for doing so, and had been arrested, beaten, and
abused by Mississippi law enforcement officers for her civil rights efforts.
Although her eyes were filled with tears, her voice remained strong. This is
how she ended her testimony:

> All of this is on account we want to register, to become first-class citizens, and if
> the Freedom Democratic Party is not seated now, I question America, is this
> America, the land of the free and the home of the brave where we have to

sleep with our telephones off the hooks because our lives be threatened daily
because we want to live as decent human beings, in America? (quoted in Mills,
pp. 120–121)

Although Hamer and the MFDP did not get to replace the Mississippi Democratic Party, her presence on television made an indelible mark on the hearts
and minds of people throughout the nation. As Mills states, "Neither MFDP
nor the national party leaders knew it, but over the long term they had just
opened the Democratic Party to greater participation by more Americans. . . .
The MFDP didn't win those two seats in 1964, but it opened many more seats
at future national conventions" (p. 132).

Reminiscing about Hamer to Bill Moyers, civil rights activist, freedom
singer, and musicologist Bernice Reagon commented:

> She looked like all of the Black women I knew. She was hefty, she was short, she
> had a singing voice very much like the women who came out of our church. She
> didn't look like my teacher; she looked like the usher on the usher board. . . .
> She looked real regular. She was so strong and insistent, and she was so mad and
> so loving. (Moyers, 1991)

Although much of Hamer's public identity was formed as a result of her
work in civil rights, she actively opposed the war in Vietnam and stated clearly
to the emerging feminist movement that the struggle of Black women was
not the same as that of White women:

> White women had been put on a pedestal, and Blacks were whacking like hell
> for the pedestal. And when you (White women) hit the ground, you're gone have
> to fight like hell, like we been fighting all this time. . . .
>   [I am] not hung up on this about liberating myself from the Black man. I'm
> not going to try that thing. I got a Black husband, six feet three, 240 pounds with
> a 14 shoe, that I don't *want* to be liberated from. But we are here to work side
> by side with this Black man in trying to bring liberation to all people. (quoted in
> Mills, 1993, pp. 273–274)

The work of Ida B. Wells, Septima Clark, and Fannie Lou Hamer exemplifies the action necessary for African American women to struggle against racism and sexism. Their stories, recorded but not unique, underscore the power
of African American women to work on their own behalf—and on their own
terms—to address the ongoing struggles of racism and sexism. All three
women demonstrated the sense of "responsibility through reciprocity; honesty and loyalty through mutuality and deference; and faith and compassion
through inner strength and self-control" that King and Mitchell (1991, p. 36)
identify as characteristics of positive African and African American family/

community relationships. Their life work, like that of Sojourner Truth and many others, was one of active struggle.

Reinventing Ourselves

> She had nothing to fall back on; not maleness, not Whiteness, not ladyhood, not anything. And out of the profound desolation of her reality she may well have invented herself.
> Toni Morrison (quoted in Giddings, 1984, p. 15)

Toni Morrison, one of the most celebrated writers of our time and a Nobel laureate, symbolizes the perceptive critic of Western scholarship. Through her writing and criticism Morrison addresses both race and gender in ways that define the uniqueness of Black womanhood:

> [Black women] look at White women and see the enemy for they know that racism is not confined to White men and that there are more White women than men in this country. [That majority] sustained an eloquent silence during times of greatest stress. . . . The faces of those White women hovering behind that Black girl at the Little Rock school in 1957 do not soon leave the retina of the mind. (quoted in Giddings, 1984, p. 307)

Morrison has created an intellectual space for Black women that marries the two oppressions into a distinct union of fighter for social justice. She writes (quoted in Lanker, 1989):

> In the beginning, people asked me a lot of questions about whether I consider myself a Black writer or a woman writer. I was fighting shy of labels that had quite other meanings. Obviously, any artist wants to feel that there is something in her work that all peoples of the world are receptive to. On the other hand, I did not want to be erased. I didn't want my Blackness to be erased, I didn't want my femininity to be erased. I wanted it to be very clear that "universal" is not for me a buzzword for not political or not ethnic. (p. 32)

One of Morrison's (1992a) most enduring contributions to intellectual/ literary discourse is the provoking of our thinking about race. She writes:

> Race has become metaphorical—a way of referring to and disguising forces, events, classes, and expressions of social decay and economic division far more threatening to the body politic than biological "race" ever was. Expensively kept, economically unsound, a spurious and useless political asset in election campaigns, racism is as healthy today as it was during the Enlightenment. It seems that it has a utility far beyond economy, beyond the sequestering of classes from

one another, and has assumed a metaphorical life so completely embedded in daily discourse that it is perhaps more necessary and more on display than ever before. (p. 63)

Morrison's work indicates that in our effort to understand difference and its representations, Blackness always represents the symbolic "other." As the women's movement gained momentum, White women "would characterize themselves as 'niggers'" (Giddings, 1984, p. 308), which Morrison views as "an effort to become Black without the responsibilities of being Black" (p. 308).

Morrison's critique of the women's movement is not an indictment of feminism (perhaps more accurately, womanism) but a call to Black women to stand firm in their insistence on a separate, self-defined identity. Her essay on the Clarence Thomas–Anita Hill hearings (Morrison, 1992b) points to the dynamism and synergy of race and gender issues:

> An accusation of such weight as sexual misconduct would probably have disqualified a White candidate on its face. Rather than any need for "proof," the slightest possibility that it was publicly verifiable would have nullified the candidacy, forced the committee members to insist on another nominee rather than entertain the necessity for public debate on so loathsome a charge. But in a racialized and race-conscious society, standards are changed, facts marginalized, repressed, and the willingness to air such charges, actually to debate them, outweighed the seemliness of a substantive hearing because the actors were Black. . . . [Anita Hill] was a mixture heretofore not recognized in the glossary of racial tropes: an *intellectual* daughter of Black *farmers;* a *Black female* taking *offense*; a Black *lady* repeating *dirty words.* (pp. xvi-xvii, emphasis original)

Patricia Hill Collins

Author of numerous articles and an important book on Black feminism, Patricia Hill Collins has been instrumental in describing an "Afrocentric feminist epistemology" (1990, p. 201). She states that the dimensions of that epistemology include (1) concrete experience as a criterion of meaning, (2) the use of dialogue in assessing knowledge claims, (3) the ethic of caring, and (4) the ethic of personal accountability.

Concrete Experience as a Criterion of Meaning. This first dimension suggests that only Black women can truly know what it is to be a Black woman. Although this notion may seem obvious, its import should not be minimized. It underscores the significance of "two types of knowing—knowledge and wisdom" (Collins, 1990, p. 208). Writes Collins, "For most African American women those individuals who have lived through the experiences about which they claim to be experts are more believable and credible than those who have merely read or thought about such experience" (p. 209).

The Use of Dialogue in Assessing Knowledge Claims. The second dimension points to the importance of creating equal status relationships via dialogue. Writes hooks (1989), "Dialogue implies talk between two subjects, not the speech of subject and object. It is a humanizing speech, one that challenges and resists domination" (p. 131). By "talking with" rather than "talking to" other Black women, African American women have the opportunity to deconstruct the specificity of their own experiences and make connections among those that are more representative of the collective experiences of Black women. Give-and-take dialogue means struggling together to make meaning a powerful experience of self-definition and self-discovery.

The Ethic of Caring. Although White feminists have identified the ethic of caring (Noddings, 1984) as a hallmark of women's scholarship, Collins (1990) reiterates its centrality to Black women's lives (and scholarship). She writes, "The ethic of caring suggests that personal expressiveness, emotions, and empathy are central to the knowledge validation process" (p. 215). Collins points out that these convergent notions of White and Black women about caring do not negate its importance to developing and understanding an Afrocentric feminist epistemology:

> The convergence of Afrocentric and feminist values in the ethic of caring seems particularly acute. White women may have access to a women's tradition valuing emotion and expressiveness, but few Eurocentric institutions except the family validate this way of knowing. In contrast, Black women have long had the support of the Black church, an institution with deep roots in the African past and a philosophy that accepts expressiveness and an ethic of caring. (p. 217)

The Ethic of Personal Accountability. The final dimension that describes an Afrocentric feminist epistemology suggests that knowledge claims must be grounded in individual character, values, and ethics. While the dispassionate, "objective," White, masculinist discourse allows people with radically differing public positions to socialize and mingle in private, an Afrocentric feminist epistemology means that private qualities have bearing on public standpoints. Thus, not only *what* was said, but *who* said it, gives meaning and interpretation to knowledge claims. Collins (1990) states:

> The ethic of personal accountability is clearly an Afrocentric value, but is it feminist as well? . . . There is a female model for moral development whereby women

are more inclined to link morality to responsibility, relationships and the ability
to maintain social ties. If this is the case, then African American women again
experience a convergence of values from Afrocentric and female institutions.
(pp. 218-219)

The Relationship Between the Womanist Tradition and Multicultural Education

Earlier in this chapter, I discussed the womanist perspective as one of
creating spaces and fighting new battles. Many other social movements and
organizations (e.g., labor unions, political organizations, church and religious
groups) also create spaces and fight new battles. The notion of creating
spaces and fighting new battles is consistent with Banks's (1993) vision of
multicultural education as a "process whose goals will never be fully realized.
. . . When prejudice and discrimination are reduced toward one group, they
are usually directed toward another group or they take new forms. . . .
Multicultural education must be viewed as an ongoing process" (p. 4).

Multicultural education is an outgrowth of the early scholarship of African American thinkers such as Williams (1882, 1883/1989), DuBois (1903),
and Woodson (1922) and the later civil rights movement that prompted the
development of Black studies, ethnic studies, and multiethnic studies (Hu-
DeHart, 1995). It has been an intellectual catalyst for the revival of feminism
and the growth of women's studies, bilingual education, antiracist education,
and the reconsideration of Woodson's ideas that spearheaded the Afrocentric
education movement. In its attempt to be inclusive, it has suffered criticism from both the right (see, for example, Bloom, 1987; D'Souza, 1991;
Schlesinger, 1991) and the left (McCarthy, 1988; Olneck, 1990). However,
that same inclusiveness allows multicultural education to embrace the Black
woman's perspective as another permutation of scholarship in the struggle.

Banks (1995) argues that multicultural education includes at least five
dimensions—content integration, knowledge construction, prejudice reduction, an equity pedagogy, and an empowering school culture. An African
American woman's perspective can and does fit each of these dimensions.
Content integration means that the lives and histories of Black women have
to be a part of curriculum transformation. Knowledge construction means that
Black women's work must be a part of an expanding epistemological consciousness. For Black women prejudice reduction means rethinking precon-
ceived notions of race, gender, and class. Equity pedagogy—the ensuring of
equal access to classroom knowledge—finds in the nexus of race and gender
an opportunity to address some of the most persistent issues of underachieve-
ment. Finally, an empowering school culture, through a womanist lens, asks

us to envision Black women outside of the cafeteria and apart from buckets and mops in school corridors.

Building the case for a womanist perspective as a part of the multicultural education movement is relatively straightforward. There are commonalities and convergences of goals and objectives. However, the issue for inclusion of the womanist perspective is not one of fighting for inclusion as much as one of fighting for visibility. By moving out from the "protective cover" of Black studies and feminist studies, the Black woman's perspective continues in its unique place as a definer of our history, a model for activism, and a path to wider epistemological truths.

REFERENCES

Adams, F. (1972). Highlander Folk School: Getting information, going back and teaching it. *Harvard Educational Review, 42* (4), 497–520.

Allen, P. G. (1986). *The sacred hoop: Recovering the feminine in American Indian traditions.* Boston: Beacon Press.

Anzaldúa, G. (1987). *Borderlands/la frontera: The new mestiza.* San Francisco: Spinsters/Ante Lute Book Co.

Asante, M. (1987). *The Afrocentric idea.* Philadelphia: Temple University Press.

Banks, J. A. (1993). Multicultural education: Characteristics and goals. In J. A. Banks & C. A. M. Banks (Eds.), *Multicultural education: Issues and perspectives* (2nd ed., pp. 3–47). Boston: Allyn & Bacon.

Banks, J. A. (1995). Multicultural education: Historical development, dimensions, and practice. In J. A. Banks & C. A. M. Banks (Eds.), *Handbook of research on multicultural education* (pp. 3–24). New York: Macmillan.

Bethel, L., & Smith, B. (Eds.). (1979). The Black women's issue [Special issue]. *Conditions, 5.*

Bleier, R. (1986). *Feminist approaches to science.* New York: Pergamon Press.

Bloom, A. (1987). *The closing of the American mind.* New York: Simon & Schuster.

Brown, C. S. (Ed.). (1986). *Ready from within: Septima Clark and the civil rights movement.* Navarro, CA: Wild Trees Press.

Butler, J. E. (1991). Difficult dialogues. In J. E. Butler & J. C. Walter (Eds.), *Transforming the curriculum: Ethnic studies and women's studies* (pp. 69–88). Albany: State University of New York Press.

Carby, H. V. (1987). *Reconstructing womanhood: The emergence of the Afro-American woman novelist.* New York: Oxford University Press.

Chan, S. (1991). *Asian Americans: An interpretive history.* Boston: Twayne.

Christian, B. (1985). *Black feminist criticism: Perspectives on Black women writers.* New York: Pergamon Press.

Code, L. (1991). *What can she know? Feminist theory and the construction of knowledge.* Ithaca, NY: Cornell University Press.

Collins, P. H. (1989). The social construction of Black feminist thought. *Signs: Journal of Women in Culture and Society, 14*, 745-773.

Collins, P. H. (1990). *Black feminist thought: Knowledge, consciousness, and the politics of empowerment*. New York: Routledge.

Cone, J. (1991). *Martin and Malcolm and America: A dream or a nightmare?* Maryknoll, NY: Orbis Press.

Davis, A. Y. (1981). *Women, race and class*. New York: Random House.

DeCosta-Willis, M. (1995). *The Memphis diary of Ida B. Wells*. Boston: Beacon Press.

D'Souza, D. (1991). Illiberal education. *Atlantic Monthly, 267*, 51-79.

DuBois, W. E. B. (1903). *The souls of Black folk*. Chicago: A. C. McClurg.

Duster, A. (Ed.). (1972). *Crusade for justice: The autobiography of Ida B. Wells*. Chicago: University of Chicago Press.

Frankenberg, R. (1993). *White women, race matters: The social construction of Whiteness*. Minneapolis: University of Minnesota Press.

Gates, H. L., Jr. (1992). The transformation of the American mind. *Social Education, 56*, 328-331.

Giddings, P. (1984). *When and where I enter: The impact of Black women on race and sex in America*. New York: Bantam Books.

Gollnick, D. M. (1995). National and state initiatives for multicultural education. In J. A. Banks & C. A. M. Banks (Eds.), *Handbook of research on multicultural education* (pp. 44-64). New York: Macmillan.

Gordon, B. (1990). The necessity of African-American epistemology for educational theory and practice. *Journal of Education, 172*, 88-106.

Grant, C. A., & Sleeter, C. E. (1986). Race, class, and gender in educational research: An argument for integrative analysis. *Review of Educational Research, 56*, 195-211.

Greaves, W., & Archambault, L. (1989). *Ida B. Wells: A passion for justice* (Video recording). Alexandria, VA: Public Broadcasting Video.

Gutiérrez, R. A. (1995). Historical and social science research on Mexican Americans. In J. A. Banks & C. A. M. Banks (Eds.), *Handbook of research on multicultural education* (pp. 203-222). New York: Macmillan.

Hendricks, H. (1989). Sojourner Truth: Her early history in slavery. *National Magazine, 16*, 24-43.

Hine, D. C. (Ed.). (1990). *Black women in United States history* (Vols. 1-16). Brooklyn, NY: Carlson.

hooks, b. (1989). *Talking back: Thinking feminist, thinking Black*. Boston: South End Press.

Hu-DeHart, E. (1995). Ethnic studies in U. S. higher education: History, development, and goals. In J. A. Banks & C. A. M. Banks (Eds.), *Handbook of research on multicultural education* (pp. 696-707). New York: Macmillan.

Joseph, G. (1981). White promotion, Black survival. In G. Joseph & J. Lewis (Eds.), *Common differences: Conflict in Black and White feminist perspectives* (pp. 19-42). Boston: South End Press.

King, D. (1987). Race, class, and gender salience in Black women's womanist consciousness. Unpublished manuscript, Dartmouth College, Hanover, NH.

King, J., & Mitchell, C. (1991). *Mothers to sons: Juxtaposing African American literature with social practice*. New York: Peter Lang.

Lanker, B. (1989). *I dream a world: Portraits of Black women who changed America*. New York: Stewart, Tabori, & Chang.

Lerner, G. (Ed.). (1972). *Black women in White America: A documentary history*. New York: Vintage Books.

Lourde, A. (1984). *Sister outsider: Essays and speeches*. Trumansburg, NY: Crossing Press.

MacKinnon, C. A. (1987). *Feminism unmodified: Discourses on life and law*. Cambridge, MA: Harvard University Press.

Maher, F. (1987). Inquiry teaching and feminist pedagogy. *Social Education, 51*, 186–192.

McCarthy, C. (1988). Rethinking liberal and radical perspectives on racial inequality in schooling: Making the case for nonsynchrony. *Harvard Educational Review, 58*, 265–279.

McIntosh, P. (1988). White privilege and male privilege: A personal account of coming to see correspondences through work in women's studies (Working Paper No. 189). Wellesley College, Center for Research on Women.

Mills, K. (1993). *This little light of mine: The life of Fannie Lou Hamer*. New York: Penguin Books.

Morris, A. (1984). *The origins of the civil rights movement: Black communities organizing for change*. New York: Free Press.

Morrison, T. (1992a). *Playing in the dark: Whiteness and the literary imagination*. Cambridge, MA: Harvard University Press.

Morrison, T. (Ed.). (1992b). *Race-ing justice, en-gendering power: Essays on Anita Hill, Clarence Thomas, and the construction of social reality*. New York: Pantheon Books.

Moyers, B. (1991, February 6). *The songs are free*. [Public Television Interview with Bernice Johnson Reagon].

Noddings, N. (1984). *Caring: A feminine approach to ethics and moral education*. Berkeley: University of California Press.

Okihiro, G. Y. (1994). *Margins and mainstreams: Asians in American history and culture*. Seattle: University of Washington Press.

Olneck, M. (1990). The recurring dream: Symbolism and ideology in intercultural and multicultural education. *American Journal of Education, 98* (2),147–174.

Painter, N. I. (1990, Spring). Sojourner Truth in life and memory: Writing the biography of an American exotic. *Gender and History, 2*, 1–26.

Schlesinger, A. M., Jr. (1991). *The disuniting of America: Reflections on a multicultural society*. Nashville, TN: Whittle Direct Books.

Sterling, D. (Ed.). (1984). *We are your sisters: Black women in the nineteenth century*. New York: W. W. Norton.

Sterling, D. (1988). *Black foremothers: Three lives* (2nd ed.). New York: Feminist Press.

Takaki, R. (1993). *A different mirror: A history of multicultural America*. Boston: Little, Brown.

Taulbert, C. L. (1989). *Once upon a time when we were colored*. Tulsa, OK: Council Oak Books.

Thompson, M. (1990). *Ida B. Wells-Barnett: An exploratory study of an American Black woman*. Brooklyn, NY: Carlson.

Truth, S. (1992). Speech to the convention of the American Equal Rights Association, New York City, 1867. In M. Busby, *Daughters of Africa* (pp. 39–40). New York: Pantheon Books.

Walker, A. (1984). *In search of our mothers' gardens: Womanist prose*. New York: Harcourt.

Warrior, R. A. (1995). *Tribal secrets: Recovering American Indian intellectual traditions*. Minneapolis: University of Minnesota Press.

Washington, M. (Ed.). (1993). *Narrative of Sojourner Truth*. New York: Vintage Books.

Weems, R. (1988). *Just a sister away: A womanist vision of women's relationships in the Bible*. San Diego, CA: Lura Media.

Williams, G. W. (1989). *History of the Negro race in America from 1619 to 1880: Negroes as slaves, as soldiers, and as citizens* (2 vols.). Salem, NH: Ayer. (Original work published 1882 and 1883)

Woodson, C. G. (1922). *The Negro in our history*. Washington, DC: Associated Publishers.

Woodson, C. G. (1933). *The mis-education of the Negro*. Washington, DC: Associated Publishers.

Yellin, J. F. (1989). *Women and sisters: The antislavery feminists in American culture*. New Haven: Yale University Press.

CHAPTER 11

Race, Gender, and Calling: Perspectives on African American Women Educators, 1861–1870

EDWARD TAYLOR

The purpose of this chapter is to describe the work and commitment of African American women teachers of newly freed Blacks in the South during and after the Civil War. The processes that affected them also will be described. A central tenet of this chapter is that cultural biases, frameworks, and perspectives influence the construction of history and the ways in which historians describe the past. Writing about African American history has undergone an evolutionary process as knowledge about race has been constructed, deconstructed, and reconstructed. I acknowledge scholars who are contributing to this transformative process. I present evidence that African American women teachers, responding to the needs of their people, served the newly freed Black men, women, and children with courage and fortitude, despite significant obstacles.

Within months after the first shot was fired at Fort Sumter in 1861, organized efforts to send teachers South began (Butchart, 1988a; Jones, 1980). During and after the Civil War, northern philanthropic and missionary groups sent teachers to the South to educate the newly freed people. Following Appomattox, they spread throughout the Confederacy and, by 1867, few towns and cities were without schools for freed men and women. Northern teachers entered the South virtually on "the heels of the soldier" (Swint, 1941/ 1967, p. 3).

One of the most engaging and perhaps neglected groups to labor for the newly freed were northern Black women educators who traveled south to teach their kindred (Butchart, 1988a). The contributions of these women in the education of freed Blacks in the South during and after the Civil War often have been overlooked or distorted in educational history. The story of the education of America's freed men and women is now becoming better documented, and the role of Black female educators in this movement is emerging. As a result of developing scholarship, we now know much more about the women who risked their lives to work among those previously denied access to literacy.

African American women educators came from various parts of the nation and from diverse backgrounds. Their teaching conferred on the newly freed African American students the power that results from knowledge and challenged prevailing notions about the abilities and educability of African Americans. Their collective commitment to uplift their people helped lay the foundation for the education of the freed men and women.

An assessment of the education of the newly freed offers perspectives on nineteenth-century American culture, the collective efforts of African Americans to act on their beliefs in their community, the faith and influence of evangelical idealism, and the belief in the capacity of education to help resolve social problems. It also illustrates the ways in which historical knowledge about African Americans has been constructed, deconstructed, and reconstructed (Banks, 1995).

When examining the contributions of African American women educators during the mid to late nineteenth century, one must proceed with caution. It is easy to misunderstand the motives of these educators and to misinterpret their actions: Were they radical educational reformers? Transformative agents? Did they challenge the dominant educational paradigms of their day? The historical evidence suggests that their actions were driven by a sense of calling and racial solidarity (Butchart, 1990). They responded to the needs of their people and did what they could to uplift their race. In spite of this, mainstream scholars typically have portrayed African American teachers of this period as largely illiterate and motivated by financial incentives (Swint, 1941/1967).

In this chapter I discuss some of the ways in which knowledge about race has been constructed, deconstructed, and reconstructed. I will identify some of the scholars who have corrected prior distortions and shed a more informed and accurate light on the nineteenth century. The aims of this chapter are to add to the emerging scholarship about African American women teachers, to reveal some aspects of their collective biographies, and to describe their actions on behalf of their community.

THE CONSTRUCTION OF KNOWLEDGE

This chapter examines knowledge as a construct with both objective and subjective influences (Banks, 1995; Code, 1991). Central to this conception of knowledge is the awareness, not only of the historical facts, but of the *position* of the knowledge producer. One's place within a social, economic, and political context produces subjectivity and affects the construction of knowledge (Tetreault, 1993). This chapter examines the social construction of knowledge and the ways in which reality is and has been explained or interpreted.

Black scholars have long understood the importance of critiquing and challenging social science scholarship intended to interpret, explain, and control individuals based on socially constructed classifications (Gordon, 1995). The ways in which dominant views have been challenged have varied, but they have shared a fundamental realization that knowledge often is constructed in ways that support inequitable, if not oppressive, actions and systems. Although postmodern and feminist theorists also challenge the construction of knowledge, some of them have not focused on epistemological issues related to race and racism (Code, 1991; Minnich, 1990).

The process of challenging knowledge about race was initiated in the United States by scholars such as Boas (1910), DuBois (1910), and Woodson (1915/1968) near the turn of the century (see Chapters 4 & 5). This process is defined by Banks (1993) as transformative; that is, it includes the "facts, concepts, paradigms, themes, and explanations that challenge mainstream academic knowledge and expand and substantially revise established canons, paradigms, theories, explanations, and research methods" (p. 7). John Hope Franklin (1989) describes this process as the "New Negro History," which is an attempt to fracture racial myths and remind the United States that the lofty ideals of this nation—justice and equality—should apply to all citizens, even scholars. As it relates to the study of the teachers of newly freed Blacks, transformative scholarship has significantly altered our understanding of this period in United States history and, especially, the role of African American women teachers.

Transformative scholarship has a long history in the United States. In the late nineteenth and early twentieth centuries Black historians and intellectuals pursued the study of African Americans as a serious intellectual activity (Banks, 1995; Franklin, 1989; Woodson, 1915/1968). Since the earliest writings about African American history, there have been at least two opposing traditions—the accounts by Black historians and those by White southern historians—asserting a "White supremacist" view (Butchart, 1988a; Phillips, 1918/1966). The latter often justified the oppression of Blacks by blaming

Blacks themselves and by using historical evidence in narrow ways to suit their purposes.

One of the first serious examinations of the history of Blacks in the United States was by George Washington Williams (1882–1883). He attempted to correct widespread distortions and propaganda with the "weapons of indisputable truth" (Franklin, 1989, p. 44). Williams dedicated years of his life to research and writing. He was keenly aware that historical scholarship about Blacks was not very reliable.

In 1915 Carter G. Woodson—with others—founded the Association for the Study of Negro Life and History and in 1916 began publishing *The Journal of Negro History*. He launched what Franklin (1989) calls the era of the "New Negro History." Woodson began an ambitious and far-reaching effort to change the way the public viewed the role of Blacks in U.S. history (Franklin, 1989). He understood well the effects of mainstream views, particularly on the teaching of history. Woodson (1933/1977) wrote:

> The teaching of history in the Negro area has had its political significance. Starting out after the Civil War, the opponents of freedom and social justice decided to work out a program which would enslave the Negroes' mind inasmuch as the freedom of body had to be conceded. It was well understood that if by the teaching of history the White man could be further assured of his superiority and the Negro could be made to feel that he had always been a failure and that the subjection of his will to some other race is necessary, the freedman, then, would still be a slave. If you can control a man's thinking, you do not have to worry about his action. (p. 84)

In 1910, W. E. B. DuBois published an important article in the *American Historical Review*, "Reconstruction and Its Benefits," a reinterpretation of the role of African Americans in education and government during the Reconstruction that diverged radically from prevalent views. He concluded that despite shortcomings, Black involvement in government had given the South three things: democratic government, free public schools, and new social legislation (Lewis, 1993). Lewis describes this article as "a note never before sounded among professional historians" (p. 384). This article laid the groundwork for DuBois's 746-page volume, *Black Reconstruction in America*, published in 1935 (DuBois, 1964). This book seriously challenged established historical accounts of the role of African Americans in Reconstruction. One of DuBois's critical and unique contributions was to analyze and interrogate the sources of oppression more forcefully than some other Black scholars were willing to do at the time (Butchart, 1988b).

The new perspectives and paradigms that underlie their work are important contributions that scholars such as Williams (1882–1883), Woodson (1915/1968), and DuBois (1953) made to the construction of historical knowledge. They laid the foundation for contemporary historians such as Louis Harlan (1983), Darlene Clark Hine (1986), John Blassingame (1972), and Sterling Stuckey (1987). These historians have continued to transform the ways in which African American history is researched and written. Franklin (1989) describes these efforts as

> a remarkable attempt to rehabilitate a whole people—to explode racial myths, to establish a secure and respectable place for the Negro in the evolution of the American social order, to develop self-respect and self-esteem among those who had been subjected to the greatest indignities known in the Western world. Finally, it was a valiant attempt to force America to keep faith with herself, to remind her that truth is more praiseworthy than power, and that justice and equality, long the stated policy of this nation, should apply to all its citizens and *even* to the writing of history. (emphasis in original; p. 45)

Scholarship, particularly since 1980, has witnessed a renewed interest in the contributions of Black and White teachers in educating America's newly freed Blacks. These efforts have corrected many of the inaccuracies of earlier views of these teachers. Henry Swint's *Northern Teachers in the South* (1941/ 1967), considered the leading authoritative work on the subject for years, remains the classic White supremacist view; it was unchallenged for several decades. He described northern teachers as misguided, fanatical, and opinionated meddlers, eager to debase southern Whites. These educators are now viewed by most historians as courageous, heroic, and visionary (Bullock, 1967; Butchart, 1988a; Horst, 1987).

Consideration of the work done by benevolent societies and the teachers of newly freed Blacks, however, should not be interpreted to imply that newly freed African Americans were passive recipients of educational opportunities brought about by legislation and missionary largesse (Butchart, 1990). Previous historical accounts have focused on northern philanthropy, not the actions of African Americans (freed and enslaved) to secure education. Such a perspective wrongly attributes the movement to educate the newly freed Blacks to Yankee benevolence (Anderson, 1988). The historic thirst for knowledge demonstrated by free and enslaved Blacks was rooted deeply in their communal values.

Enslaved and freed Blacks had made plans for systematic instruction for their people before benevolent societies entered the South in 1862, preceding the Emancipation Proclamation in 1863, and prior to the establishment of the Freedmen's Bureau in 1865. Webber (1978), in his description of education in the slave quarter community, identifies the desire to read and write as one of the strongest currents in the "deep river of slave culture" (p. 60). Numerous northern missionaries went south with the belief that the brutal and dehumanizing vestiges of slavery rendered the newly freed men, women, and children little more than uncultured and dehumanized victims who needed to be taught the rules and mores of civil society (Anderson, 1988).

When they arrived in the South, many missionaries were confounded when they discovered that many of the newly freed Blacks had established their own educational associations and schools (Anderson, 1988). In Natchez, Mississippi, for example, schools were started during the war by Negro women. In Savannah, Georgia, Blacks founded two large schools and established a Negro board of education to develop their own policies (Franklin, 1947). Black Americans, North and South, needed and accepted assistance, but it was their own action, as both teachers and students—expressing community values—that brought the walls of illiteracy and ignorance down. Recent research has helped to strengthen our understanding of a once underserved area of investigation that has implications for the fields of curriculum inquiry, critical pedagogy, and multicultural education (Beyer & Apple, 1988; Butchart, 1990).

EDUCATING FREED BLACKS IN THE SOUTH

The Sponsors

Teachers of newly freed Black men and women were selected and supported by a number of freedmen's aid societies, aid commissions, and educational organizations. The primary aims of these organizations were to abate the suffering of Black and White refugees in the South and to bring education, religion, and humanitarian relief to those formerly enslaved. When the most pressing needs were met, some of these societies began schools and commissioned teachers, "thus following the example of educational commissions" (Swint, 1941/1967, p. 3). In their work in the South, all of the societies cooperated with the Bureau of Refugees, Freedmen, and Abandoned Lands (Freedmen's Bureau). As southern towns fell under control of Union forces, representatives from northern societies, both secular and religious, arrived. Dozens of organizations (probably around 50) raised millions of dollars and sent thousands of teachers to the South to establish schools (Butchart, 1988a).

Work on behalf of the newly freed represented an extension of prewar movements for moral and institutional reform. Northern aid societies incorporated "the ideology of abolitionists, common-school reformers, Sunday school organizers, and temperance workers" (Jones, 1980, p. 14). Benevolent societies evolved in quick succession to form a complex of freedmen associations that reached cities including Boston, New York, Philadelphia, Cincinnati, and Chicago (Bullock, 1967). Secular organizations included the National Freedmen's Relief Association in New York and the New England Freedmen's

Aid Society in Boston. Many of the secular groups formed an umbrella group, the American Freedmen's Union Commission, which coordinated a national effort (Butchart, 1991). Religious groups became widely mobilized as well, and by 1866 most Protestant denominations were recruiting and sponsoring teachers.

The American Missionary Association (AMA), founded in 1846, established an early presence and played a major role in states such as Georgia, where, by 1873, it sponsored almost 80% of all the northern teachers (Jones, 1980). The AMA's purpose was not only to function as a missionary society, but also to voice an abolitionist protest against other religious groups that had been tolerant of slavery (Jones, 1985). Because of differences in record keeping and the availability of archival data, more is known about the AMA than about other groups. In spite of the AMA's dedication to the abolition of slavery and the education of Blacks, it did not necessarily promote political or social equality. Many of its White teachers viewed African Americans as inferior and were blatantly racist (Butchart, 1991).

The aid societies had the ominous task of recruiting enough teachers to meet the needs of the 4 million newly freed people, raising millions of dollars from both Whites and free Blacks, and distributing supplies to help educate the newly freed Blacks. This effort was largely voluntary; most of the aid societies were chronically underfunded. Their task was made even more formidable by southern hostility toward their efforts (Rabinowitz, 1974). In 1869, there were an estimated 9,503 teachers of the formerly enslaved in the South. Robert Morris, in *Reading, 'Riting, and Reconstruction* (1981), reminds us that many White teachers discriminated against their Black colleagues. Nevertheless, the number of Black teachers grew, and gradually they took over the supervision of some schools (Anderson, 1988). The scope of freedmen's aid groups peaked in 1866–1867; by the late 1870s, most of the schools had been closed and the teachers recalled (Jones, 1980).

Every individual who labored for the newly freed men and women deserves praise and recognition. Despite the attention paid by historians to the efforts of White teachers of the newly freed Blacks, our understanding of this group remains partial. Although exact figures are not known, available records indicate that many of the teachers of the newly freed persons were White women from the Midwest and Northeast (Rabinowitz, 1974). Early research suggested that these women "joined the cause in order to liberate themselves from the comfort and complacency of a middle class existence" (Jones, 1980, p. 8). Jones describes the archetype as "the well-educated daughter of a farmer or professional [who] was highly conscious of her duty to God and country" (p. 15).

Perkins (1984) describes the AMA women volunteers as upper- and middle-class New England White women who felt constrained by the Victorian concept of "true womanhood." These women were educated for their "proper sphere"—to become wives and mothers—and not expected to work, except in the event of financial necessity. Consequently, many young, well-educated New England women saw teaching in the South primarily as an escape from their idle and unfulfilled lives. (pp. 123–124)

Butchart (1990) has refuted some of these characterizations and has begun to paint a more accurate picture of the teachers. He suggests that although a number were well-educated, many came from modest economic backgrounds and left established teaching careers to venture South. Teaching the newly freed Blacks may have allowed a broadening of educational and geographic opportunities that these women found appealing. However, they were not particularly young. Research by Butchart (1990) indicates that the average age was almost 30. What emerges is a picture of women of lower economic status who attained some degree of higher education, had stable careers, and were able to use the opportunity to teach newly freed Blacks as a way to contribute in a courageous and meaningful way.

Until recently, studies of the educational movement to teach newly freed Blacks have made little honorable mention of the part played by Black teachers. Swint (1941/1967) leaves the impression that most of the teachers were White. What brief attention is given to Black teachers questions their competence and motives in often graphic and demeaning ways.

It is estimated that hundreds of northern teachers who went to the South were African American women (Butchart, 1988a). Of the female teachers with the AMA, at least 10% were Black. Butchart (1988a), tracing African American educators of free Blacks from New York, found that although African Americans constituted 1.2% of the population of that state, they made up more than 14% of the teachers of freed Blacks. They generally were not young women: The average age of Black teachers from New York was 31.7 years. Their educational levels were comparable to those of their White counterparts, 42.1% having some level of secondary education and 15.8% having attended college. Their parents were generally better educated and held higher-status jobs than other Blacks, although they were generally economically disadvantaged compared with their White counterparts. Black teachers spent longer in the South than Whites. Of the New York sample, African American women stayed in the South an average of 4.2 years; African American men worked 3.1 years. By contrast, White women averaged 2.6; White men around 2 (Butchart, 1990). Although these data are limited to teachers from one state and may not be generalizable, the evidence suggests that factors of race and gender did affect length of service.

It is apparent that the educational background of both Black and White teachers from New York was better than average during the period, which was 5 to 6 years of elementary schooling (Kaestle, 1983). Many teachers of newly freed men and women had completed secondary schooling, normal school, literary institute, female seminary, and, occasionally, public high school (Butchart, 1990).

Calling and Commitment

One of the more fascinating, speculative areas of research focuses on the motives of the teachers of freed men and women. Accurately gauging the motives of these "women who dared" more than 160 years ago is difficult. Ascertaining their motives requires trying to corroborate public and private statements, the ability of the historian to distinguish between intent and actions, and, perhaps most difficult, the capacity to separate the investigator's moral judgment on the effects of specific actions (Jaeger, 1988). When looking at some of the incentives of the African American teachers, however, certain themes emerge. African Americans were strongly influenced by a sense of racial solidarity and a desire to "uplift the race" (Butchart, 1990). Edmonia Highgate, of Syracuse, New York, left a principalship at a colored school in Binghamton, New York, to lecture and raise funds for the National Freedmen Relief Association of New York City before becoming an AMA teacher at the age of 20 (Perkins, 1984). She described her goal "to be a pioneer in trying to raise [the freedmen] up to the stature of manhood and womanhood" (Mansfield, 1980, p. 105). In a letter to an AMA official, Reverend George Whipple, she revealed her feelings: "I am delighted with the work and already am more than repaid in coming down to press the soil wherein the monster Slavery has its grave" (Highgate, 1864, n.p.).

Sara Stanley was a student in her third year at Oberlin College who had taught in Ohio Black schools for a number of years before going to Norfolk to teach in freedmen's schools with the AMA. She wrote to George Whipple about her convictions:

> I am, myself, a colored woman bound to that ignorant, degraded, long-enslaved race by the ties of love and consanguinity; they are socially and politically "my people," and I have an earnest and abiding conviction that the All-Father, whose loving kindness gave to me advantages which his divine wisdom withheld from them, requires me to devote every power with which he has endowed me to the work of ameliorating their condition. (Mansfield, 1980, p. 106)

In 1865, Sallie Daffin, from Philadelphia, expressed her sense of racial identification in a letter to Samuel Hunt, an AMA official:

> I presume my interest in the Freedmen and the motive that induces me to leave my home and labor for them will not be questioned when it is remembered that

they are my people. And, how muchsoever those of other races may sympathize
with them, yet none can as fully experience the strength of their needs, nor
understand the means necessary to relieve them, as we who are identified with
them. (emphasis in original; n.p.)

It is doubtful that financial compensation provided much incentive for
leaving the relative security of the North for unknown challenges in the South.
However, the meager AMA salary did not seem to deter these women from
serving (Perkins, 1984). In a letter to an AMA official, Sallie Daffin wrote that
the offer of $10 a month (about half that paid to White teachers) was short of
what she needed as she had a "mother, toward whose support I am obliged
to contribute to some extent" (Daffin, 1864a, n.p.). Although her appeal for
$12 a month was denied, she nonetheless signed the contract. She was given
the option by the AMA of going into an established school or organizing a
new one; she chose the latter option, opening the school along with two other
teachers, "Misses Harris, Smith, and myself," in a Methodist church that
began with 137 students (Daffin, 1864b, n.p.). Other teachers took a pay cut
to sign on. Edmonia Highgate's AMA salary was half of her regular pay (Perkins,
1984).

Conditions

The conditions under which all of the teachers of freed persons labored
were strenuous and hazardous. The schools were held in barns, barracks,
basements, churches, tents, and cabins (Butchart, 1988a; Swint, 1941/1967).
At Richmond, an American Union Commission school met in the Confeder-
ate naval arsenal. At Wilmington, North Carolina, the school was held in a
dilapidated church whose roof leaked so that puddles stood on the floor, and
the stove smoked so severely that students and teachers could hardly breathe
or even see one another. Another teacher "taught in what had been the poul-
try house of a plantation" (Swint, 1941/1967, p. 79). Inclement weather and
a high insect population contributed to discomfort as well.

Reaction to teachers of free persons, Black and White, was, in varying
degrees, cold, hostile, and violent. Convinced that northern teachers had the
ulterior motive of teaching social and political equality, many Southerners
rallied against them. Initial reaction included social aloofness, the refusal to
rent classroom space or provide board, and even the unwillingness to allow
teachers to buy food or attend local churches (Swint, 1941/1967). With time,
however, the backlash became more vicious and dangerous. Although exact
figures are not known, a number of teachers were threatened by the Ku Klux
Klan and physically assaulted. Some teachers left their schools after classrooms
were broken up or burned down.

When the AMA closed its schools in Norfolk, the local press was gleeful. The editor of the Norfolk *Virginian* (July 2, 1866) wrote:

> We congratulate our citizens upon a "good riddance of bad baggage" in the reported departure of these impudent missionaries. Of all the insults to which the Southern people have been subjected, this was the heaviest to bear . . . to have sent among us a lot of ignorant, narrow-minded, bigoted fanatics, ostensibly for the purpose of propagating the gospel among the heathen, and teaching our little negroes and big negroes, and all kinds of negroes . . . but whose real object was to disorganize and demoralize still more our peasantry and laboring population. (quoted in Swint, 1941/1967, p. 106)

Despite widespread opposition, there were some southern Whites who supported and contributed to the effort to educate the newly freed Blacks. In some areas, local Whites had started classes for freed persons before northern teachers arrived.

Conditions in the South were particularly precarious and wearisome for African American teachers. The AMA often sent them to areas to which White teachers would not go because they were so adverse and dangerous (Johnson, 1991). While racial conflicts, tensions, and pressures were prevalent throughout the South, they were also present within northern missionary organizations. AMA officials had already been accused (by southern Whites) of teaching social equality when they suggested housing Black and White teachers together in local mission houses. Some northern White teachers refused to live with African American teachers. In Norfolk, Mary Reed, a White Northerner, felt her Negro colleagues had "overstepped their bounds" and indicated to the AMA her unwillingness to board with them (Fen, 1967, p. 205). When assignments were made to house both races together, White teachers often treated African American teachers contemptuously and expected them to serve as maids (Perkins, 1984).

Housing arrangements were a source of significant difficulty. In Norfolk, the segregated mission house for the African American women was neither repaired nor furnished. By the summer of 1864, Black teachers had moved into the main mission house. However, this situation also proved strenuous (Perkins, 1984). Daffin objected to having to do maid's work for the White teachers (Mansfield, 1980). Clara Duncan requested some relief in the situation from the AMA:

> I came here because my heart and soul were in this work, and I am prepared to give up everything, *even life*, for the good of the cause and count it no hardship but an honor and blessing to me. Yet, I am not willing to live in an unpleasant atmosphere if it can be avoided. (emphasis in original; quoted in Mansfield, 1980, p. 111)

When the African American teachers went to teach in other areas, they discovered that the difficulties they had encountered in Virginia were not unique. When Sallie Daffin was to teach in Wilmington, North Carolina, in 1866, AMA superintendent S. S. Ashley decided she would live with a local Black family (Jones, 1985). While this arrangement was made in part to placate southern hostility, it was also a concession to the racism of the northern White teachers, who viewed their Black colleagues as subordinates (Jones, 1985). Daffin, hurt by this arrangement, refused to accept this treatment. Nonetheless, Ashley (cited in Jones, 1985) justified his position. In an 1866 letter to Samuel Hunt, he describes the dilemma:

> Colored teachers are needed at the South—they must come South. But then, it does not seem to be wise to send them in company with White teachers. There are few, very few places at the North where it would be wise to do this. Such a course at the South brings your White teachers out and in such sharp contact with the prejudices of the Southern people that their situation is made almost intolerable. (quoted in Jones, 1985)

In 1867, Daffin was sent to Arlington, where she taught 130 students (Butchart, personal correspondence, 1994). Daffin again encountered ill treatment from her White counterparts. She had been assigned to teach the advanced class when Mrs. Potter, a White teacher, demanded to teach the class herself. Daffin yielded to Potter's insistence, but the harassment did not end. She notified the AMA that despite her efforts to get along, Potter "commenced a system of persecution, by bitter taunts and cruel sarcasm, indulged in at meals and on every available occasion" (Daffin, 1867a, n.p.). The situation became unbearable and, a few days after this correspondence, Daffin wrote, "Circumstances compel me to tender to the American Missionary Association, my resignation, to take effect on the first day of June, 1867" (Daffin, 1867b, n.p.). Although available letters do not clarify the issue, the resignation appears connected to the Potter issue. Evidence suggests she accepted other teaching positions in freedmen's schools, but many details are unknown.

Blanche Harris accepted an assignment to teach in an AMA school in Natchez, Mississippi, in 1865. She was pressured to live at the mission house, where African American teachers had to room with the domestic help and were not allowed to use the sitting or dining rooms. She and the other Black teachers, including her sister, Frankie, boarded with local African American families instead (Perkins, 1984).

CONCLUSION

During the past 2 decades, significant changes have occurred in teaching, writing, and research regarding the contributions of African American women on behalf of their race. The picture that emerges of the African American women teachers of the freed persons is that of ordinary citizens who took seriously their calling and whose actions took exceptional courage. They struggled for respect from their White cohorts, yet were accorded the highest regard by their students. They experienced discrimination in their sponsoring organizations and hostility from southern Whites, but the rewards in the classroom must have been affirming.

Available evidence suggests that these teachers did not challenge the curriculum, revolutionize the philanthropic groups, or diminish the antagonism of local Whites. Far from being generals or commanders, they were the foot soldiers of the movement. They simply gave their portion. United in racial solidarity, separated from the lives of their students only by accident of circumstance or birthplace, they acted on behalf of their people. If their experience was difficult, what surely sustained them was the response of their pupils and their deep faith in the power of education. The lives spent in such service represent not so much an individual's effort or a hero's cause, but the action of a community separated by the profound barriers of slavery, humbly, yet joyfully, reunited.

Central to the goals of critical pedagogy and multicultural education are emancipation, justice, and equal educational opportunities for all students. One important aspect of historical interpretation is understanding how knowledge is constructed and how cultural biases, frameworks, and perspectives can influence what is "known" (Banks, 1993). The evolution of how the teachers of newly freed Blacks have been understood by both historians and laypeople helps illuminate how these processes operate. Scholars who have questioned widely held beliefs and stereotypes and gone beyond the mainstream "story" have allowed a fuller, more representative picture to emerge.

According to Franklin (1989), the "New Negro History" is now flourishing. Historians of all races are seeking academic and intellectual justice and balance. He notes, "For the first time in the history of the United States, there is a striking resemblance between what historians are writing and what actually happened in the history of the American Negro" (p. 47). The past 2 decades, according to modern historiographers, have had the broadest range of studies and interpretations but the greatest commitment to the emancipatory power of information (Butchart, 1988a). These historians have questioned historical processes, deepened social consciousness, and called for justice.

The multicultural initiative has developed, in part, in response to the fragmentation of American society by race, gender, and class. It is not simply an additive approach that includes the stories of a broader range of people, but a process that promotes a critical approach to matching educational practices with democratic principles. The new scholarship on the teachers of emancipated men and women during and after the Civil War represents one of the many important steps toward repairing the damage and neglect that has pervaded historical inquiry.

REFERENCES

Note: AMAA is the American Missionary Association Archives.

Anderson, J. D. (1988). *The education of Blacks in the South, 1860–1935*. Chapel Hill: University of North Carolina Press.

Banks, J. A. (1993). The canon debate, knowledge construction, and multicultural education. *Educational Researcher, 22* (5), 4–14.

Banks, J. A. (1995). The historical reconstruction of knowledge about race: Implications for transformative teaching. *Educational Researcher, 24* (2), 15–25.

Beyer, L. E., & Apple, M. W. (1988). *The curriculum: Problems, politics, and possibilities*. Albany: State University of New York Press.

Blassingame, J. W. (1972). *The slave community: Plantation life in the antebellum South*. New York: Oxford University Press.

Boas, F. (1910). The real racial problem. *Crisis, 1* (2), 22–25.

Bullock, H. A. (1967). *A history of Negro education in the South: From 1619 to the present*. Cambridge, MA: Harvard University Press.

Butchart, R. E. (1988a). We can best instruct our own people: New York African Americans in the freedmen's schools, 1861–1875. *Afro Americans in New York Life and History, 12*, 27–49.

Butchart, R. E. (1988b). Outthinking and outflanking the owners of the world: A historiography of the African American struggle for education. *History of Education Quarterly, 28*, 333–366.

Butchart, R. E. (1990). Recruits to the "army": Gender, race, class and the freedmen's teachers, 1862–1875. *Journal of Education, 172* (3), 76–87.

Butchart, R. E. (1991). Teaching the freed people, 1862–1875: Perspectives on gender, race, calling and commitment in nineteenth-century America. In R. M. Cooke & R. W. Etulain (Eds.), *Religion and culture: Historical essays in honor of Robert C. Woodward* (pp. 1–18). Albuquerque, NM: Far West Books.

Code, L. (1991). *What can she know? Feminist theory and the construction of knowledge*. Ithaca, NY: Cornell University Press.

Daffin, S. (1864a). [Daffin to G. Whipple, March 14, 1864, AMAA]. Unpublished letter.

Daffin, S. (1864b). An important letter from a teacher of the freedmen. Clipping from the *Christian Recorder* (undated), p. 62.

Daffin, S. (1865). [Daffin to S. Hunt, August 23, 1865, AMAA]. Unpublished letter.

Daffin, S. (1867a). [Daffin to G. Whipple, May 8, 1867, AMAA]. Unpublished letter.

Daffin, S. (1867b). [Daffin to E. P. Smith, May 14, 1867, AMAA]. Unpublished letter.

DuBois, W. E. B. (1910). Reconstruction and its benefits. *American Historical Review, 15*, 781–799.

DuBois, W. E. B. (1953). *The souls of Black folk*. New York: Blue Heron Press.

DuBois, W. E. B. (1964). *Black Reconstruction in America: An essay toward a history of the part which Black folk played in the attempt to reconstruct democracy in America, 1860–1880*. Cleveland: World. (Original work published

Fen, S. (1967). Notes on the education of Negroes at Norfolk and Portsmouth, Virginia, during the Civil War. *Phylon, 282,* 197–207.

Franklin, J. H. (1947). *From slavery to freedom: A history of Negro Americans.* New York: Knopf.

Franklin, J. H. (1989). *Race and history: Selected essays, 1938–1988.* Baton Rouge: Louisiana State University Press.

Gordon, B. M. (1995). Knowledge construction, competing critical theories, and education. In J. A. Banks & C. A. M. Banks (Eds.), *Handbook of research on multicultural education* (pp. 184–199). New York: Macmillan.

Harlan, L. R. (1983). *Booker T. Washington: The wizard of Tuskegee, 1901–1915.* New York: Oxford University Press.

Highgate, E. (1864). [Letter from Edmonia Highgate to G. Whipple, March 30, 1864, AMAA]. Unpublished letter.

Hine, D. C. (Ed.). (1986). *The state of Afro-American history: Past, present, future.* Baton Rouge: Louisiana State University Press.

Horst, S. L. (1987). *Education for manhood: The education of Blacks in Virginia during the Civil War.* Lanham, MD: University Press of America.

Jaeger, R. M. (Ed.). (1988). *Complementary methods for research in education.* Washington, DC: American Educational Research Association.

Johnson, W. B. (1991). A Black teacher and her school in Reconstruction Darien: The correspondence of Hettie Sabattie and J. Murray Hoag, 1868–1869. *The Georgia Historical Quarterly, 75* (1), 91–105.

Jones, J. (1980). *Soldiers of light and love: Northern teachers and Georgia Blacks, 1865–1873.* Chapel Hill: University of North Carolina Press.

Jones, M. D. (1985). "They are my people": Black American Missionary Association teachers in North Carolina during the Civil War and Reconstruction. *The Negro Educational Review, 36* (2), 78–89.

Kaestle, C. F. (1983). *Pillars of the republic: Common schools and American society, 1780–1860.* New York: Hill & Wang.

Lewis, L. L. (1993). *W. E. B. DuBois: Biography of a race.* New York: Henry Holt.

Mansfield, B. (1980). *That fateful class: Black teachers of Virginia's freedmen, 1861–1882.* Unpublished doctoral dissertation, Catholic University of America, Washington, DC.

Minnich, E. K. (1990). *Transforming knowledge.* Philadelphia: Temple University Press.

Morris, R. C. (1981). *Reading, 'riting, and reconstruction: The education of freedmen in the South, 1861–1870.* Chicago: University of Chicago Press.

Perkins, L. M. (1984). The Black female American missionary teacher in the South, 1861–1870. In J. J. Crow & F. J. Hatley (Eds.), *Black Americans in North Carolina and the South* (pp. 122–136). Chapel Hill: University of North Carolina Press.

Phillips, U. B. (1966). *American Negro slavery.* Baton Rouge: Louisiana State University Press. (Original work published 1918)

Rabinowitz, H. N. (1974). Half a loaf: The shift from White to Black teachers in the Negro schools of the urban South, 1865–1890. *Journal of Southern History, 40,* 565–594.

Stuckey, S. (1987). *Slave culture: Nationalist theory and the foundations of Black America*. New York: Oxford University Press.

Swint, H. L. (1967). *Northern teachers in the South, 1862–1870*. Nashville, TN: Vanderbilt University Press. (Original work published 1941)

Tetreault, M. K. T. (1993). Classrooms for diversity: Rethinking curriculum and pedagogy. In J. A. Banks & C. A. M. Banks (Eds.), *Multicultural education: Issues and perspectives* (2nd ed., pp. 129–167). Boston: Allyn & Bacon.

Webber, T. L. (1978). *Deep like the river: Education in the slave quarter community, 1831–1865*. New York: W. W. Norton.

Williams, G. W. (1882/83). *History of the Negro race in America from 1619 to 1880: Negroes as slaves, as soldiers, and as citizens* (2 vols.). New York: Putnam's.

Woodson, C. G. (1968). *The education of the Negro prior to 1861*. New York: Arno Press. (Original work published 1915)

Woodson, C. G. (1977). *The mis-education of the Negro*. New York: AMS Press. (Original work published 1933)

CHAPTER 12

Mary McLeod Bethune:
Feminist, Educator, and Activist

ELIZABETH F. BARNETT

This chapter discusses the life and contributions of Mary McLeod Bethune in the context of feminism, transformative education, and social activism during the early twentieth century. Bethune was born in 1875, Black, poor, female, and southern. She lived during a critical period in U.S. history, bordered by the years following the end of the Civil War and the beginning of the civil rights and feminist movements. I will tell Mary McLeod Bethune's story, placing her at the center of prominent African American women and men of this period of U.S. history. I will make explicit the connections among her applications of feminism, transformative knowledge in education, and social action.

Multicultural education in the twenty-first century goes beyond the histories of particular ethnic and cultural groups to investigate the context of oppression itself. This perspective takes into account the social, political, and economic position of the knower in terms of race, class, and gender, and foregrounds how that position influences what is known (Code, 1991). The historical foundations of this conception of multicultural education have roots in the activities of African American women, whose stories have often been silenced, lost, or untold (Skorapa, 1989). Bethune's story, while extraordinary, is only one among many such stories (Brown, 1986; Mills, 1993; Patton, 1993; Wells, 1994; White, 1979).

When I use *feminism*, I am referring to feminism as it was defined and practiced by prominent African American women who were Bethune's contemporaries. Feminist principles traditionally have been an integral part of African American culture (Davis, 1981; hooks, 1984, 1989; Moraga & Anzaldúa,

1981). Collins (1993) states that the origins of Black feminism lie in "the lived experiences that enslaved African women brought with them" (p. 418).

I am using the phrase *transformative knowledge* to mean the type of knowledge that Banks (1993) describes as "concepts, paradigms, themes, and explanations that challenge mainstream academic knowledge and that expand the historical and literary canon" (p. 9). Banks defines mainstream academic knowledge as consisting of "traditional and established knowledge in the behavioral and social sciences" (p. 9). Transformative knowledge challenges mainstream academic knowledge by questioning its basic assumptions. For example, Code (1991) challenges the mainstream academic assumption that in order for knowledge to be valid, it must be objective. She maintains that all knowledge is both objective and subjective, and that infinite variations of this objective/subjective continuum contribute to the knowledge constructed by the knower. A major tenet of transformative knowledge is that knowledge is shaped and influenced by the particular social, class, gender, and political circumstances of the knower.

I am using the term *social action* to describe the extent to which Bethune, in the context of her time, was able to educate, to build an institution, to influence national policy, and to make progress in changing mainstream perceptions of African American women. Social action was the logical extension of transformative knowledge about race and gender for Black feminist educators of the early twentieth century (Collins, 1990; Smith, 1993).

The next sections present a short biography of Mary McLeod Bethune, then discuss her activities in the context of feminism, transformative education, and social activism. Finally, I make explicit the links between Bethune's life and current theory and practice in multicultural education.

PROBLEMS IN CONSTRUCTING BETHUNE'S LIFE

Confusion surrounds many of the facts about Bethune's life. Skorapa (1989) maintains that the "existing biographical narrative is fundamentally the product of myth makers, Bethune herself among them" (pp. 33-34). She explains that Bethune's personal papers were not available for public examination or for scholarly research at the time she completed her dissertation in 1989. She describes the difficulty she had in accessing materials at the Bethune Foundation, the Bethune Museum and Archives, the National Council of Negro Women, and the Bethune-Cookman College Archives. She reports that other researchers interested in Bethune's private letters and diaries have had similar difficulties in gaining access to materials. Skorapa cautions that any published accounts of Bethune's life or work, including the biographies used in the narrative that follows, are not verifiable at this time.

The Early Years

Bethune was born July 10, 1875 near Mayesville, South Carolina, and named Mary Jane McLeod. She was the fifteenth of 17 children born to Sam and Patsy (McIntosh) McLeod, who were former slaves. In 1885, at age 10, Mary enrolled in the Trinity Presbyterian Mission School near her home. In 1888, at age 12, Bethune enrolled in the Scotia Seminary in North Carolina; she graduated in 1894 at the age of 19. She supported herself, in part, from a scholarship given to her by Miss Chrissman, a seamstress and teacher who lived in Denver, Colorado. Writes Perkins (1988), "She worked all seven years at domestic and service jobs at the school in order to supplement her scholarship" (p. 31).

Bethune spent the next year in Chicago at the Moody Institute for Home and Foreign Missions, again with a scholarship from Miss Chrissman (Holt, 1964). She was the only African American enrolled at the Moody Institute, which had a student body numbering more than a thousand (Holt, 1964). It was Bethune's dream to go to Africa to be a missionary. However, she was turned down twice by the Mission Board. They were apparently reluctant to send an African American missionary to Africa (Holt, 1964).

The School Years

In 1896 and 1897 Bethune taught at Haines Institute in Augusta, Georgia. Haines Institute was a private school for African American children opened by Lucy Craft Laney, who was to be a lifelong role model for Bethune (Holt, 1964). Laney believed that "to woman has been committed the responsibility of making the laws of society, making environments for children. She has the privilege and authority, Godgiven, to help develop into a noble man or woman the young life committed to her care. There is not nobler work entrusted to the hands of mortals" (Patton, 1993, p. 693). Teaching at Haines must have been exhilarating for Bethune, for Lucy Laney was considered a preeminent African American educator (Patton, 1993). "Bethune," writes Skorapa (1989), "was engaged in the most radical undertaking of her life, the direct empowerment of African American women through education and social intervention within her community" (p. 44).

Bethune married Albertus Bethune in 1898. Their son, Albert, was born in 1899. She stayed home with her son for a year, then became restless and anxious to return to public life (Bethune, 1972). Bethune had been inspired by her work with Lucy Laney at the Haines Institute, and she became determined to open a similar school for African American girls. She taught for several more years and searched for and dreamed of a site for the school she envisioned. Bethune (1972) later wrote about this period of her life:

I found a shabby four-room cottage, for which the owner wanted a rental of eleven dollars a month. My total capital was a dollar and a half, but I talked him into trusting me until the end of the month for the rest. This was in September. A friend let me stay at her home, and I plunged into the job of creating something from nothing. (p. 138)

On October 3, 1904, Bethune opened the Daytona Education and Industrial Institute in Daytona, Florida, with "five little girls, and a dollar and a half, and faith in God" (Smith, 1993, p. 114). In 1923, the school merged with Cookman College to become Bethune–Cookman Institute. The new school was named for Bethune and for Alfred Cookman, who was a White Methodist minister. Bethune (1972), in an essay entitled "A College on a Garbage Dump," tells a story about buying a piece of land for her school. She spoke with the owner of the property, who agreed to sell her the land for $250. He eventually accepted $5 as a down payment, with the remainder due in 2 years. Bethune sold ice cream and sweet potato pies to construction workers to raise the $5 down payment (Bethune, 1972). In 1941 Bethune–Cookman Institute officially became a liberal arts college. Bethune wrote proudly about her school:

We have fourteen modern buildings, a beautiful campus of thirty-two acres, an enrollment in regular and summer sessions of 600 students, a faculty and staff of thirty-two, and 1,800 graduates. The college property, now valued at more than $800,000, is entirely unencumbered. (p. 142)

The Women's Club Movement

During the time Bethune was building and supporting her school, she also became heavily involved in the women's club movement. The Black women's club movement emerged in response to the ever-increasing need for social programs in the African American community to resist the debilitating effects of racism (Salem, 1993). Bethune joined the National Association for Colored Women in 1912, ostensibly as a way to get publicity and support for her school (Collier-Thomas, 1993). In 1917 she became president of the Florida Federation of Colored Women; in 1920 she founded the Southeastern Federation of Colored Women; in 1924 she became president of the National Association for Colored Women, "the highest office to which a Black woman of that era could then aspire" (Smith, 1993, p. 118).

Collier-Thomas (1993) writes that Bethune became concerned about the fragmented focus of local women's groups, the "inordinate amount of time and effort raising money for male-dominated organizations and male-defined causes" and the "lack of a clear feminist focus and commitment to women's issues and especially to working-class and poor Black women" (p. 854). In

1934 she founded the National Council of Negro Women. Prior to that time, each of the regional and local women's clubs operated more or less independently, or were affiliated with White women's clubs. Skorapa (1989) suggests that the various local and national affiliates were often in disagreement, "apparently as a result of regional and class conflict" (p.76). Collier-Thomas (1993), director of the National Archives for Black Women's History and of the Mary McLeod Bethune Memorial Museum, states that "the development of the national council concept was a stroke of genius" (p. 862). The National Council for Negro Women published a newsletter, *Telefact*, and a journal, *The Aframerican Women's Journal*, and used those publications to unite and mobilize more than a million African American women for social action at the national level for the first time in U.S. history. The Council, under Bethune's leadership, became involved in working to end educational segregation, lynching, and discrimination in voting rights (Skorapa, 1989).

The Roosevelt Years

As a result of the experience and exposure she gained as president of a college and as president of the National Association of Negro Women and subsequently president of the newly formed National Council of Negro Women, Bethune became heavily involved in national politics (Skorapa, 1989). In 1935 she became special advisor on minority affairs to President Roosevelt and, in 1936, was appointed director of the National Youth Administration's Division of Negro Affairs. There were 21 million young people in the United States between the ages of 16 and 24 in 1936 (Berry, 1982). Five million of those were not in school and were not employed. Twice as many African American as White youth were on public subsidy (Berry, 1982). Bethune and her colleagues in the National Youth Administration had a profound influence on the education of African American youth. Berry writes, "Under her department, 150,000 black youths went to high school and 60,000 went to college and graduate school under the student aid program" (p. 291).

Bethune convened the group of African American men who would become the "Black Cabinet" of the Roosevelt administration. She wanted to unite as many of the African American members of the federal government as she could as part of a plan to secure federal jobs for African American women and men. Bethune believed it was essential that the perspectives of Blacks be represented in policy making and program planning at the national level. She worked throughout the later part of her life with the women's club movement and the National Youth Administration to get African Americans hired in federal jobs.

It is difficult to sustain perspective on the sheer quantity of arenas in which Bethune had influence. She was the president of a college and the highest-

ranking Black woman in the Roosevelt administration, and had personal relationships with both Eleanor and Franklin Roosevelt (Skorapa, 1989). In 1942,
when Bethune was named special assistant to the U.S. delegation at the founding conference of the United Nations, she was one of only two women of color
who attended the international conference in any official capacity. At the time
of her death she held 11 honorary advanced degrees from various colleges
and universities (Holt, 1964, p. 291). Bethune was "the preeminent leader at
large from 1936 to 1945. . . . She was tied to the leadership of the frontline
organizations, including the National Association for the Advancement of
Colored People (NAACP), the National Urban League, the Association for the
Study of Negro Life and History, and she was held in the highest esteem in
Black academia" (Smith, 1993, p. 121).

BETHUNE AS FEMINIST, EDUCATOR,
AND SOCIAL ACTIVIST

Bethune had enormous influence in many different spheres of activity. I
will now examine the breadth of her activities in three different contexts: as
feminist, as educator, and as activist. While it may be useful to separate these
arenas for discussion, they were not separate in Bethune's life. Her feminist
perspectives were central to her educational goals, and both were central to
her activities for social change.

Bethune as Feminist

Feminist principles are an integral part of African American culture. Collins
(1990) points out that "African women were socialized to be independent,
self-reliant, and resourceful" (p. 408). Because Black women in many ways
had equal status with men in their own communities, Black feminism focused
on a wider community and was "based on notions of fairness, equality, and
justice for all human beings, not just African American women" (Collins, 1993,
p. 418). The breadth of African American women's conceptualizations of feminism contrasts with a narrower version practiced by White women of the same
era (Collins, 1990; Moraga & Anzaldúa, 1981). For example, White feminists
often conceptualized the suffrage movement as concentrating primarily on
winning the vote for White women (Davis, 1981). At the same time, Black
suffragists consistently advocated voting rights for all Americans. Giddings
(1984) writes, "Afro-Americans maintained a political philosophy of universal suffrage, while Whites, including women, advocated a limited, educated
suffrage after the Civil War" (p. 119).

Because of their lived experiences, and their position in the cultural, social, economic, and political fabric of American life, African American women were often in a unique position to observe and comment on the ways in which knowledge about gender and race was constructed (Collins, 1990). When White feminists spoke about women, it was not hard for Black women to see they were talking about White women (DuBois & Ruiz, 1990; Hull, Scott, & Smith, 1982). When national leaders spoke about all men being created equal, it was obvious to Black women that they meant White men and not women of any hue (Hull, Scott, & Smith, 1982).

In the context of the multiple oppressions of race, class, and gender, Black women developed strategies to protect themselves and their families (Brewer, 1993; Ware, 1989). Collins (1990) writes,

> As mothers, othermothers, teachers, and sisters, Black women were central to the retention and transformation of the Afrocentric worldview. . . . These self-definitions enabled Black women to use African-derived conceptions of self and community to resist negative evaluations of Black womanhood advanced by dominant groups. (pp. 10–11)

Bethune had many opportunities during her own life to observe the behavior and attitudes of powerful and determined African American women. Her mother was the driving force in her family and was responsible for buying the "first five acres of the family farm" (Holt, 1964, p. 52). Her mother was also responsible for giving Bethune a strong pride in her race. Holt states: "Patsy McLeod had been fiercely determined . . . all her sons and daughters had the same father, and all were proudly black" (p. 2). Smith (1993) describes Mary McLeod's sense of herself:

> She saw herself as God's very own precious child—an equal to any other in the human family. Regardless of the limitations society imposed on her . . . , regardless of her sex, her rural southern background, and her lingering poverty, this woman believed in God and in herself. (p. 114)

Bethune's peers viewed her as a feminist; today's authors do also. Holt, Bethune's friend and biographer, called Bethune a "zealous feminist" (p. 52). McCluskey (1989), a contemporary feminist, calls Bethune "a highly focused woman who understood the limitations placed on her by racial and gender assumptions, which she exploited to her own advantage" (p. 113). Bethune's feminism centered on the dilemmas of Black family life and the roles played by Black women in protecting and strengthening their families against the debilitating effects of oppression. She came to believe that African American girls urgently needed education to help them in their multiple roles as breadwinners, caregivers, activists, social workers, educators, and preservers of African American culture.

Bethune dreamed and worked to put Black women in positions of power at local and national levels (Smith, 1993). Her perception of the role Black women should play in national politics was consistent with the role she felt they should play in their families and communities. She wanted Black women to play a role in government because she believed their wisdom and experience were required in order to ensure the survival of the race and of democracy itself.

Bethune as Transformative Educator

Bethune was a transformative leader who challenged mainstream and popular knowledge, and acted on the basis of that knowledge in order to effect social change. In a college commencement address, Bethune said, "Education is the great American adventure, the largest public enterprise in the United States, the country's most important business" (Holt, 1964, p. 192). Education was at the center of Bethune's work to end race, class, and gender inequality. In her life's work—as founder of a school and a national women's club, as a college president, and as advisor to a U. S. president—she expressed her conviction that education was essential for the survival of the African American community (McCluskey, 1989). Many of Bethune's contemporaries shared her convictions regarding the critical need for education in the Black community. Perkins (1993) makes this point:

> Viewed by society as neither humans nor citizens, they had to work together to "uplift" the race. This effort required the contributions of both men and women. Consequently, as the Black community sought to obtain whatever education was available to them . . . the education of women was included. (p. 382)

Coleman-Burns (1989) cites three reasons for the African American cultural emphasis on the education of Black women: (1) traditionally and historically, the status of the Black child was determined by the mother; (2) Black women had more access to employment and to higher-status employment than Black men; and (3) it was believed that Black women were the primary teachers of culture.

Many people in White mainstream U.S. society believed that only White men required a formal education in order to prepare them for their future status as leaders of society (Lott, 1994). They believed that women and African American men had no need for formal education because they were excluded from participation in the public life of the nation (Tyack, 1993). Middle-class White women who lived during the early years of the twentieth century were educated for the private life of housekeeping and child rearing (Perkins, 1993). Although not universally held, there were substantial differences between the educational aspirations of White and African American women. Perkins makes this distinction:

> During a period when women of the larger society were universally ridiculed for educational aspirations, within the black community, African American women received encouragement and praise for their educational efforts. (p. 382)

An urgent need for formal education for African Americans, both women and men, led eventually to an intense debate within the African American community about the nature of the curriculum for Black students in higher education (Anderson, 1988; Bullock, 1967; DuBois, 1965; Washington, 1904/1965). Booker T. Washington, one of the major figures in this controversy, was president of Tuskegee Institute, a trade school for African American youth. He was strongly in favor of industrial education that would prepare students for work. He believed that gainful employment for all African Americans eventually would lead to racial equality (Harlan, 1972, 1983; Washington, 1904/1965). W. E. B. DuBois, another eminent scholar, maintained that African Americans should be trained as scholars and intellectuals who would be able to move into and influence the White power structure (DuBois, 1965; Lewis, 1993).

The two schools of thought soon polarized into mutually exclusive positions. The accommodationists, represented by Booker T. Washington, believed that the race could best be advanced by the diligent work of each individual African American, tolerating for the moment the existing social and political system (Franklin & Meier, 1982; Skorapa, 1989). The protest movement, exemplified by W. E. B. DuBois, spoke out against race oppression and advocated aggressive demonstration and protest (Franklin & Meier, 1982).

Although the media and the community found sharp distinctions between the views of Washington and DuBois, Bethune knew that both of these men were constrained by the times (Skorapa, 1989). Harlan (1983) notes that Washington was exceptional in his ability to bridge the White and Black communities. It is conceivable that he was presenting a perspective that would be acceptable to the philanthropists who were funding his work. Skorapa (1989) suggests that Bethune learned this skill in bridging from Washington in order to get support from the charitable organizations they both depended on to continue their transformative activities. This was a tenuous position for both Washington and Bethune. They needed the support of rich White benefactors to keep the machinery of educational reform moving and, at the same time, needed the support of their own communities. Many African American activists and educators discuss the tensions inherent in this position: walking the line between the mainstream culture and the local community (Albrecht & Brewer, 1990; Collins, 1990; hooks, 1984).

Bethune's philosophy, manifested in her school and in her life, reflected aspects of both positions. The motto of her school echoed Washington's Tuskegee philosophy: head, hand, and heart. Her curriculum emphasized vocational skills that would enable her students to find jobs. At the same time, Bethune agreed with DuBois that African American youth should be educated to take their places alongside White intellectuals (Perkins, 1988). Bethune knew that her female and male students would have to take equal responsibility for the maintenance of their families and communities. African American women in particular could not afford the luxury of such debates; they needed an education for both economic and intellectual reasons.

Bethune saw no mutually exclusive categories of education; she could imagine a school where many objectives could be met simultaneously. Her thinking about the education debate can be described in modern terms as a both/and conception. Collins (1990) characterizes both/and thinking as the "art of being simultaneously a member of a group and yet standing apart from it" (p. 207). She also uses this term to describe a plurality rather than a duality to represent knowledge. Both knowledge and experience, for example, make up the phenomenon called knowing; both thought and action are necessary to the survival of African Americans, and both reason and emotion must be present in order to represent the lived experience of African American women. DuBois (1965) makes this point in his often-quoted piece on double-consciousness:

> It is a peculiar sensation, this double-consciousness, this sense of always looking at one's self through the eyes of others, of measuring one's soul by the tape of a world that looks on in amused contempt and pity. One ever feels his twoness—An American, a Negro; two souls, two thoughts, two unreconciled strivings; two warring ideas in one dark body, whose dogged strength alone keeps it from being torn asunder. (p. 215)

Bethune as Social Activist

The African American community has a long history of taking care of its own people. Second only to Jewish Americans, African Americans are the most philanthropic community in the United States (Carnoy, 1995). Service to others is and has been a cornerstone of Black culture. Black women, especially middle-class Black women, historically have seen themselves as social activists no matter what work they performed (Jones, 1985). Writes Harley (1982):

[The] vast majority of local black teachers and former teachers who involved themselves in the women's club movement . . . did so because they believed, as did most formally educated women at the time, that they had a special responsibility to their respective communities which they alone could fulfill. (p. 256)

Bethune was raised during a time when African American women "set an ambitious agenda that included not only larger roles for women but also general uplift for the race" (Ware, 1989). Social action was an essential part of that larger social agenda. Bethune the social activist was heavily involved in the women's clubs and the social welfare movement. Fannie Barrier Williams (1992), a leader in the Black women's club movement, writes about the importance of this activity: "It is nothing less than the organized anxiety of women who have become intelligent enough to recognize their own social condition and strong enough to initiate the forces of reform" (p. 492). These women recognized that they had serious responsibilities, and they took those responsibilities very seriously (Woloch, 1992). Local organizations opened, financed, and managed child-care centers, schools, healthcare agencies, and a myriad of welfare projects needed by their communities (Ware, 1989). Bethune's sense of herself and her commitment to her life's work were bound to this legacy of service (Holt, 1964; Skorapa, 1989).

Bethune believed, along with many of her contemporaries, that the education of African American girls and women was the key to equality. She wrote (quoted in McCluskey, 1989), "Very early in my life, I saw the vision of what our women might contribute to the growth and development of the race—if they were given a certain type of intellectual training. I longed to see women—Negro women—hold in their hands diplomas that bespoke achievement" (p. 119). Bethune's activism took the form of doing whatever she could to improve the lives and possibilities of African American girls and women. After 1936, this meant a life in the national spotlight as the highest-ranking African American woman in federal government. From this position of influence she worked diligently to get African Americans appointed to positions of leadership. In 1940, there was only one Black federal judge in the United States and he was in the Virgin Islands (Smith, 1993). Except for Black "Cabinet" members, who were mainly in advisory positions, Black Americans were essentially unrepresented in the federal government.

During Bethune's lifetime, most mainstream academic knowledge stated that Black families were dysfunctional, disorganized, and inferior to White families (Berry, 1982; Billingsley, 1992). Bethune was a transformative educator in that she knew and taught that Black families were strong and viable, based on her own subjective and objective experiences. Both mainstream academic and popular knowledge in the southern U.S. society where Bethune grew up held that African Americans could and should live separately from Whites (Giddings, 1984; Jones, 1985). Bethune sustained a transformative vision in that she believed in racial integration in all aspects of life. She believed adamantly in the equality of the races and sexes. Writes Holt (1964):

> In spite of the rigid segregation laws of Florida, she never submitted to them. At her school no one had precedence over another, and there was never any question of this seat or that seat, this aisle or that aisle. She violated such laws with impunity and was never called to account by any of the administrators of such laws; she simply refused to acknowledge their existence, so far as she was concerned they did not exist. (pp. 85–86)

At Bethune–Cookman College the faculty, the students, and the board of trustees were interracial. Bethune insisted that all of the women's club meetings and conventions in which she was involved be interracial (Holt, 1964). Equal status is reflected in Bethune's basic principle: "that what was good for one was good for all, the rights of one were the rights of all" (Holt, p. 141). Bethune advocated equal rights, nonsegregation, and gender equity throughout her long and impressive career as an educator and activist. She came to believe that education should teach young people to resist oppression (Perkins, 1988).

Bethune and Current Practice

Bethune's views on feminism, education, and social activism are consistent with current theories in multicultural education. Bethune envisioned that her school would include a curriculum that reflected both the lives of her students and the dominant culture. Although she lived before the term both/and was an important concept in feminist scholarship, she demonstrated pluralistic thinking in that she felt strongly that a proper education for African American students must include knowledge that would promote race-pride and race-consciousness in addition to skills for getting along in White society (Skorapa, 1989). She believed it was important for Black women to learn about their racial history. She wrote, "Negro women have always known struggle. This heritage is just as much to be desired as any other. Our girls should be taught to appreciate it and welcome it" (quoted in McCluskey, 1989, p. 120).

Black women in the United States have traditionally viewed the world through the multiple lenses of race, gender, and class (Bethune, 1972; Brewer, 1993; Collins, 1990; Hull, 1984). These perspectives facilitate the awareness that race, gender, and social class—among other factors—are socially constructed by those who have power and privilege to protect. Bethune wrote:

"Our more advanced thinkers now are beginning to point out that greatness is very largely a social accident, and almost always socially supported" (quoted in Lerner, 1973, p. xxxv).

CONCLUSION

Mary McLeod Bethune was a feminist, an educator, and a social activist within an ethnic minority community that supported and applauded her accomplishments. She conducted her activities within a larger society that constrained her movements and discounted her ideals. She learned to live her life "apart from racism without being oblivious to or untouched by it" (Jones, 1985, p. 9). Her story fills in one blank space in the historical foundations of multicultural education. It stands next to the stories of prominent African American men who laid the groundwork for the current multicultural education movement. (See Chapters 5 and 6 for discussions of Woodson and Davis.)

Multicultural education in its current manifestation acknowledges and incorporates the contributions of diverse gender, ethnic, and cultural groups into a kaleidoscope that represents many different versions of the world (Banks, 1992; Butler & Walter, 1991; Gay, 1994; Nieto, 1992; Sleeter, 1991). Alice Walker (1983) wrote, "I believe that the truth about any subject only comes when all the sides of the story are put together, and all their different meanings make one new one. Each writer writes the missing parts to the other writer's story" (p. 49). Mary McLeod Bethune's story is a piece of that truth, and I am profoundly changed in retelling it.

Acknowledgments. I am grateful to Sara Woolverton and to James A. Banks for their support and helpful comments on various drafts of this chapter.

REFERENCES

Albrecht, L., & Brewer, R. M. (1990). *Bridges of power: Women's multicultural alliances.* Philadelphia: New Society.

Anderson, J. D. (1988). *The education of Blacks in the South, 1860-1935.* Chapel Hill: University of North Carolina Press.

Banks, J. A. (1992). African American scholarship and the evolution of multicultural education. *Journal of Negro Education, 61* (3), 273-286.

Banks, J. A. (1993). The canon debate, knowledge construction, and multicultural education. *Educational Researcher, 22* (5), 4-14.

Berry, M. F. (1982). Twentieth century Black women in education. *Journal of Negro Education, 51* (3), 288-300.

Bethune, M. M. (1972). A college on a garbage dump. In G. Lerner (Ed.), *Black women in White America: A documentary history* (pp. 134-143). New York: Random House.

Billingsley, A. (1992). *Climbing Jacob's ladder: The enduring legacy of African American families.* New York: Simon & Schuster.

Brewer, R. M. (1993). Theorizing race, class, and gender: The new scholarship of Black feminist intellectuals and Black women's labor. In S. M. James & A. P. A. Busia (Eds.), *Theorizing Black feminisms: The visionary pragmatism of Black women* (pp. 13-30). New York: Routledge.

Brown, C. S. (Ed.). (1986). *Ready from within: Septima Clark and the civil rights movement.* Navarro, CA: Wild Trees Press.

Bullock, H. A. (1967). *A history of Negro education in the South: From 1619 to the present.* Cambridge, MA: Harvard University Press.

Butler, J., & Walter, J. (Eds.). (1991). *Transforming the curriculum: Ethnic studies and women's studies.* Albany: State University of New York Press.

Carnoy, M. (1995). Lecture given at the Elliott Bay Book Company, Seattle, January 19, 1995.

Code, L. (1991). *What can she know? Feminist theory and the construction of knowledge.* Ithaca, NY: Cornell University Press.

Coleman-Burns, P. (1989). African American women: Education for what? *Sex Roles: A Journal of Research, 21* (1/2), 145-160.

Collier-Thomas, B. (1993). National Council of Negro women. In D. C. Hine (Ed.), *Black women in America: An historical encyclopedia* (pp. 853-864). Brooklyn, NY: Carlson.

Collins, P. H. (1990). *Black feminist thought: Knowledge, consciousness, and the politics of empowerment.* New York: Routledge.

Collins, P. H. (1993). Feminism in the twentieth century. In D. C. Hine (Ed.), *Black women in America: An historical encyclopedia* (pp. 418-425). Brooklyn, NY: Carlson.

Davis, A. Y. (1981). *Women, race and class.* New York: Random House.

DuBois, E. C., & Ruiz, V. L. (Eds.). (1990). *Unequal sisters: A multicultural reader in U.S. women's history.* New York: Routledge.

DuBois, W. E. B. (1965). The souls of Black folk. In *Three Negro classics* (pp. 207-389). New York: Avon Books.

Franklin, J. H., & Meier, A. (1982). *Black leaders of the twentieth century.* Urbana: University of Illinois Press.

Gay, G. (1994). *At the essence of learning: Multicultural education.* West Lafayette, IN: Kappa Delta Pi.

Giddings, P. (1984). *When and where I enter: The impact of Black women on race and class in America.* New York: William Morrow.

Harlan, L. R. (1972). *Booker T. Washington: The making of a Black leader, 1856-1901.* New York: Oxford University Press.

Harlan, L. R. (1983). *Booker T. Washington: The wizard of Tuskegee, 1901-1915.* New York: Oxford University Press.

Harley, S. (1982). Beyond the classroom: The organizational lives of Black female educators in the District of Columbia, 1890-1930. *Journal of Negro Education, 51* (3), 254-265.

Holt, R. (1964). *Mary McLeod Bethune: A biography.* New York: Doubleday.

hooks, b. (1984). *Feminist theory: From margin to center.* Boston: South End Press.

hooks, b. (1989). *Talking back: Thinking feminist, thinking Black.* Boston: South End Press.

Hull, G. T. (Ed.). (1984). *Give us each day: The diary of Alice Dunbar Nelson.* New York: W. W. Norton.

Hull, G. T., Scott, P. B., & Smith, B. (Eds.). (1982). *All the women are White, all the Blacks are men, but some of us are brave: Black women's studies.* Old Westbury, NY: Feminist Press.

Jones, J. (1985). *Labor of love, labor of sorrow: Black women, work, and the family, from slavery to the present.* New York: Random House.

Lerner, G. (Ed.). (1973). *Black women in White America: A documentary history.* New York: Vintage Books.

Lewis, D. L. (1993). *W. E. B. DuBois: Biography of a race 1868-1919.* New York: Henry Holt.

Lott, B. (1994). *Women's lives: Themes and variations in gender learning.* Belmont, CA: Brooks/Cole.

McCluskey, A. T. (1989). Mary McLeod Bethune and the education of Black girls. *Sex Roles: A Journal of Research, 21* (1/2), 113-127.

Mills, K. (1993). *This little light of mine: The life of Fannie Lou Hamer.* New York: Dutton.

Moraga, C., & Anzaldúa, G. (1981). *This bridge called my back: Writings of radical women of color.* Watertown, MA.: Persephone Press.

Nieto, S. (1992). *Affirming diversity: The sociopolitical context of multicultural education.* New York: Longman.

Patton, J. O. (1993). Laney, L. C. In D. C. Hine (Ed.), *Black women in America: An historical encyclopedia* (pp. 693-695). Brooklyn, NY: Carlson.

Perkins, C. O. (1988). The pragmatic idealism of Mary McLeod Bethune. *Sage, 5* (2), 30-47.

Perkins, L. M. (1993). Education. In D. C. Hine (Ed.), *Black women in America: An historical encyclopedia* (pp. 380-387). Brooklyn, NY: Carlson.

Salem, D. (1993). National Association of Colored Women. In D. C. Hine (Ed.), *Black women in America: An historical encyclopedia* (pp. 842-851). Brooklyn, NY: Carlson.

Skorapa, O. (1989). Feminist theory and the educational endeavor of Mary McLeod Bethune. Unpublished doctoral dissertation, Georgia State University, Atlanta, GA.

Sleeter, C. E. (Ed.). (1991). *Empowerment through multicultural education.* Albany: State University of New York Press.

Smith, E. (1993). Bethune, Mary McLeod. In D. C. Hine (Ed.), *Black women in America: An historical encyclopedia* (pp. 113-127). Brooklyn, NY: Carlson.

Tyack, D. (1993). Constructing difference: Historical reflections on schooling and social diversity. *Teachers College Record, 95* (1), 8-34.

Walker, A. (1983). *In search of our mother's gardens*. San Diego: Harcourt Brace Jovanovich.

Ware, S. (1989). *Modern American women: A documentary history*. Chicago: Dorsey Press.

Washington, B. T. (1965). Up from slavery. In *Three Negro classics* (pp. 29-205). New York: Avon Books. (Original work published 1904)

Wells, I. B. (1994). *The Memphis diary of Ida B. Wells* (M. DeCosta-Willis, Ed.). Boston: Beacon Press.

White, G. M. (1979). Mary Church Terrell: Organizer of Black women. *Integrated Education, 17* (5/6), 2-8.

Williams, F. B. (1992). The Black club movement. In N. Woloch (Ed.), *Early American women: A documentary history 1600-1900* (pp. 490-493). Belmont, CA: Wadsworth.

Woloch, N. (Ed.). (1992). *Early American women: A documentary history 1600-1900*. Belmont, CA: Wadsworth.

CHAPTER 13

A Reluctant but Persistent Warrior: Eleanor Roosevelt and the Early Civil Rights Movement

ALLIDA M. BLACK

Eleanor Roosevelt was not always a champion of civil rights. For most of her life, she counseled moderation to those activists who attacked the system instead of the mentality behind it. Yet, once aroused to the racial abuses Blacks suffered at the hands of American democracy, Roosevelt reluctantly but persistently confronted this undemocratic behavior and called it by its rightful name. As she continued to grow as an individual, her insight into this "American dilemma" increased. No other noted White American spoke out so consistently, so eloquently, and so brazenly on this issue or encountered such vicious public ridicule for this stand. Consequently, by the time of her death in 1962, Martin Luther King, Jr., could write, "The courage she displayed in taking sides on matters considered controversial, gave strength to those who risked only pedestrian loyalty and commitment to the great issues of our times" (King, 1962, p. 1).

This does not imply, however, that Roosevelt always agreed with civil rights activists or endorsed their tactics. Rather, from the 1930s through the early 1960s, Black activists knew that they could trust her commitment to racial equality, her financial support to civil rights organizations, and her outspoken and honest responses to their questions and tactics. Whether serving on the Board of Directors of the National Association for the Advancement of Colored People (NAACP), financially contributing to the Congress of Racial Equality (CORE), addressing the Southern Conference on Human Welfare, supporting the Black students of Little Rock's Central High School, or campaigning tirelessly for an antilynching bill, Eleanor Roosevelt consistently

Multicultural Education, Transformative Knowledge, and Action. Copyright © 1996 by Teachers College, Columbia University. All rights reserved. ISBN 0-8077-3531-0 (pbk.), ISBN 0-8077-3532-9 (cloth). Prior to photocopying items for classroom use, please contact the Copyright Clearance Center, Customer Service, 222 Rosewood Dr., Danvers, MA 01923, USA, tel. (508) 750-8400.

acted out her commitment and challenged others to do the same. As she aged, her attitudes changed, but she did not grow conservative. She may not have done what everyone wanted her to do—for example, she did not push for a civil rights plank in the Democratic platform as hard as civil rights activists wished—but after the 1956 campaign, she realized that Adlai Stevenson's stance on the issue was equivocal and she questioned whether another candidate should take his place. When John Kennedy called on her in 1960, she spent most of the interview grilling him on his position on civil rights issues. In May 1962, just a few months before her death, she chaired the Commission of Inquiry into the Administration of Justice in the Freedom Struggle and attacked those who attacked civil rights workers in the South.

Nor was she silenced by death. In *Tomorrow Is Now* (1963), published posthumously, Eleanor Roosevelt wrote, "It is today that we must create the future of the world" (epigraph). After praising the courage of those involved in the southern freedom struggle, she compared American racists to European fascists:

> And here, too, emerged another and unmistakable similarity to the Nazism we had believed destroyed. . . . Most of the dictators of the West—Franco, Mussolini, Hitler—claimed that they were "saving" their lands from the threat of Communism. Today, as I have learned over and over to my cost, one needs only to be outspoken about the unfair treatment of the Negro to be labeled "Communist." I had regarded such expression to be the only honorable and civilized course of a citizen of the United States. (Roosevelt, 1963, p. 52)

The course Roosevelt took to reach this position was fraught with personal struggles, limitations, and political constraints. Yet once she reached a decision, she acted despite the consequences. Sometimes, a public injustice prompted a response. Other times, it was an appeal from unknown individuals who spurred action behind the scenes. I will focus on two of her early decisions—her resignation from the National Society of the Daughters of the American Revolution (DAR) in support of Marian Anderson, and her intervention on behalf of Pauli Murray and Odell Waller—and how they reflect Eleanor Roosevelt's public and private commitment to civil rights.

In 1939, Washington, DC, like most major urban areas, was a segregated city. Yet it was an erratic form of segregation in which the district government haphazardly enforced the local separatist ordinances. Although the Organic Law of 1906 mandated a dual school system for Black and White students, the DC School Board relaxed those standards in social situations. White universities and biracial community associations regularly used the recreation facilities and auditoriums of Black public schools. Black labor organizations often conducted their meetings in assembly halls of White religious and labor organizations. District citizens frequently overlooked Jim Crow customs when they attended the theater, the symphony, or a public lecture. Consequently, throughout the 1920s and 1930s, Black and White patrons integrated the audiences of numerous concerts staged at both federal auditoriums and private concert halls (Myrdal, 1944; Wender, 1949).

This elasticized form of segregation operated fairly smoothly until January 8, 1939, when the Howard University School of Music applied to the DAR for use of their auditorium, Constitution Hall, by the world-renowned contralto Marian Anderson. Unbeknownst to all initially involved in this application, this request, the subsequent struggle to lease appropriate concert space, and the concert itself merged to become the major event in the civil rights legacy of the New Deal, a pivotal battle in the campaign to end Jim Crow social practices in the nation's capital, and a crucial test of Eleanor Roosevelt's political judgment.

In 1936, after a triumphant European tour, a stunning performance at the Salzburg Music Festival, and a concert for the Roosevelts that Eleanor Roosevelt praised in her daily *My Day* column, Anderson's manager, Sol Hurok, advised his client to focus less on her European following and concentrate instead on her American tour. Following his advice, the contralto devoted 1938 and 1939 to appearances in the finest auditoriums before integrated audiences across the country, receiving rave reviews from the Atlanta, New York, Boston, St. Louis, San Francisco, New Orleans, and Memphis press. Equally praised for her talent and her poise, Anderson crossed the color line and began establishing a devoted biracial following throughout the United States ("It Happened in Memphis," 1939; Lash, 1971; "Marian Anderson to Be Honored," 1939; Whitlock, 1939; Young, 1939).

As part of her 1936 tour, Anderson had accepted Howard University's request for a benefit performance for their School of Music. For over a decade the University Concert Series had sponsored performances by renowned artists of both races as a cultural gesture to the District and as a minor fund-raising tool for the university. Marian Anderson's three performances prior to 1939 were the highlights of the series and drew successively larger integrated crowds, which forced the university to seek new concert space. By 1938, the 1,100-seat auditorium of Armstrong High School could not accommodate all the requests for tickets to Anderson's concert and the university rented the larger Rialto Theatre. Although Armstrong High School and the Rialto Theatre were Black facilities, the audience for all of Anderson's concerts was predominantly White. Therefore, in 1939 when the Rialto was in receivership and Anderson's popularity was steadily increasing, the concert series had to find another, larger location for its most popular annual event ("Anderson Episode,"1939; "Ickes Comes to Aid," 1939; Marian Anderson Citizens Committee, 1939; Smith, 1939).

Constitution Hall was the preeminent auditorium in Washington. Built in

1929 by the DAR to house its national headquarters and host its national conventions, the hall's 4,000 seats made it the largest auditorium in the District.
The National DAR Board "authorized almost immediately" public use of the
hall for "a minimum cost as a tangible contribution to life in the Nation's
Capital" (National Society, 1965). As home to the National Symphony Orchestra, the Washington Opera, and the National Geographic Society, Constitution Hall served as the focal point in the District for classical music and international culture. It was the only hall in the nation's capital comparable to those
in which Marian Anderson appeared in other cities around the nation and
throughout the world (for discussion of the purpose and history of Constitution Hall, see National Society, 1965; Strayer, 1958).

Constitution Hall was the only logical stage for the concert. On January 9,
Charles Cohen, chair of the Howard University Concert Series, and V. D.
Johnston, university treasurer, applied to the DAR for use of its concert facil-
ity on April 9. Fred Hand, manager of Constitution Hall, responded that the
hall had a standing policy of not renting concert space to Black artists. However, later that day, Hand told the press that Marian Anderson could not perform in Constitution Hall because the date requested had been booked a year
earlier by the National Symphony Orchestra and DAR regulations prohibit
rental of the hall for two engagements on the same day.

Actions were taken immediately to appeal to the DAR for reconsideration.
V. D. Johnston contacted Charles Houston, special counsel to the NAACP as
well as a Howard University board member. Houston advised Johnston to
inform the press about the dilemma and to request letters of support from
Anderson's peers. After requesting such endorsements, the university contacted the Washington press, describing the DAR's restrictive policy. Within
a day after the requests were mailed, such leading performers as Geraldine
Farrar, Kirsten Flagstad, Lawrence Tibbet, Walter Damrosh, and Leopold
Stokowski telegraphed their disapproval to the DAR. The Washington press,
however, was slower to respond. *The Washington Post* ran an editorial
expressing dismay at the DAR's action but stopping short of calling for its reversal. *The Washington Star* ignored the issue until February 1. Only *The
Washington Afro-American* and *The Washington Times-Herald* challenged
the DAR's decision and called on Congress to build a federal auditorium in
the District that would be free of racial discrimination ("Anderson Episode,"
1939; "Ban Maintained," 1939; Chronology, 1939; "Ickes Comes to Aid," 1939;
"Joins Protests Against," 1939; Smith, 1939).

Action intensified on all fronts the following week. Assured by Anderson's
manager Sol Hurok that Constitution Hall was available April 8 and April 10,
Johnston and Cohen reapplied to Hand. The DAR again refused permission,
this time stating no reason. Howard concert officials appealed the decision.
On January 16, in New York City, the Spingarn Committee of the NAACP met

and unanimously voted to present its most prestigious award to Anderson for "her special contributions in the field of music . . . and her magnificent dignity as a human being" ("Press Release," n.d.). In Washington, Charles Houston suggested that a community meeting be called to discuss the Anderson ban and to propose alternative strategies, and Walter White, secretary of the NAACP, called on Eleanor Roosevelt to ask her to present the Spingarn Medal to Anderson at the National NAACP conference in July. Roosevelt gladly accepted (Lovell, 1939a, 1939b; "Press Release," n.d.; White to Anderson, 1939; White to Roosevelt, 1939).

Three days later, Howard University applied to the Community Center Department for permission to use Central High School Auditorium for the April 9 event. The petition was referred for review to the Committee on the Use of Public Buildings of the District Board of Education. As Central High School was a White school, the committee recommended that Superintendent of Schools Frank Ballou decline the request and recommend the use of Armstrong Auditorium instead. Press coverage increased and Howard, through Johnston and Houston, asked prominent Washingtonians to lobby the DAR on its behalf. Interior Secretary Harold Ickes, Agriculture Secretary Henry Wallace, several members of Congress, and Washington Cathedral Canon Anson Phelps Stokes responded to the university's request (Ballou, 1939; Cohen et al., 1939; Statement on Application, 1939).

Thus, by February, public pressure mounted. Nevertheless, despite requests from Anderson's agents to book the hall for any date available within the first 2 weeks of April, Constitution Hall continued to ban Anderson from its stage. On February 13, the president general of the DAR, Mrs. H. M. Roberts, Jr., mailed a communiqué on the matter to her state regents, informing them that "the rules [of the DAR] are in accordance with the policy of theatres, auditoriums, hotels and public schools of the District of Columbia" (Smith, 1939, p. 167). Two days later, Fred Hand informed Charles Cohen that "the hall is not available for a concert by Miss Anderson" (Smith, 1939, p. 168). There could be no appeal. Anderson would have to find space elsewhere in the District.

Community response was swift and effective. On February 17, Johnston called a citywide meeting to discuss the board's refusal and to plan the counterattack. By the next day, local organizations were adopting resolutions protesting both the DAR and the school board's actions. Jascha Heifetz denounced the DAR from the Constitution Hall stage, saying he was ashamed to be on "a stage barred to a great singer because of her race" (Heifetz, 1939, p. 1). That same evening, five blocks away, Charles Edward Russell, a liberal White attorney, chaired an interracial gathering that agreed to circulate petitions urging the use of Central High School Auditorium. This audience, formally incorporating itself as the Marian Anderson Citizens Committee (MACC), adopted a resolution instructing its interim officers to request permission to present the petitions to the school board at its March 1 meeting. By February 22, the MACC was front-page news in the District and the national press roundly criticized the board's decision ("Ban on Anderson," 1939).

Four days later, as the MACC reconvened to assemble the 3,500 signatures it collected on its petition, Eleanor Roosevelt debated which action to take on Anderson's behalf. Howard University had been lobbying the first lady since the beginning of February to issue a public statement rebuking the DAR (Johnston, 1939), but Roosevelt refused, arguing that such a statement would do no good, as the organization "considered [her] to be too radical" (Roosevelt to Johnston, 1939). Besides, she told two friends, "she would like to make a statement . . . [but] this situation is so bad that plenty of people will come out against it" (Roosevelt to Lovell, 1939). This refusal, however, did not mean that Roosevelt sat idly along the sidelines. She carefully mapped a strategy, planning a forceful rebuttal to the snubbing that Anderson received in the nation's capital.

Roosevelt was not hiding behind the curtain of public opinion. Her position on race was already well-known. Immediately after the DAR's initial refusal to Anderson, Eleanor Roosevelt agreed to present the Spingarn Medal to the diva, met with NAACP secretary Walter White and conference chair Dr. Elizabeth Yates Webb to discuss the broadcast of the awards ceremony, planned to invite Anderson to perform for the British king and queen at the White House in June, and telegraphed her support to Howard University (Roosevelt to Lovell, 1939).

The strategical problem for Roosevelt was how to support Anderson without upstaging the local community or further angering the powerful southern Democrats. Initially, she decided to refrain from direct action and to participate only peripherally in the campaign. On February 20, less than a week after Anderson's appeals to the DAR and the school board were rejected, Roosevelt mentioned Anderson in her column for the first time. Yet, on February 25, she denied a request from V. D. Johnston to criticize the DAR in her weekly press conferences. However, the following day, she did respond to the MACC request for telegrams in support of the proposed concert. Clearly, Roosevelt did not sidestep the problem. She publicly committed herself to the Black performer, while she tried to find the most effective way to implement that commitment.

By the end of the week, Roosevelt concluded that for maximum impact her actions must be seen as a response to a national, rather than local, issue. Consequently, the National Society of the Daughters of the American Revolution and not the District of Columbia School Board should be the focus of the rebuttal. Having taken steps to ensure Anderson's eventual performance in the District and having carefully limited her association with the local groups appealing a local political decision, Eleanor Roosevelt remained free to act as an individual member of an organization responding to a decision made by that body's leadership. This masterful political strategy resounded with long-range political and public policy implications. Consequently, when Eleanor Roosevelt determined to act as an individual outside the locale directly affected by the policy, she expanded its focus from one of local leasing policies to one of national social import.

More significant than the overt actions Roosevelt took behind the scenes to facilitate Anderson's appearance in the District was the pivotal role she played in highlighting the discriminatory conduct of such a prestigious organization as the DAR. The power of understatement displayed in her *My Day* column of February 26, 1939, revealed Roosevelt's hand on the pulse of the nation. She began her column with the standard account of her social duties of the day before, rather than immediately discussing the controversy. Yet even after introducing her real topic, she refrained from naming the issue or the organization that had caused her distress.

This tactic clearly portrayed the situation in impersonal, nonthreatening terms with which the majority of her readers would identify. She introduced the dilemma simply:

> I have been debating in my mind for some time a question which I have had to debate with myself once or twice before in my life. Usually, I have decided differently from the way in which I am deciding now. (*My Day*, 1939)

She then outlined the problem and her response to it:

> The question is, if you belong to an organization and disapprove of an action which is typical of a policy, shall you resign or is it better to work for a changed point of view within the organization? In the past when I was able to work actively in any organization to which I had belonged, I have usually stayed in until I had at least made a fight and been defeated.
>
> Even then I have as a rule accepted my defeat and decided either that I was wrong or that I was perhaps a little too far ahead of the thinking of the majority of that time. I have often found that the thing in which I was interested was done some years later. But, in this case I belong to an organization in which I do no active work. They have taken an action which has been widely talked of in the press. To remain as a member implies approval of that action, therefore I am resigning. (*My Day*, 1939)

The next day, the column splashed across the front pages of American newspapers from San Francisco to New York City. Although others had resigned from the DAR over this issue, and although major public figures had publicly lamented the DAR policy, Eleanor Roosevelt placed Marian Anderson, the DAR, and racial discrimination on a national stage where it could not be ignored. By putting her political clout and personal popularity squarely behind Anderson and in front of the DAR, she moved the conflict into another arena.

On Monday, March 25, that support was formalized. The White House staff entered the battle. Assistant Secretary of the Interior Oscar Chapman presented Walter White's request to use the Lincoln Memorial to Interior Secretary Ickes. Ickes, a past president of the Chicago NAACP, phoned Franklin Roosevelt and requested an immediate appointment. Roosevelt, who was preparing to leave town that afternoon, delayed his plans and agreed to see the Interior official. When informed of Ickes's request, the president responded, "I don't care if she sings from the top of Washington Monument as long as she sings" (Ickes, 1939). Ickes called an afternoon press conference and announced that the Lincoln Memorial would be the site of the April 9 concert (Houston, 1939; Ickes, 1939; White to Houston & Johnston, 1939).

Once again the Anderson affair made the front pages of newspapers around the country. The struggle to find appropriate space for a world-famous artist outweighed the personal bias of certain members of the press corps toward Black civil rights in general and the NAACP in particular. Only the perennial Roosevelt baiter Westbrook Pegler was less than enthusiastic about the sudden turn of events ("Anderson Supporters Unsatisfied," 1939; "Anderson to Rise," 1939; "Concert in Capitol, 1939; "DAR's Ban Upset," 1939; "Marian Anderson Songs," 1939; "Marian Anderson to Sing," 1939; O'Day, 1939).

The NAACP launched a campaign to assemble as diverse a group of prominent cosponsors for the event as possible. Although Eleanor Roosevelt was the immediate first choice for chairing the event, she was not in Washington and recognized that she would upstage Anderson if she were to sponsor the event. So her close friend, Congresswoman Caroline O'Day, stepped in to assist the coordination of endorsements. Telegrams asking assistance "in sponsoring an open-air free concert by Marian Anderson under the auspices of Howard University from the Steps of the Lincoln Memorial . . . at 5p.m., Sunday, April 9" were sent to more than 500 people. By the next day, responses were flooding O'Day's office (O'Day, 1939).

By Easter Sunday, more than 300 prominent individuals had agreed to sponsor the event. The concert had become a national cause célèbre. The DAR had been rebuked throughout the 3-month campaign to stage the event, but the racial policy implications had been virtually ignored. If the event was to effect the change that the NAACP and some MACC members desired, the concert must be viewed in cultural, political, and racial terms. Few who realized the long-range implications of the event had the stature and wide-range popularity to achieve this success. Eleanor Roosevelt had both. Consequently, she was charged with carrying the mantle into the public fray. By inviting

Anderson to sing for the king and queen of Britain and agreeing to present Anderson the Spingarn Medal in the midst of the controversy, Roosevelt clearly indicated to the public she intended to stay the course.

Eleanor Roosevelt kept her word and presented the Spingarn Medal to Marian Anderson at the NAACP convention in Richmond. There she delivered a nationally broadcast address urging her audience to protect democracy actively, to ensure "the ability of every individual to be a really valuable citizen," and to strive to secure "whatever rights of citizenship are ours under the Constitution" ("Mrs. Roosevelt Awards," 1939, p. 265). By unabashedly associating herself as a primary power source behind the concert, by allowing herself to be photographed sitting next to Black political and social leaders on the stage of the NAACP national convention on Independence weekend in a stronghold of southern conservatism, Roosevelt made the event overtly political 2 months after Anderson's final encore ("Mrs. Roosevelt Awards," 1939).

The Marian Anderson venture taught Eleanor Roosevelt a valuable lesson. In 1939, she was just beginning to use *My Day* as her own political forum. The Marian Anderson controversy and the response it generated from her readers showed Roosevelt the direct impact she had when she spoke out on a political event. She received more mail supporting her resignation from the DAR than she did on any other issue she associated herself with in 1939. Consequently, this experience reinforced Mrs. Roosevelt's venture into the politics of confrontation.

Not all of Mrs. Roosevelt's actions were so public. Or so effective.

In November 1938, Franklin Roosevelt went to the University of North Carolina to receive an honorary doctor of law degree. FDR used the occasion to address those present on the need for social change. "There is change whether we will it or not," the president argued, and all citizens must recognize that the "affirmative action which we have taken in America" is the "maintenance of a successful democracy at home." The president ended his address by praising the college for "typifying as it does American liberal thought and American tradition" (Murray, 1988, pp. 110–111).

When Pauli Murray read FDR's address in *The New York Times* the following day, she was outraged. Having just applied to graduate school and been rejected by the institution the president praised for its liberalism, Murray wrote the president a stinging rebuttal:

> Yesterday, you placed your liberal approval on the University of North Carolina as an institution of liberal thought. You spoke of the necessity of change in a body of law to meet the problems of an accelerated era of civilization. You called on Americans to support a liberal philosophy based on democracy. What does this mean for Negro Americans? Does it mean that we, at last, may participate freely

. . . with our fellow citizens in working out the problems of this democracy? . . .
Or does it mean that everything you said has no meaning for us as Negroes, that
again we are to be set aside and passed over for more important problems? Do
you feel, as we do, that the ultimate test of democracy in the United States will
be the way in which it solves its Negro problem? (Murray to F. Roosevelt, 1939)

Despite her misgivings about Eleanor Roosevelt's reluctance to condemn
racial segregation, Pauli Murray mailed the first lady a copy of her letter to
the president. To her surprise, she received a reply signed by Eleanor Roosevelt
herself:

I have read the copy of the letter you sent me and I understand perfectly, but
great change comes slowly. I think they are coming, however, and sometimes it
is better to fight hard with conciliatory methods. The South is changing, but don't
push too hard. There is great change in youth, for instance, and that is a hopeful
sign. (Roosevelt to Murray, 1939)

Both women shared the same goal but differed over the methods used to
achieve a democratic society. A few weeks before writing this letter, Eleanor
Roosevelt electrified Black and White Americans by refusing to comply with
the Birmingham segregation ordinances when she attended the Southern
Conference for Human Welfare. Pauli Murray was well aware of this when
she sent her letter to Roosevelt. Consequently, Roosevelt's admonition, "don't
push too hard," was even more difficult for her to accept.

Nevertheless, Murray was impressed that the first lady took the time to
acknowledge her frustration. When Murray heard Roosevelt's radio address
on behalf of domestic workers, she again wrote the White House urging recognition of the basic human rights of Black Americans. Again, Eleanor
Roosevelt responded. Only this time, instead of replying directly to Pauli
Murray she published part of the woman's letter in her national column
(Murray, 1988). This correspondence started an almost 30-year friendship
between the young Black activist and scholar and Eleanor Roosevelt—a friendship that was as blunt and outspoken and committed as the two women were
to the causes they espoused. Although Roosevelt responded to a plea from
Murray's sister when Murray was arrested in Virginia for challenging Jim Crow
seating ordinances and called the judge involved on Murray's behalf, the two
women did not meet until January 1940, when Roosevelt invited Murray to
her New York apartment to discuss Murray's plans for National Sharecroppers Week. Impressed with Murray's presentation and well aware of the
issues involved, Roosevelt agreed to be the keynote speaker for the conference and donated $100 to the campaign (Murray, 1988).

But Roosevelt's efforts on behalf of sharecroppers were just beginning.
Not all her actions were as public as this speech and contribution. Nor were

they as effective as intervention on behalf of Marian Anderson, but they were nonetheless heartfelt.

In August 1940, Odell Waller, a Black sharecropper from Virginia, was convicted by an all-White jury (a jury from which Blacks had been excluded via the poll tax requirement) of the first-degree murder of Oscar Davis, his White landlord. Waller was sentenced to death. Pauli Murray was sent to investigate the case for the Worker's Defense League. Eleanor Roosevelt asked Murray to keep her informed.

Despite a nationwide campaign on Waller's behalf and appeals to the state courts, the death sentence stood. The Supreme Court refused to hear the case because the defense had failed to offer specific proof that those who did not pay the poll tax were excluded from jury service. The only way for Waller's sentence to be changed was for Governor Darden to commute it to life imprisonment. The governor agreed to postpone execution until all avenues for appeal were exhausted. When the Supreme Court refused to hear the case, a date for Waller's execution was set (Lash, 1971; Murray, 1988; Roosevelt to White, 1940).

To Roosevelt the parallels between the jury system Waller encountered and lynching were unmistakable. She wrote A. M. Kroeger, "Times without number Negro men have been lynched or gone to their death without due process of law. No one questions Waller's guilt, but they question the system which led to it" (Roosevelt to Kroeger, 1942, n. p.). Responding to appeals from Murray, the NAACP, and A. Philip Randolph, Eleanor Roosevelt launched a one-person crusade within the White House to have the sentence commuted. First, she called Governor Darden and pleaded the case. When that proved unsuccessful, she persistently dogged the president to write the governor requesting commutation. Finally, FDR acquiesced and wrote Darden (Lash, 1971; Murray, 1988; Roosevelt to Kroeger, 1942).

On the day of Waller's execution, Eleanor Roosevelt still would not let up. She phoned Harry Hopkins, the president's closest advisor, four or five times. FDR believed that since the governor had given reprieves while Waller appealed, he had acted constitutionally and FDR "doubted very much if the merits of the case warranted the Governor reaching any other decision." This did not deter the first lady, as this memorandum from Harry Hopkins (Lash, 1971) shows:

> Mrs. Roosevelt, however, would not take no for an answer and the President finally got on the phone himself and told Mrs. Roosevelt that under no circumstances would he intervene with the Governor and urged very strongly that she say nothing about it.
>
> I think, too, in this particular case Mrs. Roosevelt felt that I was not pressing her case with the President adequately, because in the course of the evening he

was not available on the phone and I had to act as a go-between. At any rate I felt that she would not be satisfied until the President told her himself, which he reluctantly but finally did. (pp. 865–866)

Two hours before Waller was to be executed, a dejected Eleanor Roosevelt phoned A. Philip Randolph at NAACP headquarters. As Waller's supporters listened to her over five extensions, Roosevelt in a trembling voice informed Randolph: "I have done everything I can possibly do. I have interrupted the President twice. . . . He said this is a matter of law and not of the heart. It is in Governor Darden's jurisdiction and the President has no legal power to intervene. I am so sorry, Mr. Randolph, I can't do any more" (Murray, 1988, p. 173). At 8:30 A.M., July 2, despite all the efforts on his behalf, Odell Waller was executed.

Eleanor Roosevelt was an extremely powerful person. Yet there were limits to her power. In the cases discussed, her husband was the ultimate power. Not because he was the husband and she the wife, but because Franklin Roosevelt was the president of the United States. The challenge Eleanor Roosevelt confronted on a daily basis from 1932 to 1945 was how to use her influence and her clout to the maximum, how to use her power in her own right. In the same memo in which Hopkins described Roosevelt's efforts on behalf of Odell Waller, he characterized her actions as atypical of the things that had gone on in Washington between the President and Mrs. Roosevelt since 1932 (Lash, 1971).

Once free of the constraints of the White House, Eleanor Roosevelt continued to protest injustice and demand that democracy be practiced without any limits or qualifications.

Her genius lay in her ability to know when to take a symbolic stance in favor of or in protest against an act (as she did in the Marian Anderson affair) and when to apply constant pressure behind the scenes to reach a particular end. Whether confronting the DAR, arguing strategy with Pauli Murray, or pressing the case of those denied justice, Eleanor Roosevelt had the courage of her convictions. She was not afraid to take a stand or face the consequences that stand might arouse. If she was too idealistic in her belief in education as the cure to evils of racism or too reluctant completely to endorse nonviolent resistance as a means to end injustice, she nevertheless realistically confronted the evils of a racist society and devoted her energies to defeating them.

Shortly before her death, Eleanor Roosevelt wrote: "One thing we must all do. We must cherish and honor the word *free* or it will cease to apply to us. And that would be an inconceivable situation" (Roosevelt, 1963, p. 138). It is to her everlasting credit that throughout her life, Eleanor Roosevelt practiced what she preached.

Acknowledgments. The author wishes to thank the Eleanor and Franklin Roosevelt Institute for funding this research as well as Leo Ribuffo, Helen Veit, Charlene Bickford, Kenneth Bowling, and Wendy Wolff for their encouragement and insightful criticism.

REFERENCES

The Anderson episode. (1939, February 21). *The New York Times,* editorial.

Anderson supporters unsatisfied by plan for open-air concert. (1939, April 1). *The Washington Star.*

Anderson to rise on Easter. (1939, April 8). *The Norfolk Journal and Guide*, pp. 1, 10.

Ballou, F. W. (1939, February 28). Statement on the application for the use of Central High School. Wallace, Ickes, and Stokes, telegram in Marian Anderson Controversy Collection, box 2, folder 36.

Ban maintained at Constitution Hall by DAR. (1939, January 21). *The Washington Afro-American*, p. 1.

Ban on Anderson Attacked by 6000. (1939, February, 27). *Washington Daily News*, p. 1.

Chronology Marian Anderson concert case. (1939). Citizen's Committee, Chronology: group 1, box 2, folder 35. Howard University, Moorland-Spingarn Research Center, Washington, DC.

Cohen, C., et al., to District of Columbia Board of Education. (1939, February 15). Marian Anderson Controversy Collection, collection 1, box 1, folder 21.

Concert in capitol for Marian Anderson. (1939, March 31). *The New York Times.*

DAR's ban upset; she'll sing Easter. (1939, March 31). *The New York Daily News.*

Heifetz, ashamed D.C. hall is denied Marian Anderson. (1939, February, 20). *The Washington Post*, p. 1.

Houston, C., to G. Goode. (1939, April 1). Marian Anderson Controversy Collection, box 1, folder 1.

Ickes comes to aid of colored singer in controversy. (1939, March 7). *The Washington Evening Star.*

Ickes, H. L. (1939, March 30). *The diary of Harold Ickes.* Library of Congress.

It happened in Memphis. (1939, April 4). *The Washington News.*

Johnston, V. D., to E. Roosevelt. (1939, February, 4). Eleanor Roosevelt Papers, Series 100, box 1507.

Joins protest against ban on Marian Anderson. (1939, January 31). *The Washington Star.*

King, M. L., Jr. (1962, November 24). Eulogy. *Amsterdam News*, p. 1.

Lash, J. P. (1971). *Eleanor and Franklin.* New York: W.W. Norton.

Lovell, J. (personal letters). Marian Anderson Controversy Collection, collection 1, box 2, folder 35.

Lovell, J., to E. Roosevelt. (1939a, February 25). Eleanor Roosevelt Papers, Series 100, Personal Correspondence, box 1512.

Lovell, J., to E. Roosevelt. (1939b, February 26). Eleanor Roosevelt Papers, White House Telegrams, box 2995.

The Marian Anderson Citizens Committee. (Letters to the Board of Education of the District of Columbia, March 9, 1939).

Marian Anderson songs to be heard a mile. (1939, April 4). *The Washington Daily News.*

Marian Anderson to be honored in city tonight. (1939, April 18). *The New York Daily Worker.*

Marian Anderson to sing at Lincoln Memorial. (1939, March 30). *Chicago News.*

Mrs. Roosevelt awards medal. (1939, September). *Crisis, 46* (9), p. 265.

Murray, P., to F. Roosevelt. (1939, December 19). Attached to P. Murray to E. Roosevelt, Eleanor Roosevelt Papers, Series 100, Personal Correspondence, box 1517.

Murray, P. (1988). *Song in a weary throat.* New York: Harper & Row.

My Day. (1939, February 26). Eleanor Roosevelt Papers, My Day, box 3073.

Myrdal, G. (with Sterner, R., & Rose, A.) (1944). *An American dilemma: The negro problem and modern democracy.* New York: Harper & Row.

National Society of the Daughters of the American Revolution. (1965). In *The National Society of the Daughters of the American Revolution Diamond Anniversary.* Washington, DC: NSDAR.

O'Day, C., to E. Roosevelt. (1939, April 1). Eleanor Roosevelt Papers, White House Telegrams, 2/39–12/39, box 2995.

Press Release, 24th Spingarn medal to Marian Anderson. (n.d.). NAACP Papers, Section I, Administrative Files, box C-214.

Roosevelt, E., to V. D. Johnston. (1939, February 9). Eleanor Roosevelt Papers, Series 100, box 1507.

Roosevelt, E., to J. Lovell, Jr. (1939, February 26). Eleanor Roosevelt Papers, White House Telegrams, box 2995.

Roosevelt, E., to A. M. Kroeger. (1942, August 20). Eleanor Roosevelt Papers, Personal Correspondence, box 1649.

Roosevelt, E., to P. Murray. (1939, December 19). Eleanor Roosevelt Papers, Series 100, box 1517.

Roosevelt, E. Walter White Correspondence for 1940, Eleanor Roosevelt Papers, Walter White folder, Series 100, box 1668.

Roosevelt, E. (1963). *Tomorrow is now.* New York: Harper & Row.

Smith, C. (1939, July). Roulades and cadenzas: Summing up l'affaire Anderson. *Esquire,* pp. 79, 167–168.

Statement on application for the use of Central High School auditorium for a recital by Marian Anderson. (1939, February 16). box 2, folder 38.

Strayer, M. (1958). *The DAR: An informal history.* New York: Greenwood Press.

Wender, H. S. (1949, May). *An analysis of recreation and segregation in the District of Columbia.* Washington, DC: District of Columbia Board of Education.

White, W., to M. Anderson. (1939, January 21). NAACP Papers, Administrative Files, box C-24.

White, W., to C. Houston & V. D. Johnston. (1939, March 31). Marian Anderson Controversy Collection, box 1, folder 1.

White, W., to E. Roosevelt. (1939, January 16). Eleanor Roosevelt Papers, Miscellaneous Correspondence, box 1532.

Whitlock, E. C. (1939, March 12). Marian Anderson near top in singing appeal: Negro contralto who appears here Sunday has few rivals in audience demand. *The Fort Worth Morning Star Telegram.*

Young, M. H. (1939, April 6). Marian Anderson thrills 6000 with rich voice in concert here. *The Atlanta Constitution*, p. 23.

PART IV

Intergroup Education and Racial Attitudes Research: Historical Perspectives

Near the turn of the century, massive number of immigrants entered the United States from Southern, Eastern, and Central Europe. The immigrants posed, for the old-line, Anglo-Saxon Americans, "an immigrant problem." As nativist feelings and attitudes surfaced and grew, the nation responded by establishing Americanization programs to assimilate the immigrants into the mainstream culture and to eradicate "foreign influences." The intercultural education movement incorporated some aspects of Americanization. However, the movement leaders, who were influenced by cultural pluralists such as Horace Kallen and Randolph Bourne, believed that the children of immigrants could become loyal and effective American citizens while at the same time acknowledging their cultural roots and maintaining a level of primordial attachments.

The intercultural education movement became controversial and eventually experienced near fatal blows when it became a vulnerable target of its assimilationist critics. The assimilationist critics, who were progenitors of today's Western canon defenders, feared that a focus on ethnic heritage and pride would Balkanize U. S. society. The intercultural movement experienced renewed vitality—in the form of intergroup education—when large numbers of southern Blacks and Whites rushed to northern and western cities to obtain jobs created by World War II–related industrial growth.

Racial conflict and riots developed in the cities as Blacks and Whites competed for jobs, housing, and other limited sources. Intergroup education—led by educators such as Hilda Taba, William Van Til, Lloyd Cook, and Elaine Cook—was developed to help create racial and ethnic peace through the development of school, college, and university programs. When the civil rights movement developed in the 1960s, few vital signs of the intergroup education movement remained.

In Chapter 14, Cherry A. McGee Banks describes and interprets the history of the intercultural and intergroup education movement, the ways in which this movement is related to multicultural education, and the lessons multicultural education scholars and researchers can derive from the movement's birth and death. The intergroup education period was characterized by the participation of eminent social scientists who conducted seminal research related to prejudice, prejudice reduction, and discrimination. Michael R. Hillis, in Chapter 15, provides an interpretive history of the research on racial attitudes from the 1930s through the 1950s. He states that a paradigm shift took place in the 1930s: Prejudice became viewed as a shortcoming of the prejudiced person rather than as a justified attitude toward groups who were genetically inferior. This latter view dominated social science research and theory prior to the 1930s.

CHAPTER 14

The Intergroup Education Movement

CHERRY A. MCGEE BANKS

Tensions among racial, ethnic, and religious groups have been a salient characteristic of U.S. society since its inception (Bennett, 1988; Higham, 1972; Nash, 1982). Individuals and groups in a number of institutions have worked to reduce these tensions. This chapter documents the ideas, programs, curriculum materials, and practices of scholars, teachers, and social activists who believed that education could be an important factor in combating tensions among racial, ethnic, and religious groups. These individuals constructed a movement known as intergroup education, which lasted from the mid-1920s to the early 1950s. Although their work has been largely neglected by educational historians, it represented a significant effort on the part of these educators to improve human relations. It also has important lessons for multicultural educators.

In this chapter I identify the leaders in intergroup education and describe their perspectives and assumptions. I also describe some of the distinctive ways in which intergroup leaders organized their experiences, used situated vocabularies, and interpreted the problems and reactions they encountered. The visions, views, stated goals, and achievements of intergroup leaders, however, should not be read as accurate representations of social reality, but as reflecting themes, images, and metaphors that were important to them and their work.

This chapter is divided into three parts. The nature of intergroup education is discussed in the first part. The second provides an overview of select intergroup education programs. The last part discusses the demise of intergroup education and suggests some lessons that multicultural educators can learn from the intergroup education movement. The aim of this chapter is to document the intergroup education movement. A future research agenda will examine issues such as why major educational historians have not devoted attention to the intergroup education movement, its influence on class-room practice, and the extent to which it was related to other educational movements.

THE NATURE OF INTERGROUP EDUCATION

Through materials, workshops, and college-level courses, intergroup edu-cators influenced scholars, teachers, community activists, and school admin-istrators in a number of schools throughout the United States (Committee, 1949; Taba, Brady, Jennings, & Robinson, 1949). However, intergroup edu-cation did not permeate the curriculum of most U.S. schools. Intergroup or-ganizations and programs were concentrated on the East Coast and in the Mid-west. They generally were located in communities in and within a few hours of New York City and Chicago. The Service Bureau for Intercultural Educa-tion was located in New York City; the Center for Intergroup Education was located at the University of Chicago; and the College Study in Intergroup Relations was directed from Wayne University in Detroit, Michigan (now Wayne State University). A few college programs in intergroup education were located in schools in the South such as Atlanta University in Georgia and Talladega College in Alabama. Some K–12 programs were located in school districts outside the East Coast and the Midwest, in cities such as Seattle, San Francisco, and Denver, (Cook, 1951; DuBois, 1984; Taba, Brady, & Robinson, 1952).

The American Council on Education, the American Jewish Committee, the Council on Cooperation in Teacher Education, and the National Conference of Christians and Jews were among the key organizations that provided sus-tained funding for intergroup education (DuBois, 1984; Vickery & Cole, 1943). A number of other organizations, including the National Association for the Advancement of Colored People (NAACP), the National Urban League, the China Institute, and the Japan Institute provided periodic funding for inter-group activities and materials (Montalto, 1982).

DEFINITIONS OF INTERGROUP
AND INTERCULTURAL EDUCATION

Intercultural and intergroup education were two terms that were used to describe organized efforts of educators to improve human relations. There were similarities as well as differences in the usage and meanings of the terms. Intercultural educators focused primarily on the cultures of racial, ethnic, and religious groups (Stendler & Martin, 1953). European immigrants were a pivotal group for intercultural educators, although attention also was given to people of color (DuBois, 1939). Helping new immigrants and their children maintain ties with their ancestral cultures, feel good about themselves, and make positive adjustments to their new homeland were important goals for many intercultural educators (Department of Supervisors, 1942). Much of their work involved the creation and dissemination of assembly programs and the development of materials on the cultures and contributions of various ethnic groups (DuBois, 1942).

It is difficult to date the beginning of the intercultural education movement. However, efforts to increase students' understanding of and appreciation for ethnic and racial diversity were being implemented in K–12 schools in the mid-1920s. The term *intercultural education*, however, did not officially come into being until 1935 when the Committee on Intercultural Education was established by the Progressive Education Association (DuBois, 1984).

Pinpointing the beginning of the intergroup education movement is also difficult. The intergroup education movement, however, developed after intercultural education was underway. The term *intergroup education* was commonly used in the 1940s. It described projects and programs that were implemented after race riots erupted in Detroit, Michigan, Beaumont, Texas, St. Louis, Missouri, and other cities throughout the nation. The riots increased intergroup tensions and created a sense of national urgency (Cook & Cook, 1954; Taba et al., 1952; Taba, Brady, Robinson, & Vickery, 1951; Trager & Yarrow, 1952).

One of the main distinctions between intercultural and intergroup education was that intergroup education emphasized prejudice reduction and included a focus on social class (Kilpatrick & VanTil, 1947; Stendler & Martin, 1953). African Americans frequently were highlighted in intergroup materials. However, attention also was given to European American ethnic groups, American Indians, Chinese Americans, Mexican Americans, Japanese Americans, and other groups. In general, intergroup educators highlighted similarities among groups and developed curricula to help reduce ethnic, racial, and religious conflicts (Cook & Cook, 1954).

Similarities Between Intercultural and Intergroup Education

Although intergroup and intercultural education began at different times and had somewhat different foci, the terms *intergroup* and *intercultural* were often used interchangeably (Cook & Cook, 1954; Kilpatrick & VanTil, 1947). Schools were the primary sites of intervention for both movements. Intercultural and intergroup educators conceptualized and implemented projects, programs, and materials for schools, colleges, and universities. Both groups

were instrumental in developing school knowledge that challenged the status quo (Banks, 1994; Cook & Cook, 1954; Montalto, 1982). Leaders in both
intercultural and intergroup education used democratic principles to justify
their work.

The similarities between intergroup and intercultural education appear
to have been more important to educators than were the differences (Cook
& Cook, 1954; Taba & VanTil, 1945; Trager & Yarrow, 1952; Vickery & Cole,
1943). In the 1945 National Council for the Social Studies Yearbook (Taba &
VanTil, 1945) the terms seem to be synonymous. Perhaps the overlap in the
usage of the terms is a reflection of the concerns and perspectives of key leaders in intergroup and intercultural education. Some intercultural educators,
such as H. H. Giles and William VanTil, were concerned about the movement's
focus on cultural contributions. For Giles, VanTil, and other such intercultural
educators, intergroup education may have been a name that reduced the dissonance they felt about intercultural education's emphasis on culture and their
desire to focus on prejudice reduction.

For the purposes of this chapter, intercultural and intergroup education
are conceptualized as one continuous egalitarian movement that began in the
mid-1920s with an emphasis on culture and continued into the 1950s with
an emphasis on prejudice reduction (see Table 14.1). Both terms are used
throughout this chapter. For the sake of efficiency, *intergroup* often is used
to refer to both the intergroup and intercultural education movements. It is
also important to note that intergroup educators, as well as intercultural
educators, did not speak with a single voice. Intercultural and intergroup
educators embraced several different perspectives on their work. This chapter, however, focuses on the central thrust of intergroup and intercultural
education.

EXAMPLES OF PROGRAMS DEVELOPED
BY INTERGROUP EDUCATORS

Intergroup education organizations and programs focused on legislation,
school curricula, community-based educational programs, and other activities designed to reduce prejudice, increase cross-cultural understanding,
improve the self-concepts of minorities and immigrants, and facilitate the
assimilation of minorities and immigrants into U.S. society (Cook, 1951). Several programs and organizations will be described briefly in this section. The
Springfield Plan and the Service Bureau for Intercultural Education will be
discussed in more detail than the other programs. The Springfield Plan was
selected for more detailed discussion because it is an example of a comprehensive intercultural education program involving the community at large as

TABLE 14.1 Key Events in Intercultural and Intergroup Education

1924 The Woodbury High Assembly Program was instituted by Rachel Davis DuBois in Woodbury, New Jersey.

1934 The Service Bureau for Human Relations began operations in New York City.

1935 The term *intercultural education* was coined when the Progressive Education Association established the Commission on Intercultural Education. The Commission was directed by Rachel Davis DuBois. Ruth Benedict served as a member of the Commission's Board.

1938 The first national workshop on intercultural education was held for classroom teachers. The workshop was held at Sarah Lawrence College.

The New York City Board of Education required all of its schools to hold assemblies and implement classroom activities designed to teach tolerance.

Louis Adamic's influential article, "Thirty Million New Americans," was published.

1939 "Americans All-Immigrants All," a series of 26 weekly 30-minute radio programs was aired on CBS. The series was supported by the U.S. Office of Education and the American Jewish Committee.

The first inservice course for New York City teachers in intercultural education was taught spring term at New York University.

The Springfield Plan was implemented.

1941 The Intercultural Education Workshop was founded by Rachel Davis DuBois after she left the Service Bureau.

1942 *When Peoples Meet,* a path-breaking book in intercultural education edited by Alain Locke and Bernhard J. Stern, was published.

1945 Summer workshops were held at the University of Chicago to provide teachers with the skills and knowledge necessary to implement intergroup education programs.

The Project in Intergroup Education in Cooperating Schools was established at the University of Chicago.

The College Study in Intergroup Relations was implemented by Lloyd Allen Cook at Wayne University [now Wayne State University].

1947 The Bureau for Intercultural Education cooperated with the John Dewey Society in the production of the Society's ninth yearbook, titled *Intercultural Attitudes in the Making.*

1948 The Center for Intergroup Education at the University of Chicago was established.

1954 *The Nature of Prejudice* by Gordon Allport was published.

The Service Bureau for Intercultural Education ceased operations.

The *Brown v. Board of Education of Topeka* Supreme Court decision outlawing racially segregated public schools was issued.

well as schools. The Service Bureau for Intercultural Education was selected for more detailed coverage because it was one of the first organizations to become involved in intercultural education.

Service Bureau for Intercultural Education

The Service Bureau for Education in Human Relations, later known as the Service Bureau for Intercultural Education and the Bureau for Intercultural Education, opened its office in New York City in 1934 (DuBois, 1942). An important goal of the Bureau was to improve race and ethnic group relations in the United States (Vickery & Cole, 1943). The Bureau continued in operation until 1954 (DuBois, 1984).

Rachel Davis DuBois was the primary force behind the creation of the Bureau and served as its first executive director (Montalto, 1982). Under DuBois's leadership, the Bureau mounted one of the first systematic school-based efforts to increase ethnic pride. According to Montalto (1982), DuBois's courses at Teachers College, Columbia University, were possibly the first courses offered in the field of intercultural education at a university in the United States. However, it is important to note that by the late 1920s, courses on Black history and race relations were taught in teacher-training institutes, K–12 schools, and community centers in cities throughout the United States (Dabney, 1934; Goggin, 1993). Many of the materials used in those schools were created and disseminated by Carter G. Woodson, the "father of Black history" (Dabney, 1934). Woodson is discussed in more detail in Chapter 5.

Activities of the Bureau

The Bureau disseminated literature through its clearinghouse and served as a network for individuals who were interested in intergroup education. Most of the publications selected for distribution were articles and curriculum materials. They included Louis Adamic's article on second-generation immigrants (November 1934), YWCA publications on immigration, and *Intercultural Education News*, a quarterly newsletter published by the Bureau. During its second year of operation, the Bureau distributed 900 articles on intergroup relations to school principals throughout the United States (Montalto, 1982). In addition, materials were made available to classroom teachers, community service organizations, and other interested persons.

Year-long assemblies, held at regular intervals, were a key component of the Bureau's school program (DuBois, 1984). Each assembly focused on the history, achievements, and contributions of an ethnic group, and included oratory, drama, and performance. To gain support for the assemblies and to reduce the potential for negative reaction to them, groups were presented in an order that correlated with their status in the community. High-status groups were presented first. Ethnic and racial groups that had the lowest status in the community were presented last. In general, African Americans were presented last in East coast schools, and Asians were presented last in West Coast schools (Montalto, 1982). To prevent a group from being the only ethnic group on stage, the master of ceremonies was always a person from a different ethnic group. The structure of the assemblies may have reflected DuBois's understanding that groups may be reluctant to support an activity that does not include them. It also may have reflected her subtle attempt to suggest that even powerful and highly assimilated groups in the community had ethnic ties.

Teachers from schools participating in Bureau programs frequently enrolled in university courses taught by DuBois. The classes provided teachers with information on how to implement the Bureau's programs. DuBois (1942) conceptualized three approaches for changing intergroup attitudes: the emotional approach, the situational approach, and the intellectual approach. The emotional approach appealed to feelings and was exemplified by ethnic performances and assemblies. The situational approach was implemented by bringing small groups of people together for face-to-face interactions. Teas and other social events frequently were used to implement the situational approach. DuBois believed that small informal situations provided the best environment for people to become acquainted with each other. The intellectual approach was the third and last approach. This approach focused on sharing facts about the group being studied. DuBois and her colleagues developed 74 different curriculum materials on ethnic groups. The materials were resources that teachers and students could use for information on various ethnic, racial, and religious groups. Examples of those curriculum materials are listed in Table 14.2. Plans were made, although never executed, for Thomas Nelson and Company to publish the Bureau's curriculum materials. Instead, they were mimeographed and distributed to teachers (DuBois, 1984).

The Springfield Plan

The Springfield Plan was instituted in Springfield, Massachusetts, in 1939. It was not a single plan but a series of activities, policies, and techniques. The organizers of the Plan stated that it was designed to help young people and adults acquire the skills, attitudes, and behaviors needed to embrace the principles of democracy in a pluralistic society (Alland & Wise, 1945; Chatto & Halligan, 1945). In 1939, about 30% of the 130,000 inhabitants of Springfield were considered "old" immigrants. They were descendants of immigrants who had come to North America in the 1600s and 1700s. The remaining portion

TABLE 14.2 Examples of Intercultural Education Materials Developed at Teachers College, Columbia University

German Contributions in Physics
Italians in Chemistry and Physics
Poles in American Agricultural Life
Jewish Orchestra Conductors in American Life
Lue Gim Gong: A Chinese American Horticulturist
Jewish Participation in Colonial America
Mexican Mural Painters and Their Influence in the United States
The Negro Contribution to Folk Music in America
Japanese Flower Arrangement

Source: Montalto, 1982, p. 95.

of the population was considered "new" immigrants. They included individuals who were Irish, Italian, Polish, and Greek. The population of Springfield also included Chinese and Filipino immigrants as well as Mexican Americans and African Americans. Springfield was also religiously diverse. Catholics, Orthodox Greeks, and Protestants lived in the city (Alland & Wise, 1945).

John Granrud, superintendent of schools in Springfield in 1939, is credited with providing the leadership necessary to create and implement the Plan. When he arrived in Springfield, he observed that the student population was ethnically and racially diverse but most of the teachers were Anglo-Saxon Protestants. He noted that the ethnicity of the teachers and other aspects of the hidden curriculum in Springfield schools worked against efforts that the school might take to promote brotherhood. When teaching positions opened up, he used the placement bureau at Teachers College to recruit teachers from different races and religious groups. Granrud also instituted a Committee on Education for Democracy. The Committee surveyed the community to determine the level of tension caused by prejudice and discrimination and issued a report that included the following recommendations (Alland & Wise, 1945, p. 11):

• Prejudice reflects forces and factors outside the school, such as the home, the street, the club, and the church. Therefore the program for democracy should not exclusively focus on schools. It should reach out to parents and adults in the community who condition students' environment and thinking.
• Democracy should not be presented as an idealized concept. While a positive and affirmative position on democratic ideals would be taken, it should be emphasized that we have not yet achieved our goal of a perfect democ-

racy; weaknesses in our democratic processes should be pointed out, and students should realistically discuss how these weaknesses could be corrected, and how our democratic processes could be strengthened.
- Eliminating prejudice requires that students learn about the different groups in American society, their historical backgrounds, and their contributions to American life.
- Teachers should utilize dynamic methods of instruction so that students will be excited by the prospects of a true democracy and inspired to fully embrace its ideals.

These recommendations highlight the importance of social science and educational knowledge in intergroup education. They suggest that the members of the committee had an understanding of the factors that maintained prejudice, the difference between democracy as an ideal and as a concept actually implemented, and the importance of including ethnic content as an integral part of curriculum and instruction. This kind of knowledge enabled the committee to clearly identify and lay the groundwork for responding to several complex and difficult issues.

The Adult Council and the Adult Component of the Plan. After the Committee issued its report, the Adult Council was formed. Clergy of different faiths and members of business organizations, unions, and civic and social agencies served on the Adult Council. The Council developed the Springfield Plan (Alland & Wise, 1945). In addition to programs for students, the Plan included evening classes for adults. The classes, which were offered in schools and factories, provided a forum in which community and national problems could be discussed and questions related to social, economic, and political issues examined. Classes on the duties and privileges of citizenship also were offered. In addition, adults could learn to prepare foods from different ethnic groups in cooking classes and attend concerts held in conjunction with music classes. Perhaps most important, the adult classes reflected the spirit of the Plan in that they were integrated with men and women from diverse racial, ethnic, and religious groups.

The School Component of the Plan. The K–12 component of the Plan provided opportunities for students to learn about the contributions of various ethnic, racial, and religious groups to the history of Springfield. For example, students were encouraged to find out how their great-grandparents lived, worked, and traveled and to share their stories with their classmates. One of the projects that grew out of the heritage activities was a book titled *Pioneer Spirits* (cited in Chatto & Halligan, 1945). It was written by students and printed by the school press. *Pioneer Spirits* spans several hundred years and includes stories about the students' ancestors—their experiences coming to the United States and their early years in the United States. In commenting on *Pioneer Spirits,* teachers stated that they were especially proud of the project, not only because of what the students learned but because it gave teachers an opportunity to learn more about the backgrounds of their students (Alland & Wise, 1945). Although negative comments about the school component of the Plan were not identified, it would be surprising if everyone in the school district supported the Plan. Future research will explore the possible tensions within the district related to implementing the Plan and the efforts made by district leaders to secure support for it.

Inservice Training. The designers of the Plan noted that inservice training was an important part of the Springfield Plan. Teachers were asked to work together in district-wide committees to plan curricula. They were encouraged to observe teachers in their local districts as well as in other districts. They also participated in job exchanges with teachers in other parts of the nation. School administrators believed that job exchanges provided a means for teachers to learn about promising practices in other districts and to bring new ideas to Springfield's schools.

Work in the community was another form of inservice training in Springfield. Teachers were encouraged to work in the community so that they could learn more about the homes and community life of their students. During the summer months, many Springfield teachers worked in factories, business offices, and civic agencies. They were given the same credit for work in the community as they were given for completing college courses (Chatto & Halligan, 1945).

Other Intergroup Education Projects and Programs

The College Study. Lloyd Cook, a major figure in intergroup education, implemented a 4-year cooperative project called the College Study. It began in 1945 and ended in 1949 (Cook, 1951). A major goal of the College Study was to improve teacher education. National workshops were held for faculty from the 24 colleges and universities that participated in the study (see Table 14.3). Cook intended for the colleges and universities in the study to represent all teacher-training institutions in the United States. However, the study did not include Catholic teacher-training institutions or institutions located in the Northwest. The College Study was influential and may well have been the first national effort to provide teacher educators with skills and knowledge in intergroup relations (Cook, 1951; Cook & Cook, 1954).

TABLE 14.3 Colleges and Universities That Participated in the College Study

Atlanta University	Ohio State University, Columbus
Arizona State College, Tempe	Roosevelt College, Chicago
Central Michigan College of Education, Mt. Pleasant	San Francisco State Teachers College
	Southwest Texas State Teachers College, San Marcos
Central Missouri State College, Warrensburg	Springfield College, Massachusetts
City College, New York City	State Teachers College, Eau Claire, Wisconsin
Colorado State College of Education, Greeley	State Teachers College, Milwaukee, Wisconsin
University of Denver	Moorhead State Teachers College, Minnesota
Lynchburg College, Virginia	
Marshall College, Huntington, West Virginia	Talladega College, Alabama
New Jersey State Teachers College, Trenton	University of Florida, Gainesville
	University of Pittsburgh
New York State College for Teachers, Albany	Wayne University, Detroit, Michigan
	West Virginia State College, Institute

Source: Cook, 1951, p. 8.

The Project in Intergroup Education in Cooperating Schools and the Center for Intergroup Education. The Center for Intergroup Education at the University of Chicago was directed by Hilda Taba. The Center was established in 1948 and continued until 1951. Center staff were interested primarily in experimental programs in schools and communities that could help teachers diagnose the human relations needs of their students. Taba and her colleagues (1951) stated that programs undertaken by the Center were based on the belief that "only by studying what children know, understand, feel, and can do, can teachers decide what they need to learn next" (p. 1). They reported their findings on effective ways to learn about the cultural backgrounds of students, evaluate methods used to reduce prejudice, and examine the state of intergroup education in a series of books called "Studies in Intergroup Education" (cited in Taba et al., 1951). *Diagnosing Human Relations Needs* was the first volume in the series.

Leadership Training in Intergroup Education (Taba, 1953) was the second volume in the series. In that book, Taba examines leadership training workshops as a means to change adult attitudes, build connections between knowledge and action skills, and implement a comprehensive approach to inservice training (Taba, 1953). Leadership training workshops were implemented at the University of Chicago from 1945 to 1950. In 1946, workshops also were held at Mills College in California and at Syracuse University in New

York (Taba, 1953). Eighteen school districts participated in the leadership training workshops.

The Project in Intergroup Education in Cooperating Schools also was implemented at the University of Chicago. Taba served as the director of the Project from the time that it began in January 1945 until it ended in September 1948. The Project in Intergroup Education was one of the best-known programs developed by intergroup educators. During its height, it involved more than 250 local projects in 72 schools, and 2,500 teachers, school administrators, and community members (Brady, 1992). The Project was sponsored by the American Council on Education with financial support from the National Conference of Christians and Jews. Project staff worked cooperatively with classroom teachers to develop materials, approaches, and techniques, and to identify ways to mobilize school and community resources to improve human relations and foster intergroup understanding (Taba et al., 1949).

Philadelphia Early Childhood Project. An important goal of the Philadelphia Early Childhood Project was to show that, with help from teachers, children's racial attitudes could be modified (Trager & Yarrow, 1952). This project was sponsored in part by the Bureau for Intercultural Education and was directed by Helen G. Trager. Trager—with Marian Radke Yarrow—wrote about the project in their influential book, *They Learn What They Live: Prejudice in Young Children* (1952).

KNOWLEDGE CONSTRUCTION AND THE INTERGROUP EDUCATION MOVEMENT

Knowledge is not created in a vacuum. It is created within a social context that helps shape and direct it (Code, 1991). The intergroup education movement was created within a social context where American creed values such as equality and justice were challenged by pluralism and the push by people of color and second-generation European immigrants for full inclusion in U.S. society. The growing number of immigrants and indigenous ethnic and racial groups raised questions for some Americans about the ability of the center of mainstream U.S. culture to hold (Higham, 1972). Within this context, transformative knowledge constructed by sociologists, anthropologists, and psychologists legitimized the work of intergroup educators and provided a departure point for them to develop the school knowledge reflected in the programs described above.

While it is not possible to establish a direct relationship between transformative social science knowledge and the school knowledge created by intergroup educators, it is important to note that the intergroup education movement was created and sustained in an environment where transformative social science knowledge was known and respected. Transformative knowledge is discussed in more detail in Chapter 1.

The leaders of the intergroup education movement were influential educators who were associated with prestigious institutions, such as the University of Chicago, Teachers College, Columbia University, and the New School for Social Research. These were institutions where transformative ideas were being generated and discussed. Social scientists who helped generate transformative social science knowledge, such as Ruth Benedict, Melville J. Herskovits, and Robert Redfield, influenced intergroup education through their participation in publications such as *When Peoples Meet* (Locke & Stern, 1942) and *Americans All* (Department of Supervisors and Directors of Instruction of the National Education Association, the National Council of Teachers of English, and the Society for Curriculum Study, 1942).

Transformative Social Science Knowledge and the Intergroup Education Movement

Some of the most troubling questions faced by intergroup educators were related to assimilating Southern and Eastern European immigrants and racial minorities into mainstream U.S. society. Transformative social science knowledge provided insights on these questions. It suggested that culture was a much more persistent psychic and social reality than many people previously had thought and that assimilation could not be accomplished overnight. It could take several generations (Park, 1935). Some social scientists, such as Park and Miller (1921), believed that the second generation would never become completely Americanized. Instead, they would serve as a bridge between the older unassimilated generation and the younger assimilated ones.

Park (1928) used the phrase "marginal man" to discuss the cultural conflicts experienced by first-generation immigrants. Later this term became a synonym for the second generation. Park believed that when society opened up opportunities for minorities and immigrants, they would leave the geographical, social, and psychological boundaries of their ethnic communities. However, they would psychologically remain tied to them even though they were attempting to embrace a new way of life. The dilemma for the marginal man is that he would never be able to fully return to his old way of life because he would see his old culture from a more detached and rational viewpoint. Sadly, having given up his old ways, he would not be fully accepted into his new culture because he could not or would not change his values, perspectives, or other fundamental aspects of himself. The marginal man lives in the borderlands, in between two cultures, unable to be fully a part of either.

Park and his students—who included E. Franklin Frazier, Pauline Young, Frederick Thrasher, and Louis Wirth—also developed knowledge that revealed that culture had both positive and negative effects. Culture restrained antisocial behavior and supported group cooperation as well as stifled creativity and individuality (Park & Miller, 1921). Park (1928) saw the disappearance of ethnic cultures as an advance, rather than a setback. He believed that race relations could be characterized by a cycle of four inevitable phases: "contact, conflict, accommodation, and eventual assimilation" (Park, 1950, p. 150). He warned that even though it might take many years, coercive attempts to speed the process of assimilation could backfire (Park, 1955).

Alfred Adler (1929) and other psychologists constructed knowledge that helped intergroup educators understand that the antisocial behavior that seemed to be a salient characteristic of the second generation was related to self-esteem. Adler and his colleagues provided an intellectual basis for intergroup educators to hypothesize a relationship between society's rejection of immigrant culture and immigrant children's rejection of themselves. Some intergroup educators concluded that one way to solve the second-generation problem was to increase the status of immigrants and ethnic groups by publicly acknowledging their accomplishments and by praising symbols of their cultures such as their songs, dances, and foods (Adamic, 1934; DuBois, 1930).

Franz Boas (1928) and his students at Columbia University, such as Otto Klineberg (1955), Melville J. Herskovits (1938, 1958), and Ruth Benedict (1934), created knowledge that challenged U.S. citizens to think more deeply about the role ethnic cultures could play in improving U.S. society. Their work helped create an appreciation of different cultures. They promoted a sophisticated understanding of culture not as tangible artifacts, but as an outgrowth of the historical development, psychic dispositions, and material preconditions of a society. Boas and other anthropologists helped U.S. citizens see the limitations of U.S. society from the perspective of other cultures. By showing how all great civilizations had benefited from contact with different peoples and cultures, anthropological knowledge supported intergroup educators who advocated a blending of cultural patterns in U.S. society (Benedict, 1934; Boas, 1928). Alain Locke and Bernhard J. Stern captured that insight in an important edited book, *When Peoples Meet: A Study in Race and Culture Contacts* (1942). The book was widely read by intergroup educators and used to help justify their work (Montalto, 1982).

The Nature of School Knowledge in the Intergroup Education Movement

Banks (1993) defines school knowledge as "the facts, concepts, and generalizations presented in textbooks, teacher's guides, and other forms of media designed for school use" (p. 11). Leaders in the intergroup education movement wrote books for teachers (DuBois, 1939) and students (Benedict & Welt-fish, 1948), guides for developing curriculum (Taba et al., 1949), and worked with teachers to create intergroup education programs (Taba et al., 1952).

School knowledge in intergroup education reflected the two major philosophical perspectives that were embedded in the movement: cultural contributions and prejudice reduction. I will focus only on school knowledge related to prejudice reduction because of the limited scope of this chapter.

School knowledge in the intergroup education movement developed within a context in which Taba, Wilson, and other educational leaders defined curriculum as "the total set of experiences into which schools direct pupils" (Taba & Wilson, 1946, p. 19). This broad definition of curriculum gave intergroup educators a rationale for investigating and responding to a wide range of student activities. Intergroup education curricula addressed the af-fective as well as the cognitive domains and helped students understand the psychodynamics of their attitudes and behaviors toward people who were different from themselves. In their investigations of group life in schools, Taba and her colleagues (Taba et al., 1952) examined the ways in which residen-tial segregation and stratification were paralleled by segregation and stratifi-cation in school club memberships and cross-group associations. This kind of information provided a departure point for teachers to rethink the school curriculum and for students to rethink their understanding of racial, ethnic, social-class, and religious groups.

Intergroup educators were encouraged to introduce topics that would help students understand the effects of prejudice on both prejudiced persons and their victims and to explore topics that linked social context to the develop-ment of individual values, group behaviors, and perspectives (Benedict, 1942; Taba & Elkins, 1950; Trager & Yarrow, 1952). Children's books often were used to explore these kinds of topics. Books dealing with physical character-istics, family patterns, relationships among children, and feelings of fear and rejection were used with children as early as the primary grades (Stendler & Martin, 1953). Intergroup educators believed that those kinds of topics could help reduce stereotypes and social tension.

Benedict and Weltfish's book for children titled *In Henry's Backyard* (1948) reveals how children's literature was used to break down stereotypes and high-light similarities among people. Henry, the protagonist, finds answers to ques-tions about people who are different from him. He also thinks about why dif-ferences cause people not to like each other and why people who are prejudiced seem to be fearful and anxious. *In Henry's Backyard* is an example of school knowledge that was used by intergroup educators to help reduce prejudice.

School knowledge in intergroup education also was used to help students better understand key concepts such as *segregation* and *scapegoat*. Intergroup educators used those and other concepts in discussions about prejudice and discrimination. Students were encouraged to think about segregation in terms of its legal status, effects on group and individual mores, impact on the total society, and its inconsistency with American creed ideals (Taba & Wilson, 1946). Students also were asked to identify and discuss ways in which immigrants were used as scapegoats and blamed for behaviors in which they were not involved.

Democracy, culture, race, religion, acculturation, and prejudice were some of the other important concepts that were used by intergroup educators (Vickery & Cole, 1943). Intergroup educators believed that teachers needed to have a strong background in social science knowledge to use these concepts effectively. Teachers were encouraged to read social science literature because it provided the knowledge they needed to refute claims of racial superiority, to understand the ways in which culture influences behavior, and to better understand the nature of prejudice (Vickery & Cole, 1943).

Within the context of contemporary society, the school knowledge constructed by intergroup educators may seem inappropriate or inconsequential. It is important to note, however, that at the time of the intergroup education movement, ethnocentric views were widespread in U.S. society, and immigrants and people of color often were seen as strange and different, genetically inferior, and incapable of fully participating in U.S. society (Bennett, 1988; Smedley, 1993). Institutionalized racism and apartheid were also widespread throughout the United States, particularly in the South and in the border states. The ideas that immigrants and people of color had cultures that should be honored, histories that merited study, and that they should become first-class U.S. citizens were perspectives that many mainstream Americans rejected outright or at best found challenging.

Assumptions Used to Create School Knowledge

Several assumptions undergirded the work of intergroup educators. Even though not all intergroup educators shared these assumptions, they were woven into several of the major projects and incorporated into much of the intergroup education literature. The assumptions are briefly discussed below.

1. Schools could play an important role in reducing intergroup tensions.
2. Intergroup curricula should not be canned curricula. They should be planned by classroom teachers and others who understand intergroup education and are close to the sites where the curricula will be implemented.
3. Intergroup education should not be an isolated part of the curriculum. It should be woven throughout it.
4. Students should have opportunities to experience democracy in their classrooms and schools.

5. Intergroup curricula should grow out of real-life issues and provide opportunities for students to engage in social action.

The Role of Schools in Reducing Intergroup Tensions. First and foremost, intergroup educators, such as Hilda Taba, Elizabeth Hall Brady, John T. Robinson, and William E. Vickery (1951), believed that education could make a difference in reducing intergroup tensions. They recognized that in communities where adult communication and interaction were limited by segregation and social isolation, schools were one of the few places in which students could experience the democratic principles of individual rights and equality. As educators, they understood that they had a responsibility to help improve intergroup relations in the United States. They believed the skills that could be taught in schools, such as the ability to think critically and to distinguish fact from opinion and propaganda, were important factors in reducing the potential for social conflict (Taba & Wilson, 1946).

Intergroup Curricula Should Not Be Canned Curricula. Intercultural and intergroup educators such as DuBois (1984) and Taba (Taba et al., 1952) felt strongly that classroom teachers should be involved in creating the curricula they taught. They did not believe teachers would be successful if they were not willing to cooperate in teaching intergroup skills and knowledge. Involving teachers in creating intergroup curricula would increase the probability that they would support implementation of the curricula. Intergroup educators also believed that teachers had to be informed participants in developing intergroup curricula. Therefore, it was imperative for teachers who were involved in intergroup education to take courses and participate in inservice education programs to increase their understanding of intergroup skills and knowledge. With an informed understanding of intergroup education and a firm background in their disciplines, teachers would be able to rethink the curriculum, develop new materials, and write new units and lessons (Committee, 1949; Cook & Cook, 1954; Taba & Wilson, 1946).

To provide teachers with the knowledge and skills needed to develop and implement intergroup curricula, DuBois (1984) taught intercultural education courses at Boston University; Teachers College, Columbia University; the University of California, Berkeley; and New York University. Lloyd Cook (1951) mounted an extensive national program to train teachers in intergroup education. Taba (1953) designed and implemented leadership training workshops in intergroup education at the University of Chicago from 1945 to 1950.

Intergroup Curricula Should Be Broad and Integrated. Taba and Elkins (1950) and other intergroup educators believed that thinking should be integrated into the school's core curriculum. They argued that curricula should be conceptualized as a holistic process, not as an add-on. Vickery and Cole (1943) noted that when planning intergroup education programs, it was important that the teachers on the committees represented several different disciplines. This was done to make sure that intergroup education was not viewed as the exclusive concern of one subject area or group of subjects. The goal was to weave intergroup experiences and activities throughout the curriculum, at all grade levels, and in all subjects (Taba & Wilson, 1946). Intergroup educators believed that the strength of each part of the curriculum was derived from the support each part gave to the others. They believed that isolated efforts, no matter how effective, would not achieve their goals. They also recognized that attaining the goals of the intergroup education movement required time and focused action (Brady, 1992; Taba et al., 1952; Taba & Wilson, 1946; Vickery & Cole, 1943).

Democracy Should Be Experienced. Democracy was an important concept in intergroup education. Intergroup educators who were involved in designing the Springfield Plan and the Project in Intergroup Education in Cooperating Schools assumed that democracy had to be experienced to be fully understood and embraced. They held that classrooms should be structured so that students could experience and not simply read about democratic behavior. They also recognized that teachers needed to give students opportunities to develop skills in group decision making, to provide opportunities for students to work cooperatively with people they liked and disliked, and to help students learn to consider different opinions in making decisions.

Even though intergroup educators believed that a democratic environment required the participation of all groups, they realized that it was not uncommon for minority students to be relegated to the margins of school life (Taba & Elkins, 1950). Therefore they argued that schools should make a conscious effort to make sure that all groups were able to participate in athletics, school government, clubs, and other elements of social life in schools (Taba & Wilson, 1946).

Community Involvement. The relationship between the school and the community illustrated in the Springfield Plan highlights another key assumption in intergroup education: that students should be encouraged to move outside the classroom and investigate community relationships and consider ways to improve democratic living (Chatto & Halligan, 1945). Taba (Taba & Wilson, 1946) assumed that social action was an integral part of intergroup education. She believed that tensions and group dynamics could best be explored through surveys and interviews with community leaders. Other techniques, such as letter writing to officials and journalists, holding mass meetings, and organizing forces and resources for worthy causes, were also important social action strategies.

The general assumptions discussed in this section provided a foundation for intergroup educators to develop a type of school knowledge that was grounded in a respect and appreciation for teaching and teachers. Grounded in that foundation, the assumptions served as a departure point for addressing complex social phenomena. The assumptions also provide an opportunity for readers to gain a better understaning of the values, perspectives, and beliefs of intergroup educators.

THE DEATH OF AN EGALITARIAN MOVEMENT

When the fires of Watts burned in 1964, intergroup education was only a dim memory in the minds of a few educators. Major programs in intergroup education such as the College Study and the Project in Intergroup Education in Cooperating Schools had been completed, and the Service Bureau for Intercultural Education had closed its doors. Social activists in the 1960s who demanded that educators include information on ethnic and racial groups in the curriculum were, for the most part, unaware of the curriculum materials and projects that had been developed by intergroup educators. Intergroup education had not become institutionalized in U.S. schools.

One hypothesis explaining the demise of intergroup education suggests that the movement died, in part, because key leaders in the movement moved on to other academic pursuits, thus leaving the field without leadership (Banks, 1995b). To some extent this did occur. For example, Hilda Taba is much better known for her work in curriculum and social studies than for her intergroup education activities. However, scholars such as William VanTil (1970), Gertrude Noar (1966), Charlotte Epstein (1968), and Jean Dresden Grambs (1968) continued to write in the field of intergroup education into the 1970s.

Another hypothesis about the demise of intergroup education suggests that fears related to ethnic assimilation fueled the myth of the melting pot (DuBois, 1984). The myth of the melting pot required that "good" Americans not cling to their ethnic or racial past. Assimilation was viewed as the path to full participation in U.S. society. In addition to the incentive of inclusion, there was also the fear that by focusing on ethnicity and race, groups would stir up past animosities and become targets of hate groups (DuBois, 1984).

The movement probably died in large part because the social context that spurred the development of intergroup education changed. By the early 1950s McCarthyism had spread fear throughout the United States. The threat of being accused of being un-American made a focus on ethnicity and ancestral homelands a dangerous memory for many U.S. citizens. In addition, in the 1940s economic opportunities opened up and there was more potential for inclusion for White ethnic groups. This made the promise of assimilation more attractive for those groups. By the 1960s, the grandchildren and great-grandchildren of most European immigrants had largely assimilated into U.S. society (Alba, 1990).

With economic problems affecting European immigrants waning, the assimilation of most European immigrants and their children essentially a *fait accompli*, and the fear of being accused of being un-American ever-present, educators who were using intergroup materials may have believed those perspectives were no longer needed. However, as intergroup education faded away, multicultural education, through its progenitors, ethnic studies and multiethnic studies, began to grow and gain acceptance.

The Relationship of Intergroup Education and Multicultural Education

Multicultural education began to grow as intergroup education faded, in part because the social context in which issues of difference were addressed had changed. After Watts, African American leaders, voices, and constituencies became a focal point for discussions, approaches, and concerns about inclusion. African Americans who had participated in the civil rights movement and who were influenced by the works of early African American scholars, moved into leadership roles in ethnic studies, a progenitor of multicultural education. Scholars such as James A. Banks, Geneva Gay, and Carl A. Grant served as a bridge between intergroup and multicultural education. They worked in areas that addressed equity issues in the period between the end of intergroup education and the beginning of multicultural education. Banks studied with Robert L. Green at Michigan State University. Green, a scholar in urban education, had been a confidant of Martin Luther King, Jr., and an ardent worker in the civil rights movement. Banks also co-edited *Black Self Concept* with Jean Dresden Grambs (1972), a leader in intergroup education. Grambs sought Banks out as a young African American scholar who could help her bring new insights to the revision of her influential book.

Just as European immigration was an important factor in the social upheaval that precipitated the development of intergroup education, the migration of African Americans who left the South and settled in northern cities in the 1950s and 1960s was an important factor that contributed to the development of multicultural education. For many African Americans this was an emotionally wrenching experience. Men, women, and children—old and young—left all that they had known for what they hoped would be a better life (Trotter, 1991). The job opportunities they experienced were mixed with new forms of discrimination and exclusion.

Unlike European immigrants, physical differences and societal mores prevented racial minorities from becoming structurally assimilated into U.S. society even when they were culturally assimilated (Gordon, 1964). Perhaps more important, newly arrived African Americans, Latinos, and other people of color competed with the children and grandchildren of European immigrants for jobs in northern industries (Trotter, 1991). This competition resulted in conflicts and riots. The riots in the 1960s, like those of earlier years, were a cry by African Americans for full inclusion into U.S. society.

Similarities Between Intergroup and Multicultural Education. Intergroup and multicultural educators address some of the same areas. Banks has conceptualized multicultural education as consisting of five major dimensions: *content integration, the knowledge construction process, prejudice reduction, an equity pedagogy,* and *an empowering school culture and social structure.* These dimensions are described in Chapter 18. The school knowledge that intergroup educators developed in areas such as prejudice reduction and ethnic studies exemplifies two of the dimensions: content integration and prejudice reduction. In their survey of the literature on multicultural education, Sleeter and Grant (1988) found that promoting feelings of tolerance and acceptance [or prejudice reduction] and infusing content about diverse cultures into the curriculum were approaches that were frequently used in multicultural education.

Leaders in intergroup education and multicultural education have had their motives, competence, and loyalty questioned (D'Souza, 1991; DuBois, 1984). In the mid-1920s DuBois was approached by members of the Woodbury American Legion and asked to resign her teaching position at Woodbury High School. She endured false rumors that stated that she refused to salute the U.S. flag, believed in the cult of nakedness, and supported intermarriage among the races (DuBois, 1984). Her ideas on peace and race were questioned. As a result, people she thought were her friends began to fade from her life (DuBois, 1984). In 1953, Senator Joseph McCarthy called her before the Senate Subcommittee on Government Operations. Although she ultimately received an apology from McCarthy for requiring her to come before the subcommittee, she felt victimized. She noted that after she was called before the subcommittee, requests for her work decreased and projects that had been in the making failed to materialize (DuBois, 1984). Leaders in multicultural education as well as the field as a whole also have experienced a series of attacks (D'Souza, 1991; Schlesinger, 1991). Sleeter (1995) describes some of the attacks on the field in a detailed review of the critiques of multicultural education.

Differences Between Intergroup and Multicultural Education. The intergroup education movement embraced bold and noble goals for its time.

Intergroup educators focused their efforts on increasing ethnic and racial pride and working to reduce prejudice. Their programs, for the most part, embodied what J. A. Banks (1995b) calls a contributions and additive approach. Heroes, holidays, and cultural contributions were incorporated into Irish Day, Italian Day, and Chinese Day celebrations and curriculum units (DuBois, 1942). Prejudice and discrimination were examined on an individual level (Taba et al., 1951). Intergroup educators did not, however, address structural and institutional racism, empowerment, poverty, and societal inequities. Multicultural theorists believe that these issues should be addressed in an effective multicultural education program (Banks & Banks, 1995) . They can be incorporated into the content integration, knowledge construction, and social action components of multicultural education programs.

The activities undertaken by intergroup educators were a necessary, but not sufficient, requirement for a just society. By focusing on idealized aspects of culture, defining minorities as needy individuals who required help, and not directly addressing issues of power and inclusion, intergroup educators unknowingly helped categorize minorities as the "other" and helped relegate them to the margins of society.

Lessons Multicultural Educators Can Learn from Intergroup Educators. Multiculturalists have much to learn from the intergroup education movement. Intergroup educators focused on the similarities of groups in the hope that we would be able to bridge our differences and ultimately those differences would disappear. They still haven't disappeared. Race, ethnicity, gender, and social class are important factors in human identity; attempts to deny this reality will continue to fail. Multicultural theorists can learn from intergroup educators that they must build programs in which students have opportunities to focus on differences as well as similarities. In studying differences, it is important to note that the differences that deeply divide our nation are not primarily cultural differences. Economic, educational, and other such differences block the full inclusion and participation of diverse groups in U.S. society. Those differences are embedded in institutional structures and are implicated in more visible cultural differences. Multicultural education programs must address institutional differences as well as cultural differences.

Groups excluded from full participation in U.S. society change over time, but excluded groups continue to exist. Members of groups that were discriminated against at the turn of the century are using some of the same arguments against people of color that were used against them (Banks, 1995a). Societal change requires that we name and help students better understand the societal structures and interests that maintain difference and justify exclusion.

Multicultural theorists also can learn from intergroup educators that growth in an educational movement must be handled with thought and care. As a movement expands it may have many adherents, but when difficulties come new allies sometimes become foes. To secure funding and reach out to new audiences, intercultural educators joined ranks with progressive educators. The goals and values of intercultural educators who embraced a cultural integrationist philosophy differed in some important ways from those of progressive educators. In addition, they had different alliances and different supporters. The Progressive Education Association served primarily a middle- and upper-middle-class clientele. The intergroup education movement was identified with minorities and immigrants, people who had little cultural capital. Members of the two groups had to cross multiple boundaries to try to find common ground. It is understandable that they were unsuccessful.

As multicultural education becomes increasingly popular, groups on the right are appropriating the concept (Ravitch, 1990). Multicultural educators need to work to define the field more clearly and to identify standards for professional practice (Banks & Banks, 1995). Many of the problems the field currently faces are the result of perspectives and practices that were never promoted by leaders in the field, but were attributed to the field by its detractors and critics (D'Souza, 1991; Schlesinger, 1991).

Leadership through values was an important foundation for intergroup educators and continues to be an important foundation for multicultural educators. Leadership through values is a difficult kind of leadership because values are often in conflict. Identifying and utilizing common values can motivate diverse people who are at different levels of privilege, power, and inclusion in society. However, identifying and utilizing those common values is a herculean task. To meet that challenge, multicultural educators must make their values explicit and be prepared to respond to the conflict that may result when others do not agree with the positions they take.

Multicultural leaders must be willing to express and shape conflict because leadership through values is grounded in conflict. While dysfunctional conflict can be divisive, functional conflict can help identify important issues that otherwise would remain concealed. Functional conflict cannot and should not be avoided in multicultural education. Burns (1978), an authority on leadership, states that conflict is intrinsically compelling. It galvanizes, prods, and motivates people and is an inevitable part of leadership through values. As multicultural educators identify the gap between egalitarian values and practice in the United States, they can potentially help U.S. citizens to relate their choices, commitments, decisions, and positions to reasoned, explicit, and conscious egalitarian values.

Multicultural educators are not interested in simply accumulating data about prejudice, lack of access, and other barriers to democracy and equity. They are interested in change. Through its social action component, multicultural education challenges teachers and students to engage in change. The rich legacy of the intergroup education movement provides some of the building blocks upon which change can be made. The assumptions used by intergroup educators to develop school knowledge may provide some fruitful paths for multicultural educators to follow.

More than 70 years ago leaders in the intergroup education movement envisioned a more just and humane society. They had a powerful dream and the courage, perseverance and fortitude to work to make it a reality. Even though they fell short of their dream, our schools and society are better because of their efforts. Their mantle has now passed to multicultural educators who are, in their own way, continuing the struggle for a just and humane society.

REFERENCES

Adamic, L. (November, 1934). Thirty million new Americans. *Harper's Magazine*, *169*, 684-694.

Adler, A. (1929). *The science of living*. Garden City, NY: Garden City Publishing.

Alba, R. D. (1990). *Ethnic identity: The transformation of White America*. New Haven: Yale University Press.

Alland, A., & Wise, J. W. (1945). *The Springfield plan*. New York: Viking Press.

Banks, J. A. (1993). The canon debate, knowledge construction, and multicultural education. *Educational Researcher, 22* (5), 4-14.

Banks, J. A. (1994). *Multiethnic education: Theory and practice* (3rd ed.). Boston: Allyn & Bacon.

Banks, J. A. (1995a). The historical reconstruction of knowledge about race: Implications for transformative teaching. *Educational Researcher, 24* (2), 15-25.

Banks, J. A. (1995b). Multicultural education: Historical development, dimensions, and practice. In J. A. Banks & C. A. M. Banks (Eds.), *Handbook of research on multicultural education* (pp. 3-24). New York: Macmillan.

Banks, J. A., & Banks, C. A. M. (Eds.). (1995). *The handbook of research on multicultural education*. New York: Macmillan.

Banks, J. A., & Grambs, J. D. (Eds.). (1972). *Black self concept*. New York: McGraw-Hill.

Benedict, R. (1934). *Patterns of culture*. Boston: Houghton Mifflin.

Benedict, R. (1942). American melting pot, 1942 model. In the Department of Supervisors and Directors of Instruction of the National Education Association, the National Council of Teachers of English, and the Society for Curriculum Study (Eds.), *Americans all: Studies in intercultural education* (pp. 14-24). Washington, DC: Department of Supervisors and Directors of Instruction, National Education Association.

Benedict, R., & Weltfish, G. (1948). *In Henry's backyard: The races of mankind*. New York: Henry Schuman.

Bennett, D. H. (1988). *The party of fear: From nativist movements to the new right in American history*. Chapel Hill: University of North Carolina Press.

Boas, F. (1928). *Anthropology and modern life*. New York: W. W. Norton.

Brady, E. H. (1992). Intergroup education in public schools, 1945–51. In *Jubilee conference: Hilda Taba-90* (pp. 15–29). Tartu, Estonia: Tartu University.

Burns, J. M. (1978). *Leadership*. New York: Harper & Row.

Chatto, C. I., & Halligan, A. L. (1945). *The story of the Springfield plan*. New York: Barnes & Noble.

Code, L. (1991). *What can she know? Feminist theory and the construction of knowledge*. Ithaca, NY: Cornell University Press.

Committee on the Study of Teaching Materials in Intergroup Relations. (1949). *Intergroup relations in teaching materials: A survey and appraisal*. Washington, DC: American Council on Education.

Cook, L. A. (1951). *Intergroup relations in teacher education* (College Study in Intergroup Education, Vol. 11). Washington, DC: American Council on Education.

Cook, L. A., & Cook, E. (1954). *Intergroup education*. New York: McGraw-Hill.

Dabney, T. L. (1934). The study of the Negro. *The Journal of Negro History, 19*, 266–307.

Department of Supervisors and Directors of Instruction of the National Education Association, the National Council of Teachers of English, and the Society for Curriculum Study. (Eds.). (1942). *Americans all: Studies in intercultural education*. Washington, DC: Department of Supervisors and Directors of Instruction, National Education Association.

D'Souza, D. (1991). *Illiberal education: The politics of race and sex on campus*. New York: Free Press.

DuBois, R. D. (1930). *The contributions of racial elements to American life* (2nd ed.). Philadelphia: Women's International League for Peace and Freedom.

DuBois, R. D. (1939). *Adventures in intercultural education: A manual for secondary school teachers*. New York: Intercultural Education Workshop.

DuBois, R. D. (1942). Conserving cultural resources. In the Department of Supervisors and Directors of Instruction of the National Education Association, the National Council of Teachers of English, and the Society for Curriculum Study (Eds.), *Americans all: Studies in intercultural education* (pp. 148–159). Washington, DC: Department of Supervisors and Directors of Instruction, National Education Association.

DuBois, R. D. (with Okorodudu, C.). (1984). *All this and something more: Pioneering in intercultural education*. Bryn Mawr, PA: Dorrance.

Epstein, C. (1968). *Intergroup relations for the classroom teacher*. Boston: Houghton Mifflin.

Goggin, J. (1993). *Carter G. Woodson: A life in Black history*. Baton Rouge: Louisiana State University Press.

Gordon, M. (1964). *Assimilation in American life: The role of race, religion, and national origins*. New York: Oxford University Press.

Grambs, J. D. (1968). *Intergroup education: Methods and materials*. Englewood Cliffs, NJ: Prentice-Hall.

Herskovits, M. J. (1938). *Acculturation: The study of culture contact*. New York: J.J. Augustin.

Herskovits, M. J. (1958). *The myth of the Negro past*. Boston: Beacon Press.

Higham, J. (1972). *Strangers in the land: Patterns of American nativism 1860-1925*. New York: Atheneum.

Kilpatrick, W. H., & VanTil, W. (Eds). (1947). *Intercultural attitudes in the making: Ninth yearbook of the John Dewey Society*. New York: Harper & Brothers.

Klineberg, O. (1955). *Race differences*. New York: Harper & Brothers.

Locke, A., & Stern, B. J. (Eds.). (1942). *When peoples meet: A study in race and culture contacts*. New York: Progressive Education Association.

Montalto, N. V. (1982). *A history of the intercultural education movement 1924-1941*. New York: Garland.

Nash, G. B. (1982). *Red, white and black: The people of early America* (2nd ed.). Englewood Cliffs, NJ: Prentice-Hall.

Noar, G. (1966). *The teacher and integration*. Washington, DC: National Education Association.

Park, R. E. (1928). Human migration and the marginal man. *American Journal of Sociology, 33*, 881-893.

Park, R. E. (1935). Assimilation. In *Encyclopedia of the social sciences*, II (pp. 281-283). New York: Macmillan.

Park, R. E. (1950). *Race and culture*. New York: Free Press.

Park, R. E. (1955). *Society: Collective behavior, news, and opinion, sociology and modern society*. Glencoe, IL: Free Press.

Park, R. E., & Miller, H. A. (1921). *Old world traits transplanted*. New York: Harper & Brothers.

Ravitch, D. (1990, October 24). Multiculturalism, yes, particularism, *The Chronicle of Higher Education, 37* (8), 44.

Schlesinger, A. M., Jr. (1991). *The disuniting of America*. Knoxville, TN: Whittle Direct Books.

Sleeter, C. E. (1995). An analysis of the critiques of multicultural education. In J. A. Banks & C. A. M. Banks (Eds.), *Handbook of research on multicultural education* (pp. 81-94). New York: Macmillan.

Sleeter, C. E., & Grant C. A. (1988). *Making choices for multicultural education: Five approaches to race, class, and gender*. Columbus, OH: Merrill.

Smedley, A. (1993). *Race in North America: Origin and evolution of a worldview*. Boulder, CO: Westview Press.

Stendler, C. B., & Martin, W. E. (1953). *Intergroup education in kindergarten-primary grades*. New York: Macmillan.

Taba, H. (1953). *Leadership training in intergroup education*. Washington, DC: American Council on Education.

Taba, H., Brady, E. H., Jennings, H. H., & Robinson, J. T. (1949). *Curriculum in intergroup relations: Case studies in instruction for secondary schools*. Washington, DC: American Council on Education.

Taba, H., Brady, E., & Robinson, J. (1952). *Intergroup education in public schools*. Washington, DC: American Council on Education.

Taba, H., Brady, E., Robinson, J. T., & Vickery, W. E. (1951). *Diagnosing human relations needs*. Washington, DC: American Council on Education.

Taba, H., & Elkins, D. (1950). *With focus on human relations*. Washington, DC: American Council on Education.

Taba, H., & VanTil, W. (Eds.). (1945). *Democratic human relations: Promising practices in intergroup and intercultural education in the social studies*. Washington, DC: National Council for the Social Studies.

Taba, H., & Wilson, H. E. (1946). Intergroup education through the school curriculum. *Annals of the American Academy of Political and Social Science, 244*, 19–25.

Trager, H. G., & Yarrow, M. R. (1952). *They learn what they live: Prejudice in young children*. New York: Harper & Brothers.

Trotter, J. W., Jr. (Ed.). (1991). *The great migration in historical perspective*. Bloomington: Indiana University Press.

VanTil, W. (1970). *Prejudiced: How do people get that way?* (rev. ed.). New York: Anti-Defamation League.

Vickery, W. E., & Cole, S. G. (1943). *Intercultural education in American schools: Proposed objectives and methods*. New York: Harper & Brothers.

CHAPTER 15

Research on Racial Attitudes: Historical Perspectives

MICHAEL R. HILLIS

Understanding race as a socially constructed concept is fundamental to a historical analysis of research on racial attitudes (Banks, 1993a, 1995a). Therefore, I begin this chapter with a brief introduction to critical theory and knowledge construction, then present the results of my analysis of the race relations literature. I review how the investigation of racial attitudes underwent a dramatic theoretical shift in the 1920s and 1930s. My discussion focuses on the state of the field prior to 1920 and the manner in which it evolved. Next, I examine the work of the major researchers during the 1920s and 1930s. This section is organized around the components of an attitude as traditionally conceptualized: affect, behavior, and cognition. I then assess the methods used to measure racial attitudes and discuss their strengths and limitations. The implications of this research for multicultural education will be considered in the final part of this chapter.

CRITICAL THEORY AND KNOWLEDGE CONSTRUCTION

Critical theory is a philosophical movement that attempts to "understand why the social world is the way it is and, more importantly, through a process of critique, strives to know how it should be" (Ewert, 1991, p. 346). A major tenet of the theory is that knowledge is socially constructed (Weiler, 1988); objective "reality" is constrained and influenced by the subjective forces of human interaction (Code, 1991). This interactional process, between objectivity (knowledge) and subjectivity (knower), occurs through dialogic communication in which ideas are presented, challenged, debated, and modified. The resulting product is what a discourse community (i.e., the community in dialogue) agrees upon as *knowledge*. Critical theorists maintain that questions assessing this process of knowledge construction must be raised. An examination of the historical literature on racial attitudes indicates that many of the changes in the race relations field were the result of voices that challenged a socially constructed understanding of race.

The construction of knowledge is not a neutral process (Banks, 1993a, 1995a, 1995b; Giroux, 1983). When individuals are involved in the creation of knowledge, they carry into it personal biases. As a result, knowledge is not objective in the sense that people observe and draw uniform, unbiased conclusions. Rather, knowledge is a product of both the subjective meanings and objective reality upon which people agree (Code, 1991; Grady & Wells, 1987). Since knowledge is constructed in a discourse community, to understand the positionality of the knowledge, it is essential to examine who belongs to that community. Because a discourse community cannot encompass all perspectives, the production of knowledge is influenced by omissions. Knowledge in relation to race prior to the 1920s was strongly influenced by the omission of the voices of people of color.

RESEARCH PRIOR TO THE 1920S

Gould, in his significant book, *The Mismeasure of Man* (1981), chronicles research that examined differences among the races. One avenue of research that scientists conducted during the nineteenth century was craniometry—the examination of human skull size in order to infer individual and group characteristics. Many researchers during this period tried to scientifically prove the existence of biologically superior and inferior races. (I use the term *race* because of its historical importance. Contemporary scholars [e.g., Banks, 1991] have noted that the term is limited in its usefulness.) By measuring the cranial capacities of different racial groups, these researchers attempted to provide evidence that the White race had the largest cranial capacity and, therefore, was the superior race. One researcher, Broca (cited in Gould, 1981), concluded that White men had a capacity that exceeded other "less-advanced" groups, including women.

Gould (1981) reanalyzed Broca's findings and concluded that his data either had been altered, contained serious methodological flaws, or was characterized by flawed logic. Gould reasoned that because of the *zeitgeist* (i.e., the general intellectual climate of the period) that existed in the United States and Europe during this period, researchers had attempted to confirm their previously held beliefs about racial superiority, rather than to construct objective scientific knowledge.

The idea that Whites are the superior race remained strong throughout the late 1800s and early 1900s. If we ask ourselves why, one answer becomes apparent: Whites were in power and wanted to justify their oppression of other groups (Fairchild & Gurin, 1978). As a consequence, prior to the 1920s, the mainstream academic community failed to examine racial prejudice. This period was not without any writing on prejudice (e.g., DuBois, 1901; Thomas, 1904). However, these were exceptions to a trend that had emerged. Most mainstream scientists conducted studies that demonstrated the deficiencies of racial and ethnic minorities (e.g., Bean, 1906; Cope, 1887). These studies reinforced the idea of superior and inferior races. As Duckitt (1992) states, "White attitudes of paternalistic superiority or open antipathy to blacks were widely accepted as inevitable and natural responses to the seemingly obvious 'inferiority' and 'backwardness' of blacks and other colonial peoples" (p. 49).

The research paradigm that described Whites as the superior race was challenged in the 1920s by a new paradigm that emerged. The mainstream scientific community started to question the innate superiority of Whites (Samelson, 1978) and began to examine issues of equality. Rather than being concerned exclusively about how the races might be different, researchers initiated an examination of relations among the races. However, the sociological situation (i.e., prejudice, discrimination, and racism that existed before the 1920s) had not changed. Whereas a person could have "justifiable feelings of racial superiority" (Duckitt, 1992) at the turn of the century, these same feelings in the 1920s often were labeled racial prejudice. What began to change was the socially constructed idea of race and race relations.

The reasons for this change in research focus are complex and difficult to understand completely. However, Samelson (1978) outlines a number of factors that contributed to the shift. In 1924, the United States Congress passed the Johnson–Reed Act, which, by establishing a nationality quota system, effectively discriminated against immigrants who were not from Northern Europe and Great Britain (Banks, 1991). This act helped to shift the emphasis from providing a rationale for the exclusion of immigrant groups to trying to solve the problems that existed within the nation. This shift caused Bogardus (1928) to state, "Few Americans realize the importance or the extent of what is probably the greatest single issue confronting America, that of race relationships" (p. vii).

During the 1920s and 1930s a number of researchers entered the field of race studies who were not of White, Northern European descent. The new researchers, many of them Jewish, had been victimized by anti-Semitism and discrimination. Consequently, they entered the field of race relations from a different position than earlier psychologists, a position that emanated from the margins rather than the center (Okihiro, 1994). As they entered the research community, their work helped move the focus to racial attitude research (Adorno, Frenkel-Brunswik, Levinson, & Stanford, 1950; Herskovits, 1941/1967; Samelson, 1978).

Finally, Samelson (1978) notes that in the 1920s and 1930s, the Western nations experienced Hitler's rise to power in Germany. Hitler was often viewed with alarm and as an enemy that had to be overcome. This fear, coupled with Hitler's doctrine of racial purity and Aryan superiority, influenced the scientific community in the United States. Witnessing the terrible manifestation of the belief in racial superiority, a group of social scientists (e.g., Bogardus, 1925a; Katz & Braly, 1933) focused their attention on the racial attitudes of U.S. citizens. Their motivation arose from a desire to understand race prejudice in order to prevent its future development.

The research community that evolved during the 1920s and 1930s began to question the fundamental assumptions that had been made in previous decades. Rather than focus on racial superiority, scientists began to assess the racial prejudices of individuals. This shift was a dramatic one, for it moved the emphasis from one of domination to one that more closely reflected ideas of equality.

STUDIES OF PREJUDICE IN THE 1920S AND 1930S

Affect, Behavior, and Cognition

Researchers traditionally have conceptualized attitudes as having *affective*, *behavioral*, and *cognitive* antecedents and consequences (Borg & Gall, 1989; Chein, 1951; Harding, Proshansky, Kutner, & Chein, 1969; Sears, Peplau, & Taylor, 1991). When examining prejudice within this traditional paradigm, researchers may observe an affective component (dislike for another ethnic group), a behavioral component (discriminatory behavior toward another ethnic group), or a cognitive component (a stereotype about the members of that ethnic group). Although contemporary theorists (Greenwald, 1989; Olson & Zanna, 1993; Stroebe & Insko, 1989) maintain that the tripartite model gives an incomplete picture of attitudes, the affect–behavior–cognition (ABC) model is still a useful way to conceptualize prejudice.

Affective Studies of Prejudice

When researchers discuss the affective component of attitudes, they are trying to understand the feeling response people have toward an object. In racial attitude studies, researchers have attempted to assess people's feelings toward groups other than their own. Some of the earliest studies of this component were conducted by Bogardus (1925a).

Bogardus (1925a) developed an instrument he called the *Social Distance Scale* (SDS). (See Figure 15.1.) The idea of social distance was based on the work of Robert E. Park (1924) and was one of the first systematic measures of attitudes (Watson, 1973). Bogardus assumed that prejudiced people would desire less social intimacy among themselves and other ethnic groups; tolerant people, on the other hand, would show this tendency less. To measure social distance, Bogardus asked subjects to respond to a scale measuring the desired level of social distance among themselves and other ethnic groups. This scale ranged from "would exclude from my country" to "kinship through marriage."

Bogardus published two studies on social distance in 1925. In the first study (1925b), 248 college-age students rated 36 "ethnic" groups according to three categorizations: (1) friendly feelings toward the group, (2) feelings of neutrality, and (3) feelings of dislike. Following this, they ordinally rated all of the ethnic groups for each category. The subjects then selected the group they felt the greatest dislike toward and the reasons why. Bogardus identified four broad categories for why this dislike arose: (1) the subjects accepted the opinions and traditions of others, (2) unpleasant personal experiences with the race as a child, (3) disgust associated with sensory impressions of other groups, and (4) unpleasant personal experiences with the race as an adult.

Although this study did not use the SDS, Bogardus described a number of interesting pieces of qualitative data that the SDS would not have been able to reveal. For example, Bogardus noted that "sometimes a single sensory image engendering fear or disgust or both, and experienced in childhood, is the basis of a generalization against a whole race" (p. 226). What is important to note

TABLE 15.1 Social Distance Scale

(This is a modified version of the Bogardus Social Distance Scale)

According to my first feeling reaction I would willingly admit members of each race (as a class, and not the best I have known, nor the worst members) to one or more of the classifications under which I have placed an (x).

	As part of my family by marriage	As personal friends	As neighbors	As a fellow worker at my job	As a citizen of the United States	As visitors only to the United States	Would exclude from my country
Blacks							
Chinese							
Japanese							

Source: Adapted from Bogardus, 1925. Used with permission of the Society for Applied Sociology.

here is that Bogardus challenged the notion that a racially prejudiced generalization was valid. Instead, he maintained that prejudice was the result of a number of experiences that produced *irrational* belief systems.

As a supplement to this study, Bogardus (1925a) attempted to show the validity of the SDS as a measurement technique. He defined social distance as the "understanding and feeling that persons experience regarding each other. It explains the nature of a great deal of their interaction. It charts the character of social relations" (p. 299). The SDS, he reasoned, is a way to measure this affective response in individuals.

Zeligs and Hendrickson (1933), following the work of Bogardus, investigated the affective responses of children. They used a modified version of the SDS, the *Racial Attitudes Indicator*, to determine how children would respond to a social distance measure. By modifying the language of the SDS, Zeligs and Hendrickson developed a measure that produced results similar to those of Bogardus (1928).

Realizing the limitations of a survey method in determining attitudes, Zeligs and Hendrickson (1934) conducted a number of personal interviews with the children. Unfortunately, the results of these interviews were not carefully analyzed by the authors (at least not in their article). Instead, they used the interviews to establish the validity of the *Racial Attitudes Indicator*.

Although Bogardus (1926, 1927, 1928, 1968) and other researchers (e.g., Bethlehem, 1977) continued to develop and refine the social distance concept, the SDS has a number of problems. The most difficult problem with this form of assessment is that it often elicits socially desirable responses in subjects (Aboud & Skerry, 1984; Edwards, 1957; Hillis, 1994; Katz, 1976). Measures that directly ask for information may not elicit valid responses (Dovidio & Fazio, 1992).

Interestingly, Bogardus (1926, 1927) wrote a number of articles that conceptualized social distance apart from the SDS. In one study, Bogardus (1927) assessed how "race friendliness," which decreases social distance, develops. The importance of Bogardus's work is critical to our understanding of how the knowledge of race relations was constructed prior to his work. Rather than simply measuring the prejudices of people, Bogardus suggested that positive relationships among the races were desirable. The suggestion of social intimacy breached a new area of race relations—a movement away from divisiveness and negativity toward racial unity and tolerance.

Behavioral Studies of Prejudice

One of the major problems that attitude theorists have tried to solve is the issue of correspondence between attitudes and behaviors (Ajzen & Fishbein, 1980). Intuitively, one would assume that an individual's attitude is manifested in his or her behavior. However, researchers have shown that this relationship is a complex phenomenon that is mediated by a number of factors.

In one of the earliest studies, LaPiere (1934) sought to determine whether expressed attitudes always correspond with actual behavior. LaPiere and a Chinese couple traveled across the United States together, staying in hotels and eating in restaurants. Throughout their travels, they were refused service only once out of 251 instances. To follow up this behavioral assessment, LaPiere sent letters to the same hotels and restaurants asking if they would be willing to "accept members of the Chinese race as guests" (p. 233). The response that LaPiere received was overwhelmingly negative; 92% stated that they would refuse service to a member of the Chinese "race." As LaPiere states, questionnaires are only symbolic representations of social reality and may not be accurate gauges of how people will behave. As a result, there is a lack of correspondence between expressed attitudes and behavior.

The importance of this study is twofold. As LaPiere (1934) noted in an earlier study, the verbalization of an attitude is not the same as the observance of behavior. As attitude theorists (e.g., Ajzen & Fishbein, 1980; Greenwald, 1989; Warner & LaFleur, 1969) have continued to maintain, the relationship between attitudes and behavior is mediated by many variables. The studies by LaPiere were among the first that questioned this relationship.

Second, LaPiere (1934) stated that qualitative data were needed in the assessment of attitudes. He wrote:

> Quantitative measurements are quantitatively accurate; qualitative evaluations are always subject to the errors of human judgment. Yet it would seem far more worth while to make a shrewd guess regarding that which is essential than to accurately measure that which is likely to prove quite irrelevant. (p. 237)

This second point remains an important one for the field of racial attitude assessment. As Stephan (1985) stated 50 years later, there is still a need for behavioral observation.

Interestingly, one study, conducted soon after LaPiere's (1934), used observation as a preliminary device for the development of quantitative measures. In 1938, Eugene and Ruth Horowitz published a report of field work they had conducted in a U.S. border state. Their work consisted of first becoming participant-observers within the community, and from this vantage point developing hypotheses that were later tested. The Horowitz and Horowitz preliminary data, based on observations of the community, produced an array of notable findings.

Horowitz and Horowitz (1938) observed that there was a deep separation in the community that was based primarily on racial grouping. Although this was not an unexpected observation, it does point to a social organization that was beginning to be analyzed rather than taken for granted. As part of their analysis, Horowitz and Horowitz assessed the development of racial attitudes in children.

Horowitz and Horowitz (1938) interviewed both parents and children. The parents were asked, indirectly, what their role was in the development of their children's racial attitudes. Horowitz and Horowitz found that the parents minimized their role in attitude development: "Parents felt that children were naive about race distinction, felt that they [the parents] had never said nor done anything to influence the children, felt that the children were discriminating of their own volition" (p. 334). However, when the researchers asked the children about their parents, they heard something quite different. One first-grade White girl said, "Mamma tells me not to play with black children, keep away from them" (p. 333).

Based on their analysis, Horowitz and Horowitz (1938) detailed how parents shape children's racial attitudes. When parents restrict who the child can and cannot play with, the child learns the in-groups and out-groups. The restrictions, Horowitz and Horowitz observed, come from community pressures that limit intergroup contact. Furthermore, the investigators stated that "the children tend to forget the origins of their attitudes just as parents forget having taught them to the children. As the origins are forgotten, rationalizations are developed to support the attitudes" (p. 336).

Based on these observations, both Eugene Horowitz (1936) and Ruth Horowitz (1939) conducted studies using quantitative measures. The instrumentation for these studies included a categories test and a picture identification test. In the categories test, the investigators presented the children with five pictures of differing arrangements (e.g., pictures of two White girls, one African American girl, and two African American boys). The children were then asked to determine which pictures did not belong together. As Campbell (1950) has noted, the strength of this method is that it allows the investigators to determine the categorization processes of children. However, as Katz (1976) points out, this method has never been assessed using measures of reliability and validity. The second measure used by Horowitz and Horowitz, a picture identification test, asked children to identify their ethnic affiliation.

Following the work of Horowitz and Horowitz, Kenneth and Mamie Clark (1939, 1947) began a series of racial attitude studies that have subsequently become influential and widely known. Using what has become known as the doll technique, Clark and Clark (1939) described how a large percentage of African American children in their studies rejected black dolls in favor of white dolls. They hypothesized that African American children were symbolically rejecting themselves because of the socially negative associations with black skin color. Banks (1993b) has noted that this "self-hate hypothesis" was the dominant paradigm for understanding the racial attitudes of African American children until the 1970s.

This method of assessing children's racial attitudes has remained one of the dominant methodologies used in the field (Spencer, 1982, 1984). Although the technique has shown a consistent pattern of response, scholars (e.g., Aboud, 1988) have severely criticized this methodology and theoretical framework (Cross, 1991). The problems associated with this technique include the use of forced choice (Aboud, 1987; Aboud & Skerry, 1984), more than one variable being altered at a time (e.g., skin and eye color changing; Katz, 1976), no reliability or validity data (Aboud, 1988), and questionable interpretation of the results (Spencer, 1982, 1984).

Spencer (1982, 1984) maintains that African American children could reject the black dolls while retaining a high self-esteem. She argues that researchers must distinguish between *personal* identity and *group* identity: Personal identity refers to the self-concept or self-esteem of an individual, while group identity refers to the reference group with which individuals identify. Spencer (1982) demonstrates that African American children can express both White bias and a positive personal identity.

A second measure Clark and Clark (1947) used was a coloring test. They gave the children sheets of paper with drawings of a leaf, an apple, an orange, a mouse, a boy, and a girl, along with crayons for coloring. The investigators then asked the children to color each object to determine whether they knew the correct color. If the children did know the color of the objects, they were asked to color the child with the same color as themselves. If they refused to color themselves an appropriate color, Clark (1955) hypothesized it "was an indication of emotional anxiety and conflict in terms of their own skin color" (p. 43).

An African American child coloring herself orange might indicate self-rejection and anxiety, as the Clarks hypothesized. However, other reasonable interpretations exist. During the 1930s and 1940s when the Clarks conducted most of their research, there were few positive reinforcements of the color black in the mainstream popular culture. As a result, the child may have been rejecting the color black on a group rather than an individual level (Spencer, 1982).

The importance of these behavioral studies is that researchers had begun to assess the racial attitudes of different ethnic and racial groups. Clark and Clark and Horowitz and Horowitz attempted to understand racial attitudes from a minority perspective. Their work contributed to the dialogue on how racial attitudes develop and their negative consequences (Cross, 1991; Phinney & Rotheram, 1987). As an indication of their historical importance, the Supreme Court cited the Clarks's findings in footnote 11 of the decision when it declared racially segregated schools unconstitutional (Salley, 1993). When the Supreme Court handed down its decision on May 17, 1954, Justice Earl Warren (1969) stated:

> To separate them from others of similar age and qualifications solely because of their race generates a feeling of inferiority as to their status in the community that may affect their hearts and minds in a way unlikely ever to be undone. (p. 288)

Cognitive Studies of Racial Attitudes

Rather than focusing on affective responses or behavioral consequences, cognitive studies try to assess how individuals think about other racial groups. What researchers are essentially describing is the stereotypes that individuals hold. As Aboud (1988) writes, "Stereotypes are rigid, overgeneralized beliefs about the attributes of ethnic group members" (p. 5).

Although Lippman (1922) generally is credited for the construction of the idea of stereotypes, it was the work of Katz and Braly (1933) that popularized the idea in racial attitude studies (Brigham, 1971). Katz and Braly gave 100 students a list of 10 ethnic groups and a separate list of 84 adjectives. The subjects were asked to mark those words that "seem to you typical of [ethnic group]" (p. 282). Following this step, the subjects were asked to review their selections for each group and pick the five that they viewed as being the most typical.

Katz and Braly (1933) found that the students they studied had a high level of agreement on the stereotypes for different groups. For example, 78% of them viewed Germans as scientifically minded and 79% thought Jews were shrewd. Based on these results, the researchers discussed how people hold stereotypes in the face of disconfirming evidence. Stereotypes are broadly conceived; all people at one time or another exhibit many kinds of behavior (Katz & Braly, 1933). Consequently, when a person holds a stereotypical view of a group, it is quite easy to find evidence that confirms the belief. Moreover, when confronted with disconfirming evidence, individuals can easily dismiss it as being an exception. Katz and Braly wrote, "By thus omitting cases which contradict the stereotype, the individual becomes convinced from association with a race that its members are just the kind of people he always thought they were" (p. 288).

The Katz and Braly (1933) study challenged the view that popular conceptions of ethnic groups reflected enlightened thinking. This notion was common among social scientists during the 1930s. The research by Katz and Braly (1933) indicated that people create conceptions of other groups based on a number of factors, including class position, social makeup, and images in the media. As a result, stereotypical thinking provides a "fertile field for the fiction to produce distorted and fallacious observations" (Katz & Braly, 1933, p. 289), distortions that serve to marginalize groups of color and other groups on the margins of society.

IMPLICATIONS FOR MULTICULTURAL EDUCATION

As the work and theories of scholars during the 1920s and 1930s indicated, one of the ways that oppression manifests itself is through racial prejudice. As these scholars entered the scientific community, they argued that racial prejudice and discrimination were, and continue to be, a widespread problem—one that had not been thoroughly addressed in the mainstream academic community prior to the 1920s. Their work raised the consciences of social scientists and suggested that work needed to be done to reduce prejudice and discrimination in the nation. The field of education became a site where these issues were addressed. Chapter 14 discusses the development of the intergroup education movement as a means to reduce prejudice and discrimination in the schools (Taba, Brady, & Robinson, 1952).

Critical theorists have suggested that education can serve one of two functions in a society (Giroux, 1983; Weiler, 1988). Schools that are reproductive generate citizens to reproduce the existing social order. As a result, societal change will not occur because the existing system perpetuates itself. In a productive system, schools attempt to produce citizens who will critically examine society. Critical theorists view citizen action as having the potential to transform the social order, creating one that is more democratic and just.

Reducing prejudice and discrimination is one of the major goals of multicultural education. Banks (1995b) has described multicultural education as having five interrelated dimensions: (1) *content integration*—a movement away from Eurocentric and additive models of curriculum to one that is infused with diverse voices; (2) *knowledge construction process*—a recognition that knowledge is a socially constructed phenomenon; (3) *prejudice reduction*—to "help students develop more positive attitudes toward different racial and ethnic groups" (Banks, 1994, p. 16); (4) *an equity pedagogy*—classroom instruction that adapts to the unique talents and needs of a diverse student population; and (5) *an empowering school culture and social structure*—schools that reflect the pluralistic nature of society through a reformed school culture that promotes equity for students from diverse groups.

When we examine these five dimensions, they constitute an "antiracist education." Some scholars (Mattai, 1992; McCarthy, 1990) have criticized multicultural education for not directly addressing racism. However, each dimension described by Banks (1995b) contributes to freeing our educational system from oppressive and racist tendencies that have manifested themselves throughout the history of U.S. society. Ultimately, the goal is to give all people an equal chance to succeed (Payne, 1984). The manner in which multicultural education has been conceptualized by Banks (1995b) is a movement that would help produce a reduction in prejudice if implemented in an authentic way.

Multicultural theorists have devoted much attention to curriculum reform and transformation (Banks, 1995b; Gay, 1995; Nieto, 1992). Theorists such as Banks, Gay, and Nieto maintain that the mainstream curriculum fails to describe the experiences and perspectives of people of color. A Eurocentric curriculum is a reflection of dominant group hegemony; groups outside of the mainstream community are marginalized and stripped of voice. The result is a monocultural curriculum—a curriculum that breeds arrogance and ideas of racial superiority (Parekh, 1986).

Multicultural education undermines students' prejudices through a transformation of the curriculum. A diverse curriculum allows students the opportunity to view ideas, history, and social relations from unique and fresh perspectives (Hillis, 1993). As a result, the knowledge that is constructed more closely reflects the experiences of traditionally disenfranchised groups. This is not to suggest that a multicultural curriculum will eliminate racial prejudice. Rather, it may help students "understand the intellectual and moral roots of racism and weaken it" (Parekh, 1986, p. 31).

The remaining dimensions of multicultural education described by Banks (1995b) work similarly to reduce prejudice and racism. Beneath each dimension is the implicit belief that the current state of education is inequitable. Consequently, multicultural education assumes that the entire educational system must be reformed in order to achieve equity. Although Mattai (1992) argues that "mainstream" multicultural education does not directly address racism, a broad multicultural approach may be the only way to achieve comprehensive change. As the historical work of the researchers discussed above indicates, racial prejudice is a complex phenomenon that manifests itself in complex and diverse forms. Consequently, an approach that focuses on only prejudice reduction might end up severing one head of a "societal Hydra," rather than attacking the beast where it is most vulnerable. The comprehensiveness of Banks's dimensions addresses these complex issues; racial prejudice will be effectively reduced only through a transformative approach to school reform. Havel (1992) reflects on the relationship between the state and society:

> The state is not something unconnected to society, hovering above it or outside it, a necessary and anonymous evil. The state is a product of society, an expression of it, an image of it. It is a structure that a society creates for itself as an instrument of its own self-realization. If we wish to create a good and humane society, capable of making a contribution to humanity's "coming to its senses,"

we must create a good humane state. That means a state that will no longer suppress, humiliate, and deny the free human being, but will serve all the dimensions of that being. (pp. 121–122)

If we desire in U.S. society what Havel proposes, then it is imperative that we, as educators, work for justice in the schools. If we do not, then education remains a reproductive system that limits the development of both individuals and society (Giroux, 1983). The investigation of prejudice and racism is part of a critical and transformative multicultural education designed to move schools from a means of reproduction to one of production. By continuing to raise our voices in the critical dialogue of race relations, we can continue to challenge the manifestation of hegemonic institutions.

REFERENCES

Aboud, F. E. (1987). The development of ethnic self-identification and attitudes. In J. S. Phinney & M. J. Rotheram (Eds.), *Children's ethnic socialization: Pluralism and development* (pp. 32–55). Newbury Park, CA: Sage.

Aboud, F. E. (1988). *Children and prejudice*. Cambridge, MA: Blackwell.

Aboud, F. E., & Skerry, S. A. (1984). The development of ethnic attitudes: A critical review. *Journal of Cross-Cultural Psychology, 15* (1), 3–34.

Adorno, T. W., Frenkel-Brunswik, E., Levinson, D. J., & Stanford, R. N. (1950). *The authoritarian personality*. New York: W. W. Norton.

Ajzen, I., & Fishbein, M. (1980). *Understanding attitudes and predicting social behavior*. Englewood Cliffs, NJ: Prentice-Hall.

Banks, J. A. (1991). *Teaching strategies for ethnic studies* (5th ed.). Boston: Allyn & Bacon.

Banks, J. A. (1993a). The canon debate, knowledge construction, and multicultural education. *Educational Researcher, 22* (5), 4–14.

Banks, J. A. (1993b). Multicultural education for young children: Racial and ethnic attitudes and their modification. In B. Spodek (Ed.), *Handbook of research on the education of young children* (pp. 236–250). New York: Macmillan.

Banks, J. A. (1994). *Multiethnic education: Theory and practice* (3rd ed.). Boston: Allyn & Bacon.

Banks, J. A. (1995a). The historical reconstruction of knowledge about race: Implications for transformative teaching. *Educational Researcher, 24* (2), 15–25.

Banks, J. A. (1995b). Multicultural education: Historical development, dimensions, and practice. In J. A. Banks & C. A. M. Banks (Eds.), *Handbook of research on multicultural education* (pp. 3–24). New York: Macmillan.

Bean, R. B. (1906). Some racial peculiarities of the Negro brain. *American Journal of Anatomy, 5*, 353–432.

Bethlehem, D. W. (1977). Validity of social distance scales: A Zambian study. *The Journal of Social Psychology, 101*, 157–158.

Bogardus, E. S. (1925a). Measuring social distance. *Journal of Applied Sociology, 9*, 299–308.

Bogardus, E. S. (1925b). Social distance and its origins. *Journal of Applied Sociology, 9*, 216–226.

Bogardus, E. S. (1926). Social distances between groups. *Journal of Applied Sociology, 10*, 473–479.

Bogardus, E. S. (1927). Race friendliness and social distance. *Journal of Applied Sociology*, 11, 278–279.

Bogardus, E. S. (1928). *Immigration and race attitudes*. New York: Heath.

Bogardus, E. S. (1968). Comparing racial distance in Ethiopia, South Africa, and the United States. *Sociology and Social Research, 52* (2), 149–156.

Borg. W. R., & Gall, M. D. (1989). *Educational research: An introduction* (5th ed.). New York: Longman.

Brigham, J. C. (1971). Ethnic stereotypes. *Psychological Bulletin, 76* (1), 15–38.

Campbell, D. T. (1950). The indirect assessment of social attitudes. *Psychological Bulletin, 47*, 15–38.

Chein, I. (1951). Notes on a framework for the measurement of discrimination and prejudice. In M. Jahoda, M. Deutsch, & S. W. Cook (Eds.), *Research methods in social relations* (pp. 382–390). New York: Dryden.

Clark, K. B. (1955). *Prejudice and your child*. Boston: Beacon Press.

Clark, K. B., & Clark, M. P. (1939). The development of consciousness of self and the emergence of racial identification in Negro preschool children. *Journal of Social Psychology, 10*, 591–599.

Clark, K. B., & Clark, M. P. (1947). Racial identification and preference in Negro children. In T. M. Newcomb & E. L. Hartley (Eds.), *Readings in social psychology* (pp. 169–178). New York: Holt, Rinehart, and Winston.

Code, L. (1991). *What can she know? Feminist theory and the construction of knowledge*. Ithaca, NY: Cornell University Press.

Cope, E. D. (1887). *The origin of the fittest*. New York: Macmillan.

Cross, W. E., Jr. (1991). *Shades of Black: Diversity in African American identity*. Philadelphia: Temple University Press.

Dovidio, J. F., & Fazio, R. H. (1992). New technologies for the direct and indirect assessment of attitudes. In J. M. Tanur (Ed.), *Questions about questions: Inquiries into the cognitive bases of surveys* (pp. 204–240). New York: Russell Sage Foundation.

DuBois, W. E. B. (1901). The relation of the Negroes to the Whites in the south. *Annals of the American Academy of Political and Social Science, 18*, 121–140.

Duckitt, J. (1992). *The social psychology of prejudice*. New York: Praeger.

Edwards, A. L. (1957). *The social desirability variable in personality assessment and research*. New York: Dryden.

Ewert, G. D. (1991). Habermas and education: A comprehensive overview of the influence of Habermas in educational literature. *Review of Educational Research, 61*(3), 345–378.

Fairchild, H., & Gurin, P. (1978). Traditions in the social psychological analysis of race relations. *American Behavioral Scientist, 21*, 757–778.

Gay, G. (1995). Curriculum theory and multicultural education. In J. A. Banks & C. A. M. Banks (Eds.), *Handbook of research on multicultural education* (pp. 25–43). New York: Macmillan.

Giroux, H. (1983). *Theory and resistance in education: A pedagogy for the opposition*. South Hadley, MA: Bergin & Garvey.

Gould, S. J. (1981). *The mismeasure of man*. New York: W. W. Norton.

Grady, H. G., & Wells, S. (1987). Toward a rhetoric of intersubjectivity: Introducing Jürgen Habermas. *Journal of Advanced Composition, 6*, 33–47.

Greenwald, A. G. (1989). Why are attitudes important? In A. R. Pratkanis, S. J. Breckler, & A. G. Greenwald (Eds.), *Attitude structure and function* (pp. 1–10). Hillsdale, NJ: Lawrence Erlbaum.

Harding, J., Proshansky, H., Kutner, B., & Chein, I. (1969). Prejudice and ethnic relations. In G. Lindzey & E. Aronson (Eds.), *The handbook of social psychology* (Vol. 5, pp. 1–76). Reading, MA: Addison-Wesley.

Havel, V. (1992). *Summer meditations* (P. Wilson, Trans.). New York: Knopf.

Herskovits, M. J. (1967). *The myth of the Negro past* (4th ed.). Boston: Beacon Press. (Original work published 1941)

Hillis, M. R. (1993). Multicultural education and curriculum transformation. *The Educational Forum, 58* (1), 50–56.

Hillis, M. R. (1994). The development of a free association technique for measuring prejudice. Unpublished doctoral dissertation, University of Washington, Seattle.

Horowitz, E. L. (1936). The development of attitudes toward the Negro. *Archives of Psychology, 194*, 1–47.

Horowitz, E. L., & Horowitz, R. E. (1938). Development of social attitudes in children. *Sociometry, 1*, 301–338.

Horowitz, R. E. (1939). Racial aspects of self-identification in nursery school children. *Journal of Psychology, 7*, 91–99.

Katz, D., & Braly, K. (1933). Racial stereotypes of one hundred college students. *Journal of Abnormal and Social Psychology, 28*, 280–290.

Katz, P. A. (Ed.). (1976). *Towards the elimination of racism*. New York: Pergamon Press.

LaPiere, R. T. (1934). Attitudes versus actions. *Social Forces, 13*, 230–237.

Lippman, W. (1922). *Public opinion*. New York: Harcourt, Brace.

Mattai, P. R. (1992). Rethinking the nature of multicultural education: Has it lost its focus or is it being misused? *Journal of Negro Education, 61*(1), 65–77.

McCarthy, C. (1990). *Race and curriculum: Social inequality and the theories and politics of difference in contemporary research on schooling*. New York: Falmer Press.

Nieto, S. (1992). *Affirming diversity: The sociopolitical context of multicultural education*. New York: Longman.

Okihiro, G. Y. (1994). *Margins and mainstreams: Asians in American history and culture*. Seattle: University of Washington Press.

Olson, J. M., & Zanna, M. P. (1993). Attitudes and attitude change. *Annual Review of Psychology, 44*, 117–154.

Parekh, B. (1986). The concept of multicultural education. In S. Modgil, G. K. Verma,

K. Mallick, & C. Modgil (Eds.), *Multicultural education: The interminable debate* (pp. 19–31). London: Falmer Press.

Park, R. E. (1924). The concept of social distance. *Journal of Applied Sociology, 8,* 339–344.

Payne, C. (1984). Multicultural education and racism in American schools. *Theory Into Practice, 23* (2), 126–131.

Phinney, J. S., & Rotheram, M. J. (Eds.). (1987). *Children's ethnic socialization: Pluralism and development.* Newbury Park, CA: Sage.

Salley, C. (1993). *The Black 100: A ranking of the most influential African Americans, past and present.* New York: Citadel Press.

Samelson, F. (1978). From "race psychology" to "studies in prejudice": Some observations on the thematic reversal in social psychology. *Journal of the History of the Behavioral Sciences, 14* (3), 265–278.

Sears, D. O., Peplau, L. A., & Taylor, S. E. (1991). *Social psychology* (7th ed.). Englewood Cliffs, NJ: Prentice-Hall.

Spencer, M. B. (1982). Personal and group identity of Black children: An alternative synthesis. *Genetic Psychology Monographs, 106,* 59–84.

Spencer, M. B. (1984). Black children's race awareness, racial attitudes, and self-concept: A reinterpretation. *Journal of Child Psychology and Psychiatry, 25,* 433–441.

Stephan, W. G. (1985). Intergroup relations. In G. Lindzey & E. Aronson (Eds.), *Handbook of social psychology* (3rd ed., Vol. 2, pp. 233–346). New York: Random House.

Stroebe, W., & Insko, C. A. (1989). Stereotype, prejudice, and discrimination: Changing conceptions in theory and practice. In D. Bar-Tal, C. F. Graumann, A. W. Kruglanski, & W. Stroebe (Eds.), *Stereotyping and prejudice: Changing conceptions* (pp. 3–36). New York: Springer-Verlag.

Taba, H., Brady, E. H., & Robinson, J. T. (1952). *Intergroup education in public schools.* Washington, DC: American Council on Education.

Thomas, W. I. (1904). The psychology of race-prejudice. *The American Journal of Sociology, 9* (5), 593–611.

Warner, L. L., & LaFleur, M. L. (1969). Attitudes as an interactional concept: Social constraint and social distance as intervening variables between attitudes and action. *American Sociological Review, 34,* 153–159.

Warren, E. (1969). Brown et al. v. Board of Education of Topeka et al. In M. J. Adler, C. Van Doren, & G. Ducas (Eds.), *The Negro in American history: Black Americans 1928–1968* (Vol. 1, pp. 282–288ff., 305–306). Chicago: Encyclopaedia Britannica Educational Corporation.

Watson, P. (1973). *Psychology and race.* Chicago: Aldine.

Weiler, K. (1988). *Women teaching for change: Gender, class, and power.* South Hadley, MA: Bergin & Garvey.

Zeligs, R., & Hendrickson, G. (1933). Racial attitudes of two hundred sixth-grade children. *Sociology and Social Research, 18,* 26–36.

Zeligs, R., & Hendrickson, G. (1934). Checking the social distance technique through personal interviews. *Sociology and Social Research, 18,* 420–430.

PART V

Language Revitalization, Curriculum Reform, and Action

The attempt by the multiculturalists to incorporate transformative knowledge into the school, college, and university curriculum evoked a bitter controversy during the late 1980s and early 1990s. Equally contentious has been the attempt by transformative educators and policy makers to legitimize primordial languages and to institutionalize them within the common civic culture and the schools. Groups on the margins have fought hard battles and initiated language revitalization movements to preserve their native languages and to maintain their ethnic and cultural identities.

In Chapter 16 Carlos J. Ovando and Karen Gourd use the idea of transformative knowledge to guide their discussion of language revitalization, language policies, and school language practices and programs. They examine four case studies of language revitalization movements: (1) the Navajo at Rough Rock and Rock Point (in Arizona); (2) the Hualapai, a Native American group in Arizona; (3) the Maori of New Zealand; and (4) Native Hawaiians in Hawaii.

Curriculum transformation and language revitalization efforts challenge dominant group hegemony in the United States as well as White privilege. Curriculum transformation and the revitalization of primordial languages require that power be shared, the center be transformed, and a new conception of the *unum* be formulated. America must be re-envisioned and re-imagined. Transforming the center will tax the commitment, imagination, and tenacity of each individual and group. However, it will pose special problems and challenges for individuals and groups who have power and privilege. In his personalized, reflective, and empowering chapter, Gary Howard (Chapter 17) gives sage advice regarding actions Whites who are committed to transforming the center can take to help the United States to actualize the ideals stated in the Declaration of Independence, the Constitution, and the Bill of Rights.

In Chapter 18, James A. Banks encapsulates the major themes in this book by describing the dimensions of multicultural education, a conceptualization that can be used to guide curriculum transformation, school reform, and student action. He describes a unit on the Montgomery bus boycott to illustrate how the major themes discussed in this book can be implemented by classroom teachers.

CHAPTER 16

Knowledge Construction, Language Maintenance, Revitalization, and Empowerment

CARLOS J. OVANDO AND KAREN GOURD

"All the way through school, I was told they just wanted to make me a white person, so I'd succeed. The teachers would tell me everything about me was bad. I'd go home and think about it: 'What in the hell got me to be an Indian? Why?'" (Rose Chesarek, quoted in Crawford, 1991, p. 143). With these thoughts Rose Chesarek, a Crow Indian educator, has captured the essence of educational policies toward U.S. cultural and linguistic minorities during the pre-civil rights era. In carrying out such policies, educators expected these groups to replace their native languages with standard English.

There have been many accounts suggesting that the United States generally has had a history of national tolerance for languages other than English (Fitzgerald, 1993; Heath, 1981; Heath & Mandabach, 1983; Kloss, 1977). However, Schlossman (1983) points out that there has been too little research to substantiate these claims because immigration historians have had little interest in language issues. Few scholars would argue that the Mexicans in the Southwest, Puerto Ricans in Puerto Rico, African Americans, American Indians, or Pacific Islanders experienced language and cultural tolerance as part of federal policies or educational practices prior to the civil rights movement of the 1960s and 1970s.

We use the concept of transformative knowledge to guide our analysis. We examine four representative indigenous minority cultures and consider two sets of questions: What have been the effects (intended or unintended) of language educational policies and practices aimed at indigenous cultures? Conversely, how have indigenous language groups in the United States and other nations affected government policies and educational practices? We approach these questions using a historical-social framework (Tollefson, 1991). We use this framework to examine the purposes that language policies and educational practices serve and to consider whom they are meant to benefit. We also explore the effects of these policies when measured by criteria outside mainstream society.

To address these issues, we first review briefly the nature of knowledge construction and transformative knowledge. We then survey the current process of language loss as it is occurring throughout the world. We consider the implications of the rapid loss of language diversity. We then look more closely at U.S. hegemony and language issues in Native American education. With our perspective established, we take a closer look at four cases of language revitalization efforts: Navajo, Hualapai, Maori, and Hawaiian. As we look at these four cases, we can see that transformative knowledge provides the intellectual rationale for deconstructing dominant group hegemony, structures, and institutions, including dominant and institutionalized languages (Fishman, 1991; Newmeyer, 1986). Language maintenance and revitalization are major vehicles that marginalized and dominated groups use to attain power within society, to create a sense of peoplehood, and to challenge institutionalized structures, paradigms, and languages (Crawford, 1991; Minami & Ovando, 1995). To attain power, linguistic minority groups try to institutionalize and legitimize their languages within the mainstream society (Labov, 1972; Labov, Cohen, Robins, & Lewis, 1968). Transformative knowledge about languages, language use, and the validity of languages is essential to these attempts.

KNOWLEDGE CONSTRUCTION
AND TRANSFORMATIVE KNOWLEDGE

People perceive and understand the world based on their experiences and previous knowledge; they construct their understandings of the world by interpreting new information based on what they already know and believe. Two basic assumptions underlie knowledge construction: (1) there is no single truth, and (2) reality is defined by positionality (Code, 1991; Teterault, 1993). Each person's experiences and roles (based in part on nationality, ethnicity, language, social class, education, religion, and gender) work jointly to adjust the lens through which he or she views the world. Language plays an important part in the knowledge construction process in at least two major ways: (1) the language that individuals and groups are familiar with and use affects their perceptions of the world and of others (Whorf, 1959); and (2) the language individuals or groups choose to use or to not use sends powerful messages to others (Newmeyer, 1986). A critical issue in language maintenance and revitalization is who defines and interprets the needs of ethnic groups and who decides what languages a group uses.

Language can serve as a concrete example of how the mind accommodates new knowledge. For example, Navajo, an indigenous language in America, has at its disposal all the words to describe a modern car. These words were not borrowed from other languages; they were constructed from words already available in Navajo (Bunge, 1992). The existence of a Navajo car lexicon illustrates the tendency of languages to develop as information, needs, and the experiences of individuals or groups change.

Individuals may not be aware of the implicit forces that influence their views and how they construct knowledge. However, people who construct transformative knowledge are keenly aware of both the dominant view and their alternative interpretations or resistance to it. Transformative knowledge challenges mainstream academic knowledge and institutions, expands and substantially revises established canons and paradigms, and supports social, economic, and political reform (Banks, 1993).

The Mayas are a group that have used transformative knowledge to resist the image of Mayan culture presented by linguists studying their language. We briefly consider their situation as an example of how knowledge construction can occur. England (1992) explains that linguists traditionally have been trained to "be true to [their] data" (p. 31), meaning that they should report data accurately and thoroughly and remain apolitical. However, at two Mayan linguistics workshops in 1985 and 1989, a group of Mayas suggested that linguists consider both the negative and positive consequences of their research on the people whose language they study. Linguistics is not apolitical; it affects important issues such as language maintenance, literacy, and bilingualism. Furthermore, in choosing what data to report and which examples to include, linguists have the power and expert authority to represent the Mayan language, culture, and people positively or negatively (England, 1992). For instance, linguists using only violent verbs as examples of the Mayan language, without commenting on the political struggle at the time of data collection, misrepresent Mayas as a violent cultural group (England, 1992).

England (1992) argues that investigating a language with low prestige requires sensitivity and a concern that exceeds scientific objectivity. The Mayas resent the "take-the-data-and-run" habit of many linguists and pointedly ask why linguists publish in a language they do not understand. In exchange for the specialized knowledge the Mayas provide to the linguists about their language, linguists might provide the Mayas with the specialized knowledge of linguistics that would enable them to do linguistics. As Jeanne (1992) reminds readers, anthropological linguistics originated with the study of Native American languages by Boas (1911), Sapir (1921), and Bloomfield (1933), "but despite the large contribution of Native American languages to formal language scholarship, tribal communities themselves have been involved primarily as a source of data and have not reaped the benefits of Native American language scholarship" (p. 24).

In effect, Mayas are asking linguists to view them not in the traditional Western view of the subordinate role of "uneducated and unsophisticated" informants (England, 1992, p. 30) but rather as co-researchers with equally valuable knowledge and skills. Through their activism, the Mayas have influenced an academic discipline to change how it interprets and presents data. Similar requests are being made by other indigenous groups throughout the world as they struggle to redefine how mainstream cultures view and interact with their cultures.

Marginalized ethnic groups such as the Mayas have actively developed various oppositional responses to the threatened status of their languages and thus have strengthened their cultural identity. Freire (1970/1992) discusses liberation of the oppressed, not as a gift that is bestowed or as a victory taken, but as a reciprocal process that unfolds as marginalized groups struggle for their rights. In so doing, marginalized groups alter mainstream thinking as well as their own.

But what is at stake as marginalized groups use knowledge about languages and political strategies to revitalize, reconstruct, and institutionalize their ancestral languages? In the next section we examine the extensive language loss that is occurring throughout the world and consider its serious implications.

LANGUAGE LOSS AND LANGUAGE MAINTENANCE

When we discuss language loss, we mean the process of language extinction. Krauss (1992), Hale (1992), and Crawford (1994, 1995) make the analogy between biological and language extinction. Krauss (1992) explains that when children cease to learn the mother tongue of their parents, "unless the course is somehow dramatically reversed, they are already doomed to extinction, like species lacking reproductive capacity" (p. 4). When a language ceases to have reproductive capacity it is said to be moribund (Diamond, 1993; Krauss, 1992). In 1992 Krauss estimated that the following percentages of languages were moribund: 90% of the remaining 50 indigenous languages of Alaska and the Soviet North; 90% of the remaining 250 Australian aboriginal languages; 80% of the 187 remaining North American indigenous languages; and about 30% of the 900 remaining South American indigenous languages. Accurate figures on the number of languages spoken in the world today do not exist. However, Krauss and other linguists estimate that during the next century half of the approximately 6,000 languages spoken in the world today will become extinct.

Writes Hale (1992), "Language loss is a serious matter . . . it is part of a much larger process of loss of cultural and intellectual diversity in which politically dominant languages and cultures simply overwhelm indigenous local languages and cultures, placing them in a condition which can only be described as embattled" (p. 1). An ever-increasing number of cultures are shifting their language of communication from their ancestral language to the language of those in power. Krauss (1992) lists some of the factors that contribute to language loss as ranging "from outright genocide, social or economic or habitat destruction, displacement, demographic submersion, language suppression in forced assimilation or assimilatory education, to electronic media bombardment, especially television" (p. 6). In addition, other recent trends such as "urbanization, deforestation, desertification, and AIDS" contribute to language loss (Krauss, 1992, p. 7).

The thoughts of Athapaskan youths, whom Ovando (1994) interviewed, illustrate that indigenous groups are aware of the language loss in their communities. One eighth grader stated, "We can't afford to lose any more of our Native ways. There is only a handful of elders who know the old culture" (quoted in Ovando, 1994, p. 46). An eleventh grader from the same village stated: "None of the students at my high school can speak our native language, Athabascan [an alternative spelling of Athapaskan]. Instead of learning to speak it we are being taught English. None of us care to sit and try to learn our native language from the elders in our community; we are all busy watching television and listening to music by Mr. Big and Nirvana" (quoted in Ovando, 1994, p. 46). Education has provided a new knowledge base to the younger generation, but that new knowledge has been purchased at a high price: loss of ancestral languages and cultures.

Historically, schools have played an important part in efforts to assimilate linguistic minority groups and have been places where language loss is accelerated. However, schools can encourage and influence the reversal of language loss (Dick & McCarty, 1994; Holm & Holm, 1995). Language preservation has become a pressing issue for some groups. These groups have developed school programs to help preserve their languages and cultures. Although school programs alone cannot reverse language shifts, as part of the complex sociocultural system, school programs can influence what language indigenous groups select for communicative and academic purposes.

McLaughlin (1989) recommends "the creation of conditions in schools whereby students and teachers alike participate in the creation and recreation of knowledge" (p. 42). School knowledge that fits the model described by Banks (1993) will reflect personal/cultural knowledge, popular knowledge, and transformative knowledge, as well as mainstream academic knowledge. The status of a language, which is determined by when, where, and by whom it is used, greatly influences the type of knowledge transmitted.

The use of indigenous languages only within the school classroom probably will not raise the status of a language, but when school programs permit the exchange of personal/cultural knowledge using the indigenous language, the perceived value of both the personal/cultural knowledge and the indigenous language is enhanced. The status of a language (which is determined by location, situation, and by whom it is used) greatly influences the type of knowledge transmitted. With increased individual and group identity on the part of local community members, school programs can more easily become vehicles for strengthening cultures and for increasing opportunities for languages to be used outside the school, thus improving the status of the indigenous languages from within.

McLaughlin (1989) suggests that schools must recognize their role in the power relations between mainstream academic knowledge and the lived experiences of the local people. School programs should reflect the experiences of the community and provide students with the tools to "interrogate and selectively appropriate knowledge, values and skills from the dominant culture which can provide them with a basis for changing their existing circumstances" (McLaughlin, 1989, p. 44). Although language programs in schools often are reduced to debate over the linguistic effectiveness of bilingual programs, McLaughlin (1989) and Ovando (1990) have attempted to move the debate to a level that recognizes the complexity of language revitalization efforts, focusing on issues related to hegemony. Ovando (1990) believes that before we can evaluate a school program's effectiveness, we must ask how language diversity fits into the existing national ideology. If the goals of the program include transferring power by allowing the local community to use their knowledge gained through lived experiences to organize school programs, then the success of the school programs cannot be determined solely by standardized test scores. In the past, school programs may have been expected to correct years of inappropriate federal policies (Collier, 1988). However, they alone cannot be responsible for reversing language shifts. It is only through bottom-up, community strength that school programs can help to reverse language shifts.

In addition to local support, other factors are needed to make a language safe from extinction. Krauss (1992) states that "official state support and very large numbers of speakers" are needed (p. 7). However, even though ethnic groups may experience population growth, this growth does not automatically translate into large numbers of speakers of indigenous languages. The Maori in New Zealand and the Navajo in the United States, for example, experienced population growth during the 1980s, while the number of native speakers drastically declined (Fishman, 1991; McLaughlin, 1992). Education in English and the "assimilative power of the English language" (Ovando, 1993, p. 219) have negatively affected Navajo and Maori language maintenance, despite population growth.

The loss of ancestral languages is a concern for many complex reasons. As Krauss (1992) again asks, using the analogy to the biological kingdom, "Should we mourn the loss of [the languages] Eyak or Ubykh any less than the loss of the panda or California condor?" (p. 8). Crawford (1994) believes that language loss does not just mean a loss of data sources for linguists. It increases the general loss of human diversity and therefore will negatively influence human progress in unknown ways; it also causes serious damage to a group's identity. When a language is lost, the issue of identity is the greatest concern, as Crawford (1994) has stated.

Despite the negative consequences of language loss that many scholars perceive, both Diamond (1993) and Crawford (1994) have pointed out that some people argue that language loss may be a good thing, and that fewer languages will promote easier communication and provide more opportunities for world peace. Diamond believes that people need a common language to communicate, but that does not preclude them from knowing more than one language. People do not need to give up their native language; they only need to acquire a second one. Diamond also notes that most minority cultures learn the majority language and usually do not ask majority cultures to learn their languages. A common language does not ensure peaceful relations between groups of people because there are many other factors that are sources of conflict, such as religion, ethnicity, and territorial disputes.

UNITED STATES HEGEMONY
AND NATIVE AMERICAN EDUCATION

It is estimated that between 250 and 300 languages were spoken by the indigenous people of North America when the Europeans arrived (J. Crawford, personal communication, May 7, 1995). As the United States expanded its borders, the indigenous people generally were viewed with hostility by the European Americans who went west (Duchene, 1988; Holm, 1979). Key leaders, including George Washington, Patrick Henry, John Marshall, and Secretary of War Henry Knox, expected that the "Indian *problem* would eventually be solved very largely by the mere pressure of civilization upon *barbarism*, and that the economy of the savage would not be able to survive against that of the white man" (emphasis added; Mohr, 1933, p. 174). Hundreds of Native American languages moved toward extinction "as White settlers carried out polices of Indian enslavement, extermination, removal, containment, and repression" (Crawford, 1991, p. 142).

The policy of assimilating Indian youth through education is clearly reflected in this 1887 statement by J. D. C. Atkins, Commissioner of Indian Affairs: "If we expect to infuse into the rising generation the leaven of American citizenship, we must remove the stumbling blocks of hereditary customs and manners, and of these language is one of the most important elements" (quoted in Adams, 1988, p. 8). Atkins apparently understood the importance of language and that stripping the native languages from American Indians would significantly change their lives. He viewed these changes as positive, explaining that "no unity or community of feeling can be established among different peoples unless they are brought to speak the same language and thus become imbued with the like ideas of duty" (Adams, 1988, p. 8).

The removal of Indian children from their families was considered appropriate because a major concern of mainstream society was that Indian children replace tribal languages and customs with the more "civilized" language and culture of European Americans. Adams (1988) states that "education for citizenship focused on language instruction and political socialization" (p. 8). Ironically, most American Indians did not gain citizenship until 1924. It was 1927 before the practice of taking Indian children from their home and community was considered inconsistent with contemporary views of mainstream education (Reyhner, 1992).

Missionary schools often tried to "civilize" the Indians through education. Missionaries found that their attempts to convert the indigenous peoples to Christianity and to teach literacy skills were more successful when they used the native languages of the Native Americans (Reyhner, 1992). While a pro-indigenous language stance on the part of missionaries did not necessarily mean an affirmation of indigenous cultural values, it probably did help to maintain the indigenous languages. By the late 1800s, however, most schools that had been started by missionaries and had used native languages to educate Choctaws, Creeks, Chickasaws, Seminoles, and Cherokees were closed (McDonald, 1989; Noley, 1979). During the 1850s the Cherokee had a literacy rate in Cherokee of 90% (McDonald, 1989) and had high levels of English literacy (Medicine, 1979). They had their own printing press and produced a newspaper in both languages (Spicer, 1980a). However, after the takeover of their schools by the federal government, their literacy levels in both Cherokee and English dropped precipitously. The Cherokee were among the least educated population in the United States in the 1970s (Medicine, 1979).

Between 1889 and 1930, the majority of American Indians learned to speak English. McLaughlin (1992) describes the Navajo situation: "As recently as 1946, two-thirds of the Navajo Tribe, which then numbered seventy thousand members, had no school experience whatsoever; there were only fifty high-school graduates; and the median number of years of schooling for tribal members as a whole was less than one" (p. 6). Illiteracy in both English and Navajo was common. Navajo was the primary means for oral communication in the community (McLaughlin, 1992). Once the children started attending schools that used English as the language of instruction, the erosion of Navajo was accelerated (McLaughlin, 1992).

The general mission of boarding schools was to assimilate Indian children. However, educators complained that despite all that was done for them, and their acquisition of Western education and English language skills, many Indians went "back to the blanket" (Spicer, 1980b, p. 118). Many chose to live in Indian communities and to follow Indian customs (Spicer, 1980b). However, an often overlooked fact is that the communities the students returned to had changed in important ways (Henze & Vanett, 1993). Their traditional cultures and means of livelihood were not sitting patiently awaiting their return, and those who returned had been influenced by their experiences away from the reservations (Spicer, 1980b). When Indians returned to the reservations, new problems arose, including increased hostility toward Whites (Spicer, 1980a, 1980b). The boarding school experience had managed to replace their native languages with English and had changed many of their Indian ways. However, as Spicer (1980a) explains, "as Indians borrowed white modes of behavior, belief, and organization, they did not necessarily come to admire whites or identify with them. Rather they identified themselves more intensely as Indians" (p. 63).

The assimilationist policies of educating Indian youth had allowed, ironically, avenues for increased American Indian political militancy during the 1960s. Indians made the conditions of their lives known by demonstrating and demanding restitution for broken treaties (Spicer, 1980b). The Indians living away from the reservations (who supposedly were more assimilated) were less under the control of the federal government than Indians living on reservations and were more successful in publicizing their message. Increased interaction with Whites tended to result in more negative attitudes toward non-Indian ways. It also gave Indians opportunities to resist mainstream cultural penetration (Fuchs & Havighurst, 1972). Contrary to what was expected, living with Whites and receiving a White education did not necessarily imbue Native Americans with a desire to assimilate. Despite tremendous language loss over the course of several hundred years of European contact, the embers of native language revitalization are alive.

LANGUAGE REVITALIZATION EFFORTS AND EMPOWERMENT: FOUR CASES

We now examine four cases of language revitalization efforts and community empowerment (see Fishman, 1991, for additional examples). We look first at two examples involving Native American languages: Navajo revitalization efforts at Rough Rock and Rock Point, and the Hualapai Bilingual/Bicultural Program in Peach Springs, Arizona. We then describe language revitalization among the Maori of New Zealand. In the final case we consider briefly the efforts being undertaken to revitalize the Hawaiian language. The struggle of these disparate groups to legitimize their languages within mainstream society are informative examples of the transformative possibilities of language maintenance and revitalization. Comparisons of the struggles of indigenous people in diverse locations help us to better understand how attempts to reverse language loss are empowering to the indigenous groups. Comparisons also can redefine the dominant and the indigenous perspectives on the importance of language and culture in education.

Language Revitalization Efforts at Rough Rock and Rock Point

Galena Sells Dick, the coordinator and former bilingual teacher for the Title VII Program at Rough Rock Elementary School, stressed the contrasts between traditional Indian boarding schools and the Rough Rock School on the Navajo reservation in northeastern Arizona:

> Unlike the boarding schools which tried to make us lose our Indian characteristics and made us ashamed of our language and culture, the Rough Rock School [formerly the Rough Rock Demonstration School] views Navajo language and culture as sources of great pride. (Galena Sells Dick, in Dick & McCarty, 1994, p. 17)

In 1966, 2 years before the enactment of the Bilingual Education Act, Rough Rock Demonstration School became the first Native American school to contract for Indian control of a school (Lipka & McCarty, 1994; McCarty, 1989). It was also the first Native American-operated school to use the community's language and culture for instruction (Lipka & McCarty, 1994). From the beginning, the school's teachers and administrators viewed Navajo language and culture as valuable tools and sought to build on the Navajo children's strengths by using their language and culture in instruction (Dick & McCarty, 1994).

There were few certified Navajo teachers at Rough Rock in 1966. Consequently, culturally sensitive instruction was a major undertaking. The school board approved a training program for local community members to become certified teachers. This commitment to Navajo teacher training is given major credit for building the foundation that made a strong bilingual/bicultural program possible at Rough Rock (Dick & McCarty, 1994; Lipka & McCarty, 1994). As more Navajo speakers became certified teachers, they could more easily address the needs of Navajo students. It was easier to get things accomplished when more people with similar ideas were working together. Teachers became more confident as they saw themselves as competent, trained educators, and local community members trusted teachers because of their outside training and inside status (Dick & McCarty, 1994).

A second important development that contributed to Rough Rock Demonstration School's success was the involvement of teachers in a 5-year, collaborative research project with the Hawaiian Kamehameha Early Education Program (KEEP). KEEP began in 1971 with money from the estate of the former royal family of Hawaii (Au, 1980; Jordan, 1984, 1995). KEEP had two purposes: "(1) to discover ways to improve the educational achievement of Hawaiian children; and (2) to influence the public schools of Hawaii in their behalf" (Jordan, 1984, p. 60). Although KEEP uses standard English, not the home language of the children, it is characterized by culturally compatible classroom practices and has been credited with the improvement of the reading test scores of Hawaiian students (Au & Mason, 1983; Jordan, 1984, 1995). The KEEP researchers were interested in finding out whether the well-documented, culturally sensitive literacy strategies would be as effective with Navajo as with Hawaiian children (Jordan, 1995; Lipka & McCarty, 1994). As the KEEP researchers and the Rough Rock teachers worked together over 5 years, the Navajo teachers' view of themselves was transformed. The Navajo teachers became "more willing to take new pedagogical risks; [their] concerns moved . . . from simply replicating KEEP to modifying it to address language development in both Navajo and English" (Lipka & McCarty, 1994, p. 270).

The Kamehameha Early Education Program—a culturally sensitive, monolingual program—aided the development of the Rough Rock English–Navajo Language Arts Program (RRENLAP), a bilingual/bicultural program. As the Rough Rock Community School moved away from prepackaged, Western-dominated, English-only curricula, it developed a role for Navajo literacy (Dick & McCarty, 1994), creating a place for the Navajo language in the modern world. The English literacy abilities of students improved as their Navajo proficiency increased (Dick & McCarty, 1994). With improved Navajo and English proficiency and improved reading test scores, Navajo children have taken new pride in themselves and their language.

Rough Rock has served as a model of local control for other Indian-operated schools, such as that at Rock Point (Collier, 1988), a Navajo reservation–interior community located in northeastern Arizona (Rosier & Holm, 1980; Begay et al., 1995). The following description of the Rock Point Community School program is based on Holm and Holm's work (1990, 1995). Rock Point was established as a Bureau of Indian Affairs (BIA) day community school in the mid-1930s (Holm & Holm, 1995). Ninety to 95% of all students entering the school system from Rock Point homes were, until the early 1970s, Navajo monolingual. Because few Navajos could read or write Navajo, it was not easy to move to a bilingual literacy education program. The Rock Point program operated with a Navajo teacher (initially without a diploma) and an English-speaking teacher in each classroom (Holm & Holm, 1990). The two teachers had equal responsibility for instruction and planning, a model that challenged the teacher and aide model, which still dominates much of bilingual education in U.S. mainstream schools. (For a description of the Rock Point program, see Holm and Holm, 1990, 1995.)

Development of a Navajo teaching staff was an important part of the Rock Point program, as it was at Rough Rock (Holm & Holm, 1990). In 1995, teachers already employed by the Rock Point Community School District without their degrees were required to take 12 hours per contract year at a university. This option, however, is no longer available to newly hired teachers, who must already be certified (R. Livingstone, personal communication, June 1, 1995). More than 40 Navajo teachers had earned their degrees in this program when Holm and Holm published their work.

As the Rock Point program was initiated, English language teachers were quickly hired and given an orientation. However, while the English language teachers were going through orientation, the Navajo language teachers, without the aid of "Anglos or diplomas," were in charge of all instruction. The experience of being on their own helped them to realize how much they were capable of teaching. Their success during the orientation made the Navajo teachers question the mainstream knowledge that gave little value to their Indian ways. Although they did not totally reject the schooling process that resulted in diplomas, they viewed themselves from a new perspective. With that new perspective and the support of Public Law 93-638 (self-determination), the Navajo community had the strength in 1975 to negotiate control of the school.

The Navajo bilingual programs at Rough Rock and Rock Point challenge the conventional expectation that the more exposure to English, the sooner English proficiency will be acquired. Research at Rock Point supports bilingual education as an important pedagogical approach for language development and as a positive way to effectively educate students labeled "at risk" of school failure because they come from homes that use a language other than English. Navajo bilingual programs provide documentation that academic knowledge and English skills are enhanced through the use of the native language to give a firm foundation in literacy, particularly in the early years (Rosier & Holm, 1980; Tharp, Dalton, & Yamauchi, 1994). Furthermore, through such bilingual programs, local communities can learn to value and use their knowledge and skills for education in the community.

Hualapai Bilingual/Bicultural Program

In existence since 1975 and located in Peach Springs, Arizona, the Hualapai Bilingual/Bicultural Education Program was initiated by Akira Yamamoto, a linguist, who in collaboration with a Hualapai elder named Jane Honga began to learn and document the Hualapai language and culture with the intent of producing storybooks that could be used to help children write in Hualapai and English (Watahomigie, 1995; Watahomigie & McCarty, 1994; Watahomigie & Yamamoto, 1987). According to Watahomigie and McCarty (1994), Hualapai remained an unwritten language until the Hualapai Bilingual/Bicultural Program began. Affirming the importance of bilingual and bicultural parents in the socialization process of their children, the community-based, bilingual/bicultural program in the local public elementary school (K–8) served about 230 students in 1995, 90% of whom were Hualapai; the non-Hualapai students also learn Hualapai (L. J. Watahomigie, personal communication, June 1, 1995). Content is presented in both English and Hualapai and focuses on understanding the local community and environment through a variety of means, including computer and video technology (Watahomigie & McCarty, 1994).

The Hualapai program continues to serve as an important example of language revitalization, transformation, and empowerment. It became a training program for anthropologists to learn a new type of research, the kind of collaborative research the Mayas proposed at their linguistic workshops, discussed at the beginning of this chapter. Anthropologists and linguists in the Hualapai project worked toward bilingualism/biculturalism, not just for the sake of their research but for the needs of the local community (Watahomigie & McCarty, 1994; Watahomigie & Yamamoto, 1992). The project has led to a deeper understanding of collaborative research. Watahomigie and Yamamoto (1992) explain, "The goal of collaborative research is not only to engage in a team project but also, and perhaps more importantly, to provide opportunities for local people to become researchers themselves" (p. 12).

As Watahomigie and others began this project, it became clear that they needed more resources than the community could contribute. They wrote a successful grant proposal for a training program through the American Indian Language Development Institute (AILDI), which provided collaborative opportunities for language and cultural maintenance for many other Indian groups. Because of AILDI's fundamental view of language and culture, American Indian communities have begun to change their expectations of school.

The collaborative approach has led to the training of local community members and the inclusion of a native language or cultural component in many elementary and secondary teacher preparation programs (Watahomigie, 1995; Watahomigie & McCarty, 1994; Watahomigie & Yamamoto, 1992). However, there are still obstacles to be overcome. The teacher-training programs are not at convenient times and locations for the local community members to attend. In some instances, students who are seeking teaching certification programs may have to drive 7 hours to the nearest university. A combination of family responsibilities and financial hardships often prevent such students from becoming certified within 4 years. As a result, the Hualapai teachers may take as long as 15 years to complete their college training (L. J. Watahomigie, personal communication, June 1, 1995). Despite these obstacles, there have been modest gains in producing "homegrown" Hualapai teachers.

The Hualapai program has shown that collaborative, cooperative projects have great potential. Watahomigie and Yamamoto (1992) believe that collaborative projects can "ensure that intellectual wealth of local communities can achieve a position of dignity in education and other aspects of life. Another effect, in some areas at least, is to bring local language literacy to people who have never before experienced it, to enable people to express themselves in the written form of their own language, even if only to give voice to feelings of mild despair" (pp. 16–17).

In 1990, 15 years after the Hualapai Bilingual/Bicultural Education Program began, the Native American Languages Act was enacted. Members of the American Indian Language Development Institute, along with another organization on the international level, the Native American Language Issues Institute, worked together to initiate political support for the endangered languages of the United States and helped lead the way to the Native American Languages Act, Public Law 101-477. This act, drafted with input from participants of the American Indian Language Development Institute, serves at a minimum as symbolic support of indigenous languages. It also provides incentives for many more indigenous communities to take local action toward maintaining their language (McCarty, 1992). For the mainstream policy makers and the indigenous community members who look to the mainstream for direction, the Native American Languages Act is a powerful instrument that can affect how Indians and non-Indians view indigenous languages.

Language Revitalization Among Maori

When we examine the Maori struggle to reverse language shift through new programs in public schools, we find many parallels between the situation of indigenous languages in the United States and New Zealand. Although in many ways different from indigenous groups living in North America, the Maori of New Zealand experienced European colonialism in some ways similar to Native Americans (Havighurst, 1984). In the 1800s, missionary schools provided many Maori with their first formal education, and as often occurred in the United States, the missionary schools used the indigenous language as the language of instruction. In 1867, with the passage of the Native Schools Act, the government began to take responsibility for the education of Maori children. The government committed itself to these goals: (1) promoting local interests and control of the rural Maori schools; and (2) making English a part of all government-supported schools. Although native language missionary schools continued to exist, many more Maori children were educated in government schools (Smith, 1983).

Unlike government boarding schools for Native Americans in the United States, the government schools for the Maori in New Zealand were not intent on eradicating the ancestral culture. The purpose of the government schools was to prepare the students for the modern world while allowing them to continue Maori traditions (Middleton, 1992; Smith, 1983). Thus the Maori to some degree maintained a level of cultural self-respect that was denied Native Americans. This double focus of schools to prepare Maori children for the modern world and to maintain Maori cultural values created, as early as the 1900s, an educated indigenous population in New Zealand that could assume leadership roles supporting Maori people (Havighurst, 1984). Havighurst (1984) suggests that this combination of a Western education and cultural self-respect paved the road for the later Maori grass-roots movement to reform New Zealand schools.

Prior to the early 1900s, Maori children were largely segregated in Maori schools. From the early 1900s on, however, segregation decreased and fewer Maori children attended schools where Maori traditions were respected. After World War II, many Maori moved to urban areas, seeking better living conditions, jobs, and education. Ironically, the move to the urban areas for a better education meant that Maori children attended *pakeha* (White descendants of British and other European colonists) schools and, as the minority population, relinquished the Maori-sensitive cultural traditions of the segregated Maori rural schools. In the urban contexts, Maori children tended to give up their language and cultural traditions in the process of becoming schooled. Although their population increased in the 1900s, as with the Navajo, the population increase did not mean that there was a higher percentage of Maori who could use the language (Fishman, 1991).

As this culture and language loss developed, the Maori Social and Economic Advancement Act was passed in 1945. Fishman (1991), however, describes it as mere tokenism. The Act established the Maori Tribal Executives to preserve Maori art, crafts, language, and history. However, the Act neglected to provide a plan of action or funding resources. Although there was no specific plan for *preserving* the culture, the Act detailed procedures for *controlling* Maori behavior and for regulating and licensing billiard rooms operated by Maori (Fishman, 1991).

In the 1960s, the implicit government policy, described by Fishman (1991) as "seek the knowledge of the *pakeha*" (p. 232), was questioned by Maori who had gained the knowledge of the *pakeha* and were keenly aware of the continuing disadvantaged state of the Maori people. The Maori became less tolerant of the tokenism offered by the *pakeha* and took steps toward revital-

ization of their language and culture. Three important steps toward revitalization were (1) a movement to protect the *taonga*, which Fishman (1991)
describes as "all those things of material and spiritual value of the Maori"
(p. 235), including the language, (2) the *aatarangi* movement that began in
1979 as a community-based program focusing on adult learning (or relearning)
of the Maori language, and (3) the *Tu Tangata Whanau,* the Family Development Program using the traditional concept of extended families to re-
establish what Fishman (1991) referred to as the "norms of hospitality,
caring, spirituality and sharing, behavioral norms for which spoken Maori
language is considered essential" (p. 237).

The *Tu Tangata Whanau* program was the birthplace of the *kohanga
reos*, or 'language nests'. Language nests, which continue in operation today,
are provided by Maori-speaking parents or grandparents who volunteer as
child-care workers for preschoolers. These language nests provide a natural
Maori language setting for children during their primary language learning
years. Additional benefits of the program are community-building and good
child care for young Maori children. (For a thorough and in-depth analysis of
the structure, operation, and style of the *kohanga reos*, see Fleras, 1989; Irwin,
1990.) However, as Fishman (1991) has pointed out, more than the *kohanga
reo* program is needed. In order for the Maori language to become safe from
extinction, the young children leaving preschool for elementary school need
bilingual programs that will maintain their Maori fluency and build Maori literacy skills. Again it is the Maori community that has identified the lack of
attention to continuing Maori language education, and in 1987 400 *kohanga
reo* teachers took these concerns to the Education Department, demanding
government funding for Maori schooling (Fishman, 1991). Many Maori educational activists are now pushing for withdrawal from the *pakeha* education
system and for the establishment of separate Maori education systems
(Middleton, 1992).

Language revitalization efforts have transformed knowledge by challenging previous implicitly held views of both Maori and mainstream New
Zealanders (Middleton, 1992). Before the revitalization efforts, most New
Zealanders believed that educating Maori children meant providing them with
the same education and opportunities as non-Maori children (Smith, 1983).
However, Maori increasingly are doubting the efficacy of a traditional Western education system for their children, and the non-Maori population is
beginning to understand the difference between equitable and equal education. The new policies based on this new thinking include teacher-training
programs in Maori language and culture as part of all teacher preparation
programs, recruitment of Maori teachers, and training sessions for experienced
teachers and principals. Many of the courses for educators use the Maori
extended family concept, thus legitimizing it and providing the opportunity

for the Maori community to have a major role in expanding teacher knowledge (Smith, 1983). Thus the Maori are no longer just a group of people to be educated and assimilated; they are sharing their culture and language and changing the mainstream interpretation of Maori knowledge. (*The New Zealand Annual Review of Education* is a good resource for continually updated articles on Maori education.)

Language Revitalization in Hawaii

Unlike many other indigenous languages, Hawaiian, a Polynesian language similar to Maori, has a history of use in written form. A written script was introduced by missionaries in the early nineteenth century, and the language was used exclusively in public education during the Hawaiian monarchy (Wilson, 1991). Unlike many of the other languages we have discussed, there are textbook materials, a dictionary, cultural pieces, printing presses, legal records, and manuscripts in Hawaiian (Kimura & 'Aha Punana Leo Incorporated, 1987; Wilson, 1991).

Despite this strong legacy, with Hawaiian statehood in 1959 came legislation outlawing the use of Hawaiian in public schools. Like linguistic minority students in the mainland U.S., Hawaiians were punished for using their home language at school (Kimura & 'Aha Punana Leo Incorporated, 1987). This policy had a devastating effect. In a short time, Hawaiian changed from being the primary language of all people born in Hawaii (including non-Hawaiians) to being the native language of fewer than 2,000 people. In 1987, many of the remaining native speakers were over the age of 70, and most Hawaiians actually spoke Hawaii Creole rather than Hawaiian (Kimura & 'Aha Punana Leo Incorporated, 1987). In 1987, there were only about 30 native Hawaiian-speaking children in the islands (Wilson, 1991).

With this precipitous and alarming loss, however, have come a variety of revitalization efforts. Spearheaded by leaders of Hawaiian ancestry who saw the need for Hawaiian families to take a leadership role in the education of their children, a *kupuna*-based program was conceived in 1976 by Queen Lili'uokalani Children's Center (QLCC), a private social work agency designed to serve Hawaiian orphan children and grass-roots groups on the island of O'ahu. (*Kupuna* means elder in Hawaiian.) After overcoming intense resistance from the school establishment, the Hawaiian Language Program was initiated in 1979, in the Windward District, under the sponsorship of the State of Hawaii Department of Education, QLCC, and the Joint Residents' Hawaiian Language Committee (H. Bernardino, personal communication, May 30, 1995). *Kupuna* who were also native speakers of Hawaiian taught Hawaiian culture, music, and language to 1,435 students from kindergarten through fifth grade. However, developing fluency in Hawaiian was not the focus of the program. That is, students could count and sing in Hawaiian, for example, but they could not carry on a conversation in Hawaiian (L. Kimura, personal communication, May 30, 1995). Rather, the program was intended to be a community development effort to enable parents to become active participants in making decisions that affected their children's education and the community (H. Bernardino, personal communication, May 30, 1995). Now called the Hawaiian Studies Program, it is completely funded and delivered by the public school system throughout the state.

The most serious attempts to revitalize the Hawaiian language have been implemented by the Punana Leo Schools, begun in 1984 by a private nonprofit group. These schools serve children ages 2 to 6 by providing them with quality, native Hawaiian language exposure. It is interesting to note that these preschools were modeled after the Maori language nests (Kimura & 'Aha Punana Leo Incorporated, 1987). Punana Leo Schools were granted the same privilege as foreign language schools to hire teachers fluent in Hawaiian even if they did not have all the necessary college courses to teach in the Hawaiian language (Kimura & 'Aha Punana Leo Incorporated, 1987). Along with this development, Hawaiians have succeeded in having the Hawaiian language taught as a university language course, giving the language more legitimacy in the academic world. Although there has been some resistance by the English-dominant government, Hawaiian has been named an official language of Hawaii and indigenous group members have had some success in bringing the indigenous community and the academic community closer together (Kimura & 'Aha Punana Leo Incorporated, 1987). Through lobbying and protest from families and friends involved with the Punana Leo Schools, the 1959 legislation outlawing the use of Hawaiian in the schools was finally overturned in 1987 (Wilson, 1991).

The influence of such language revitalization programs across thousands of miles is impressive. The KEEP researchers from Hawaii were influential in helping the Navajo at Rough Rock develop a new approach to literacy. Hawaiians, in turn, have borrowed the language nest idea from the Maori. Since then, individuals involved in the language nest movement in Hawaii have helped Alaskan Natives, whose languages are threatened with extinction, to develop their own nesting programs (Demmert, 1993; Lipka & McCarty, 1994).

IMPLICATIONS FOR LANGUAGE MAINTENANCE AND REVITALIZATION IN DIVERSE CONTEXTS

Holm and Holm (1990, 1995) capture the common characteristics of the Rock Point program and many of the other examples we have described of education of indigenous children: (1) a commitment to bilingual instruction,

(2) a culturally relevant curriculum, and (3) strong involvement in and control of education by parents and the local community. These programs also lend support to modern school reforms that focus on shared decision-making models in which teachers are viewed as professionals able to make appropriate decisions. In addition, the programs reveal the importance of teacher training that prepares educators to teach in culturally and linguistically sensitive ways.

The approach underlying these programs is very different from those in traditional programs. Instead of operating from a highly functionalist curriculum that is driven by a nationalistic ideology and market forces (see Goodman, 1995), these programs do not require a factory model approach to school in order to achieve a particular end product. Instead, their leaders and teachers ask: "What do parents and grandparents want for their children?" "What will work for these students?" "How can the school prepare the students for what the students need?" This need must be assessed by including the local cultural perspective rather than relying solely on the dominant one. From a cultural perspective, many of the problems that language minority students experience in mainstream programs can be attributed to the school's devaluing of the home and culture of the students rather than to their cultural differences. In culturally and linguistically sensitive programs students are not labeled "at risk"—a cultural deficit approach. Culturally sensitive programs have moved beyond home–school discontinuity, cultural relativity, or cultural difference theory and have made room for more equitable, culturally sensitive schooling defined in cooperation with the community.

Tharp, Dalton, and Yamauchi (1994) discuss important general principles of culturally sensitive schooling that have been derived from research on ethnic and cultural groups like those involved in the programs described in this chapter. The authors suggest that work with ethnic groups has increased the dominant culture's understanding of cognition, motivation, and language development in general. Although there is no single, proven effective method for all students, the knowledge gained from research focusing on ethnic communities can guide mainstream schooling as well as schooling for minority groups.

Research with a cross-cultural focus has shown that ways of perceiving, processing, and storing information are culturally influenced. Although there is no evidence that all individual members of any particular group use the same cognitive style, cognitive styles are "culturally supported"—that is, strongly influenced by cultural norms and experiences (Irvine & York, 1995). Instruction for students who learn best in a holistic cognitive style requires very different approaches from instruction for students operating from an analytical cognitive style. Likewise, research on cultural influences on motivation has shown that different cultural groups are motivated in significantly different ways. Motivation research reveals that culturally compatible classrooms increase student participation and result in higher levels of academic achievement (Tharp, Dalton, & Yamauchi, 1994).

One of the most important principles that Tharp, Dalton, and Yamauchi (1994) discuss is the importance of developing language competence in the language of instruction. Although attempts to revitalize languages have provided evidence to support bilingual education as a way to promote school success and to improve English skills, there is a larger conclusion to be made: Language is crucial to the development of cognitive skills. The implication is that all school instruction should have a strong language component.

As important and relevant as these conclusions are, there is a prescriptive nature to them that leaves the authors uncomfortable. Attributing the success of the educational programs that we have described to the concrete explanations of local control, cultural compatibility, and an empowered teaching force seems to provide a simple formula for indigenous schooling. However, in order to understand the significance of the programs, the tendency to accept a simple, quick explanation should be avoided. Stairs (1994) presents a preliminary model of school as cultural negotiation. The model examines context (classrooms, community, region, and state/national levels, including the political-social history of power relations), meaning (the what, how, and why of teaching as defined by the culture), and depth of process (the level of participation of students, teachers, and the community). Viewing these programs through this educational model fits with the historical-social framework we set out to use to uncover the purpose of the policies and practices of schools.

The significance of Stairs's cultural negotiation model is seen, as one example, in local conflicts over language maintenance and revitalization efforts. An important part of the historical context of educating indigenous groups in the United States is forced assimilation. Self-determination is now the legislated federal policy that supports local control over Native American schools in the United States, but local control does not automatically translate into bilingual and bicultural education. Many authors writing about indigenous languages (e.g., Ayoungman, 1995; Begay et al., 1995; Holm & Holm, 1990, 1995; Lipka, 1994; McLaughlin, 1992; Ovando, 1984, 1994; Silentman, 1995) have made it clear that all members of indigenous communities do not necessarily support language and culture revitalization efforts. The reasons for this lack of total support range from the existence of Native American traditionalists who consider their language an oral language and resist the creation of literacy events in the language (McLaughlin, 1992), to pragmatists who for economic and professional success want to put all their efforts into learning standard English (Ayoungman, 1995), the nation's language of power.

The value of Stairs's cultural negotiation model begins long before the students enter the classroom, as the questions of what languages will be taught and who will teach them are legitimized by their negotiation in community forums. Successful language revitalization programs in one community have important implications for other communities and settings. It is not necessarily the particular elements of the programs that should be duplicated, but rather the recognition of the complex, interactive model of education and the acknowledgment of the centrality of language and culture as an educational issue. The depth of the process has been instrumental in changing the context of schooling not only by changing the outcomes—teaching the ancestral language and culture in school—but by addressing the issue of whose language will be valued. This is the question, simultaneously asked at the federal, state, local, and individual levels, that ultimately may decide the fate of language revitalization efforts.

We would like to be optimistic about the future—to think that educational programs will be viewed as having multidimensional layers that need to develop and interact with the community rather than as rules and formulas for transmitting language and culture. And we would like to think that the culturally sensitive programs developed by indigenous groups will influence mainstream ways of perceiving education. However, the swing toward conservative politics that leaves the financial backing of these and similar programs in jeopardy, accompanied by the pressure of groups like English Only, affirms both the complexity of and the need for ongoing struggles for educational reforms that focus on cultural and linguistic equity and revitalization.

Acknowledgments. We are grateful to James A. Banks, Haunani Bernardino, James Crawford, Larry Kimura, Kristina J. Lindborg, Masahiko Minami, and Jon Reyhner for their insightful comments on earlier drafts of this chapter.

REFERENCES

Adams, D. W. (1988). Fundamental considerations: The deep meaning of Native American schooling, 1880–1900. *Harvard Educational Review, 58* (1), 1–28.

Au, K. H. (1980). Participation structures in a reading lesson with Hawaiian children: Analysis of a culturally appropriate instructional event. *Anthropology and Education Quarterly, 11* (2), 91–115.

Au, K. H., & Mason, J. M. (1983). Cultural congruence in classroom participation structures: Achieving a balance of rights. *Discourse Processes, 6* (2), 145–167.

Ayoungman, V. (1995). Native language renewal: Dispelling the myths, planning for the future. *Bilingual Research Journal, 19* (1), 183–187.

Banks, J. A. (1993). The canon debate, knowledge construction, and multicultural education. *Educational Researcher, 22* (5), 4–14.

Begay, S., Dick, G. S., Estell, D. W., Estell, J., McCarty, T., & Sells, A. (1995). Change from the inside out: A story of transformation in a Navajo community school. *Bilingual Research Journal, 19* (1), 121-139.

Bloomfield, L. (1933). *Language.* New York: Henry Holt.

Boas, F. (Ed.). (1911). *Handbook of American Indian languages* (Part I) (Bureau of American Ethnology Bulletin 40). Washington, DC: Smithsonian Institution Press.

Bunge, R. (1992). Language: The psyche of a people. In J. Crawford (Ed.), *Language loyalties: A source book on the official English controversy* (pp. 376-380). Chicago: University of Chicago Press.

Code, L. (1991). *What can she know? Feminist theory and the construction of knowledge.* Ithaca, NY: Cornell University Press.

Collier, J., Jr. (1988). Survival at Rough Rock: A historical overview of Rough Rock Demonstration School. *Anthropology & Education Quarterly, 19* (3), 253-269.

Crawford, J. (1991). *Bilingual education: History, politics, theory, and practice* (2nd ed.). Los Angeles: Bilingual Education Services.

Crawford, J. (1992). *Hold your tongue: Bilingualism and the politics of "English Only."* Reading, MA: Addison-Wesley.

Crawford, J. (1994). Endangered Native American languages: What is to be done and why? *Journal of Navajo Education, XI* (3), 3-11.

Crawford, J. (1995). Endangered Native American languages: What is to be done, and why? *Bilingual Research Journal, 19* (1), 17-38.

Demmert, W. G., Jr. (1993). Language, learning, and national goals: A Native American view. In *The issues of language and culture: Proceedings of a symposium convened by the Center for Applied Linguistics.* Washington, DC. (ERIC Document Reproduction Service No. ED 355 781)

Diamond, J. (February, 1993). Speaking with a single tongue. *Discover,* pp. 78-85.

Dick, G. S., & McCarty, T. L. (1994). Navajo language maintenance and development: Possibilities for community-controlled schools. *Journal of Navajo Education, 11* (3), 15-20.

Duchene, M. (1988). Giant law, giant education, and ant: A story about racism and American Indians. *Harvard Educational Review, 58* (3), 354-362.

England, N. C. (1992). Doing Mayan linguistics in Guatemala. *Language: Journal of the Linguistic Society of America, 68* (1), 29-35.

Fishman, J. A. (1991). *Reversing language shift.* Clevedon, U.K.: Multilingual Matters.

Fitzgerald, J. (1993). Views on bilingualism in the United States: A selective historical review. *Bilingual Research Journal, 17* (1/2), 35-56.

Fleras, A. J. (1989). Te Kohanga Reo: A Maori language renewal program. *Canadian Journal of Native Education, 16* (2), 78-88.

Freire, P. (1992). *Pedagogy of the oppressed.* New York: Continuum. (Original work published 1970)

Fuchs, E., & Havighurst, R. J. (1972). *To live on this earth.* Garden City, NY: Doubleday.

Goodman, J. (1995). Change without difference: School restructuring in historical perspective. *Harvard Educational Review, 65* (1), 1-29.

Hale, K. (1992). Endangered languages: On endangered languages and the safeguarding of diversity. *Language: Journal of the Linguistic Society of America, 68* (1), 1-3.

Havighurst, R. J. (1984). Anglo-Native relations in Australia, New Zealand, and the USA. *Educational Research Quarterly, 8* (4), 103-112.

Heath, S. B. (1981). English in our language heritage. In C. A. Ferguson & S. B. Heath (Eds.), *Language in the USA* (pp. 6-20). London: Cambridge University Press.

Heath, S. B., & Mandabach, F. (1983). Language status and the law in the United States. In J. Cobarrubias & J. A. Fishman (Eds.), *Progress in language planning: International perspective* (pp. 87-105). New York: Mouton.

Henze, R. C., & Vanett, L. (1993). To walk in two worlds or more? Challenging a common metaphor of Native education. *Anthropology & Education Quarterly, 24* (2), 116-134.

Holm, A., & Holm, W. (1990). Rock Point, a Navajo way to go to school: A valediction. *The Annals of the American Academy of Political and Social Science, 508,* 170-184.

Holm, A., & Holm, W. (1995). Navajo language education: Retrospect and prospects. *Bilingual Research Journal, 19* (1), 141-167.

Holm, T. (1979). Racial stereotypes and government policies regarding the education of American Indians, 1879-1920. In *Multicultural education and the American Indian* (pp. 15-24). Los Angeles: University of California, American Indian Studies Center.

Irvine, J. J., & York, D. E. (1995). Learning styles and culturally diverse students: A literature review. In J. A. Banks & C. A. M. Banks (Eds.), *Handbook of research on multicultural education* (pp. 484-497). New York: Macmillan.

Irwin, K. (1990). The politics of Kohanga Reo. In S. Middleton, J. Codd, & A. Jones (Eds.), *New Zealand educational policy today: Critical perspectives* (pp. 110-120). Auckland, New Zealand: Allen and Unwin.

Jeanne, L. M. (1992). An institutional response to language endangerment: A proposal for a Native American language center. *Language: Journal of the Linguistic Society of America, 68* (1), 24-28.

Jordan, C. (1984). Cultural compatibility and the education of Hawaiian children: Implications for mainland educators. *Educational Research Quarterly, 8* (4), 59-71.

Jordan, C. (1995). Creating cultures of schooling: Historical and conceptual background of the KEEP/Rough Rock collaboration. *Bilingual Research Journal, 19* (1), 83-100.

Kimura, L. L., & 'Aha Punana Leo Incorporated. (1987). The Hawaiian language and its revitalization. In *Our language, our survival: Proceedings of the Seventh Annual Native American Language Issues Institute.* Saskatoon: Saskatchewan Indian Languages Institute.

Kloss, H. (1977). *The American bilingual tradition.* Rowley, MA: Newbury House.

Krauss, M. (1992). The world's languages in crisis. *Language: Journal of the Linguistic Society of America, 68* (1), 4-10.

Labov, W. (1972). *Language in the inner city.* Philadelphia: University of Pennsylvania Press.

Labov, W., Cohen, P., Robins, C., & Lewis, J. (1968). *A study of the nonstandard English of Negroes and Puerto Rican speakers in New York City* (Vol. 2) (Cooperative Research Project No. 3280). Washington, DC: Office of Education.

Lipka, J. (1994). Language, power, and pedagogy: Whose school is it? *Peabody Journal of Education, 69* (2), 71–93.

Lipka, J., & McCarty, T. L. (1994). Changing the culture of schooling: Navajo and Yup'ik cases. *Anthropology & Education Quarterly, 25* (3), 266–284.

McCarty, T. L. (1992). Federal language policy and American Indian education. Revised version of a paper presented at the annual meeting of the American Educational Research Association, San Francisco. (ERIC Document Reproduction Service No. RC 018 999)

McCarty, T. L. (1989). School as community: The Rough Rock Demonstration. *Harvard Educational Review, 59* (4), 484–503.

McDonald, D. (1989, August 2). Stuck in the horizon: A special report on the education of Native Americans. *Education Week,* pp. 1–16.

McLaughlin, D. (1989). Power and the politics of knowledge: Transformative leadership and curriculum development for minority language learners. *Peabody Journal of Education, 66* (3), 41–60.

McLaughlin, D. (1992). *When literacy empowers: Navajo language in print.* Albuquerque: University of New Mexico Press.

Medicine, B. (1979). Bilingual education and public policy: The cases of the American Indian. In R. V. Padilla (Ed.), *Ethnoperspectives in bilingual education research: Bilingual education and public policy in the United States* (pp. 395–407). Ipsilanti: Eastern Michigan University.

Middleton, S. (1992). Equity, equality, and biculturalism in the restructuring of New Zealand schools: A life-history approach. *Harvard Educational Review, 62* (3), 301–322.

Minami, M., & Ovando, C. J. (1995). Language issues in multicultural contexts. In J. A. Banks & C. A. M. Banks (Eds.), *Handbook of research on multicultural education* (pp. 329–344). New York: Macmillan.

Mohr, W. H. (1933). *Federal Indian relations 1774–1788.* New York: AMS Press.

Newmeyer, F. J. (1986). *The politics of linguistics.* Chicago: University of Chicago Press.

Noley, G. (1979). Choctaw bilingual and bicultural education in the 19th century. In *Multicultural education and the American Indian* (pp. 25–39). Los Angeles: University of California, American Indian Studies Center.

Ovando, C. J. (1984). School and community attitudes in an Athapaskan bush village. *Educational Research Quarterly, 8* (4), 12–29.

Ovando, C. J. (1990). Politics and pedagogy: The case of bilingual education. *Harvard Educational Review, 60* (3), 341–356.

Ovando, C. J. (1993). Language diversity and education. In J. A. Banks & C. A. M. Banks (Eds.), *Multicultural education: Issues and perspectives* (2nd ed., pp. 215–235). Boston: Allyn & Bacon.

Ovando, C. J. (1994). Change in school and community attitudes in an Athapaskan village. *Peabody Journal of Education, 69* (2), 43-59.

Reyhner, J. (1992). Policies toward American Indian languages: A historical sketch. In J. Crawford (Ed.), *Language loyalties: A source book on the official English controversy* (pp. 41-47). Chicago: University of Chicago Press.

Rosier, P., & Holm, W. (1980). *The Rock Point experience: A longitudinal study of a Navajo school program* (Saad Naaki Bee Na'nitin). Washington, DC: Center for Applied Linguistics.

Sapir, E. (1921). *Language: An introduction to the study of speech.* New York: Harcourt, Brace, and World.

Schlossman, S. L. (1983). Is there an American tradition of bilingual education? German in the public elementary schools, 1840-1919. *American Journal of Education, 91* (2), 139-186.

Silentman, I. (1995). Revaluing indigenous languages through language planning. *Bilingual Research Journal, 19* (1), 179-182.

Smith, A. F. (1983). A response for the Maori population of New Zealand. In Centre for Educational Research and Innovation Organization for Economic Co-operation and Development (Ed.), *The education of minority groups: An enquiry into problems and practices of fifteen countries* (pp. 348-360). Hampshire, England: Gower.

Spicer, E. (1980a). American Indians. In S. Thernstrom (Ed.), *Harvard encyclopedia of American ethnic groups* (pp. 58-114). Cambridge, MA: Harvard University Press.

Spicer, E. (1980b). American Indians, federal policy toward. In S. Thernstrom (Ed.), *Harvard encyclopedia of American ethnic groups* (pp. 114-122). Cambridge, MA: Harvard University Press.

Stairs, A. (1994). The cultural negotiation of indigenous education: Between micro-ethnography and model-building. *Peabody Journal of Education, 69* (2), 154-171.

Teterault, M. K. T. (1993). Classrooms for diversity: Rethinking curriculum and pedagogy. In J. A. Banks & C. A. M. Banks (Eds.), *Multicultural education: Issues and perspectives* (2nd ed., pp. 129-148). Boston: Allyn & Bacon.

Tharp, R. G., Dalton, S., & Yamauchi, L. A. (1994). Principles for culturally compatible Native American education. *Journal of Navajo Education, 11* (3), 33-39.

Tollefson, J. W. (1991). *Planning language, planning inequality: Language policy in the community.* London: Longman.

Watahomigie, L. J. (1995). The power of American Indian parents and communities. *Bilingual Research Journal, 19* (1), 189-194.

Watahomigie, L. J., & McCarty, T. L. (1994). Bilingual/bicultural education at Peach Springs: A Hualapai way of schooling. *Peabody Journal of Education, 69* (2), 26-42.

Watahomigie, L. J., & Yamamoto, A. Y. (1987). Linguistics in action: The Hualapi Bilingual/Bicultural Education Program. In D. D. Stull & J. J. Schensul (Eds.), *Collaborative research and social change* (pp. 77-98). Boulder, CO: Westview Press.

Watahomigie, L. J., & Yamamoto, A. Y. (1992). Local reactions to language decline. *Language: Journal of the Linguistic Society of America, 68* (1), 10-17.

Whorf, B. L. (1959). Linguistics as an exact science. In L. F. Dean & K. G. Wilson (Eds.), *Essays on language and usage.* New York: Oxford University Press.

Wilson, W. H. (1991, December 15). American Indian bilingual education: Hawaiian parallels. *NABE News, 15* (3), 9-10.

CHAPTER 17

Whites in Multicultural Education: Rethinking Our Role

GARY HOWARD

How does an ethnic group that historically has been dominant in its society adjust to a more modest and balanced role? Put differently, how do White Americans learn to be positive participants in a richly pluralistic nation? These questions have always been a part of the agenda of multicultural education but are now coming more clearly into focus. Most of our work in race relations and multicultural education in the United States has emphasized—and appropriately so—the particular cultural experiences and perspectives of Black, Asian, Hispanic, and American Indian groups. These are the people who have been marginalized to varying degrees by the repeated assertion of dominance by Americans of European ancestry. As the population of the United States shifts to embrace ever larger numbers of previously marginalized groups, there is an emerging need to take a closer look at the changing role of White Americans.

Part of this need is generated by the growing evidence that many White Americans may not be comfortable with the transition from their dominant status. As our population becomes more diverse, we have seen an alarming increase in acts of overt racism. The number and size of hate groups in the United States are rising. Groups such as the Aryan Nation, neo-Nazis, and skinheads tend to play on the anger, ignorance, and fears of the more alienated, disenfranchised, and uneducated segments of White society.

Too many segments of our White American population remain committed to their position of dominance; they are willing to defend it and legitimize it, even in the face of overwhelming evidence that our world is rapidly changing (Hacker, 1992). Taken as a whole, these realities strongly suggest that a peaceful transition to a new kind of America, in which no ethnic or cultural group is in a dominant position, will require considerable change in education and deep psychological shifts for many White Americans. Attempting to effect these changes is part of the work of multicultural education, and that challenge leads us to a central question: What must take place in the minds and hearts of White Americans to convince them that now is the time to begin their journey from dominance to diversity?

There is much that needs to be said to help us understand our collective past, as well as the present. In a sense we are all victims of our history, some more obviously and painfully than others. It is critical that we White Americans come to terms with our reality and our role. What does it mean for White people to be responsible and aware in a nation where we have been the dominant cultural and political force? What can be our unique contribution, and what are the issues we need to face? How do we help create a nation where all cultures are accorded dignity and the right to survive?

I explore these questions here from the perspective of a White American. Each nation, of course, has its own special history to confront and learn from, but the depth and intensity of our struggle with diversity in the United States have significant lessons to teach both our own people and the rest of the world.

AMERICAN IMMIGRANTS

European Americans share at least one commonality: We all came from somewhere else. In my own family, we loosely trace our roots to England, Holland, and perhaps Scotland. However, with five generations separating us from our various "homelands," we have derived little meaning from these tenuous connections with our ancestral people across the water. This is true for many White Americans, who often are repulsed by the appellation "European American" and would never choose such a descriptor themselves. They simply prefer "American" and to forget the past.

On the other hand, many White Americans have maintained direct and strong ties with their European roots. They continue after many generations to draw meaning and pride from those connections. In the Seattle region there is an Ethnic Heritage Council composed of members of 103 distinct cultural groups, most of them European. These people continue to refer to themselves as Irish American, Croatian American, Italian American, or Russian American— terminology that acknowledges the two sides of their identity.

European Americans are a diverse people. We vary broadly across extremely different cultures of origin, and we continue here in the United States to be diverse in religion, politics, economic status, and lifestyle (Alba, 1990). We also vary greatly in the degree to which we value the notion of the melting pot. Many of us today are ignorant of our ethnic history because our ancestors worked so hard to dismantle their European identity in favor of what they perceived to be the American ideal. The further our immigrant ancestors' cultural identities diverged from the White Anglo-Saxon Protestant image of the "real" American, the greater was the pressure to assimilate. Jews, Catholics, Eastern Europeans, Southern Europeans, and members of minority religious sects all felt the intense heat of the melting pot. From the moment they arrived on American soil, they received a strong message: Forget the home language, make sure your children don't learn to speak it, change your name to sound more American—or, if the immigration officials can't pronounce it, they'll change it for you.

In dealing with the history and culture of European Americans, it is important to acknowledge the pain, suffering, and loss that often were associated with their experiences. For many of these groups, it was a difficult struggle to carve out a niche in the American political and economic landscape and at the same time preserve some sense of their own ethnic identity. Some White Americans resist the multicultural movement today because they feel that their own history of suffering from prejudice and discrimination has not been adequately addressed.

Family Realities

Like many White Americans, I trace my roots in this country back to the land—the Minnesota farm my mother's great-grandparents began working in the 1880s. My two uncles still farm this land, and I spent many of the summers of my youth with them. It was there that I learned to drive trucks and tractors at the age of 12. I learned the humor and practical wisdom of hard-working people. I learned to love the land—its smell and feel; its changing moods and seasons; its power to nourish the crops, the livestock, and the simple folks who give their lives to it. On this land and with these people I have known my roots, my cultural heritage, much more deeply than through any connection with things European. The bond of my Americanness has been forged in my experience with the soil.

Yet, as I have grown to understand more of the history of this country, a conflict emerged in my feelings about our family tradition of the land. I have a close friend and colleague, Robin Butterfield, whose traditional Ojibwa tribal lands once encompassed the area now occupied by my family's farm. This farm, which is the core experience of my cultural rootedness in America, is for her people a symbol of defeat, loss, and domination. How do I live with this? How can I incorporate into my own sense of being an American the knowledge that my family's survival and eventual success on this continent were built on the removal and near extermination of an entire race of people?

And to bring the issue closer to the present, many of my relatives today hold prejudicial attitudes about cultural differences. The racist jokes they tell at family gatherings and the ethnic slurs that punctuate their daily chatter have been an integral part of my cultural conditioning. It was not until my college years, when I was immersed in a rich multicultural living situation, that these barriers began to break down for me. Most of my relatives have not had that opportunity. They do not understand my work in multicultural education. "You do what?" The racist jokes diminish in my presence, but the attitudes remain. Yet, I love these people. They are my link with tradition and the past, even though many of their beliefs are diametrically opposed to what I have come to know and value about different cultures.

My family is not atypical among White Americans. Internal contradictions and tensions around issues of culture and race are intrinsic to our collective experience. For most White Americans, racism and prejudice are not theoretical constructs; they are members of the family.

When we open ourselves to learning about the historical perspectives and cultural experiences of other races in America, much of what we discover is incompatible with our image of a free and democratic nation. We find conflicting realities that do not fit together easily in our conscious awareness, clashing truths that cause train wrecks in the mind. In this sense, White Americans are caught in a classic state of cognitive dissonance. Our collective security and position of economic and political dominance have been fueled in large measure by the exploitation of other people. The physical and cultural genocide perpetrated against American Indians, the enslavement of African peoples, the exploitation of Mexicans and Asians as sources of cheap labor—on such acts of inhumanity rests the success of the European enterprise in America.

This cognitive dissonance is not dealt with easily. We can try to be aware. We can try to be sensitive. We can try to deal with the racism in our own families, yet the tension remains. We can try to dance to the crazy rhythms of multiculturalism and race relations in the United States, but the dissonant chords of this painful past and present keep intruding.

The Luxury of Ignorance

Given the difficulty of dealing with such cognitive dissonance, it is no mystery why many White Americans simply choose to remain unaware. In fact, the possibility of remaining ignorant of other cultures is a luxury uniquely available to members of any dominant group. Throughout most of our history, there has been no reason why White Americans, for their own survival or success, have needed to be sensitive to the cultural perspectives of other groups. This is not a luxury available to people of color. If you are Black,

Indian, Hispanic, or Asian in the United States, daily survival depends on knowledge of White America. You need to know the realities that confront you in the workplace, in dealing with government agencies, in relation to official authorities like the police. To be successful in mainstream institutions, people of color in the United States need to be bicultural—able to play by the rules of their own cultural community and able to play the game according to the rules established by the dominant culture. For most White Americans, on the other hand, there is only one game, and they traditionally have been on the winning team.

The privilege that comes with being a member of the dominant group, however, is invisible to most White Americans (McIntosh, 1988). Social research repeatedly has demonstrated that if Jessie Myles, an African American friend, and I walk into the same bank on the same day and apply for a loan with the same officer, I will be more likely to receive my money—and with less hassle, less scrutiny, and less delay. This is in spite of the fact that Jessie has more education and is also more intelligent, better looking, and a nicer person. Likewise, if I am turned down for a house purchase, I don't wonder whether it was because of the color of my skin. And if I am offered a new job or promotion, I don't worry that my fellow workers may feel that I'm there not because of my qualifications, but merely to fill an affirmative action quota. Such privileged treatment is so much a part of the fabric of our daily existence that it escapes the conscious awareness of most White Americans. From the luxury of ignorance are born the culturally encapsulated neighborhoods of our nation, which remain painfully out of touch with the experiences and sensibilities of multicultural America.

Emotions That Kill

The most prevalent strategy that White Americans adopt to deal with the grim realities of history is denial. "The past doesn't matter. All the talk about multicultural education and revising history from different cultural perspectives is merely ethnic cheerleading. My people made it, and so can yours. It's an even playing field and everybody has the same opportunities, so let's get on with the game and quit complaining. We've heard enough of your victim's history."

Another response is hostility, a reaction to cultural differences that we have seen resurfacing more blatantly in recent years. The Aryan Nation's organizing in Idaho, the murder of a Black man by skinheads in Oregon, the killing of a Jewish talk show host by neo-Nazis in Denver, cross burnings and Klan marches in Dubuque, and the increase in racist incidents on college campuses all point to a revival of hate crimes and overt racism in the United States. We can conjecture why this is occurring now: the economic downturn, fear of job competition, the rollback on civil rights initiatives by recent administrations. Whatever the reason, hostility related to racial and cultural differences has always been a part of American life and only once again was brought into bold relief by the first Rodney King decision and its violent aftermath in Los Angeles.

Underlying both the denial and the hostility is a deep fear of diversity. This fear is obvious in the Neanderthal violence and activism of White supremacist groups. Because of their personal and economic insecurities, they seek to destroy that which is not like them.

The same fear is dressed in more sophisticated fashion by Western traditionalists and neoconservatives who campaign against multicultural education. They fear the loss of European and Western cultural supremacy in the school curriculum (Ravitch, 1990; Schlesinger, 1992). With their fraudulent attempt to characterize "political correctness" as a new form of McCarthyism and with their outcries against separatism, particularism, reverse racism, and historical inaccuracy in multicultural texts, they defend cultural turf that is already lost. The United States was never a White European Christian nation and is becoming less so every day. Most public school educators know the curriculum has to change to reflect this reality, but many guardians of the traditional canon still find it frightening to leave the Old World.

Denial, hostility, and fear are literally emotions that kill. Our country—indeed, the world—has suffered endless violence and bloodshed over issues of racial, cultural, and religious differences. And the killing is not only physical, but emotional and psychological as well. With this hostility toward diversity, we threaten to destroy the precious foundation of our national unity, which is a commitment to equality, freedom, and justice for all people. It is not multiculturalism that threatens to destroy our unity—as some neoconservative academics would have us believe—but rather our inability to embrace our differences and our unwillingness to honor the very ideals we espouse.

Ironically, these negative responses to diversity are destructive not only for those who are the targets of hate but also for the perpetrators themselves. Racism is ultimately a self-destructive and counterevolutionary strategy. As is true for any species in nature, positive adaptation to change requires a rich pool of diversity and potential in the population. In denying access to the full range of human variety and possibility, racism drains the essential vitality from everyone, victimizing our entire society.

Another emotion that kills is guilt. For well-intentioned White Americans guilt is a major hurdle. As we become aware of the realities of the past and the present—of the heavy weight of oppression and racism that continues to drag our nation down—it is natural for many of us of European background to feel a collective sense of complicity, shame, or guilt. On a rational level, of course, we can say that we didn't contribute to the pain. We weren't there.

We would never do such things to anyone. Yet, on an emotional level, there is a sense that we were involved somehow. And our membership in the dominant culture keeps us connected to the wrongs, because we continue to reap the benefits of past oppression.

There is a positive side to guilt, of course. It can be a spur to action, a motivation to contribute, a kick in the collective conscience. Ultimately, however, guilt must be overcome, along with the other negative responses to diversity—for it, too, drains the lifeblood of our people. If we are finally to become one nation of many cultures, then we need to find a path out of the debilitating cycle of blame and guilt that has occupied so much of our national energy.

Responses That Heal

How do we as White Americans move beyond these negative responses to diversity and find a place of authentic engagement and positive contribution? The first step is to approach the past and the present with a new sense of honesty. Facing reality is the beginning of liberation. As White Americans, we can face honestly the fact that we have benefited from racism. The point is simply to face the reality of our own privilege. We also can become supportive of new historical research aimed at providing a more inclusive and multidimensional view of our nation's past. Scholars and educators are searching for the literature, the experiences, the contributions, and the historical perspectives that have been ignored in our Eurocentric schooling. It is important that White Americans become involved in and supportive of this endeavor, which is, of course, highly controversial.

Many White Americans feel threatened by the changes that are coming. One of our responsibilities, therefore, is to help them understand that our nation is in a time of necessary transition. This is part of the honesty we are trying to address. It took 500 years for our present curriculum to evolve, and in spite of its many fine qualities, it is still flawed and inaccurate and excludes most non-European perspectives and influences. The new multicultural curricula also will have to go through a process of evolution toward balance and accuracy. The appropriate role for aware White Americans is to participate in this evolution, rather than to attack it from the outside, as many critics of multicultural education have chosen to do.

Along with this honesty must come a healthy portion of humility. It is not helpful for White Americans to be marching out in front with all the answers for other groups. The future belongs to those who are able to walk and work beside people of many different cultures, lifestyles, and perspectives. The business world is embracing this understanding. We now see top corporate leaders investing millions of dollars annually to provide their employees with skills to function effectively in a highly diverse workplace (Thomas, 1991). They are forced to make this expenditure because schools, frankly, have not done an adequate job. Diversity is a bottom-line issue for employers. Productivity is directly related to our ability to deal with pluralism. Whenever power, truth, control, and the possibility of being right are concentrated in only a few people, a single perspective, one culture, or one approach, the creativity of an entire organization suffers.

Honesty and humility are based on respect. One of the greatest contributions White Americans can make to cultural understanding is simply to learn the power of respect. In Spanish, the term *respeto* has a deep connotation. It goes far beyond mere tolerance or even acceptance. *Respeto* acknowledges the full humanness of other people, their right to be who they are, their right to be treated in a good way. When White Americans learn to approach people of different cultures with this kind of deep respect, our own world becomes larger and our embrace of reality is made broader and richer. We are changed by our respect for other perspectives. It is more than just a nice thing to do. In the process of respecting other cultures, we learn to become better people ourselves.

But all of this is not enough. As members of the majority population, we are called to provide more than honesty, humility, and respect. The race issue for White Americans is ultimately a question of action: What are we going to do about it? Racism is not a Black problem or an Indian problem or an Asian problem or a Hispanic problem—or even a White problem. The issue of racism and cultural diversity in the United States is a human problem, a struggle we are all in together. It cannot be solved by any one group. We have become embedded in the problem together, and we will have to deal with it together.

This brings us to the issue of co-responsibility. The way for us to overcome the denial, hostility, fear, and guilt of the past and present is to become active participants in the creation of a better future. As White Americans, once we become aware of the heavy weight of our oppressive past, our role is not to fall into a kind of morose confessionalism about the sins of our ancestors. The healing response for ourselves, as well as for those who have been the victims of oppression, is involvement, action, contribution, and responsibility. The healing path requires all of us to join our efforts, resources, energy, and commitment. No one group can do it alone. Together we are co-responsible for the creation of a new America.

THE SEARCH FOR AUTHENTIC IDENTITY

Before White Americans can enter fully into this active partnership for change, however, we need to come to terms with who we are as a people. One problem that arises from an honest appraisal of the past is that it sometimes becomes difficult for us as White people to feel good about our own history. Where do we turn to find positive images for ourselves and our children? In the 1960s and early 1970s we saw a revolution in positive identity for Blacks, American Indians, Hispanics, and Asians. During this period there was an explosion of racial and cultural energy—what Banks (1994) refers to as the ethnic revitalization movement. What were White youths doing at this time? There was a revolution happening with them as well: a revolution of rejection. As the civil rights movement, the antiwar movement, and the women's liberation movement were bringing to the public's attention many of the fundamental flaws of a culture dominated by White males, the youths of White America were searching for an alternative identity.

At this time in our history, White America was at war with itself. The children of affluence and privilege, the very ones who had benefited the most from membership in the dominant culture, were attacking the foundation of their own privilege. In creating a new counterculture of rebellion and hope, they borrowed heavily from Black, Indian, Hispanic, and Asian traditions. Their clothing, ornamentation, hairstyles, spiritual explorations, jargon, values, and music defined an eclectic composite culture that symbolized identification with the oppressed. In their rejection of the dominant culture, they sought to become like those whom the dominant culture historically had rejected.

Thus we have the essence of the "wannabe" phenomenon: White Americans trying to be someone else. When the limitations of privilege, of affluence, of membership in the dominant group become apparent to us as White Americans, we often turn to other cultural experiences to find identity, purpose, meaning, and a sense of belonging. When the truth of our collective history is brought home to us, we turn to other traditions for a new place to be.

But there is another alternative for White identity, one that resides within our own cultural roots. It became clear to me during my sabbatical study tour around the world in 1990–1991. I began the trip with the goal of gaining some new insights about education from the First Peoples in several countries. During a 7-month period I was immersed in the rich contexts of the Navajo, Hopi, Maori, Australian Aboriginal, Balinese, and Nepalese cultures. I gained much from my exposure to the traditional perspectives of these cultures, but the most powerful personal experiences came for me in the place I least expected them—my own ancestral Europe.

In the Basque country of northern Spain, in the Pyrenees Mountains near the French border, I entered a prehistoric cave that was one of the sacred sites of the ancient people of Europe. I was amazed by the beauty and the power this cave held for me. I had been in the sacred caves of the Anasazi, those people who preceded the Navajo and Hopi in what is now Arizona and

New Mexico. I had been in the ceremonial caves of the Aboriginal people of Australia. In both of these previous experiences, I had been drawn to the handprints on the walls, created there by ancient artists blowing pigment through a bone or reed to leave images of their hands on the surface of the stone.

When I discovered, in the deepest part of a cave in the Pyrenees, 21 hand-prints created by ancient Europeans in the exact style of the Anasazi and the Aborigine, I knew I had connected with a profound source of my own identity. There was a sense of the universality of all human experience. In the projection of our hands on stone walls, in the desire to express ourselves and find meaning in life, we are all one. And then came an even deeper lesson. In my journey around the world, I had been searching for meaning in other people's cultures. Here in a cave in Europe was a connection with my own.

After leaving the Pyrenees, I spent the next 3 weeks exploring the ancient sacred sites of England and Scotland. In the company of Peter Vallance, a story-teller, dancer, and modern version of the old Celtic bard, I continued to grow more deeply into a sense of rootedness in my own past. I learned that the old Celts and other ancient ones of Great Britain were a fascinating people. They had spread over a large area in Europe and were, in fact, some of the people who worshipped in those magnificent caves in northern Spain.

I also learned that the Celts became the victims of the imperialistic expansion of Roman Christianity. Their culture was overwhelmed by the two-fold aggression of the Roman army and the church. Consequently, much of their history is lost to us today. The amazing stone circles, like Stonehenge, which are still evident throughout the British Isles, stand as powerful reminders of the Celtic vision of nature and of the people's sacred connection with both the earth and the sky.

What does my experience in Europe mean for us as White Americans? First, there is no need to look to other cultures for our own sense of identity. Any of us who choose to look more deeply into our European roots will find there a rich and diverse experience waiting to be discovered. Second, the history of oppression and expansionism perpetrated by European nations is only part of our past. It is a reality that must be acknowledged and dealt with, but it is not our only heritage as White Americans. In fact, many of our own ancestral groups, like the Celts, have themselves been the victims of the same kind of imperialistic drives that have been so devastating to other indigenous populations around the world. And third, when we push the human story back far enough, we come to a place of common connection to this earth, to a place where people of all races are brothers and sisters on the same planet. It is in this recognition of both our uniqueness as European Americans and our universality as human beings that we can begin to make an authentic contribution to the healing of our nation.

WHO ARE MY PEOPLE?

As a result of my world tour and of my lengthy struggle with the issues discussed here, I have come to a new sense of my own identity as a White American. I have seen that I have deep connections with this earth through my own cultural ancestry. I also have become aware of a complex, painful, yet rich history of connections to all other peoples. I have seen that White Americans can be drawn together with people everywhere who are struggling with the questions of cultural and human survival. We can develop a deep commitment to and a strong stake in the preservation and strengthening of diversity at home and throughout the world. We can become aware that our energy and vision, along with those of other Americans of all cultures, are essential to the healing that must take place if we are to survive as a pluralistic and just nation.

It is time for a redefinition of White America. As our percentage of the population declines, our commitment to the future must change. It is neither appropriate nor desirable to be in a position of dominance. Even though we are undeniably connected by history and ethnicity with a long legacy of oppression, this identification with the oppressor is not our only means of defining ourselves. We can choose now to contribute to the making of a new kind of nation. Young White students need to see that they, too, can be full participants in the building of a multicultural America.

Because the music of the United States is propelled by such a rich mixture of cultural rhythms, it is time for all of us to learn to move with grace and style to the new sounds. The future calls each of us to become partners in the dance of diversity, a dance in which everyone shares the lead. Because we have been separated by race and ethnicity for so long, we all may feel awkward at first with the new moves. It will take time to learn to embrace fully our emerging multicultural partnerships. But with a little help from our friends in other cultures, even White folks can learn to dance again, as we once did among the great stone circles of ancient Europe. Rather than being isolated in the dance hall of the dominant, we now have an exciting opportunity to join with Americans of all cultures in creating a nation that actually tries to move to the tune of its own ideals. These are my people, and this could be our vision.

REFERENCES

Alba, R. D. (1990). *Ethnic identity: The transformation of White America*. New Haven: Yale University Press.

Banks, J. A. (1994). *Multiethnic education: Theory and practice* (3rd ed.). Boston: Allyn & Bacon.

Hacker, A. (1992). *Two nations*. New York: Macmillan.

McIntosh, P. (1988). White privilege and male privilege: A personal account of coming to see correspondences through work in women's studies. Unpublished paper, Wellesley College, Wellesley, MA.

Ravitch, D. (Spring, 1990). Multiculturalism: E Pluribus Plures. *American Scholar*, pp. 337–354.

Schlesinger, A. M., Jr. (1992). *The disuniting of America: Reflections on a multicultural society*. New York: W. W. Norton.

Thomas, R. R., Jr. (1991). *Beyond race and gender*. New York: Amacon.

CHAPTER 18

Transformative Knowledge, Curriculum Reform, and Action

JAMES A. BANKS

The rich student diversity in today's schools is a challenge as well as an opportunity. Complex diversity related to gender, race, ethnicity, culture, and language characterizes a growing number of classrooms and schools in the United States. In addition, diversity related to social class and sexual orientation is becoming increasingly important as the gap between the rich and the poor widens and as more and more gay students and teachers publicly proclaim their sexual orientations.

CREATING AN AUTHENTIC *UNUM*

A significant challenge posed by the increasing recognition of diversity within U.S. society is how to create a cohesive and democratic society while at the same time allowing citizens to maintain their ethnic, cultural, and primordial identifications and affiliations. Our goal should be to create a nation-state that actualizes the concept of *e pluribus unum*—out of many, one. Historically the United States has tried to create the one out of the many by attempting to eradicate ethnic and cultural diversity and to force all citizens to become assimilated into an idealized Anglo-Saxon Protestant culture (Higham, 1972; Olneck, 1995). This coercive process has not and will not result in an authentic *unum*.

An imposed *unum* is not authentic, is not perceived as legitimate by the nation's diverse population, and does not have moral authority. It is also inconsistent with the ideals of a democratic society. The *pluribus* (the diverse people) must participate in a process of negotiation and power sharing in order to create an authentic *unum* that has moral authority and legitimacy.

The United States has done better than most other nations in creating a society that actualizes a just and authentic *unum*. Yet citizen expectations for a just society have far outpaced the nation's progress in attaining its democratic ideals. Many of our citizens—including many youths who are poor, who speak a language other than English, and who are of color—are alienated, and feel left out, abandoned, and forgotten by U.S. mainstream institutions (Bialystok & Hakuta, 1994; Igoa, 1995). The inclusion of these youths into U.S. mainstream culture and institutions not only will help them to become effective and productive citizens, but will strengthen the nation's mainstream institutions. These institutions will be forced to transform and consequently enrich themselves as they structurally incorporate citizens from the nation's diverse groups.

Within the past 2 decades, multicultural education has emerged as a vehicle to facilitate the transformation of the nation's educational institutions and the structural inclusion of the nation's diverse groups into U.S. society (Banks, 1994a; Banks & Banks, 1993, 1995). Multicultural education tries to create equal educational opportunities for all students by changing the total school environment so that it will reflect the diverse groups in U.S. society and in the nation's schools and classrooms.

THE DIMENSIONS OF MULTICULTURAL EDUCATION

I have identified and described five dimensions of multicultural education that educators can use to guide the implementation and assessment of programs designed to respond to student diversity, and to incorporate transformative scholarship into the curriculum and pedagogy (Banks, 1994b, 1995). They are: content integration, the knowledge construction process, prejudice reduction, an equity pedagogy, and an empowering school culture and social structure (see Figure 18.1).

Content integration deals with the extent to which teachers use examples and content from a variety of cultures and groups to illustrate key concepts, generalizations, and issues within their subject area or discipline. The *knowledge construction process* refers to the extent to which teachers help students to understand, investigate, and determine how the biases, frames of reference, and perspectives within a discipline influence the ways in which knowledge is constructed within it. Students also learn how to create knowledge themselves. The previous chapters in this book focus on knowledge construction and transformative action.

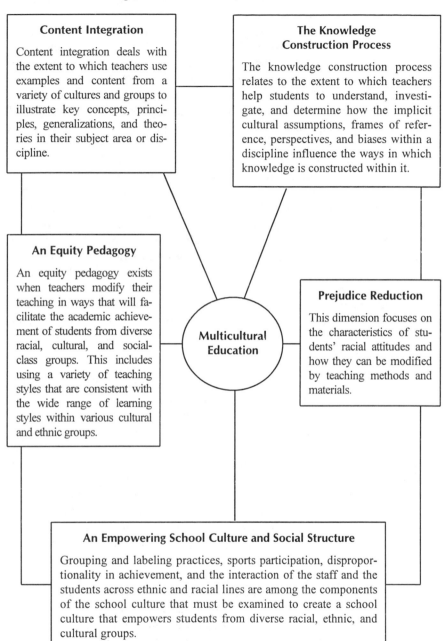

Content Integration

Content integration deals with the extent to which teachers use examples and content from a variety of cultures and groups to illustrate key concepts, principles, generalizations, and theories in their subject area or discipline.

The Knowledge Construction Process

The knowledge construction process relates to the extent to which teachers help students to understand, investigate, and determine how the implicit cultural assumptions, frames of reference, perspectives, and biases within a discipline influence the ways in which knowledge is constructed within it.

An Equity Pedagogy

An equity pedagogy exists when teachers modify their teaching in ways that will facilitate the academic achievement of students from diverse racial, cultural, and social-class groups. This includes using a variety of teaching styles that are consistent with the wide range of learning styles within various cultural and ethnic groups.

Multicultural Education

Prejudice Reduction

This dimension focuses on the characteristics of students' racial attitudes and how they can be modified by teaching methods and materials.

An Empowering School Culture and Social Structure

Grouping and labeling practices, sports participation, disproportionality in achievement, and the interaction of the staff and the students across ethnic and racial lines are among the components of the school culture that must be examined to create a school culture that empowers students from diverse racial, ethnic, and cultural groups.

FIGURE 18.1 The Dimensions of Multicultural Education

Prejudice reduction describes lessons and activities used by teachers to help students to develop positive attitudes toward different racial, ethnic, and cultural groups. Research indicates that children come to school with many negative attitudes toward and misconceptions about different racial and ethnic groups (Phinney & Rotheram, 1987). Research also indicates that lessons, units, and teaching materials that include content about different racial and ethnic groups can help students to develop more positive intergroup attitudes if certain conditions exist in the teaching situation (Banks, 1991a). These conditions include positive images of the ethnic groups in the materials and the use of multiethnic materials in a consistent and sequential way.

An *equity pedagogy* exists when teachers modify their teaching in ways that facilitate the academic achievement of students from diverse racial, cultural, and social-class groups. Research indicates, for example, that the academic achievement of African American and Mexican American students increases when cooperative teaching activities and strategies, rather than competitive ones, are used in instruction (Aronson & Gonzalez, 1988).

An *empowering school culture and social structure* exists when the culture and organization of the school have been restructured so that students from diverse racial, ethnic, social-class, and gender groups will experience educational equality and cultural empowerment. To create a school culture that empowers all students, the entire school must be conceptualized as the unit of change and the reform must be systemic. Variables that need to be examined and changed include grouping practices, the social climate of the school, assessment practices, extracurricular activities and participation, and staff expectations and responses to students from diverse cultural, ethnic, racial, and income groups.

To implement multicultural education effectively, educators must attend to each of the five dimensions described above. They should use content from diverse groups when teaching concepts and skills, help students to understand how knowledge is constructed (Banks, 1994a; Cortés, 1995; Gordon, 1995), help students to develop positive intergroup attitudes and behaviors, modify their teaching strategies so that students from diverse racial, cultural, and social-class groups will learn effectively, and restructure the culture and organization of the school so that it promotes educational equity.

Educators also should create processes and possibilities whereby parents and other members of the community can become involved in meaningful ways in the implementation of school multicultural programs and activities. Since the early history of ethnic studies in the United States, minority communities have played pivotal supportive roles in the success of school programs related to diversity. The African American public strongly supported Woodson's Association for the Study of Negro Life and History and Negro

History Week. At an important point in its history, the African American community provided most of the financial support for the Association.

Although the five dimensions of multicultural education are highly interrelated, each requires deliberate attention and focus. The reminder of this chapter focuses on two of the five dimensions described above: *content integration* and the *knowledge construction process*. Readers can examine two previous publications by the author for detailed discussions of each of the five dimensions (Banks, 1994b, 1995).

Content Integration

Teachers use several different approaches to integrate content about racial, ethnic, and cultural groups into the school, college, and university curriculum (Banks, 1991b). One of the most popular is the *contributions approach*. When this approach is used, teachers insert isolated facts about ethnic and cultural group heroes and heroines into the curriculum without changing the structure of their lesson plans and units. The *additive approach* also is frequently used by teachers to integrate content about ethnic and cultural groups into the curriculum. In this approach, the organization and structure of the existent curriculum remain unchanged. Special units on gender, cultural, and ethnic groups are added to the curriculum, such as units on African Americans in the West, the women's rights movement, and famous Americans with disabilities. While an improvement over the contributions approach, the additive approach is problematic because groups such as women, African Americans, and people with disabilities remain on the margin of the curriculum.

Knowledge Construction and Transformation

The *transformation approach* brings content about cultural, ethnic, and racial groups—and about women—from the margin to the center of the curriculum. It helps students to understand how knowledge is constructed and how it reflects the experiences, values, and perspectives of its creators. In this approach, the structure, assumptions, and perspectives of the curriculum are changed so that the concepts, events, and issues taught are viewed from the perspectives and experiences of a range of groups, including men and women from different social-class, ethnic, and racial groups.

The center of the curriculum no longer focuses on mainstream Americans, but on an event, issue, or concept that is viewed from many different perspectives and points of view. This is done while at the same time helping students to understand our common U.S. heritage and traditions. Teachers should help students to understand that while we live in a diverse nation, as Americans we share many cultural traditions, values, and political ideals that cement us as a nation. The goals of the transformation approach include: (1) helping students to develop an understanding of the complex ways in which the interaction of different ethnic, racial, and cultural groups have resulted in the development of U.S. culture and civilization; (2) helping students to understand how knowledge is constructed; and (3) helping students to learn how to construct knowledge themselves, including the formulation of interpretations, concepts, and generalizations.

TEACHING HOW KNOWLEDGE IS CONSTRUCTED: REWRITING THE HISTORY OF THE MONTGOMERY BUS BOYCOTT

A major goal of this book is to link transformative multicultural education practice in today's classroom with the work of transformative scholars and activists of the past. I will use a unit on the history of the Montgomery bus boycott that began on December 5, 1955 to illustrate how the transformation approach can be used to teach students how knowledge is constructed and how to create their own interpretations. This unit focuses on race and gender. However, the approach illustrated in the unit can be used to teach about groups differentiated by social class, religion, gender, race, culture, and ethnicity.

A careful study of these events from different perspectives will give students an opportunity to understand how history is written and rewritten and how historians construct interpretations and determine who gets included in written history. Popular and widespread views of the Montgomery bus boycott that often are repeated in textbooks are: (1) *the arrest of Mrs. Rosa Parks was the cause of the boycott*; and (2) *Mrs. Parks refused to give up her seat when asked by the bus driver because she was tired from working hard all day.*

Two important autobiographies by women who played key roles in the boycott enable historians to rewrite the history of the boycott. One is by Jo Ann Gibson Robinson (Garrow, 1987), who was an English professor at Alabama State College and who served as president of the Women's Political Council (WPC). The other autobiography is by Rosa Parks (with Haskins, 1992).

The WPC was founded in 1946 by professional African American women in Montgomery to provide leadership, support, and improvement in the Black community and to work for voting rights for African Americans. Many of the

WPC members were professors at Alabama State College; others were Black public school teachers.

In 1953, African Americans in Montgomery brought to the WPC more than 30 complaints about abuses they had experienced from bus drivers. Robinson and the other WPC members worked with the city leaders to improve the treatment of Black bus riders, but to no avail. About 70% of the bus riders in Montgomery were African Americans.

African American bus riders continued to experience intimidation and demeaning and hostile encounters with bus drivers, such as being asked to give up their seats to Whites even when they were seated in the "Negro" section of the bus. They often had to pay their fares in the front of the bus and were forced to exit and re-enter through the back door. Sometimes the bus drove off and left them before they could make it to the back entrance. In 1951, an African American man who had been drinking was killed by a police officer after he was involved in an encounter with a bus driver.

As the negative incidents directed against African American bus riders mounted, the WPC concluded that only a boycott against the bus system would end hostile bus incidents toward Blacks and bus segregation. It began to plan for a boycott and to wait for the "right" incident to use to launch it.

On March 2, 1955, Claudette Colvin, a 15-year-old high school student, was arrested when she refused to give up her seat for a White rider. She was seated in the "Negro" section of the bus. Mrs. Robinson observes: "When she refused, they dragged her, kicking and screaming hysterically, off the bus. Still half-dragging, half-pushing, they forced her into a patrol car which had been summoned, put handcuffs on her wrists so she would do no physical harm to the arresting police, and drove her to jail. There she was charged with misconduct, resisting arrest, and violating the city segregation laws" (Garrow, 1987, p. 38). Claudette Colvin was later found guilty and released on probation. The African American community was enraged by the verdict.

Mary Louise Smith, an 18-year-old, was arrested and fined for refusing to give up her seat in October 1955. Then, on December 1, 1955, Rosa Parks was arrested for refusing to give up her seat for a White rider. Parks (with Haskins, 1992) writes:

> People always say that I didn't give up my seat because I was tired, but that isn't true. I was not tired physically, or no more tired than I usually was at the end of a working day. I was not old, although some people have an image of me being old then. I was forty-two. No, the only tired I was, was tired of giving in.
>
> The driver of the bus saw me still sitting there, and he asked was I going to stand up. I said, "No." He said, "Well, I'm going to have you arrested." Then I said, "You may do that." These were the only words we said to each other.

As I sat there, I tried not to think about what might happen. I knew that anything was possible. I could be manhandled or beaten. I could be arrested. People have asked me if it occurred to me that I could be the test case the NAACP had been looking for. I did not think about that at all. In fact if I had let myself think too deeply about what might happen to me, I might have gotten off the bus. But I chose to remain. (p. 116)

Fed up with mistreatment, intimidation, and the violence they experienced daily from bus drivers, the African American women of Montgomery, led by the WPC, called for a boycott of the city buses that would take place the day after Rosa Parks was arrested, Friday, December 2, 1955. Robinson (Garrow, 1987) describes how she prepared for the boycott:

I sat down and quickly drafted a message and then called a good friend and colleague John Cannon, chairman of the business department of the college, who had access to the college's mimeograph equipment. When I told him that the WPC was staging a boycott and needed to run off the notices, he told me that he too had suffered embarrassment on the city buses. Like myself, he had been hurt and angry. He said that he would happily assist me. Along with two of my most trusted students, we quickly agreed to meet almost immediately, in the middle of the night, at the college's duplicating room. We were able to get three messages to a page, greatly reducing the number of pages that had to be mimeographed in order to produce the tens of thousands of leaflets we knew would be needed. By 4 A. M. on Friday, the sheets had been duplicated, cut in thirds, and bundled. Each leaflet read (in part):

Another Negro woman has been arrested and thrown in jail because she refused to get up out of her seat on the bus for a white person to sit down. . . . This has to be stopped. Negroes have rights, too, for if Negroes did not ride the buses, they could not operate. Three-fourths of the riders are Negroes, yet we are arrested, or have to stand over empty seats. If we do not do something to stop the arrests, they will continue. The next time it may be you, your daughter, or mother. This woman's case will come up on Monday. We are, therefore, asking every Negro to stay off the buses Monday in protest of the arrest and trial. Don't ride the buses to work, to town, to school, or anywhere else on Monday. (p. 45)

Reinterpreting the Past

When students study about the construction of knowledge using the Montgomery bus boycott as a case study, they can compare *mainstream* accounts of the events (such as those in textbooks) with *transformative* accounts (see Chapter 1 for the definition of transformative knowledge), such as those given by Jo Ann Gibson Robinson and Rosa Parks. They can discuss why people who often played significant roles in historical events, such as those played by Robinson and the Women's Political Council in the Montgomery bus boycott, often remain invisible in history. The work of men and organizations headed by men such as Martin Luther King, Jr., and Ralph D. Abernathy are emphasized in most textbook and popular accounts of the Montgomery bus boycott. The work of women like Jo Ann Gibson Robinson and her female colleagues in the Women's Political Council remains invisible in most textbooks. It is significant that Robinson's memoir is entitled *The Montgomery Bus Boycott and the Women Who Started It*. Another source that describes the role of women in the civil rights movement is *Women in the Civil Rights Movement: Trailblazers and Torchbearers 1941–1965* (Crawford, Rouse, & Woods, 1993).

A comparison of Rosa Parks's account of why she did not give up her seat to a White rider with the accounts in textbooks will help students to understand not only how *written history* can be highly discrepant from *actual past events* but how history is rewritten when people who have been excluded from its production begin to play active roles in its construction. Jo Ann Gibson Robinson and Rosa Parks have written accounts of the Montgomery bus boycott that challenge institutionalized accounts in significant ways.

Incorporating Transformative Scholarship into the Curriculum

As Robert Merton (1972) has perceptively observed, *insiders* and *outsiders* often have different perspectives on the same events. Merton points out that both insider and outsider perspectives are needed to give us a total view of social and historical reality. Since the 1970s, people of color—who historically have been outsiders and transformative scholars—have produced a prodigious amount of scholarship that teachers need to incorporate into the curriculum in order to give students the total view of social reality described by Merton and to enable students to construct their own interpretations of reality.

Recent examples of this new scholarship include Ronald Takaki's thoughtful and informative *A Different Mirror: A History of Multicultural America* (1993); *The Color Line: Legacy for the Twenty-First Century* by John Hope Franklin (1993); *Borderlands/La Frontera* by Gloria Anzaldúa (1987); *Black Feminist Thought: Knowledge, Consciousness, and the Politics of Empowerment* by Patricia Hill Collins (1990); and *The Sacred Hoop* by Paula Gunn Allen (1986). Other important recent examples are *Margins and Mainstreams: Asians in American History and Culture* by Gary Y. Okihiro (1994) and *Revelations: American History, American Myths* by Nathan Irvin Huggins (1995).

When identifying transformative scholarship (defined in Chapter 1) that will be used to transform the school, college, and university curriculum, a special effort needs to be made by teachers to include works that deal with women of color, such as those by Anzaldúa, Collins, and Allen. Scholarship by men of color often has been as silent on women's issues as that by White men (hooks & West, 1991). Fortunately, recent transformative scholarship on women of color is rich in insights and concepts. Important new works include *Unequal Sisters: A Multicultural Reader in U. S. Women's History,* edited by DuBois and Ruiz (1990), and *Black Women in America: A Historical Encyclopedia,* edited by Darlene Clark Hine, with Elsa Barkley Brown and Rosalyn Terborg-Penn (1993).

Teaching for Personal, Social, and Civic Action

Transformative scholarship has been in the past and is today tightly related to action designed to reform society and to make it more democratic. An important goal of multicultural education is to help students acquire the knowledge and commitments needed to make reflective decisions and to take personal, social, and civic action to promote democracy and democratic living. Opportunities for action help students to develop a sense of personal and civic efficacy, to develop faith in their ability to make changes in the institutions that are part of their lives, and to handle situations in which they apply the knowledge they have learned (Banks, with Clegg, 1990).

Action activities and projects should be tuned to the cognitive and moral developmental levels of students. Practicality and feasibility also should be important considerations. Students in the primary grades can take action by making a commitment to stop laughing at ethnic jokes that sting; students in the early and middle grades can act by reading books about other racial, ethnic, and cultural groups. Upper-elementary-grade students can make friends with students who are members of other racial, ethnic, and cultural groups and participate in cross-racial activities and projects with students who attend a different school in the city. Upper-grade-students also can participate in projects that provide help and comfort to people in the community with special needs. They also can participate in local political activities such as school bond elections and elections on local initiatives. Lewis (1991) has written a helpful guide that describes ways to plan and initiate social action activities and projects for students. Guidelines for citizen action projects are presented in Table 18.1.

When students study content, concepts, and events from the perspectives of the diverse groups that shaped the events, they can be taught how to construct their own interpretations of the past and present. Transformative teaching enables students to take actions that will help to reform U.S. society so that its *unum* will be authentic and have moral authority among the nation's diverse groups. A reformed U.S. society will help to liberate and empower all of the nation's citizens. Transformative teaching constitutes what bell hooks (1994) calls "the practice of freedom."

TABLE 18.1 Guidelines for Citizen Action Projects

1. The activities should be *meaningful* experiences, not merely projects in which students become involved just to say that they are participating in citizen action projects.

2. The *primary* goal of citizen action projects should be to provide experiences for the students whereby they can attain a sense of political effectiveness, and not just serve the community. However, the most effective projects contribute to the attainment of both goals.

3. Charity and other kinds of community help experiences are legitimate and potentially meaningful activities, although the projects should, as often as possible, help students to gain a sense of political effectiveness.

4. Students should participate in citizen action activities only after they have studied the related issue from the perspectives of the social sciences, analyzed and clarified their values regarding it, identified the possible consequences of their actions, and expressed a willingness to accept those consequences.

5. When problems within the school can be resolved through student action, participation in school activities should have priority over participation in projects in the wider community.

6. While group decision-making is legitimate and often desirable, no individual student should be required to participate in an action project that he or she feels is contrary to his or her values and beliefs.

7. The experience and age of the students should be considered when action projects are planned and implemented. Young children should confine their actions to their classroom, school, and family, or to other primary groups or secondary institutions in which they feel secure and that are supportive of their actions.

8. When citizen action projects are planned, the support of other teachers, students, school administrators, related community agencies, and members of the community should be solicited.

9. Students who wish to participate in citizen action projects should be allowed to have schedules conducive to such participation. The concept of the school should be broadened; activities need not necessarily take place within the four walls of the school room.

10. When a community is seriously divided over a social issue and feelings within the community are intense, action projects should be confined to the classroom, school, family, or to other supportive institutions in which students feel secure.

11. Citizen action projects planned by students should not violate the laws and mores of the community.

12. Citizen action projects planned within the school should be consistent with American creed values and human dignity.

(Continued overleaf)

TABLE 18.1, *continued*

13. When citizen action projects are planned, the teacher should make every effort to help the students identify all the possible consequences of their actions, especially those actions that may have adverse consequences, either for the individual or the group.
14. Students who wish to engage in individual projects should not be discouraged, but should be helped to realize the fact that group action is usually more politically effective than individual action.
15. When citizen action projects are planned, the teacher should make every effort to minimize any physical, emotional, or psychological damage to the students. This can be accomplished largely by soliciting the cooperation of other persons in the school and wider community, and by carefully considering the possible consequences of different courses of action.
16. Citizen action projects should be nonpartisan. Although groups of students may decide to campaign for a particular candidate or issue, students with other beliefs and goals should have the option to plan parallel projects to support their beliefs and political choices.

Source: Reprinted with the publisher's permission from Banks with Clegg, 1990, pp. 461–462.

REFERENCES

Allen, P. G. (1986). *The sacred hoop: Recovering the feminine in American Indian traditions*. Boston: Beacon Press.

Anzaldúa, G. (1987). *Borderlands/la frontera: The new mestiza*. San Francisco: Spinsters/Aunt Lute Book Co.

Aronson, E., & Gonzalez, A. (1988). Desegregation, jigsaw, and the Mexican-American experience. In P. A. Katz & D. A. Taylor (Eds.), *Eliminating racism: Profiles in controversy* (pp. 301–314). New York: Plenum Press.

Banks, J. A. (1991a). Multicultural education: Its effects on students' racial and gender role attitudes. In J. P. Shaver (Ed.), *Handbook of research on social teaching and learning* (pp. 459–469). New York: Macmillan.

Banks, J. A. (1991b). *Teaching strategies for ethnic studies* (5th ed.). Boston: Allyn & Bacon.

Banks, J. A. (1994a). *An introduction to multicultural education*. Boston: Allyn & Bacon.

Banks, J. A. (1994b). *Multiethnic education: Theory and practice* (3rd ed.). Boston: Allyn & Bacon.

Banks, J. A. (1995). Multicultural education: Historical development, dimensions, and practice. In J. A. Banks & C. A. M. Banks (Eds.), *Handbook of research on multicultural education* (pp. 3–24). New York: Macmillan.

Banks, J. A., & Banks, C. A. M. (Eds.). (1993). *Multicultural education: Issues and perspectives* (2nd ed.). Boston: Allyn & Bacon.

Banks, J. A., & Banks, C. A. M. (Eds.). (1995). *Handbook of research on multicultural education*. New York: Macmillan.

Banks, J. A., with Clegg, A. A., Jr. (1990). *Teaching strategies for the social studies: Inquiry, valuing and decision-making* (4th ed.). New York: Longman.

Bialystok, E., & Hakuta, K. (1994). *In other words: The science and psychology of second-language acquisition*. New York: Basic Books.

Collins, P. H. (1990). *Black feminist thought: Knowledge, consciousness, and the politics of empowerment*. New York: Routledge.

Cortés, C. E. (1995). Knowledge construction and popular culture: The media as multicultural educator. In J. A. Banks & C. A. M. Banks (Eds.), *Handbook of research on multicultural education* (pp. 169-183). New York: Macmillan.

Crawford, V. L., Rouse, J. A., & Woods, B. (Eds.). (1993). *Women in the civil rights movement: Trailblazers and torchbearers 1941-1965*. Bloomington: Indiana University Press.

DuBois, E. C., & Ruiz, V. L. (Eds.). (1990). *Unequal sisters: A multicultural reader in U.S. women's history*. New York: Routledge.

Franklin, J. H. (1993). *The color line: Legacy for the twenty-first century*. Columbia: University of Missouri Press.

Garrow, D. J. (Ed.). (1987). *The Montgomery bus boycott and the women who started it: The memoir of Jo Ann Gibson Robinson*. Knoxville: University of Tennessee Press.

Gordon, B. M. (1995). Knowledge construction, competing critical theories, and education. In J. A. Banks & C. A. M. Banks (Eds.), *Handbook of research on multicultural education* (pp. 184-199). New York: Macmillan.

Higham, J. (1972). *Strangers in the land: Patterns of American nativism 1860-1925*. New York: Atheneum.

Hine, D. C. (with Brown, E. B., & Terborg-Penn, R.). (Eds.). (1993). *Black women in America: An historical encyclopedia*. Brooklyn, NY: Carlson.

hooks, b. (1994). *Teaching to transgress: Education as the practice of freedom*. New York: Routledge.

hooks, b., & West, C. (1991). *Breaking bread: Insurgent Black intellectual life*. Boston: South End Press.

Huggins, N. I. (1995). *Revelations: American history, American myths*. New York: Oxford University Press.

Igoa, C. (1995). *The inner world of the immigrant child*. New York: St. Martin's Press.

Lewis, B. A. (1991). *The kid's guide to social action*. Minneapolis: Free Spirit.

Merton, R. K. (1972). Insiders and outsiders: A chapter in the sociology of knowledge. *The American Journal of Sociology, 78* (1), 9-47.

Okihiro, G. Y. (1994). *Margins and mainstreams: Asians in American history and culture*. Seattle: University of Washington Press.

Olneck, M. R. (1995). Immigrants and education. In J. A. Banks & C. A. M. Banks (Eds.), *Handbook of research on multicultural education* (pp. 310-327). New York: Macmillan.

Parks, R. (with Haskins, J.). (1992). *Rosa Parks: My story*. New York: Dial Books.

Phinney, J. S., & Rotheram, M. J. (Eds.). (1987). *Children's ethnic socialization: Pluralism and development*. Beverly Hills, CA: Sage.

Takaki, R. (1993). *A different mirror: A history of multicultural America*. New York: Little, Brown.

About the Contributors

James A. Banks is professor and director of the Center for Multicultural Education at the University of Washington, Seattle. He has written or edited 15 books in multicultural education and in social studies education. His books include *Teaching Strategies for Ethnic Studies, Multiethnic Education: Theory and Practice, Teaching Strategies for the Social Studies,* and *An Introduction to Multicultural Education.* He is the editor (with Cherry A. McGee Banks) of *Multicultural Education: Issues and Perspectives* and *Handbook of Research on Multicultural Education.*

Professor Banks has received fellowships from the National Academy of Education, the Kellogg Foundation, and the Rockefeller Foundation. In 1986, he was named a Distinguished Scholar/Researcher on Minority Education by the American Educational Research Association (AERA). In 1994, he received the AERA Research Review Award. A past president of the National Council for the Social Studies, he received an honorary Doctorate of Humane Letters (L.H.D.) from the Bank Street College of Education in 1993.

Cherry A. McGee Banks is assistant professor of education at the University of Washington, Bothell. Her current research interest focuses on race and gender in educational leadership. She has contributed to such journals as *Phi Delta Kappan, Social Studies and the Young Learner, Educational Policy, Theory Into Practice,* and *Social Education.* Professor Banks is associate editor of *Handbook of Research on Multicultural Education,* co-editor of *Multicultural Education: Issues and Perspectives,* contributing author of *Education in the 80s: Multiethnic Education,* and co-author of *March Toward Freedom: A History of Black Americans.* She serves on several national committees and boards, including the American Bar Association's Special Committee on Youth Education for Citizenship and the Board of Examiners for the National Council for the Accreditation of Teacher Education. Professor Banks serves on the editorial boards of *The Social Studies* and *Educational Foundations.*

Elizabeth F. Barnett is a professor of multicultural studies and early childhood education at Shoreline Community College. She also is heavily involved in research on outcomes assessment of multicultural education. She holds a bachelor's degree in psychology (and French language and literature) from Seattle University and a master's degree in special education from the University of Washington. She is enrolled in a Ph.D. program in multicultural education at the University of Washington and is currently working on her dissertation.

Allida M. Black is visiting assistant professor of history and American studies at Pennsylvania State University, Harrisburg, and a lecturer in history at George Washington University. She is the author of *Casting Her Own Shadow: Eleanor Roosevelt and the Shaping of Postwar Liberalism* (1995) and *"What I Hope to Leave Behind:" The Selected Articles of Eleanor Roosevelt* (1995). She lives in Arlington, Virginia, where she is researching *"Who Elected Her Anyway?" First Ladies and Politics from Betty Ford Through Hillary Rodham Clinton.*

Karen Gourd is a doctoral candidate in curriculum and instruction at the University of Washington, Seattle. Her area of teaching and research interest is teacher education with focuses on multicultural education and bilingual education. Her dissertation work is in liberatory education. She has taught English as a foreign language in Taiwan, and English as a second language in K–12 public schools and colleges in the United States, and has been involved in numerous curriculum development projects.

Michael R. Hillis is an assistant professor of education at East Tennessee State University, where he teaches courses in the foundations of education and multicultural education. Professor Hillis received his Ph.D. in educational psychology at the University of Washington, where he focused on the cognitive and developmental aspects of racial prejudice. His dissertation research investigated the use of free association techniques for assessing prejudice. Professor Hillis's current research interests and publications include the moral dimensions of multicultural education and the connections between technology and diversity.

Gary Howard is president and founder of the REACH Center for Multicultural Education in Seattle, Washington. Over the past 25 years he has provided extensive training in cultural awareness to schools, universities, and businesses throughout the United States, Canada, and Australia. He is the author of numerous articles on multicultural and diversity issues. His work related to the role of White Americans in a multicultural society is considered pioneering. In his keynote addresses at regional and national conferences, Mr. Howard draws on a wide range of experiences exploring multicultural issues throughout the world. He often approaches these talks from the perspective of one central question: "What does it mean to be an educated person at the dawn of the twenty-first century?"

Gloria Ladson-Billings is associate professor of curriculum and instruction at the University of Wisconsin–Madison. She specializes in issues of multicultural education and culturally relevant pedagogy. Professor Ladson-Billings has written extensively on successful teachers of African American students, including the book *The Dreamkeepers: Successful Teachers of African American Children.* She is a 1989 recipient of the National Academy of Education's Spencer postdoctoral fellowship, the 1995 recipient of the National Association of Multicultural Education's Outstanding Research Award, and the 1995 recipient of the American Educational Research Association's Committee on the Role and Status of Minorities Early Career Contribution Award. Her latest research interest is in critical race theory and its application to education. At the University of Wisconsin–Madison she teaches courses in multicultural perspectives in education, culturally relevant pedagogy, and social studies methods.

Carol Miller is an associate professor in the department of American Indian studies and the program in American studies at the University of Minnesota, Twin Cities. She is a former coordinator of a Bush Foundation Faculty Development Program on Excellence and Diversity in Teaching. Her research focuses on American Indian literature. Professor Miller is completing a book-length study of converging themes and teaching–learning outcomes in narratives by contemporary Native women writers. She is a member of the Cherokee Nation of Oklahoma.

Nathan Murillo is professor emeritus, California State University, Northridge. Until his retirement in 1992, he was a counselor and professor, teaching courses in psychology and Chicano studies. He has taught at the University of California, Santa Cruz, and was an invited speaker at Stanford University in 1970. Professor Murillo was on the faculty at the University of Southern California School of Medicine and has served on various site-visiting teams for the American Psychological Association. He was a consultant to the Peace Corps in Central and South America and in Southeast Asia. His publications include *The Mexican American Family, The Works of George. I. Sánchez: An Appreciation,* and a videotape (with Elizabeth Shon), *Cross-Cultural Training in Counseling and Psychotherapy, Series I: Asian Americans.*

Carlos J. Ovando is professor of education and chair of the Department of Curriculum and Instruction at Indiana University, Bloomington. He has taught at Oregon State University, the University of Alaska, Anchorage, and the University of Southern California. Professor Ovando specializes in bilingual and multicultural education and has contributed to numerous publications in these fields. He has served as guest editor of two special issues of *Education Research Quarterly* and contributed to *Handbook of Research on Multicultural Education, Peabody Journal of Education, Bilingual Research Journal, Phi Delta Kappan, Kappa Delta Pi Record,* and *Harvard Educational Review.* He is the co-author of *Bilingual and ESL Classrooms.* Professor Ovando has presented papers in Canada, Egypt, England, Guam, Mexico, Nicaragua, the Netherlands, and the Philippines.

Agnes M. Roche is a doctoral candidate specializing in literacy and multicultural education at the University of Washington, Seattle. An organist and choir director, she is a former music teacher and a former research assistant at the Center for Multicultural Education at the University of Washington. She served as a research assistant to the editors in the preparation of *Handbook of Research on Multicultural Education.* Ms. Roche has been involved in advocacy work for the Mien (Laotian) community in Seattle since 1987. Her research interests include family literacy, parental involvement, and multicultural curriculum history and theory.

Edward Taylor is assistant professor in leadership and policy studies at the University of Washington, Seattle. His areas of teaching and research are related to the sociocultural foundations of education, multicultural education, policy issues related to special needs populations, and leadership and organizational change. His dissertation focused on the academic and social fit between African American students and traditionally White institutions. Professor Taylor was formerly an instructor/program director in the Department of Education at the University of San Diego, where he received an Administrator of the Year Award in 1990. He served as a reviewer for *Handbook of Research on Multicultural Education.*

Henry Yu is assistant professor of history at the University of California, Los Angeles. He received his doctorate in history from Princeton University. Professor Yu teaches courses in modern American intellectual history and Asian American history, and is also a member of the Asian American Studies Center at UCLA. While researching his dissertation, *Thinking About Orientals: Race, Migration, and Modernity in Twentieth-Century America,* he held fellowships from the Social Sciences and the Humanities Research Council of Canada, the Mellon Foundation, and the Woodrow Wilson Society.

Index

Abernathy, Ralph, 343
Aboud, F. E., 283, 286, 287
Academic knowledge
  mainstream, 9, 10, 14-16, 71-72, 76-77,
    299, 342-343
  transformative. *See* Transformative
    knowledge
Activism. *See* Social activism
Acuña, Rodolfo, 8, 9, 17, 18
Adamic, Louis, 255, 256, 264
Adams, D. W., 304
Adams, F., 189
Adler, Alfred, 264
Adorno, T. W., 281
Affective studies of prejudice, 281-283
Aframerican Womens Journal, The, 221
African American(s), vii, ix
  and construction of knowledge about
    race, 68-71, 73-77
  and cultural knowledge, 11-12
  differences between Whites and, 77-84
  educating freed blacks in the South, 206-
    213
  history of, 17, 203-213, 340-346
  intelligence tests and, 117-121, 123-
    124
  and Montgomery bus boycott, 340-346
  "naming dilemma" of, 181-182
  poverty of, 79
  production and dissemination of
    transformative scholarship on, 95-
    98
  protest movement, 225
  and self-hate hypothesis, 285-286
  sharecroppers, 242-244
  and slavery. *See* Slavery
  social activism of, 70, 189-190, 218, 220-
    222, 225, 226-228, 340-346
  and Whiteness, 81
  women. *See* African American women
African American community, 50-51, 94, 97
African American sociology, 50, 71-72, 74

African American studies, 31-39, 196
  dilemma of scholars in, 34-35
  early scholarship, 31-34, 39, 46-60, 73-
    75, 77-78, 93-109
  early teaching of, 35-36
  ethnic studies, 36-39
  and meta-narratives, 49-51
  "New Negro History" (Franklin), 203-
    204, 213
  urban communities, 33, 50-51, 55, 59, 75
  Carter Godwin Woodson in, 17, 33, 36-
    37, 59, 93-109
African American women, 177-216
  Bethune, Mary McLeod, 217, 219-229
  Clark, Septima, 187-190
  Collins, Patricia Hill, 194-196
  feminist scholars, 64-65
  Hamer, Fannie Lou, 190-193
  Truth, Sojourner, 183-185
  as teachers of freed blacks in the South,
    208-213
  Wells, Ida B., 185-187
  women's club movement, 220-221, 227
African Heroes and Heroines (Woodson),
  101
African Myths, Together with Proverbs
  (Woodson), 36, 101
Afrocentrism, 4, 72-73, 196
  and early African American studies, 31, 35
  and womanist tradition, 182, 194-196
'Aha Punana Leo Incorporated, 313, 314
Ajzen, I., 283, 284
Alba, R. D., 22, 69, 270, 324
Albrecht, L., 226
Alienation, 336
Alland, A., 257-260
Allen, Paula Gunn, 18, 179, 343
Allport, Gordon W., 119, 255
*All the Women Are White, All the Blacks
  Are Men, but Some of Us Are Brave*
  (Hull et al.), 177
Altbach, P. G., 20

Please remember that this is a library book,
and that it belongs only temporarily to each
person who uses it. Be considerate. Do
not write in this, or any, library book.

DATE DUE

AP 6 '04			
JE 9 '04			
FE 27 05			
AP 5 06			